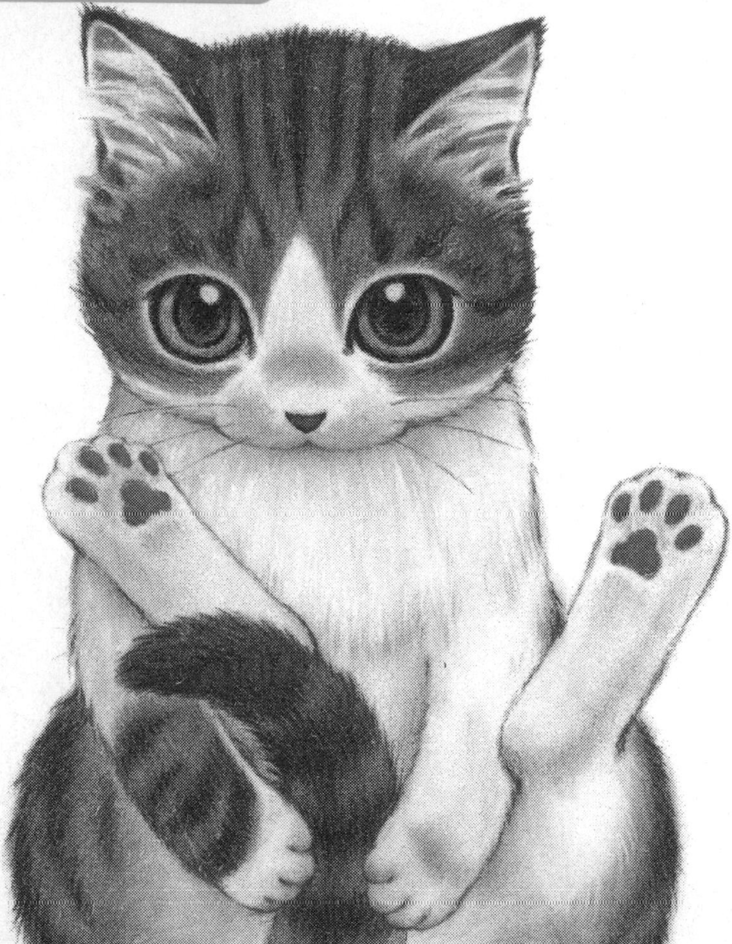

Plum Crazy! tales of a tiger-striped cat

4

story & art by
HOSHINO NATSUMI

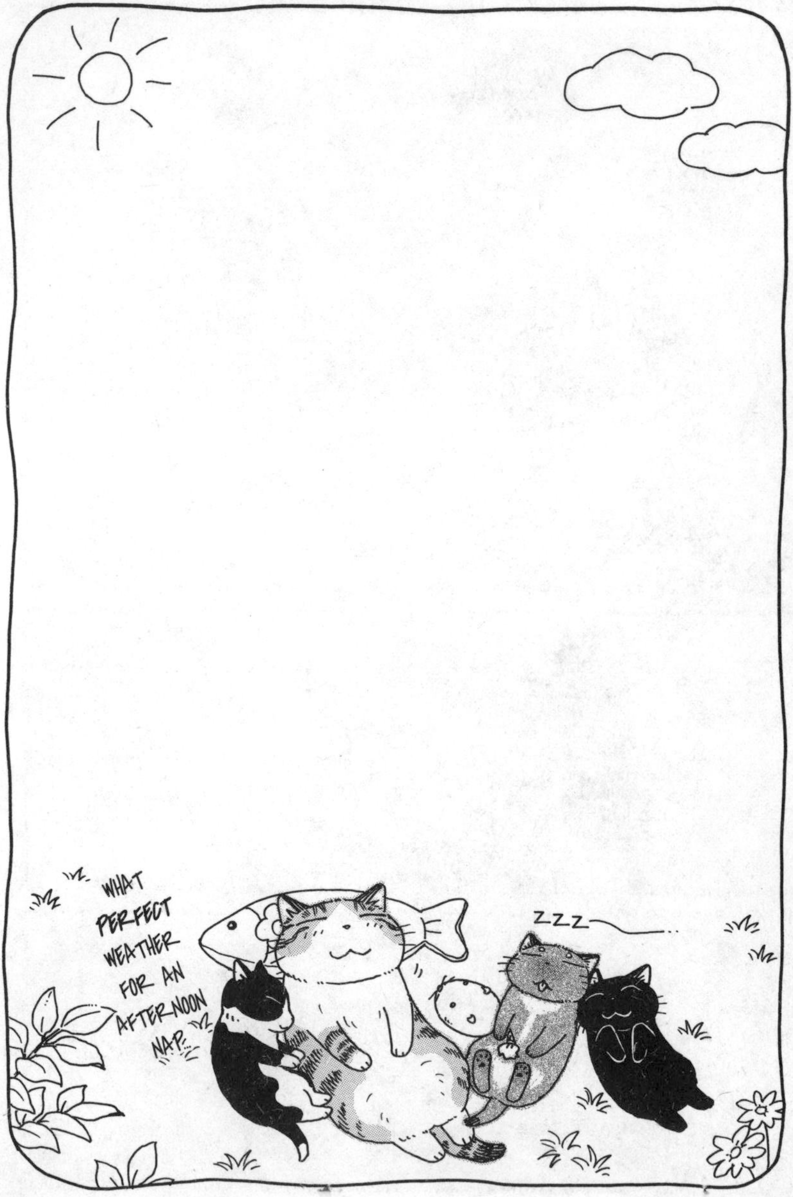

WHAT PERFECT WEATHER FOR AN AFTERNOON NAP...
ZZZ

SHORT.17

"Because It's the Fall"

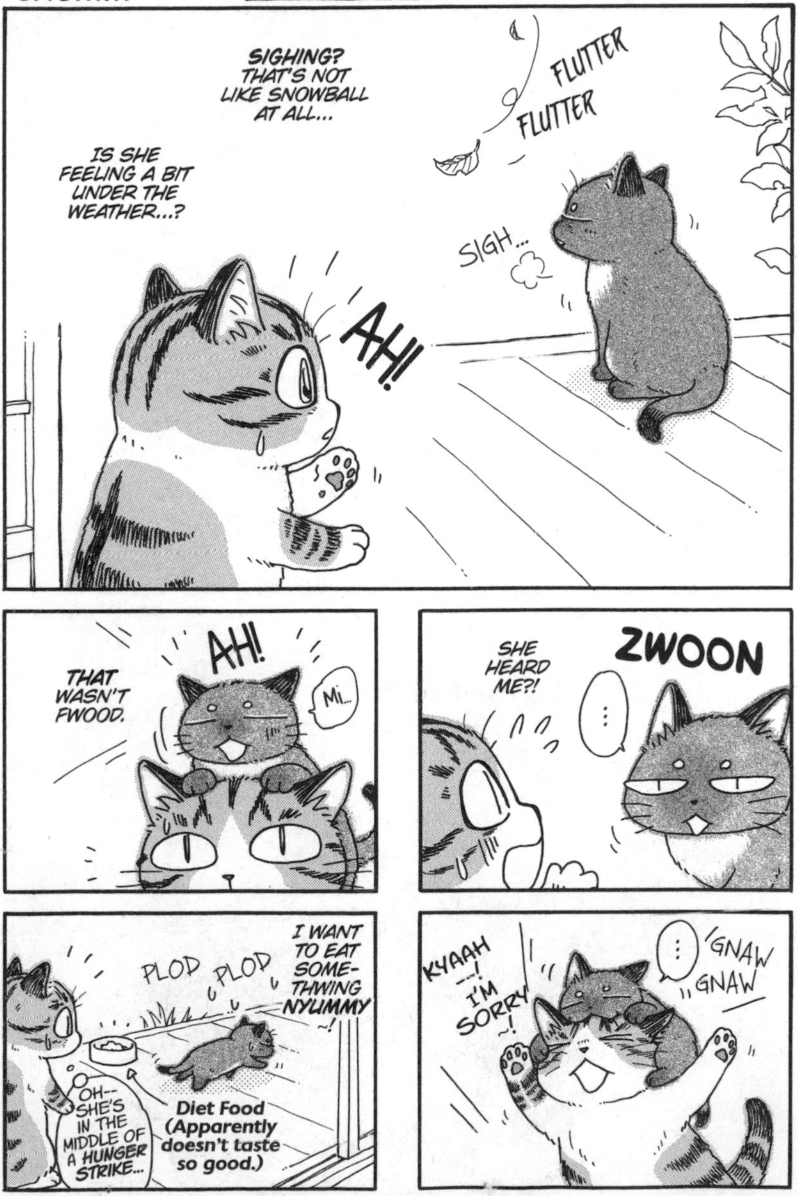
FLUTTER
FLUTTER
SIGHING? THAT'S NOT LIKE SNOWBALL AT ALL...
IS SHE FEELING A BIT UNDER THE WEATHER...?
SIGH...
AH!!
ZWOON
...
SHE HEARD ME?!
AH!
Mi...
THAT WASN'T FWOOD.
GNAW GNAW
...
KYAAH--! I'M SORRY~!
I WANT TO EAT SOME-THWING NYUMMY~!
PLOD PLOD
Diet Food (Apparently doesn't taste so good.)
OH--SHE'S IN THE MIDDLE OF A HUNGER STRIKE...

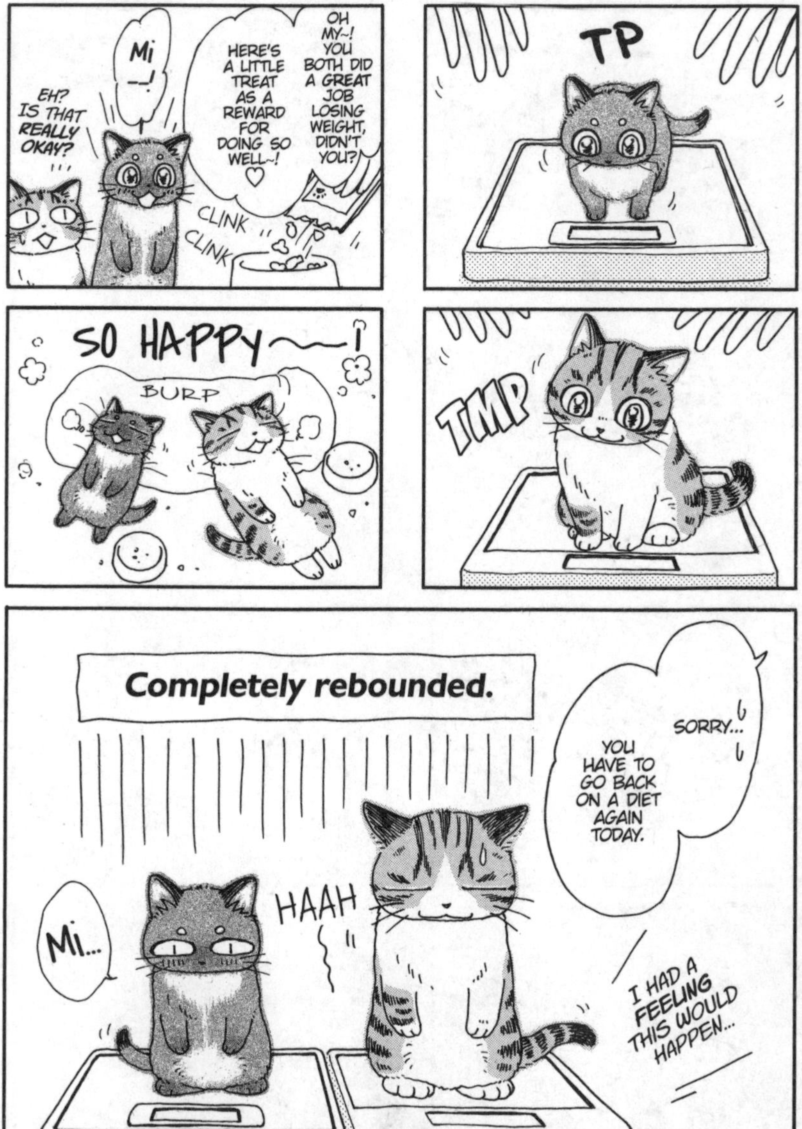
TP
OH MY~! YOU BOTH DID A GREAT JOB LOSING WEIGHT, DIDN'T YOU?
HERE'S A LITTLE TREAT AS A REWARD FOR DOING SO WELL~! ♡
Mi —!
EH? IS THAT REALLY OKAY?
CLINK
CLINK
TMP
SO HAPPY~~!
BURP
SORRY...
YOU HAVE TO GO BACK ON A DIET AGAIN TODAY.
Completely rebounded.
I HAD A FEELING THIS WOULD HAPPEN...
HAAH
Mi...

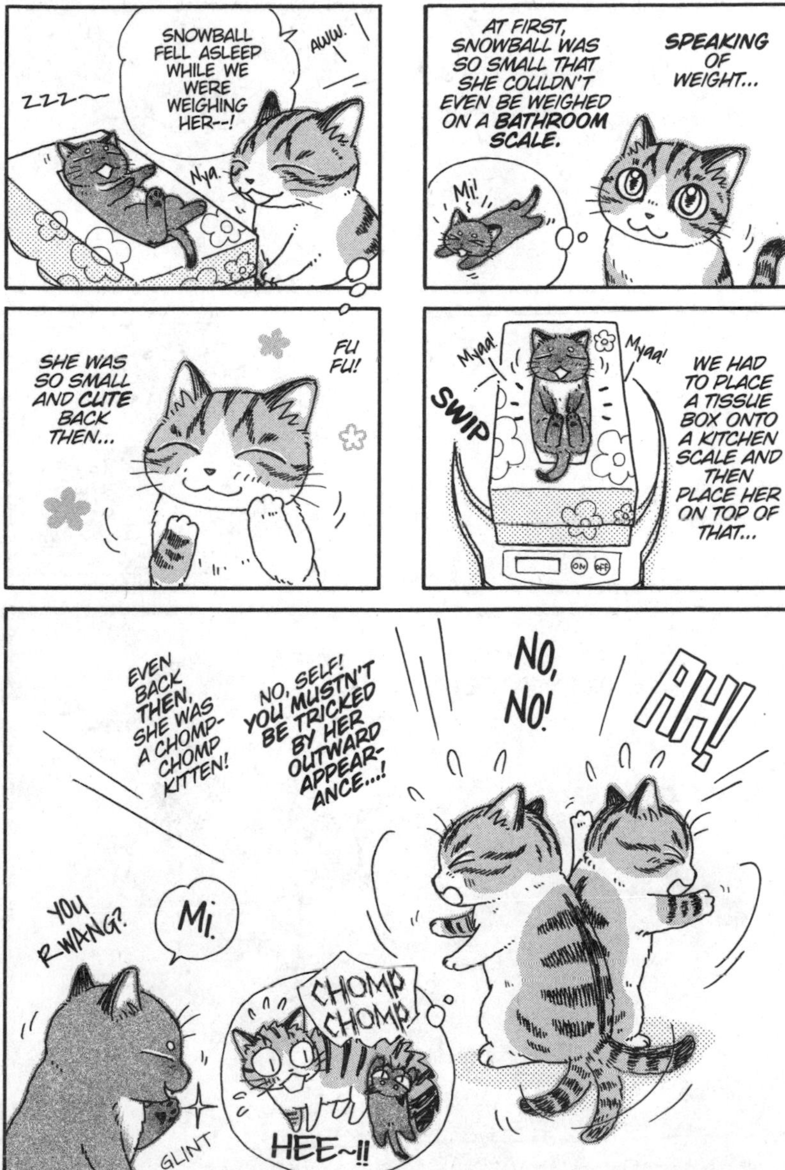
SPEAKING OF WEIGHT...
AT FIRST, SNOWBALL WAS SO SMALL THAT SHE COULDN'T EVEN BE WEIGHED ON A BATHROOM SCALE.
Mi!
AWW.
SNOWBALL FELL ASLEEP WHILE WE WERE WEIGHING HER--!
Nya.
ZZZ~~
WE HAD TO PLACE A TISSUE BOX ONTO A KITCHEN SCALE AND THEN PLACE HER ON TOP OF THAT...
Myaa!
Myaa!
SWIP
ON
OFF
FU FU!
SHE WAS SO SMALL AND CUTE BACK THEN...
AH!
NO, NO!
NO, SELF! YOU MUSTN'T BE TRICKED BY HER OUTWARD APPEARANCE...!
EVEN BACK THEN, SHE WAS A CHOMP-CHOMP KITTEN!
CHOMP CHOMP
HEE~!!
Mi.
YOU R-WANG?
GLINT

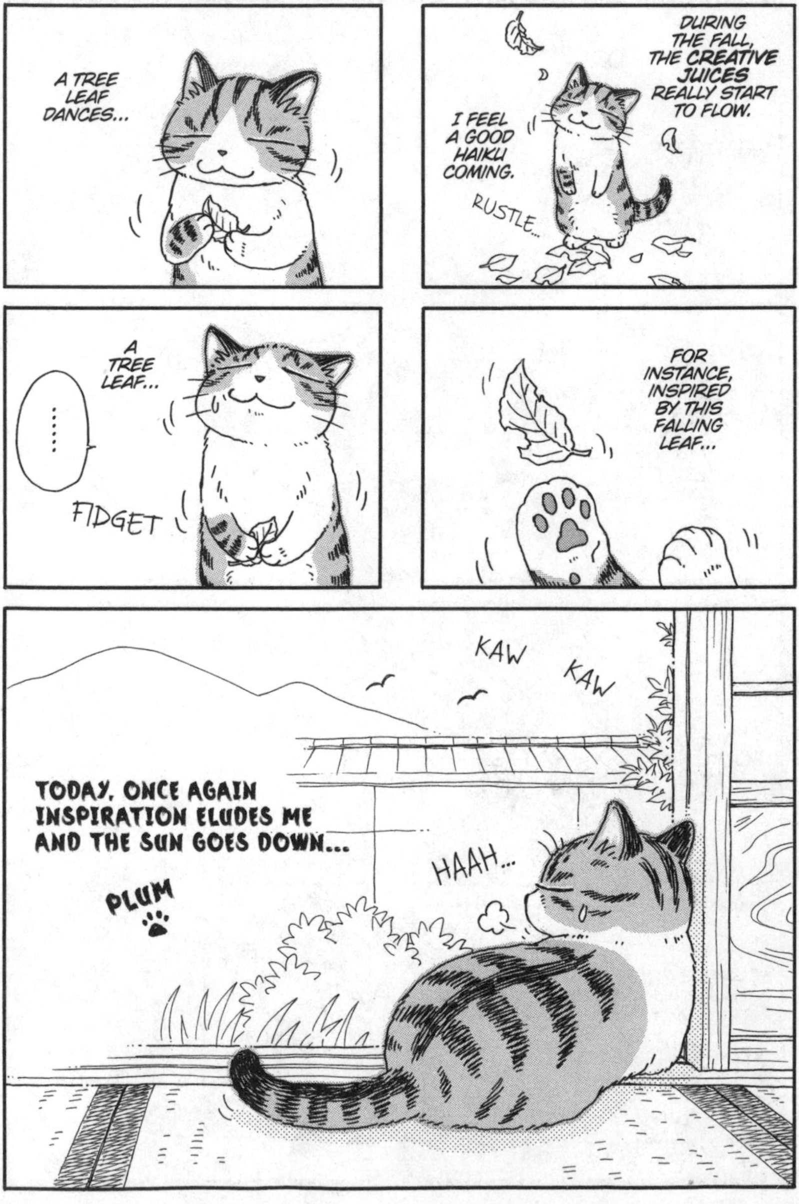
DURING THE FALL, THE CREATIVE JUICES REALLY START TO FLOW.
I FEEL A GOOD HAIKU COMING.
RUSTLE...
A TREE LEAF DANCES...
FOR INSTANCE, INSPIRED BY THIS FALLING LEAF...
A TREE LEAF...
......
FIDGET
KAW
KAW
TODAY, ONCE AGAIN INSPIRATION ELUDES ME AND THE SUN GOES DOWN...
HAAH...
PLUM

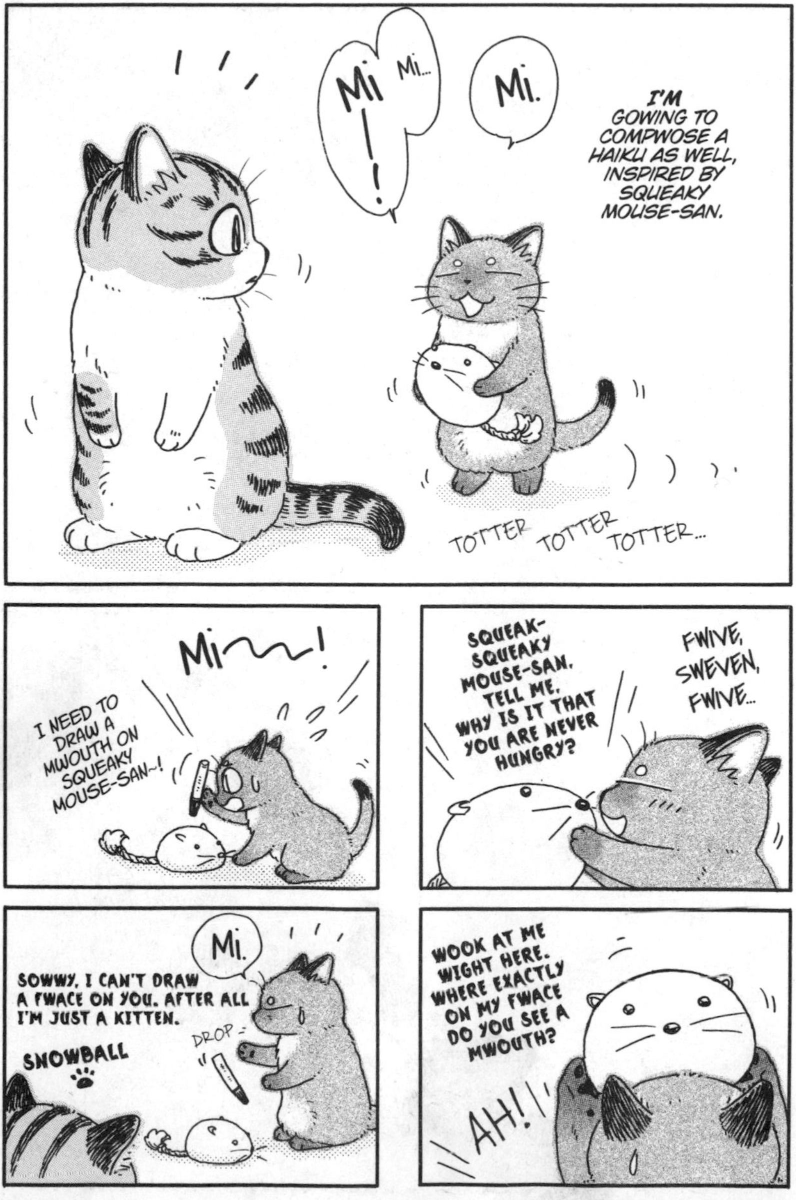
I'M GOWING TO COMPWOSE A HAIKU AS WELL, INSPIRED BY SQUEAKY MOUSE-SAN.
Mi.
Mi...
Mi!!
TOTTER TOTTER TOTTER...
FWIVE, SWEVEN, FWIVE...
SQUEAK-SQUEAKY MOUSE-SAN, TELL ME, WHY IS IT THAT YOU ARE NEVER HUNGRY?
Mi~~!
I NEED TO DRAW A MWOUTH ON SQUEAKY MOUSE-SAN~!
WOOK AT ME WIGHT HERE. WHERE EXACTLY ON MY FWACE DO YOU SEE A MWOUTH?
AH!!
Mi.
SOWWY, I CAN'T DRAW A FWACE ON YOU. AFTER ALL I'M JUST A KITTEN.
DROP
SNOWBALL

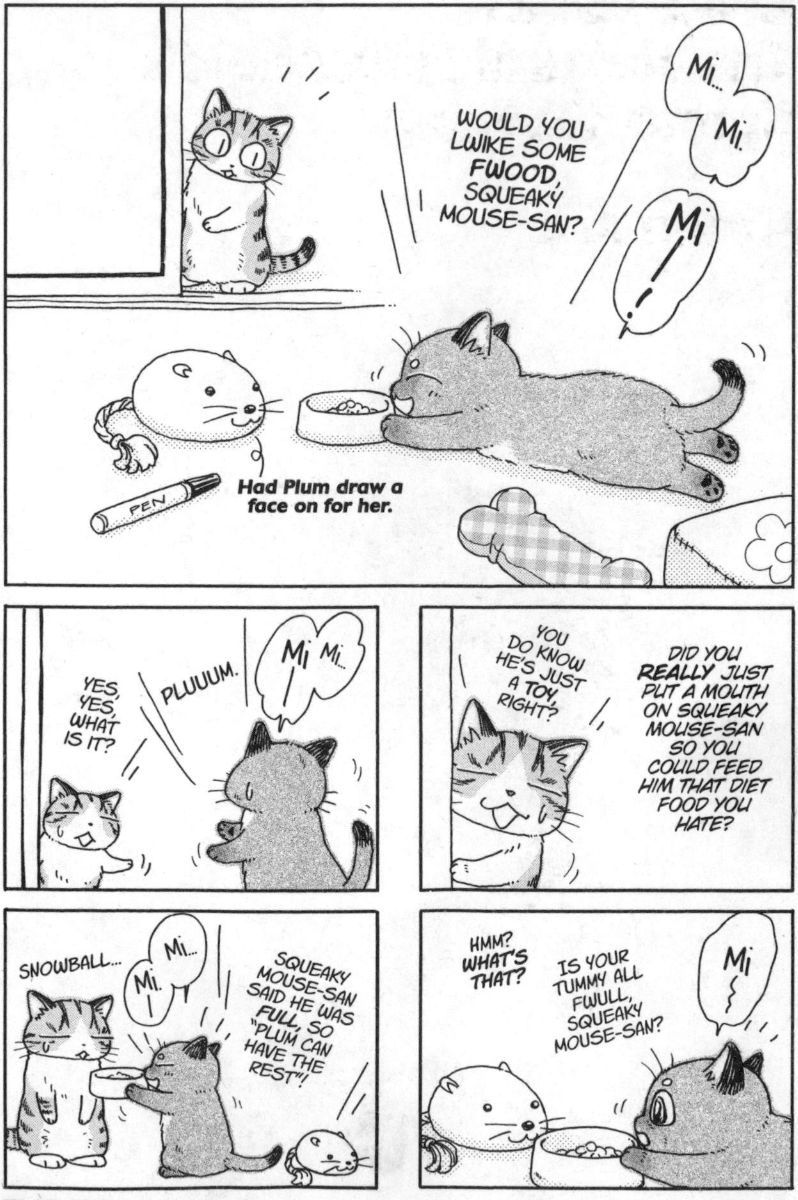
Mi... Mi.
Mi!
WOULD YOU LWIKE SOME FWOOD, SQUEAKY MOUSE-SAN?
PEN
Had Plum draw a face on for her.
DID YOU REALLY JUST PUT A MOUTH ON SQUEAKY MOUSE-SAN SO YOU COULD FEED HIM THAT DIET FOOD YOU HATE?
YOU DO KNOW HE'S JUST A TOY, RIGHT?
Mi Mi...
PLUUUM.
YES, YES, WHAT IS IT?
Mi
IS YOUR TUMMY ALL FWULL, SQUEAKY MOUSE-SAN?
HMM? WHAT'S THAT?
SQUEAKY MOUSE-SAN SAID HE WAS FULL, SO "PLUM CAN HAVE THE REST"!
Mi... Mi.
SNOWBALL...

THE END

CHAPTER 21
The Nakarai Household's Spring Cleaning

Kitten Arc

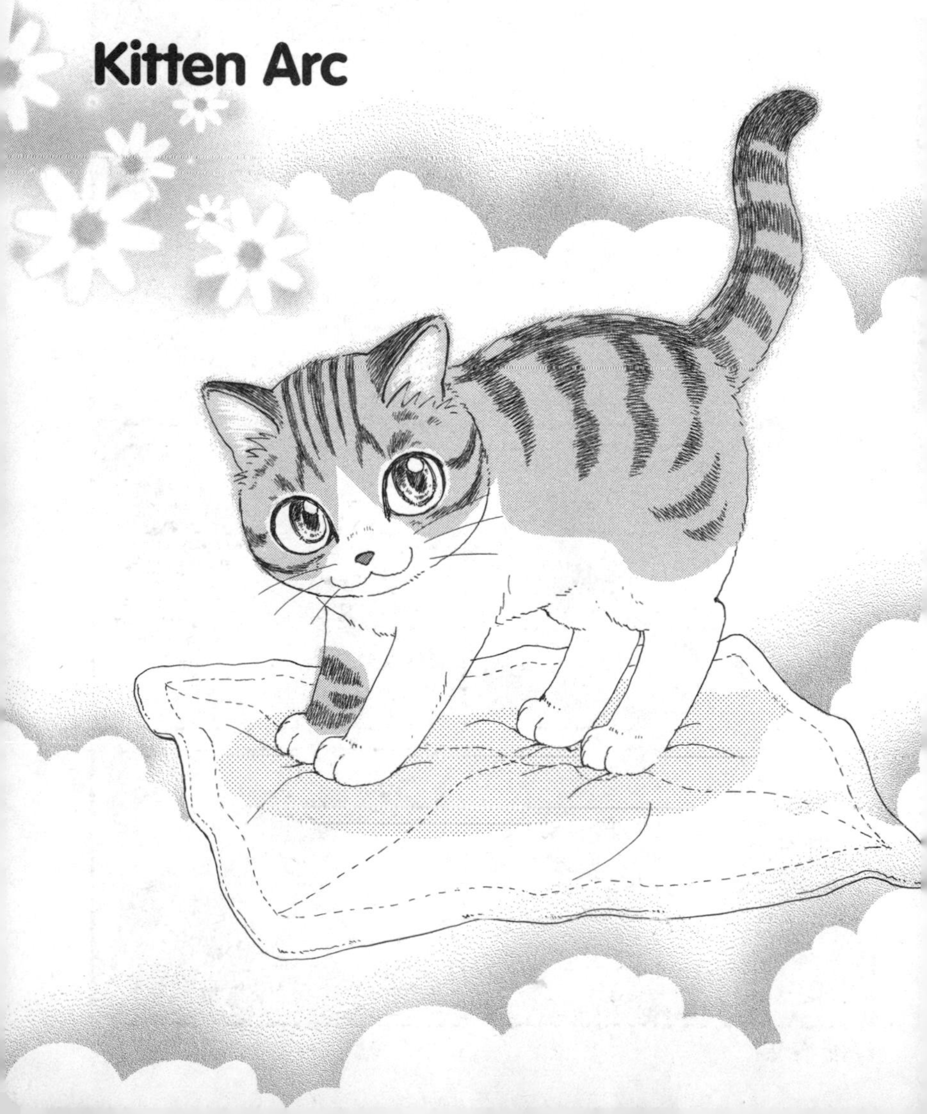

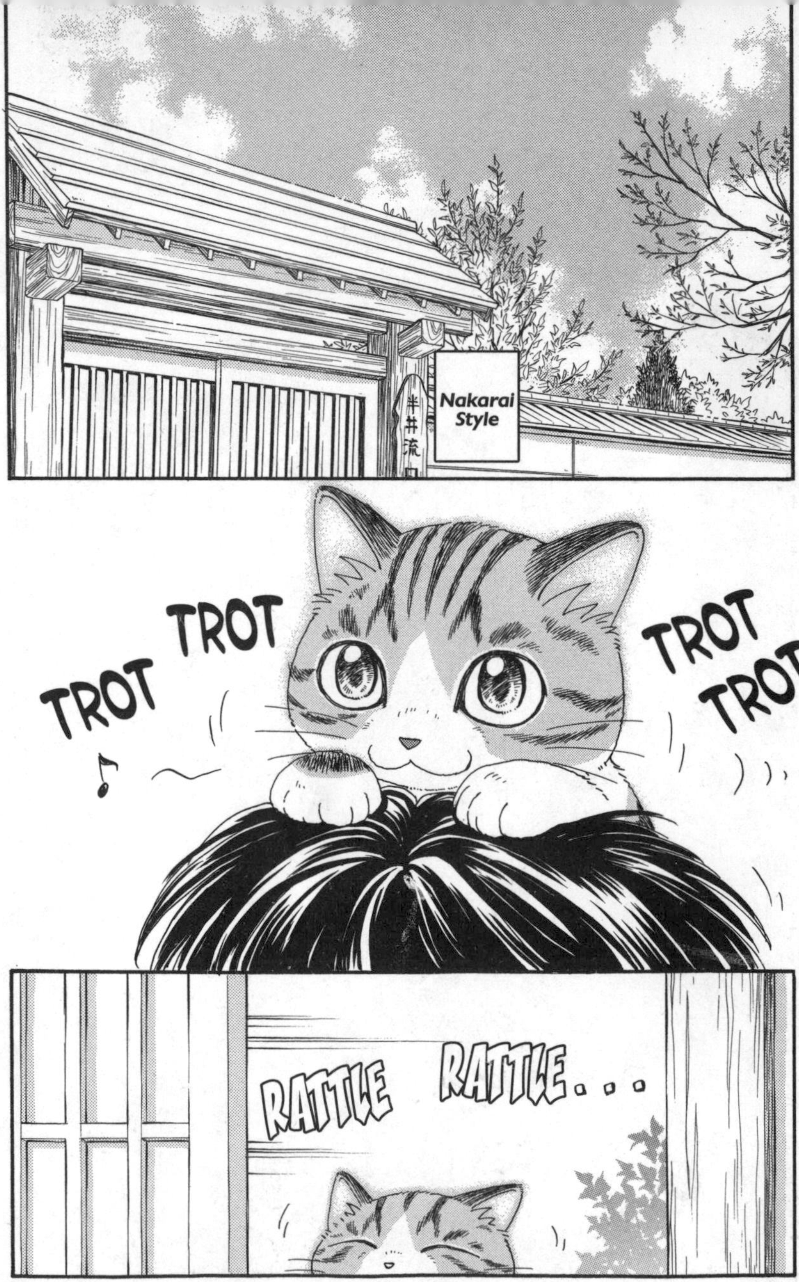
半井流
Nakarai Style
TROT TROT
TROT TROT
RATTLE RATTLE...

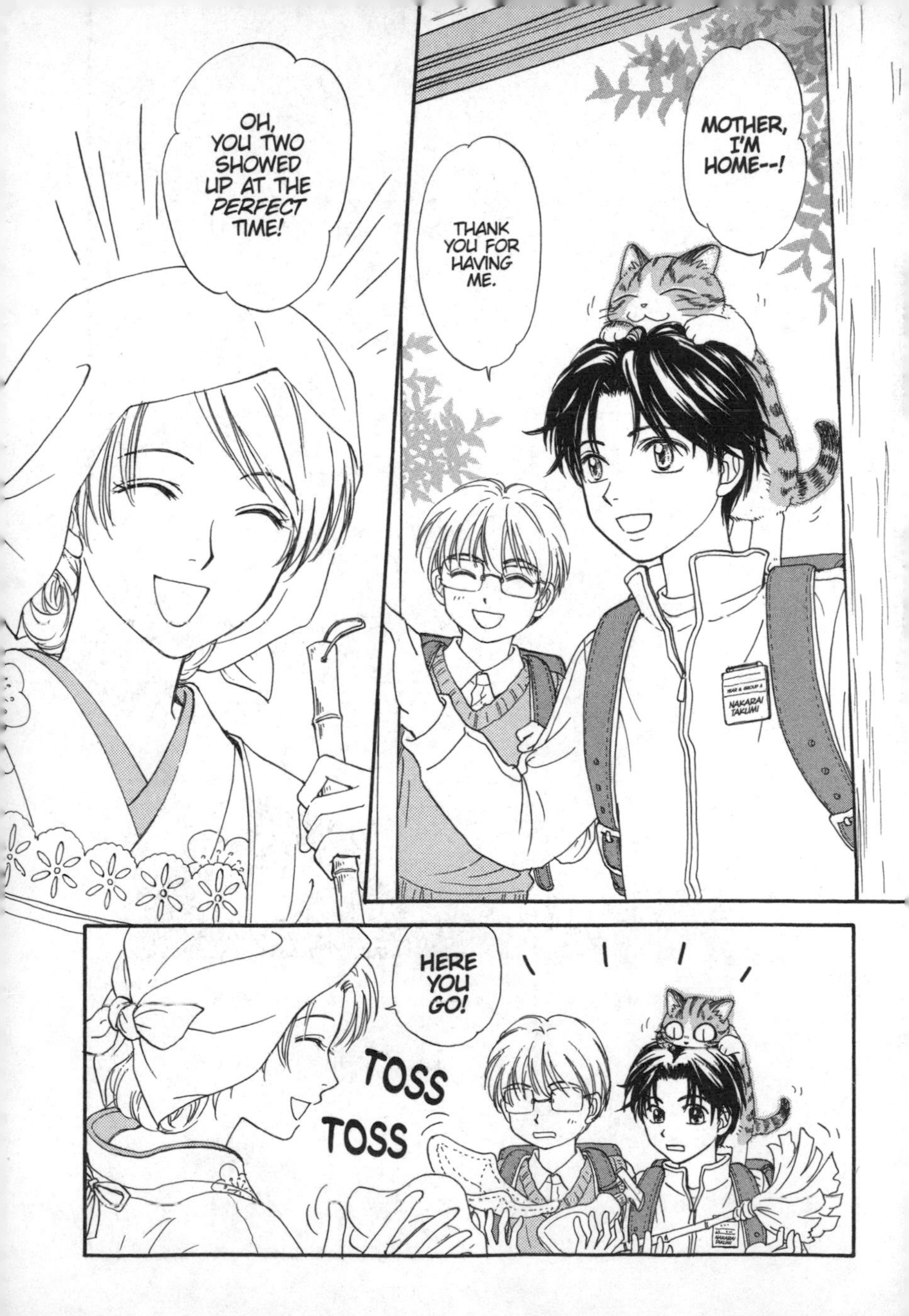
MOTHER, I'M HOME--!
THANK YOU FOR HAVING ME.
NAKARAI TAKUMI
OH, YOU TWO SHOWED UP AT THE *PERFECT* TIME!
HERE YOU GO!
TOSS
TOSS

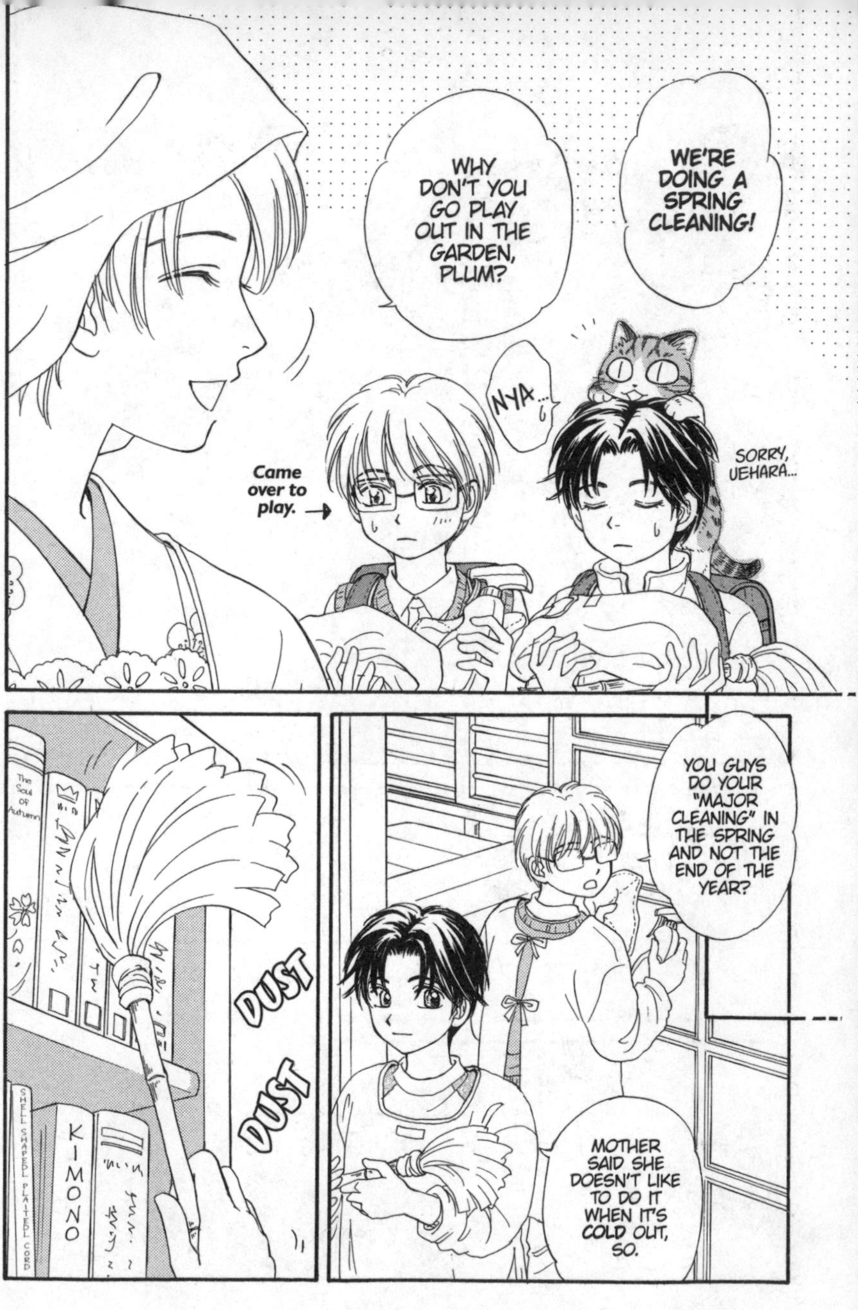
WE'RE DOING A SPRING CLEANING!
WHY DON'T YOU GO PLAY OUT IN THE GARDEN, PLUM?
NYA...
SORRY, UEHARA...
Came over to play.
YOU GUYS DO YOUR "MAJOR CLEANING" IN THE SPRING AND NOT THE END OF THE YEAR?
MOTHER SAID SHE DOESN'T LIKE TO DO IT WHEN IT'S COLD OUT, SO.
The Soul of Autumn
DUST
DUST
SHELL SHAPED PLAITED CORD
KIMONO

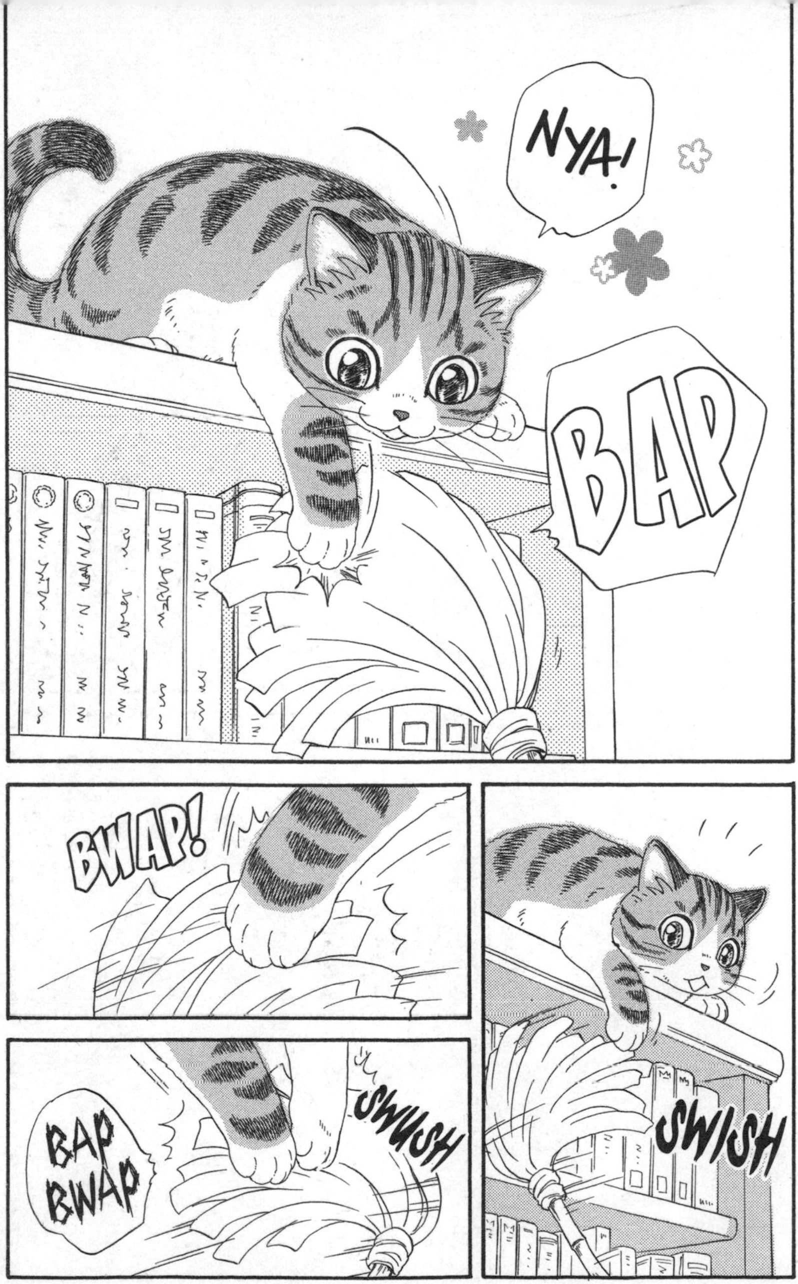
NYA!
BAP
SWISH
BWAP!
SWUSH
BAP
BWAP

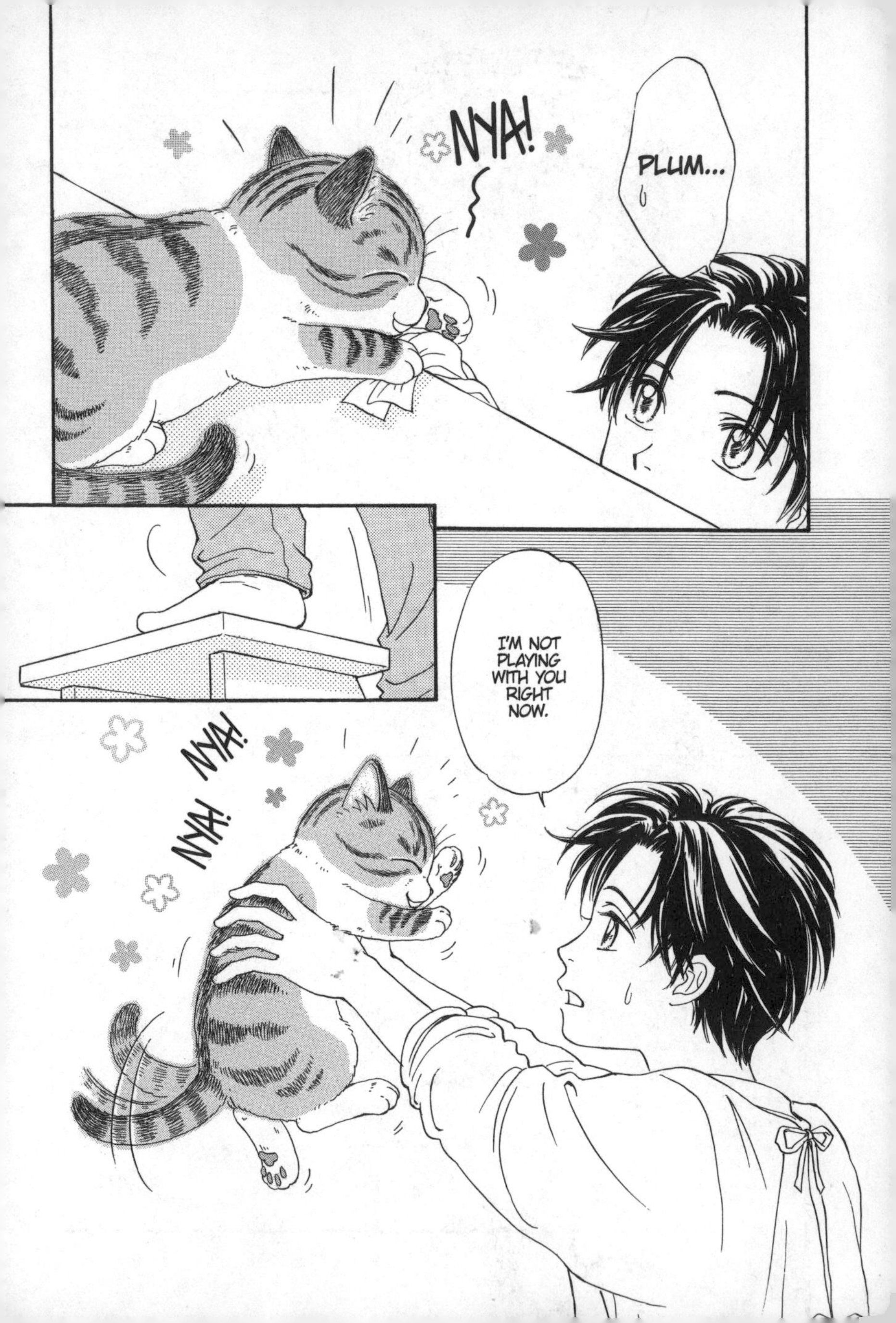
PLUM...
NYA!
I'M NOT PLAYING WITH YOU RIGHT NOW.
NYA!
NYA!

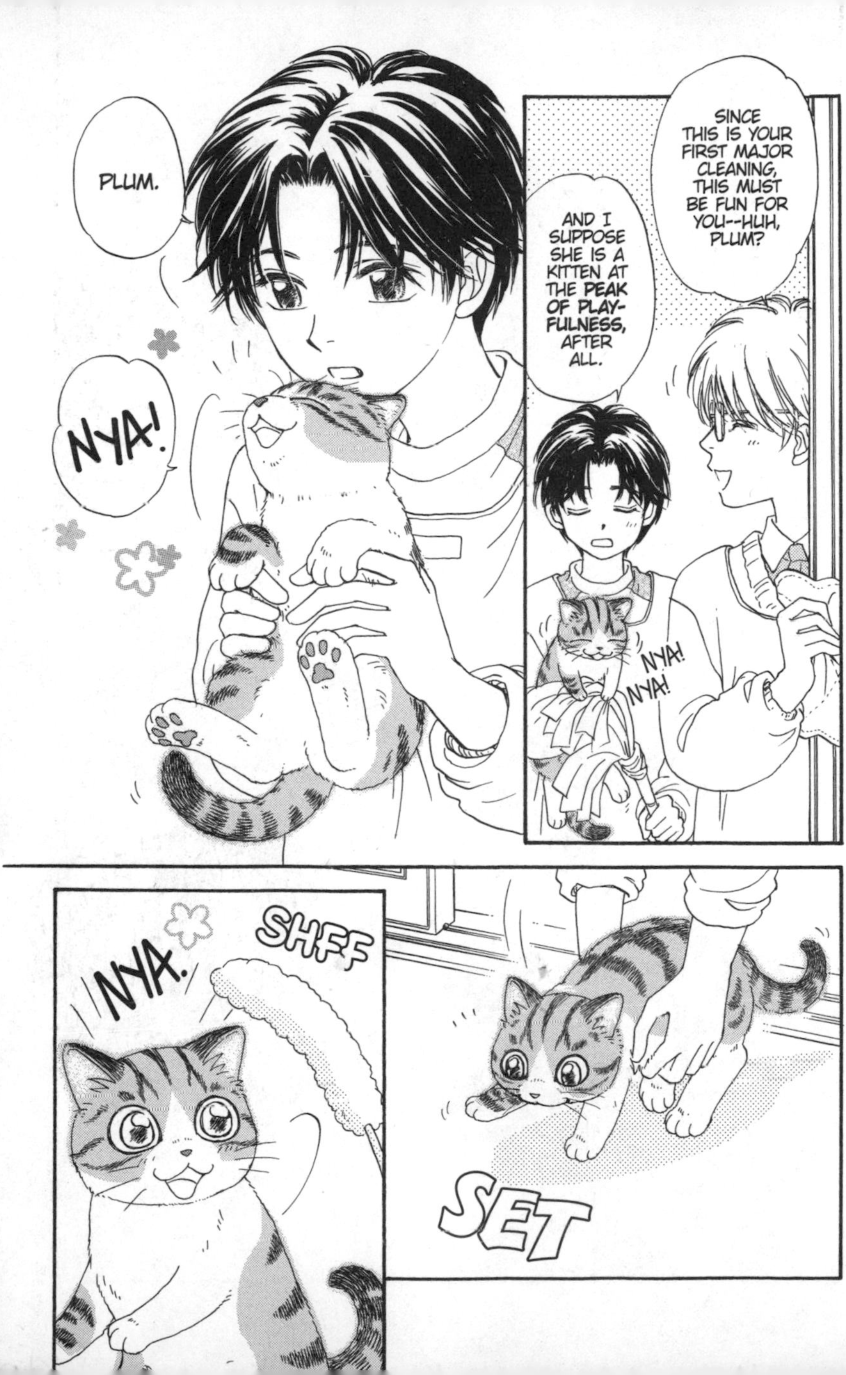
SINCE THIS IS YOUR FIRST MAJOR CLEANING, THIS MUST BE FUN FOR YOU--HUH, PLUM?
AND I SUPPOSE SHE IS A KITTEN AT THE PEAK OF PLAY-FULNESS, AFTER ALL.
NYA! NYA!
PLUM.
NYA!
SET
SHFF
NYA.

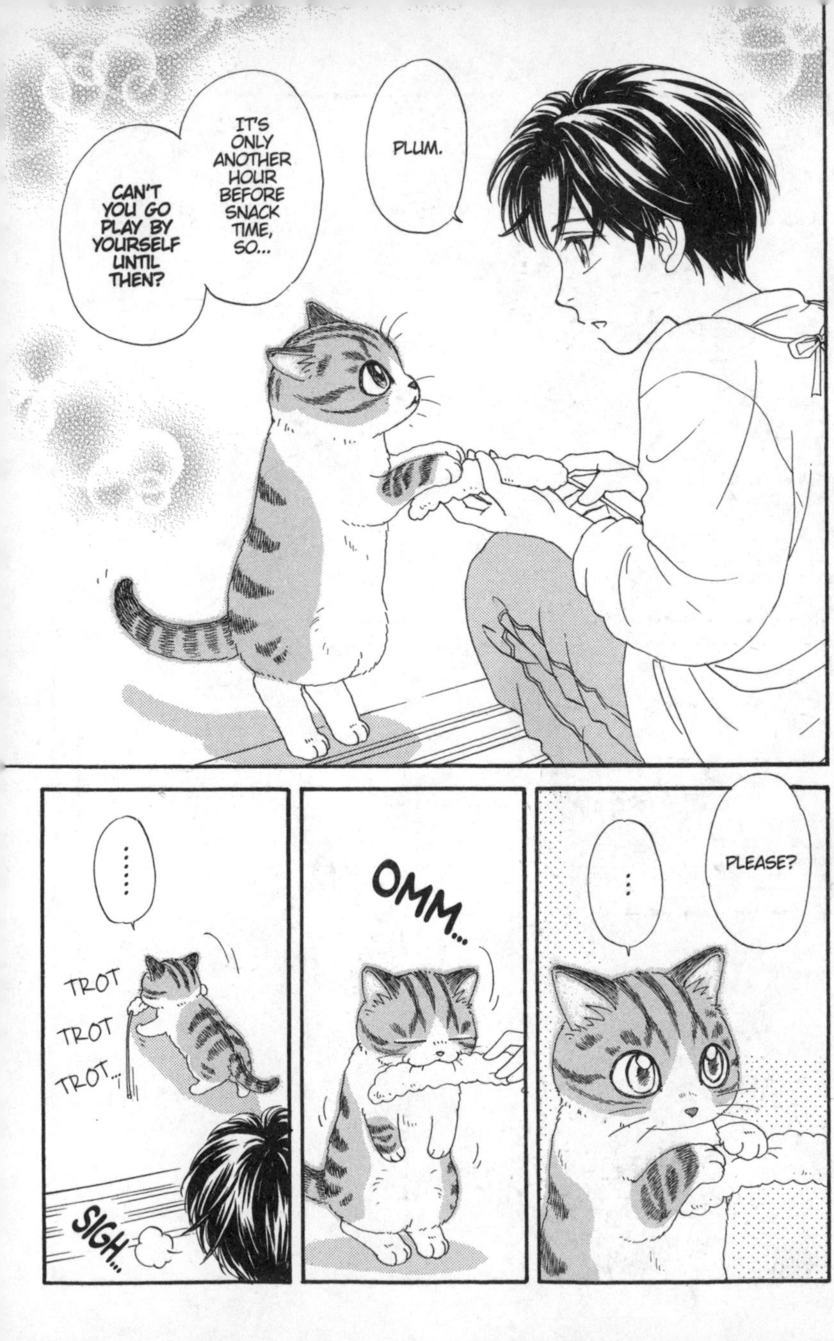
PLUM.
IT'S ONLY ANOTHER HOUR BEFORE SNACK TIME, SO...
CAN'T YOU GO PLAY BY YOURSELF UNTIL THEN?
PLEASE?
...
OMM...
......
TROT
TROT
TROT...
SIGH...

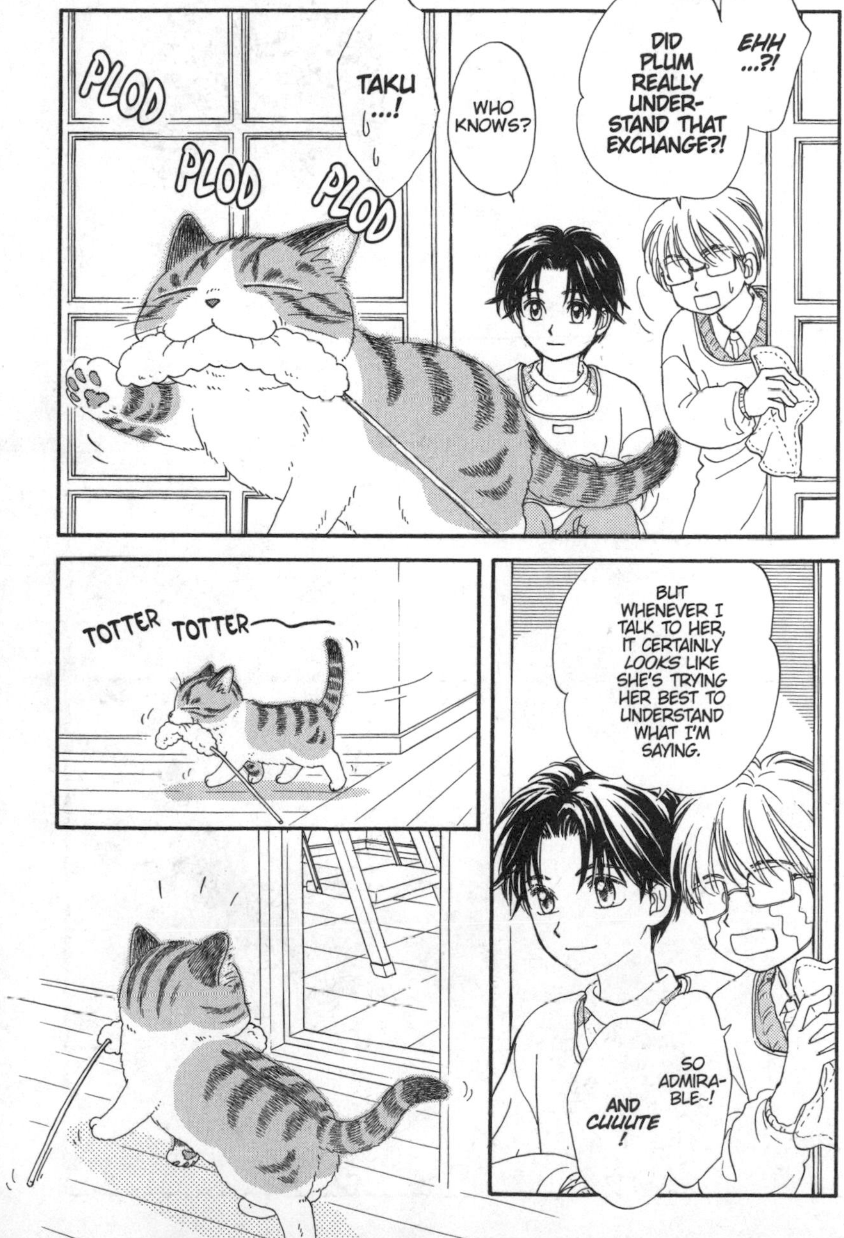
EHH ...?!
DID PLUM REALLY UNDER-STAND THAT EXCHANGE?!
WHO KNOWS?
TAKU ...!
PLOD
PLOD
PLOD
BUT WHENEVER I TALK TO HER, IT CERTAINLY *LOOKS* LIKE SHE'S TRYING HER BEST TO UNDERSTAND WHAT I'M SAYING.
SO ADMIRA-BLE~!
AND CUUUTE!
TOTTER TOTTER—

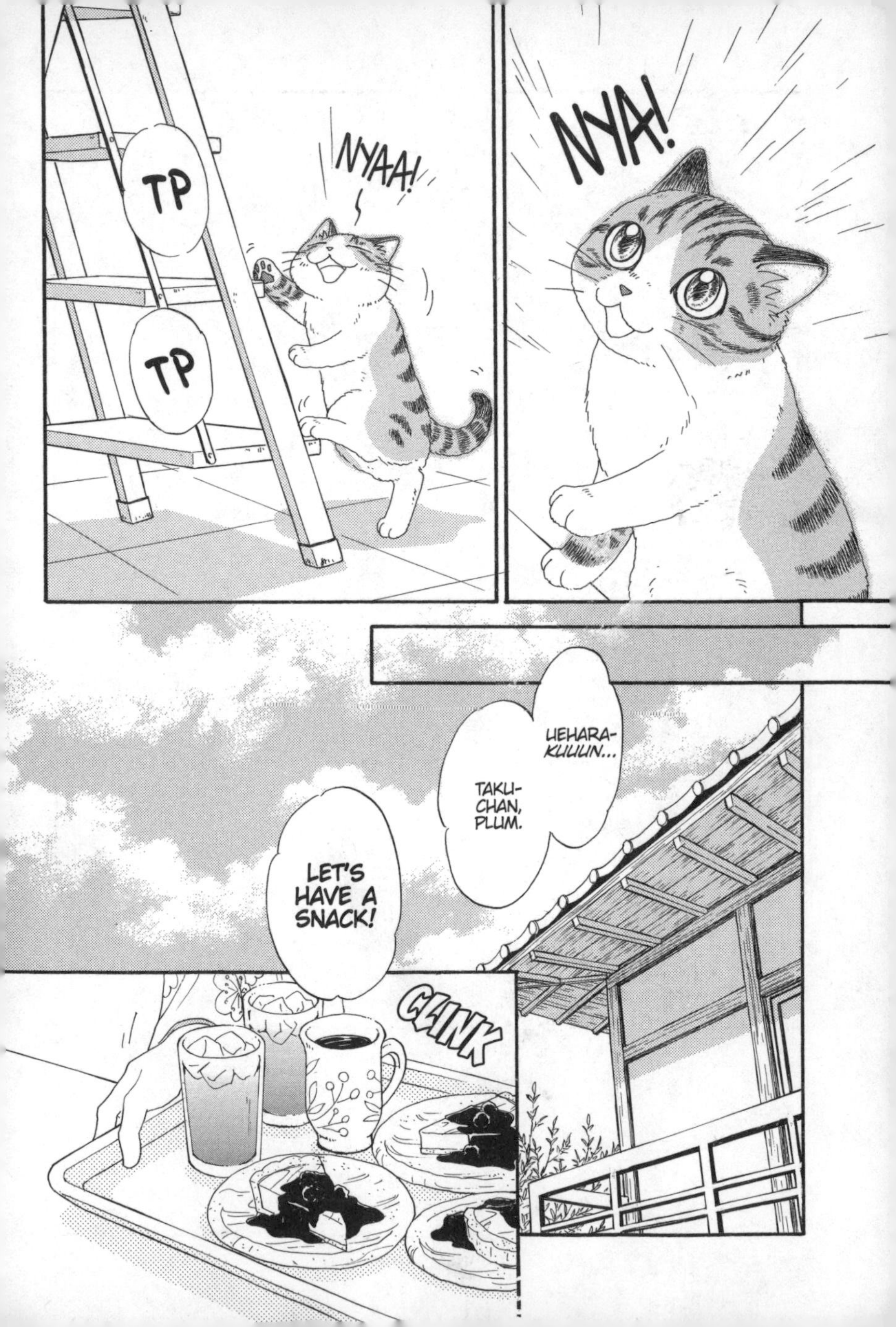
NYA!
NYAA!
TP
TP
UEHARA-KUUUN...
TAKU-CHAN, PLUM.
LET'S HAVE A SNACK!
CLINK

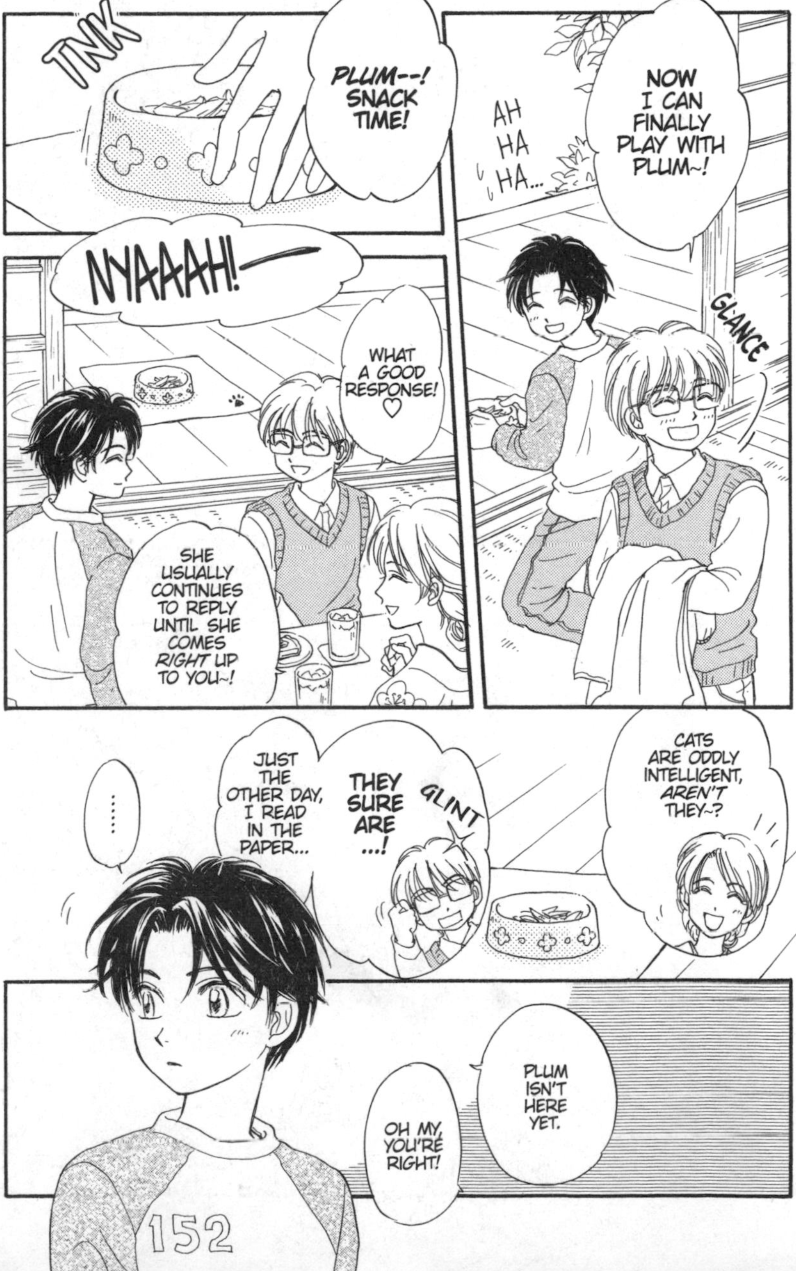
NOW I CAN FINALLY PLAY WITH PLUM~!
AH HA HA...
GLANCE
TNK
PLUM--! SNACK TIME!
NYAAAH!—
WHAT A GOOD RESPONSE! ♡
SHE USUALLY CONTINUES TO REPLY UNTIL SHE COMES RIGHT UP TO YOU~!
CATS ARE ODDLY INTELLIGENT, AREN'T THEY~?
GLINT
THEY SURE ARE ...!
JUST THE OTHER DAY, I READ IN THE PAPER...
......
PLUM ISN'T HERE YET.
OH MY, YOU'RE RIGHT!
152

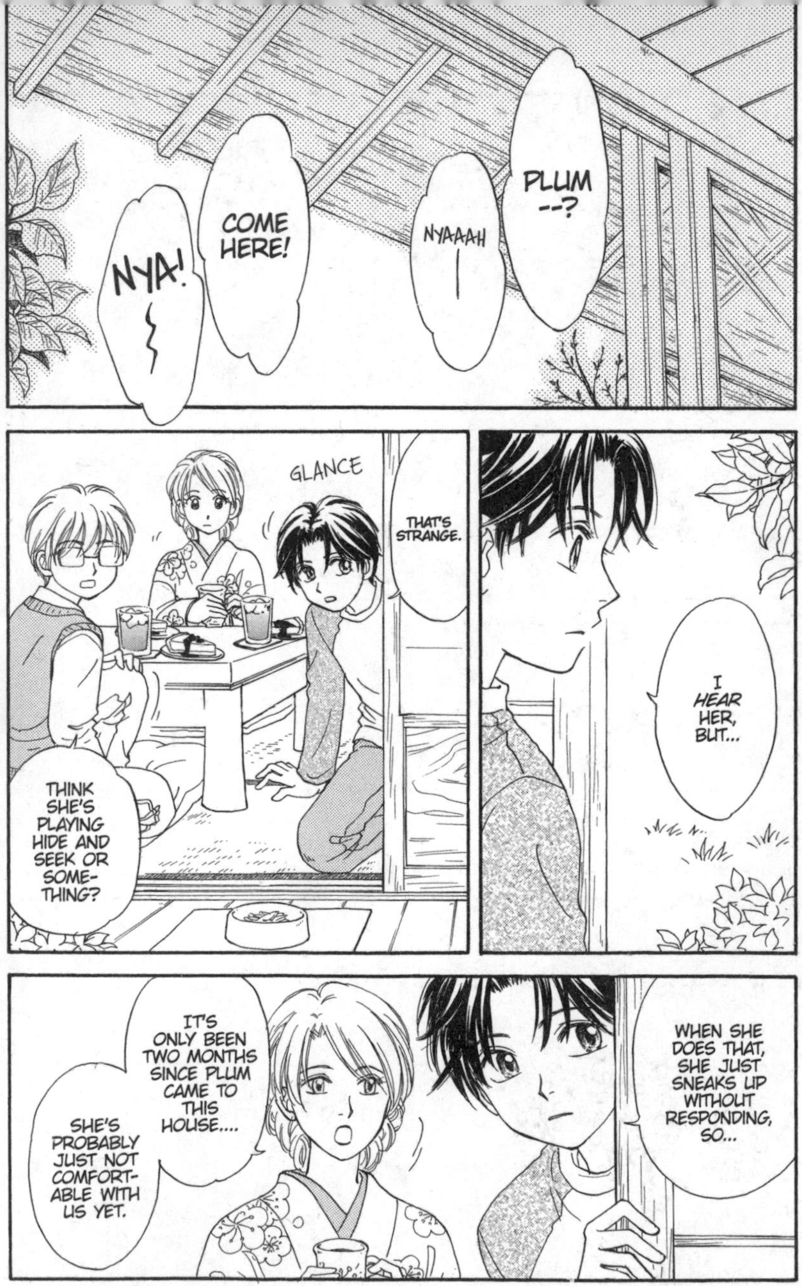
PLUM --?
NYAAAH
COME HERE!
NYA!
I HEAR HER, BUT...
THAT'S STRANGE.
GLANCE
THINK SHE'S PLAYING HIDE AND SEEK OR SOME-THING?
WHEN SHE DOES THAT, SHE JUST SNEAKS UP WITHOUT RESPONDING, SO...
IT'S ONLY BEEN TWO MONTHS SINCE PLUM CAME TO THIS HOUSE....
SHE'S PROBABLY JUST NOT COMFORT-ABLE WITH US YET.

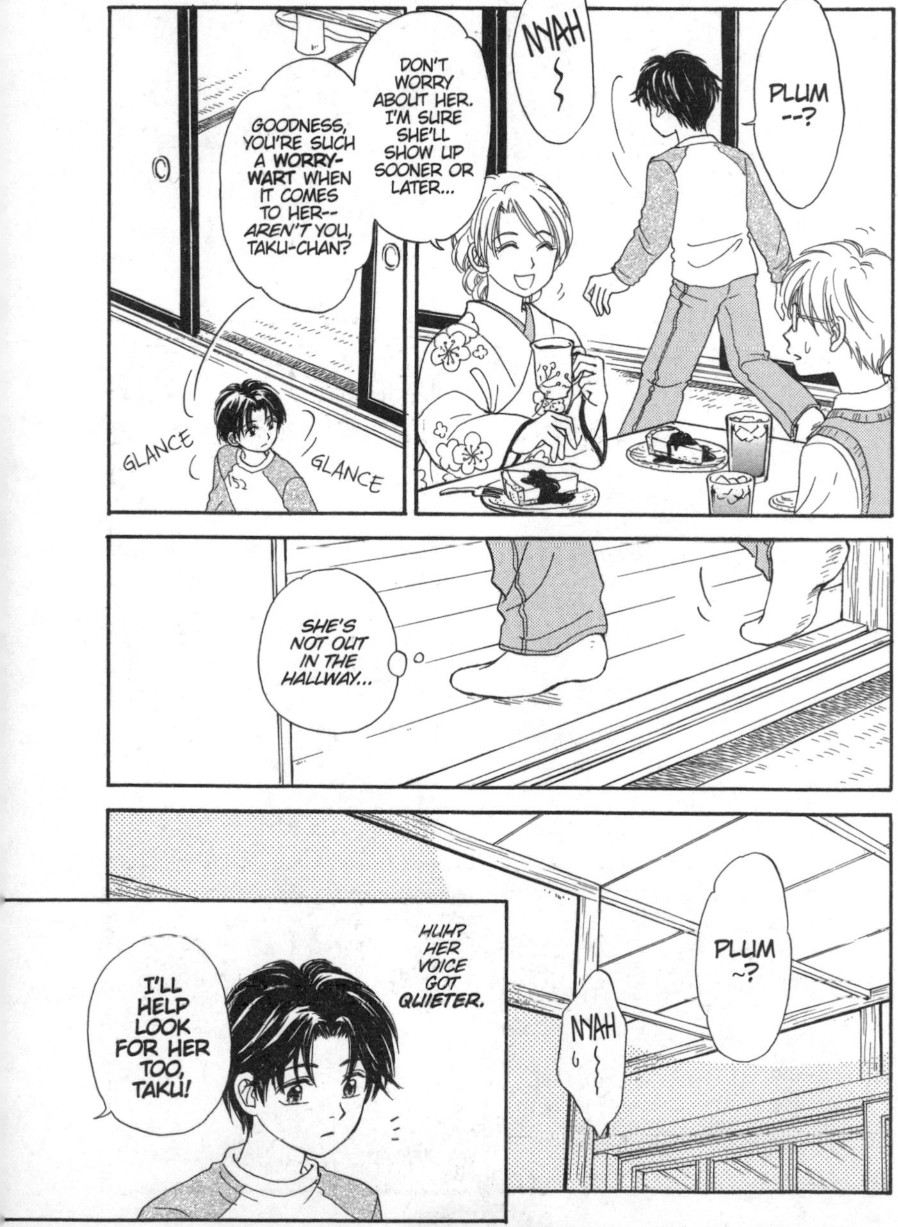
PLUM --?
NYAH ~
DON'T WORRY ABOUT HER. I'M SURE SHE'LL SHOW UP SOONER OR LATER...
GOODNESS, YOU'RE SUCH A WORRY-WART WHEN IT COMES TO HER-- AREN'T YOU, TAKU-CHAN?
GLANCE
GLANCE
SHE'S NOT OUT IN THE HALLWAY...
PLUM ~?
NYAH ~
HUH? HER VOICE GOT QUIETER.
I'LL HELP LOOK FOR HER TOO, TAKU!

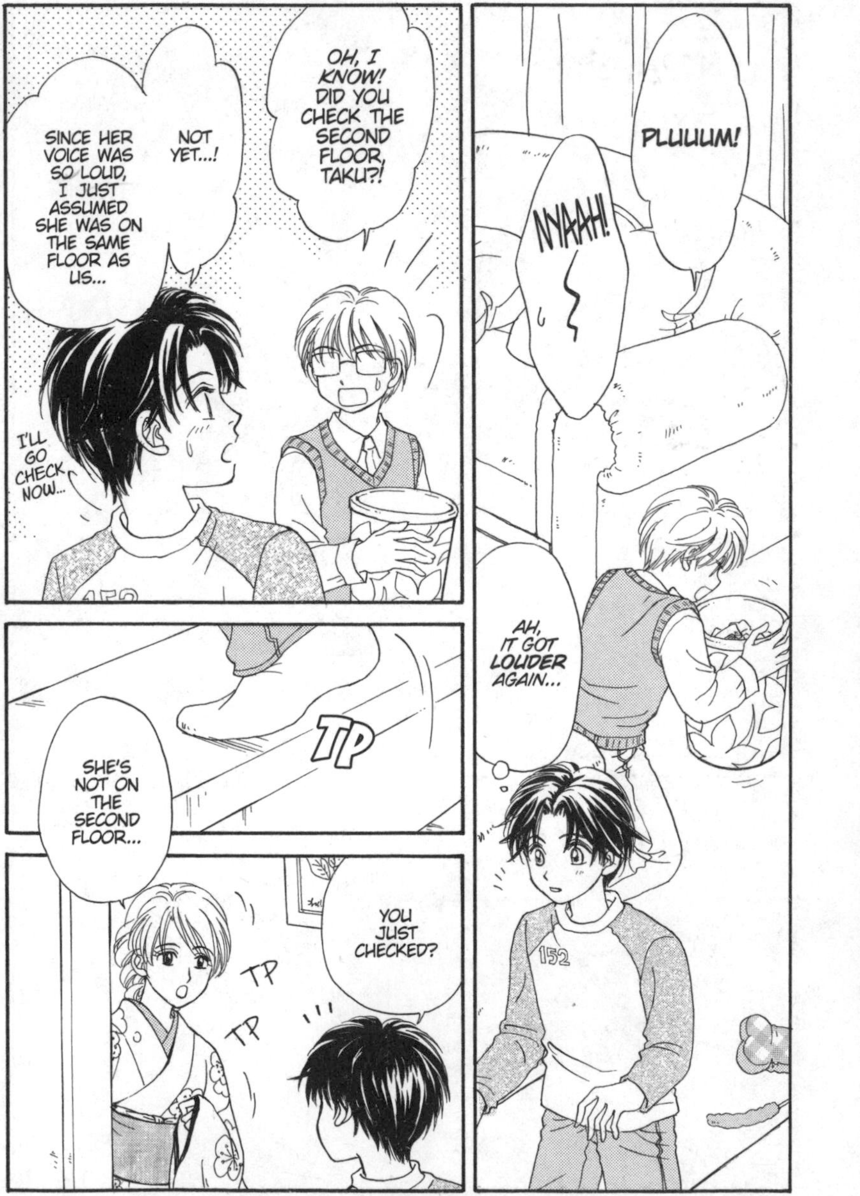
PLUUUM!
NYAAH!
AH, IT GOT LOUDER AGAIN...
OH, I KNOW! DID YOU CHECK THE SECOND FLOOR, TAKU?!
NOT YET...!
SINCE HER VOICE WAS SO LOUD, I JUST ASSUMED SHE WAS ON THE SAME FLOOR AS US...
I'LL GO CHECK NOW...
TP
SHE'S NOT ON THE SECOND FLOOR...
YOU JUST CHECKED?
TP
TP

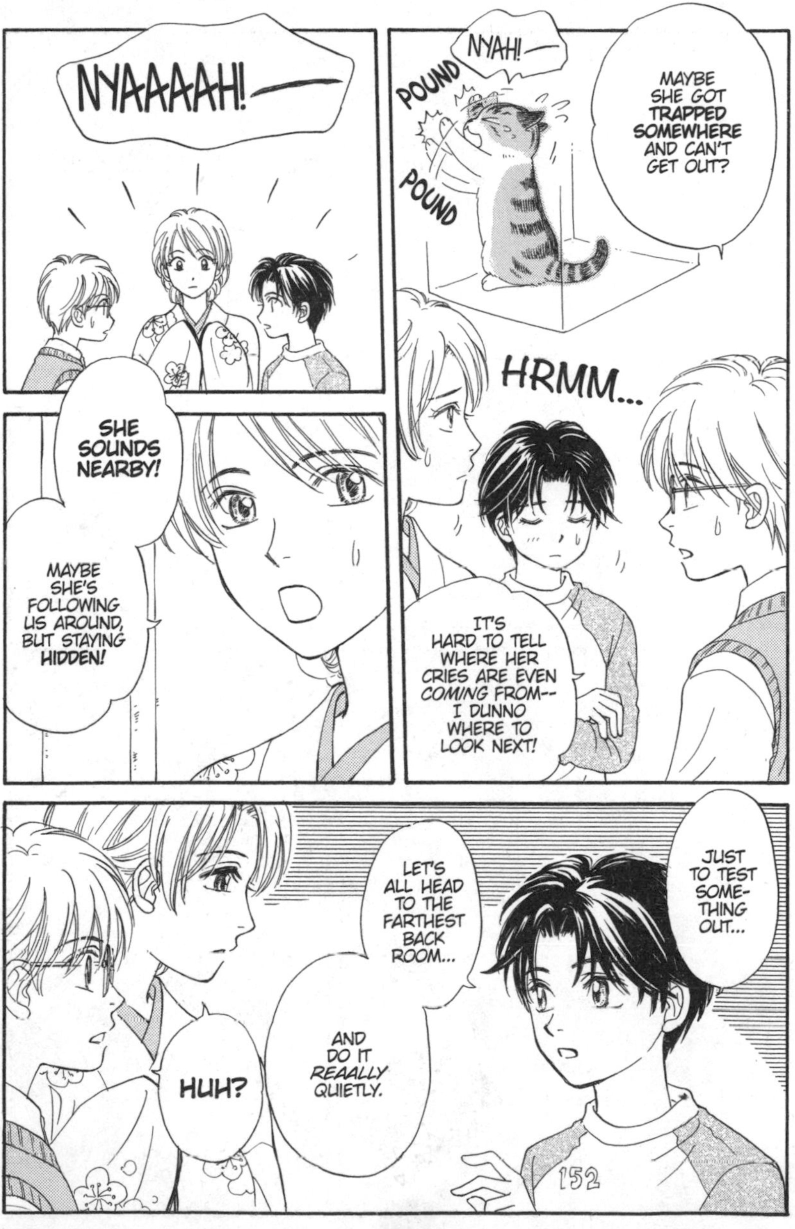
NYAH!——
POUND
POUND
MAYBE SHE GOT TRAPPED SOMEWHERE AND CAN'T GET OUT?
HRMM...
IT'S HARD TO TELL WHERE HER CRIES ARE EVEN COMING FROM-- I DUNNO WHERE TO LOOK NEXT!
NYAAAAH!——
SHE SOUNDS NEARBY!
MAYBE SHE'S FOLLOWING US AROUND, BUT STAYING HIDDEN!
JUST TO TEST SOME-THING OUT...
LET'S ALL HEAD TO THE FARTHEST BACK ROOM...
AND DO IT REAALLY QUIETLY.
HUH?
152

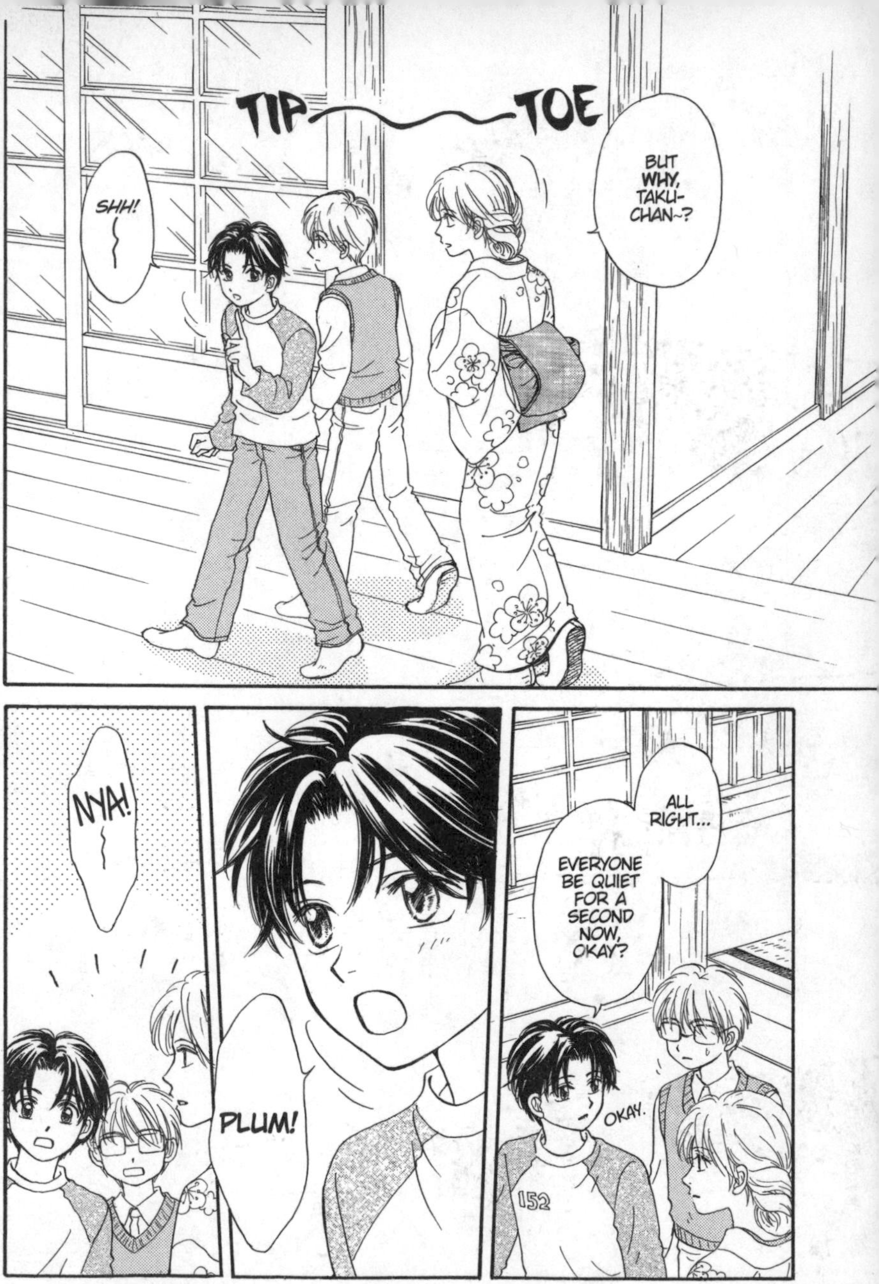
TIP—TOE
BUT WHY, TAKU-CHAN~?
SHH!
ALL RIGHT...
EVERYONE BE QUIET FOR A SECOND NOW, OKAY?
OKAY.
PLUM!
NYA!

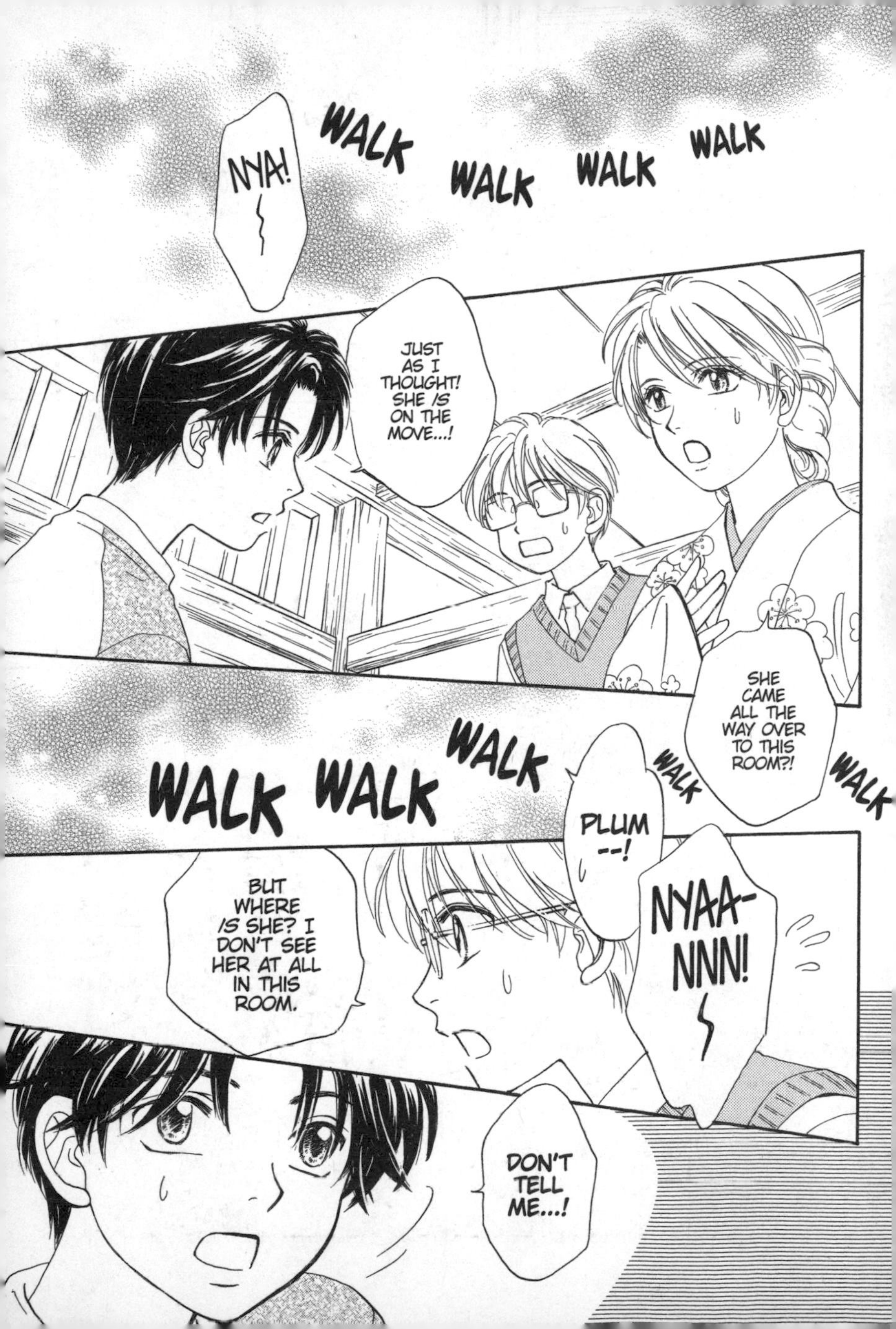
WALK
WALK
WALK
WALK
NYA!
JUST AS I THOUGHT! SHE IS ON THE MOVE...!
WALK
SHE CAME ALL THE WAY OVER TO THIS ROOM?!
WALK
WALK
WALK
WALK
PLUM--!
NYAA-NNN!
BUT WHERE IS SHE? I DON'T SEE HER AT ALL IN THIS ROOM.
DON'T TELL ME...!

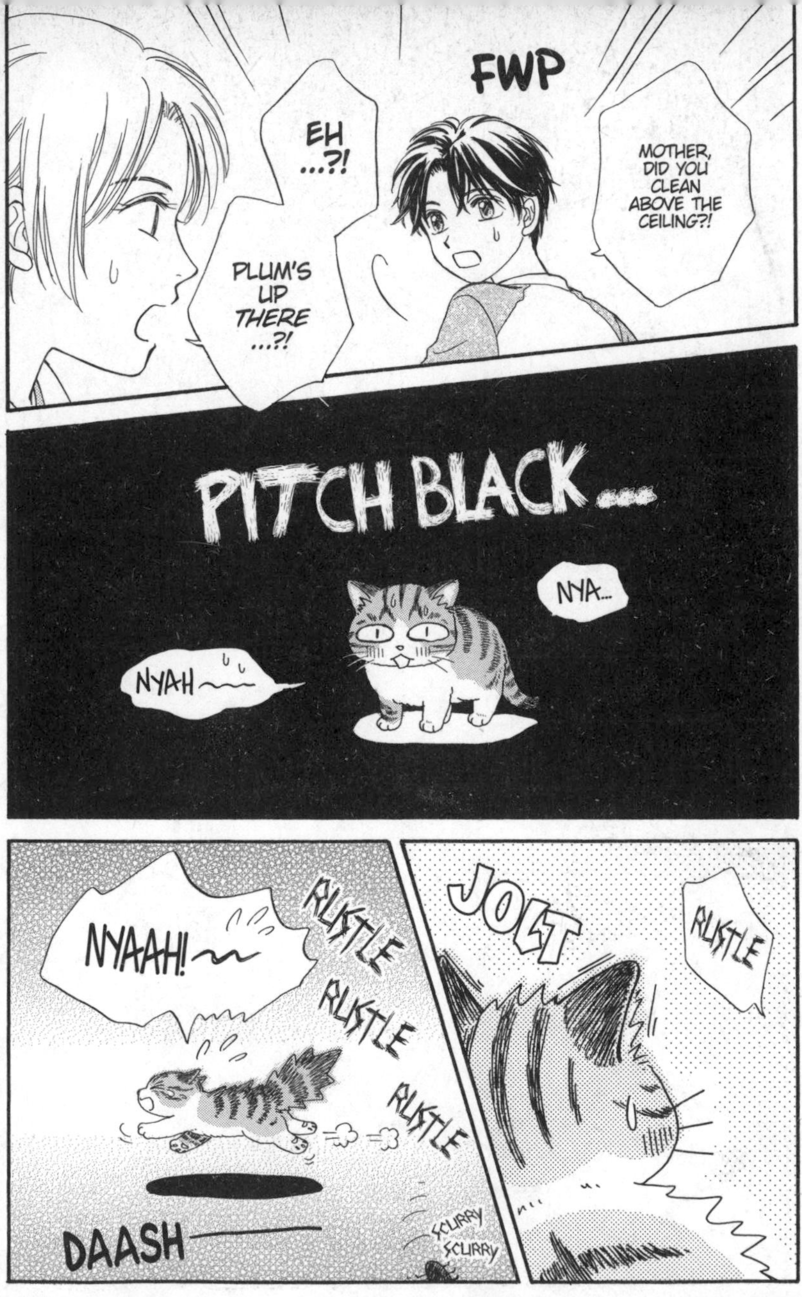
FWP
MOTHER, DID YOU CLEAN ABOVE THE CEILING?!
EH ...?!
PLUM'S UP THERE ...?!
PITCH BLACK...
NYA...
NYAH~~~
JOLT
RUSTLE
RUSTLE
RUSTLE
RUSTLE
NYAAH!~
SCURRY SCURRY
DAASH

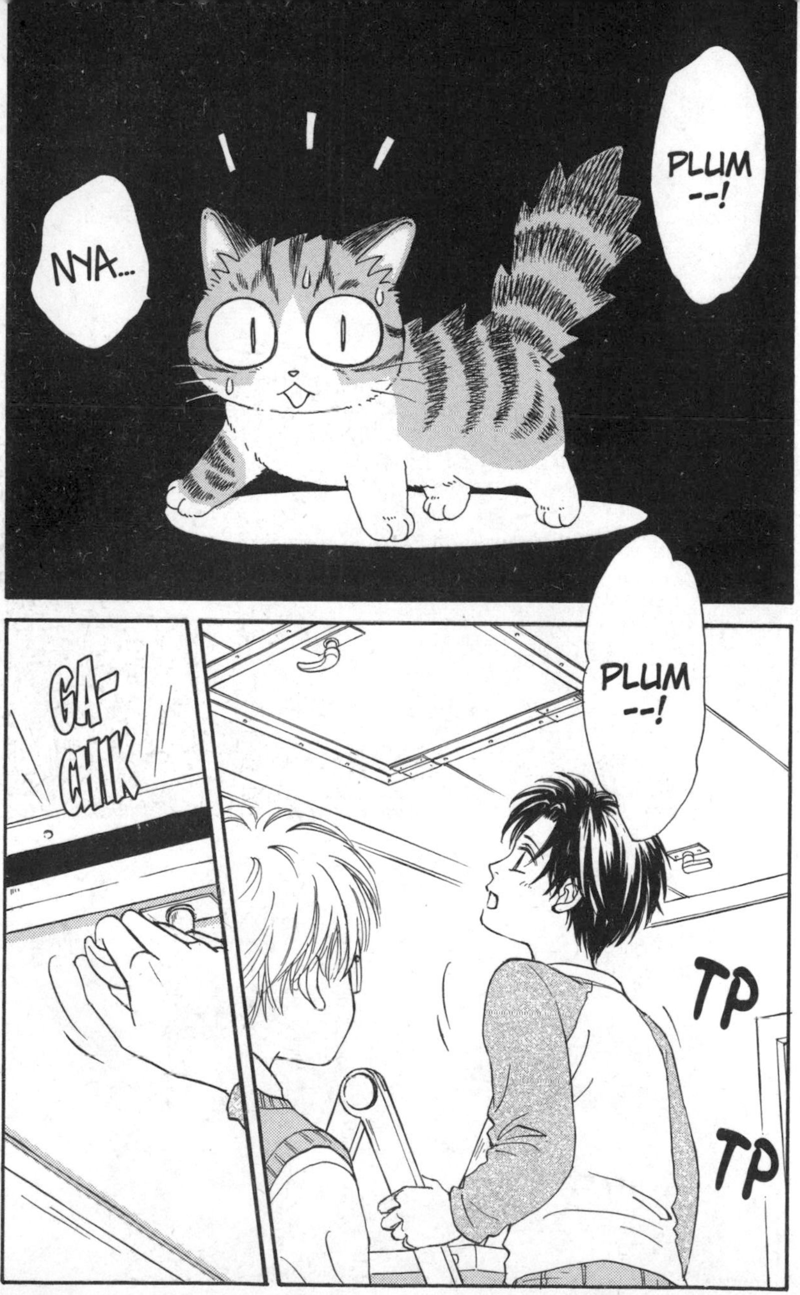
PLUM --!
NYA...
PLUM --!
TP
TP
GA-CHIK

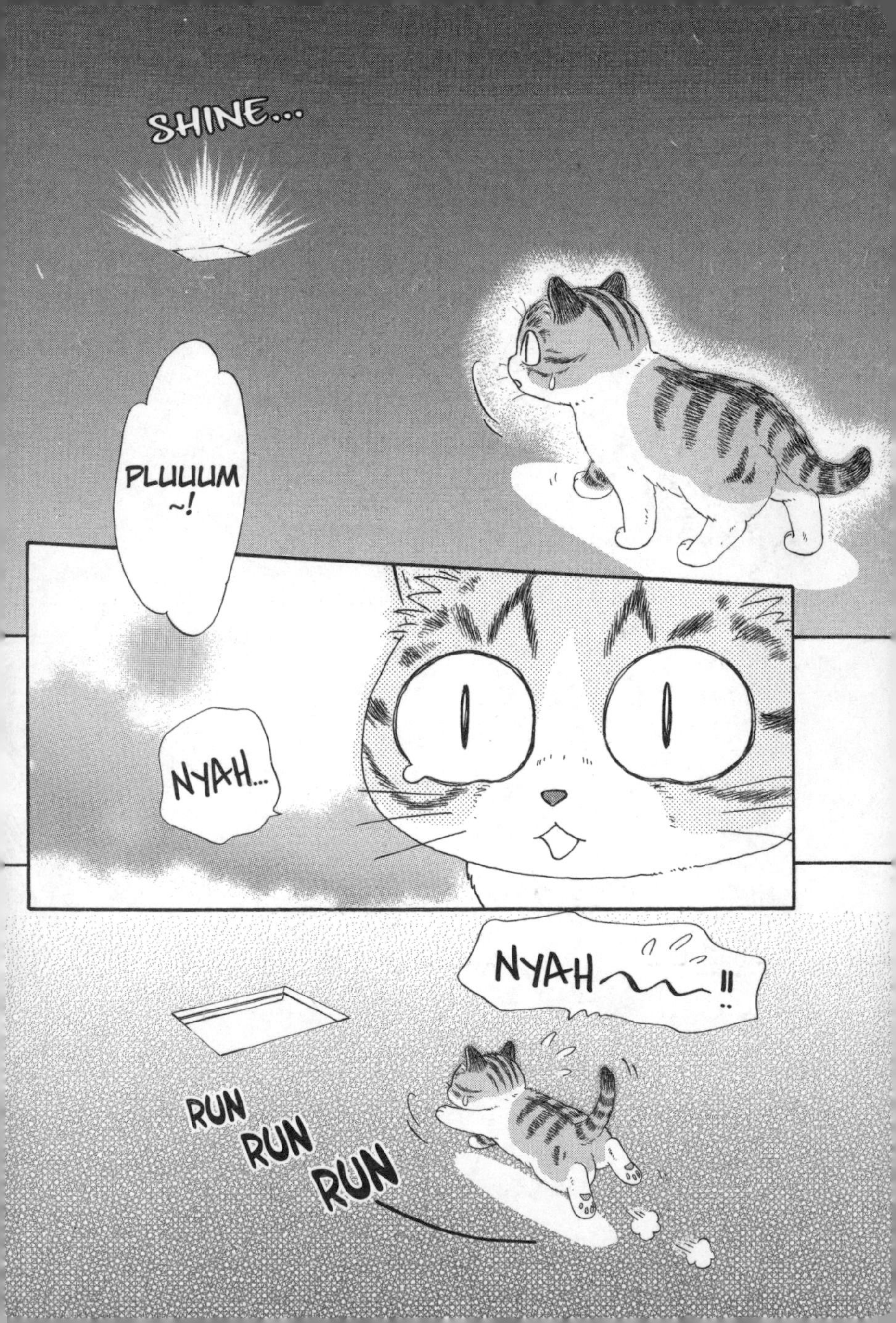
SHINE...
PLUUUM ~!
NYAH...
NYAH~~!!
RUN RUN RUN

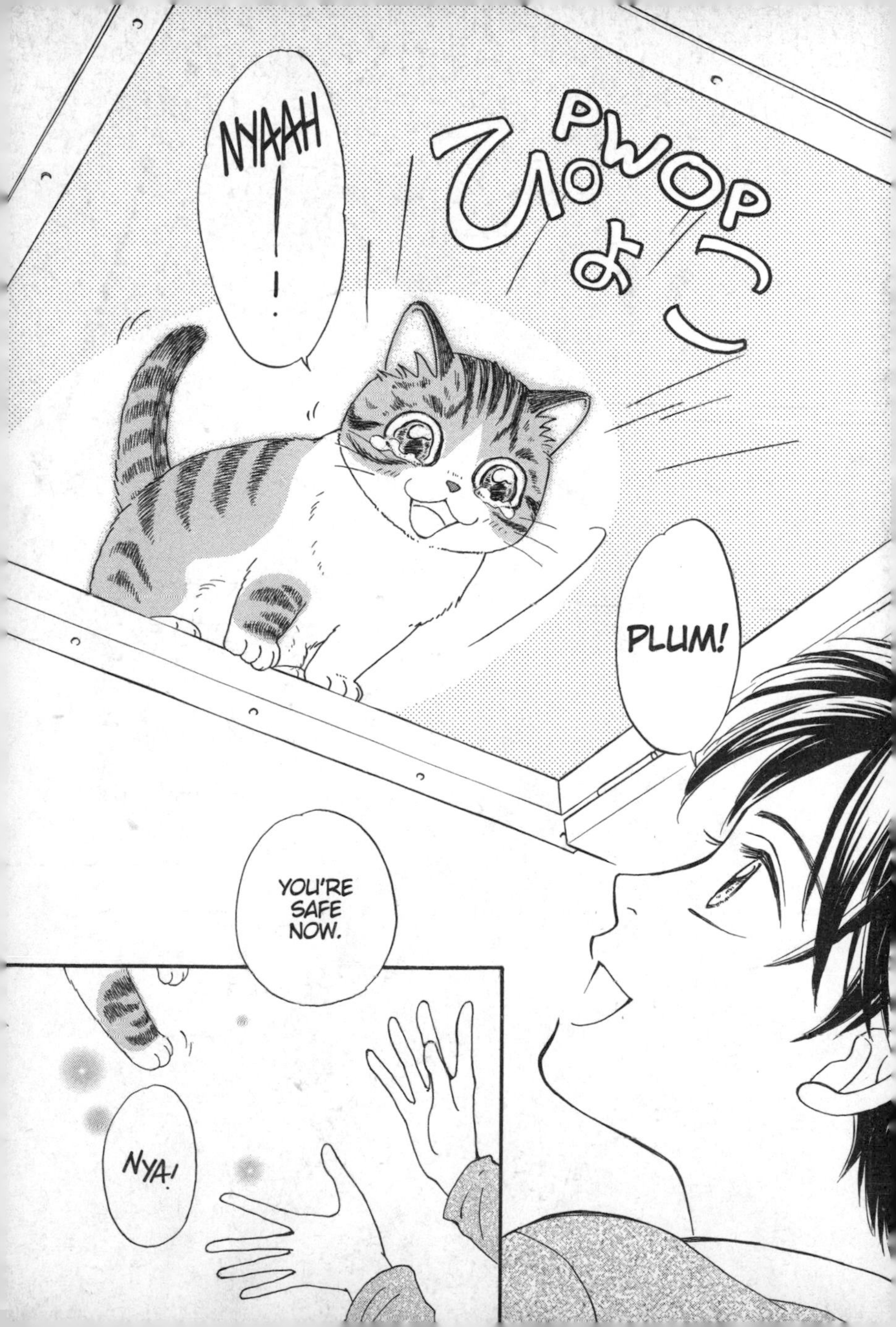
PWOP
ぴよこ
NYAAH!!
PLUM!
YOU'RE SAFE NOW.
NYA!

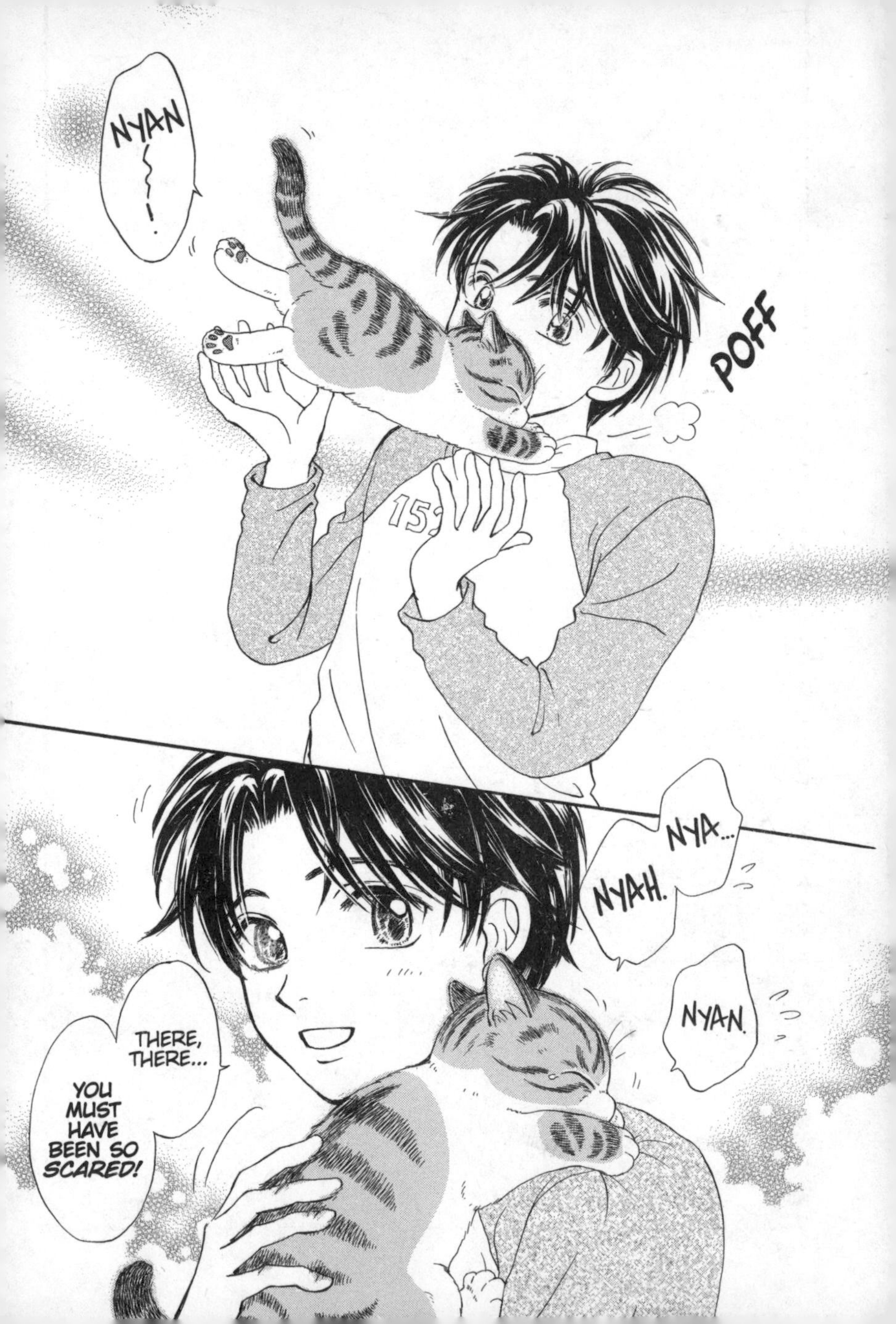
NYAN~!
POFF
NYA...
NYAH.
NYAN.
THERE, THERE... YOU MUST HAVE BEEN SO SCARED!

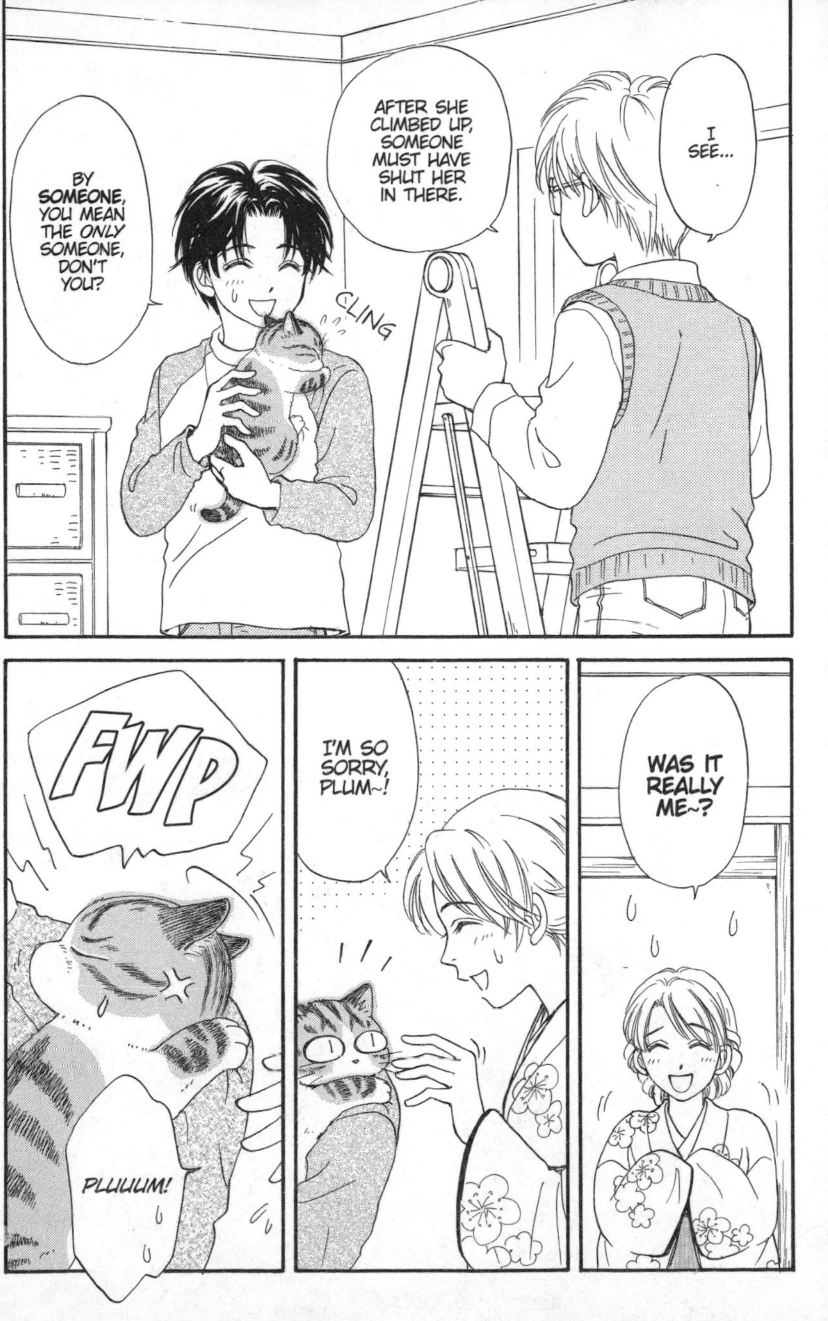
I SEE...
AFTER SHE CLIMBED UP, SOMEONE MUST HAVE SHUT HER IN THERE.
BY SOMEONE, YOU MEAN THE *ONLY* SOMEONE, DON'T YOU?
CLING
WAS IT REALLY ME~?
I'M SO SORRY, PLUM~!
FWP
PLUUUM!

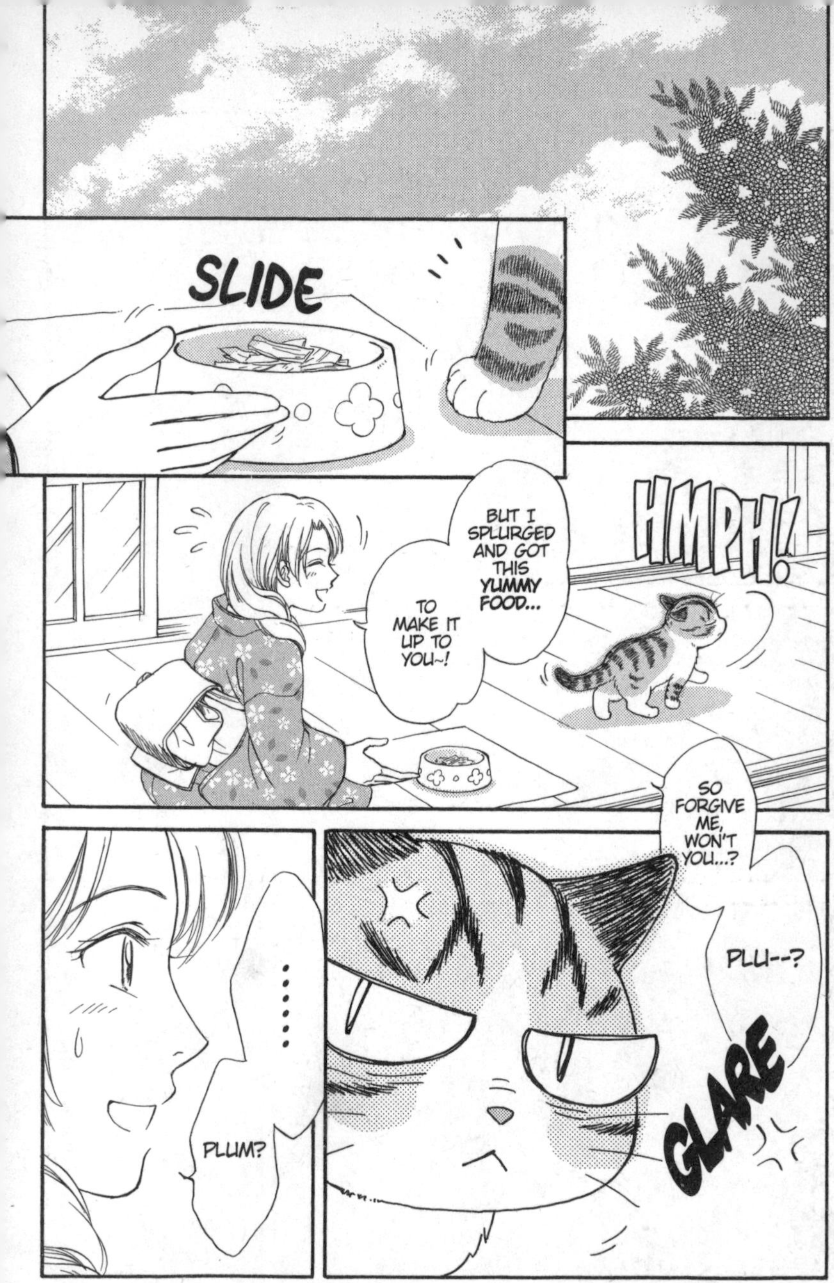
SLIDE
HMPH!
BUT I SPLURGED AND GOT THIS YUMMY FOOD...
TO MAKE IT UP TO YOU~!
SO FORGIVE ME, WON'T YOU...?
PLU--?
GLARE
......
PLUM?

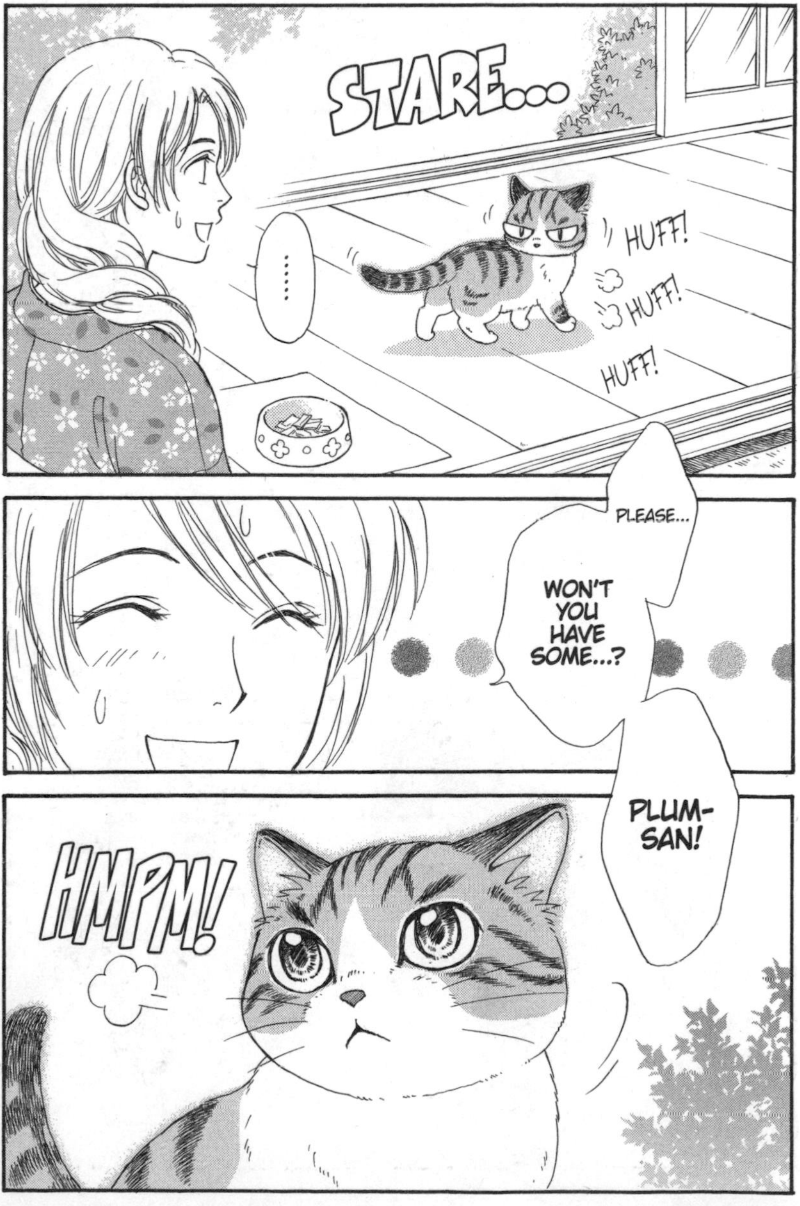
STARE...
......
HUFF!
HUFF!
HUFF!
PLEASE...
WON'T YOU HAVE SOME...?
PLUM-SAN!
HMPM!

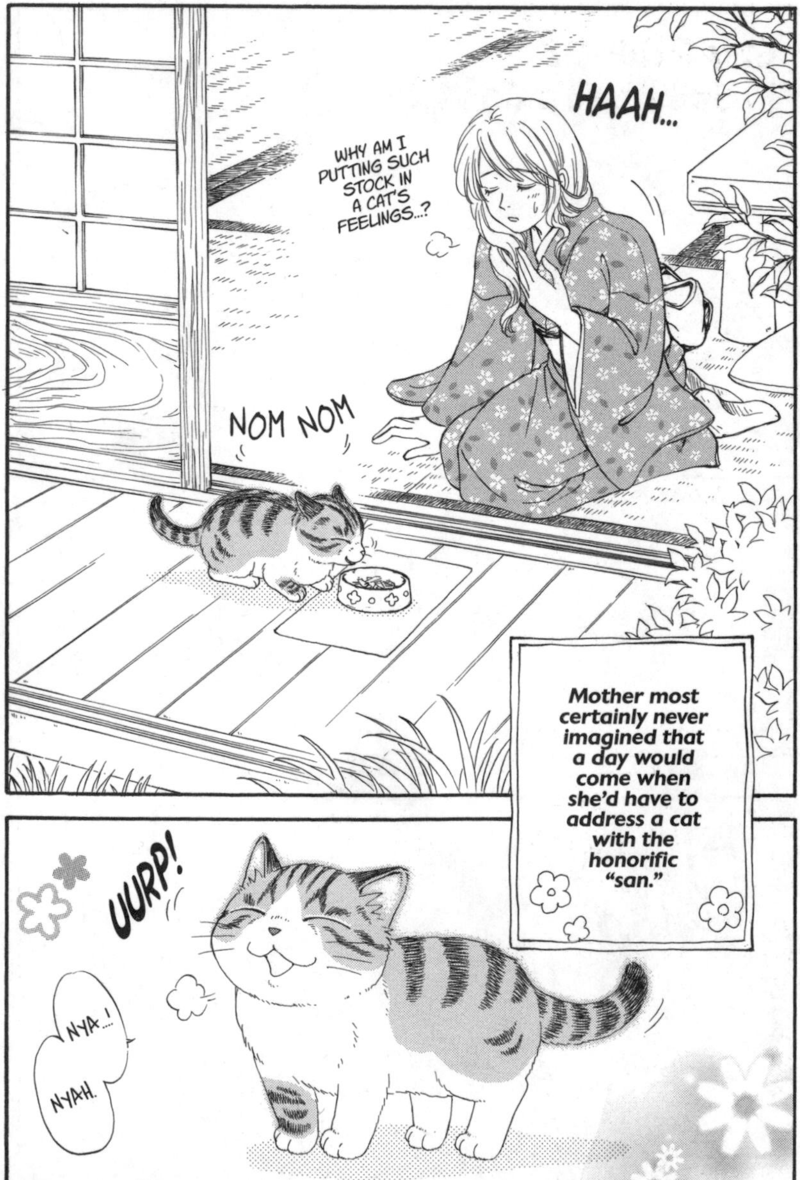
HAAH...
WHY AM I PUTTING SUCH STOCK IN A CAT'S FEELINGS...?
NOM NOM
Mother most certainly never imagined that a day would come when she'd have to address a cat with the honorific "san."
UURP!
NYA...!
NYAH.

THE END

CHAPTER 22
In Snowball's Case

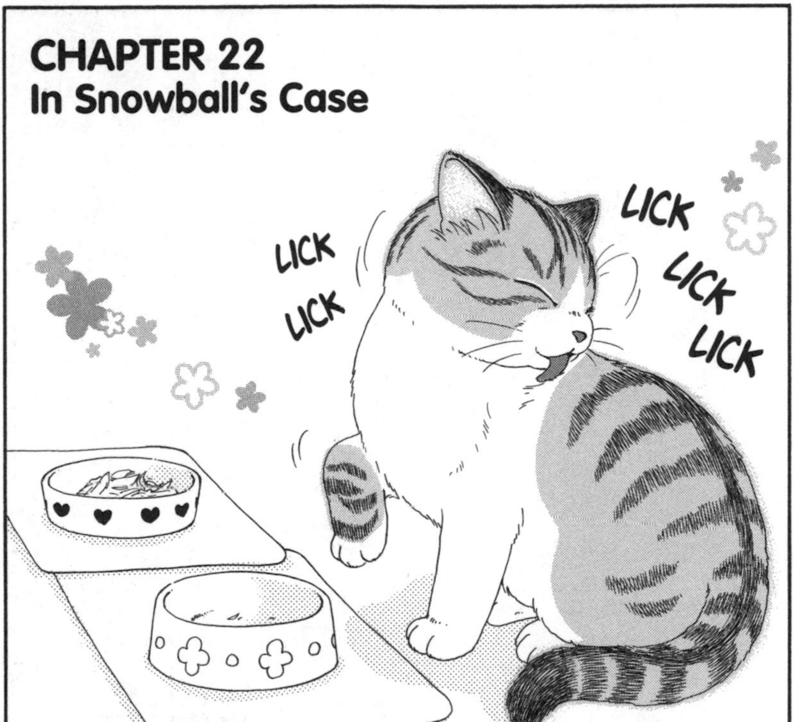
LICK
LICK
LICK
LICK
LICK

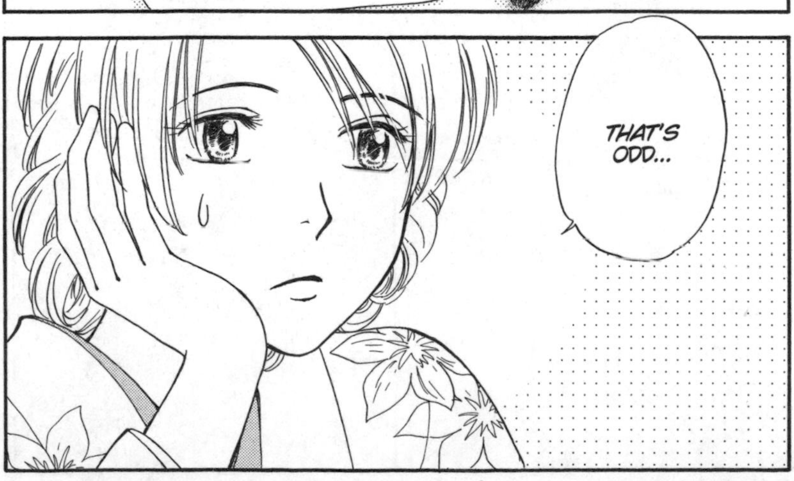
THAT'S ODD...

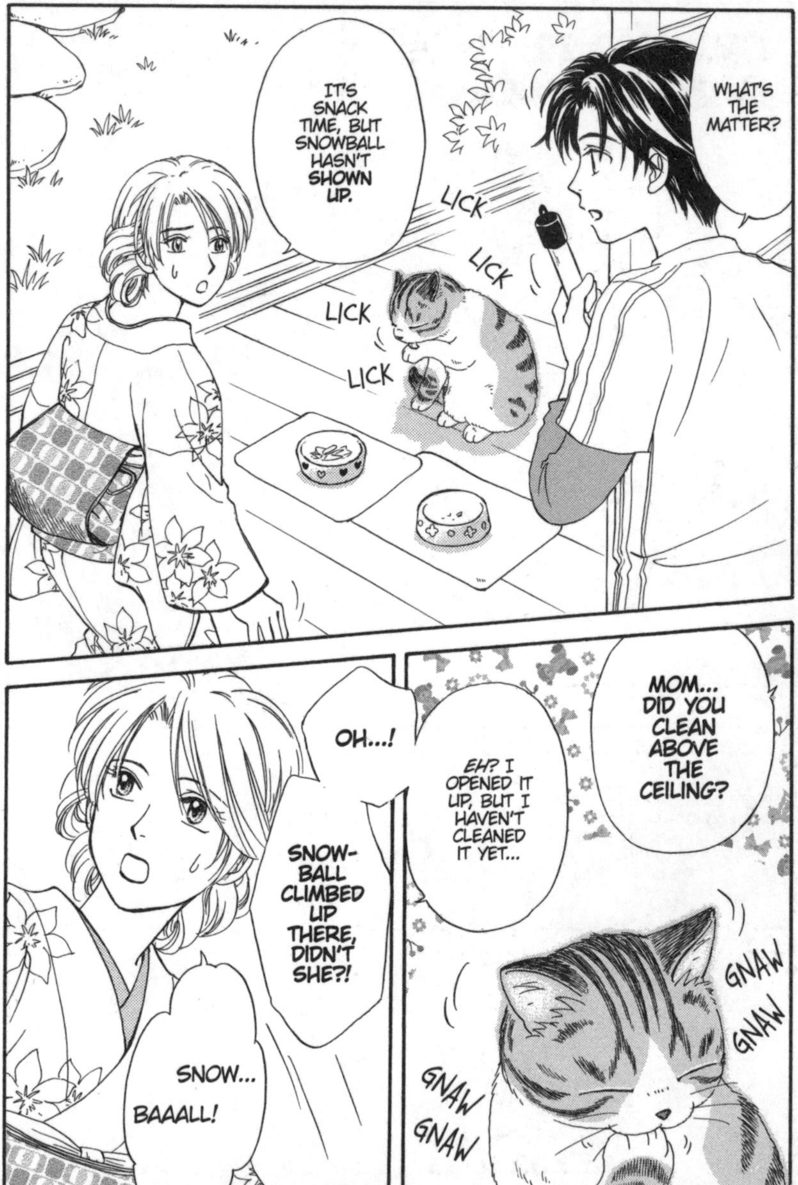
WHAT'S THE MATTER?
IT'S SNACK TIME, BUT SNOWBALL HASN'T SHOWN UP.
LICK
LICK
LICK
LICK
MOM... DID YOU CLEAN ABOVE THE CEILING?
EH? I OPENED IT UP, BUT I HAVEN'T CLEANED IT YET...
GNAW
GNAW
GNAW
GNAW
OH...!
SNOW-BALL CLIMBED UP THERE, DIDN'T SHE?!
SNOW...
BAAALL!

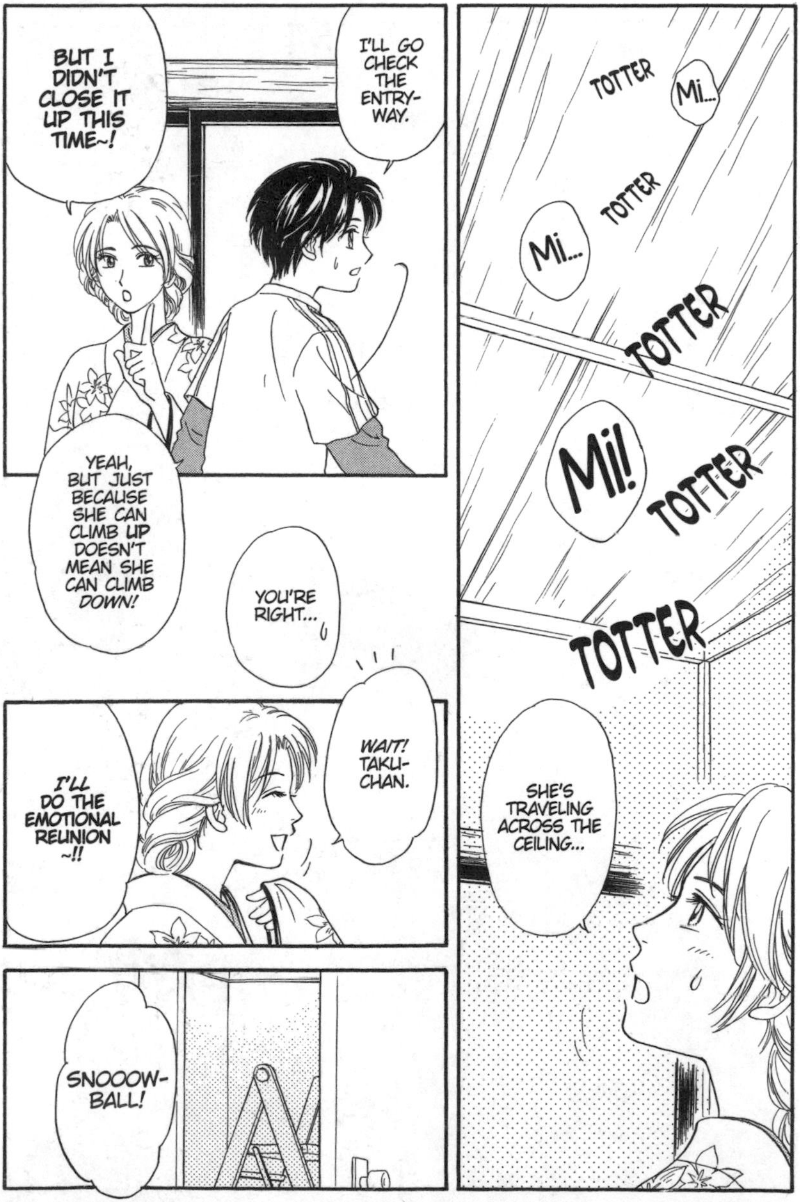
TOTTER
Mi...
TOTTER
Mi...
TOTTER
Mi!
TOTTER
TOTTER
SHE'S TRAVELING ACROSS THE CEILING...
I'LL GO CHECK THE ENTRY-WAY.
BUT I DIDN'T CLOSE IT UP THIS TIME~!
YEAH, BUT JUST BECAUSE SHE CAN CLIMB UP DOESN'T MEAN SHE CAN CLIMB *DOWN!*
YOU'RE RIGHT...
WAIT! TAKU-CHAN.
I'LL DO THE EMOTIONAL REUNION ~!!
SNOOOW-BALL!

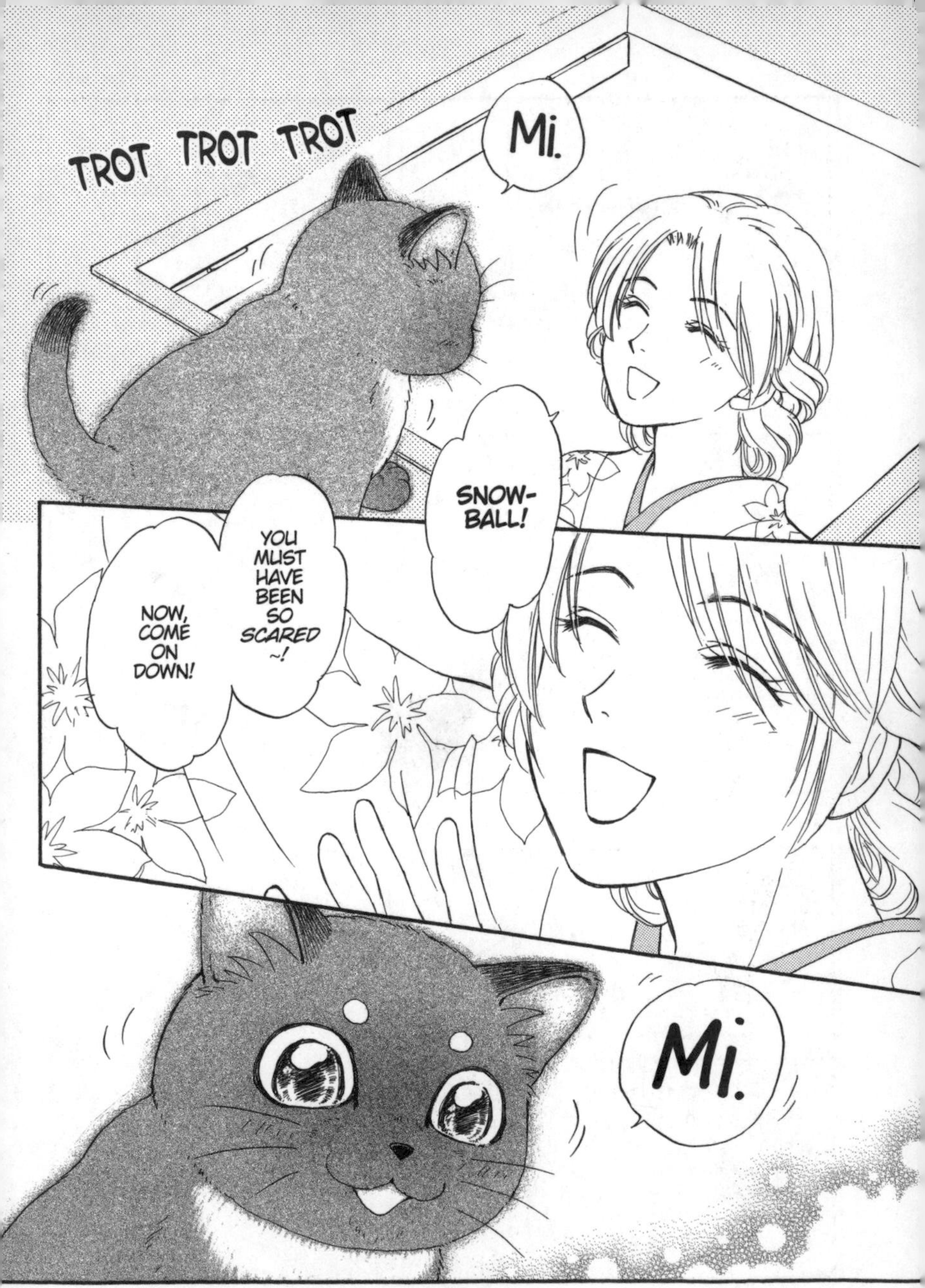
Mi.
TROT TROT TROT
SNOW-BALL!
YOU MUST HAVE BEEN SO SCARED ~!
NOW, COME ON DOWN!
Mi.

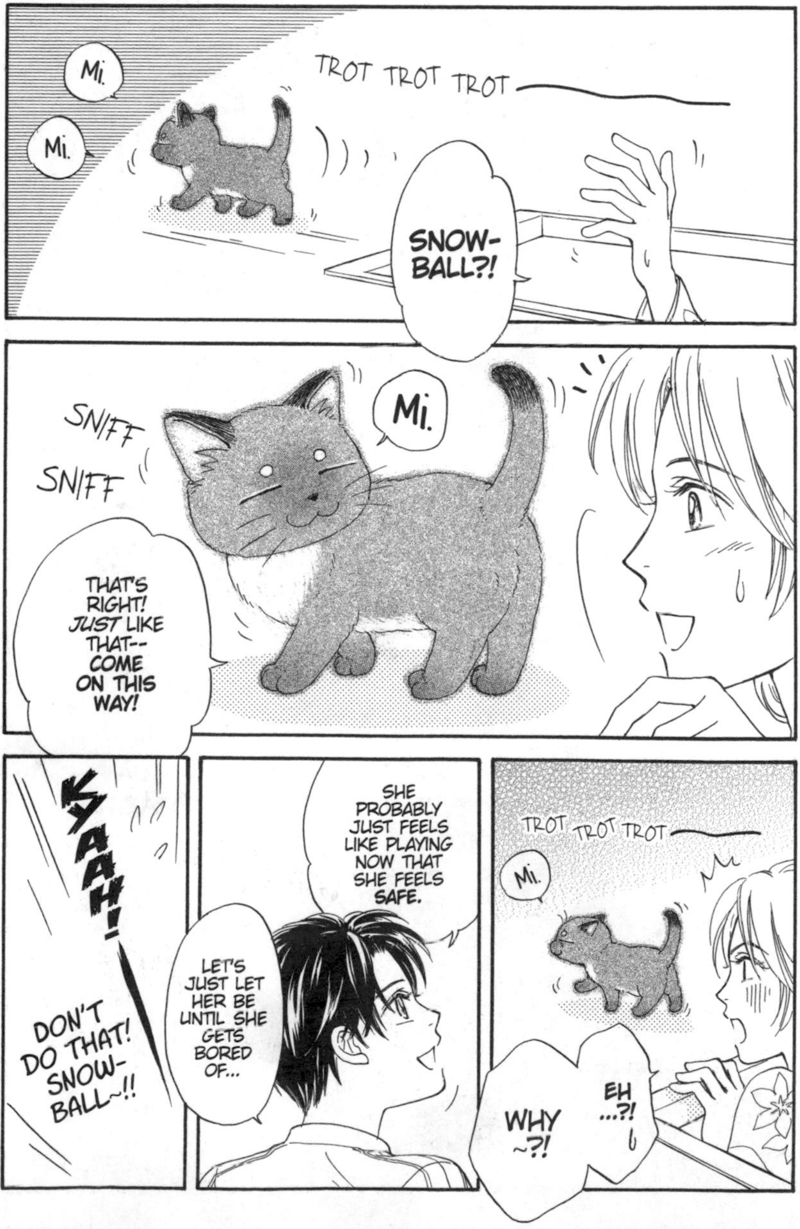
TROT TROT TROT——
SNOW-BALL?!
Mi.
Mi.
Mi.
SNIFF SNIFF
THAT'S RIGHT! *JUST* LIKE THAT-- COME ON THIS WAY!
TROT TROT TROT——
Mi.
EH ...?!
WHY ~?!
SHE PROBABLY JUST FEELS LIKE PLAYING NOW THAT SHE FEELS SAFE.
LET'S JUST LET HER BE UNTIL SHE GETS BORED OF...
KYAAAH!
DON'T DO THAT! SNOW-BALL~!!

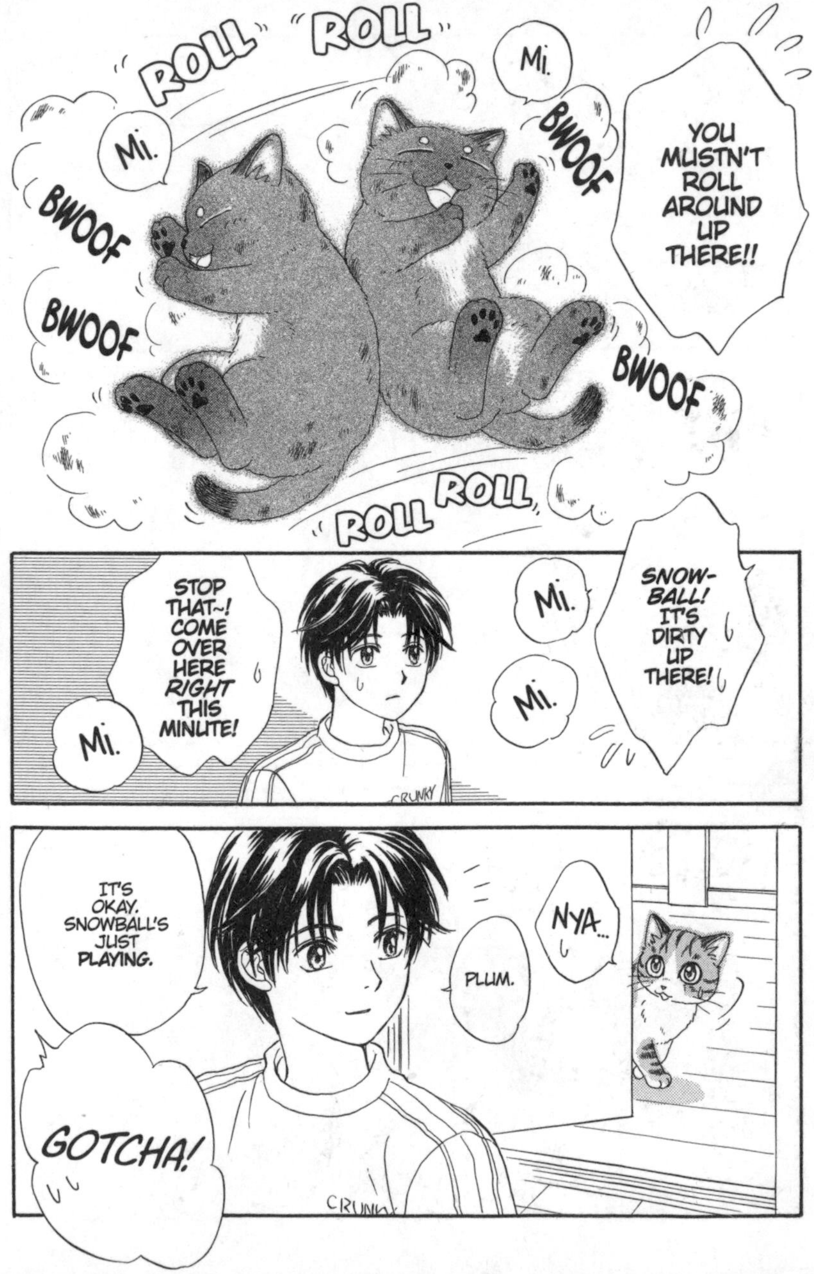
YOU MUSTN'T ROLL AROUND UP THERE!!
Mi.
BWOOF
ROLL
ROLL
Mi.
BWOOF
BWOOF
BWOOF
ROLL
ROLL
SNOW-BALL! IT'S DIRTY UP THERE!
Mi.
Mi.
STOP THAT~! COME OVER HERE RIGHT THIS MINUTE!
Mi.
CRUNKY
NYA...
PLUM.
IT'S OKAY. SNOWBALL'S JUST PLAYING.
GOTCHA!
CRUNKY

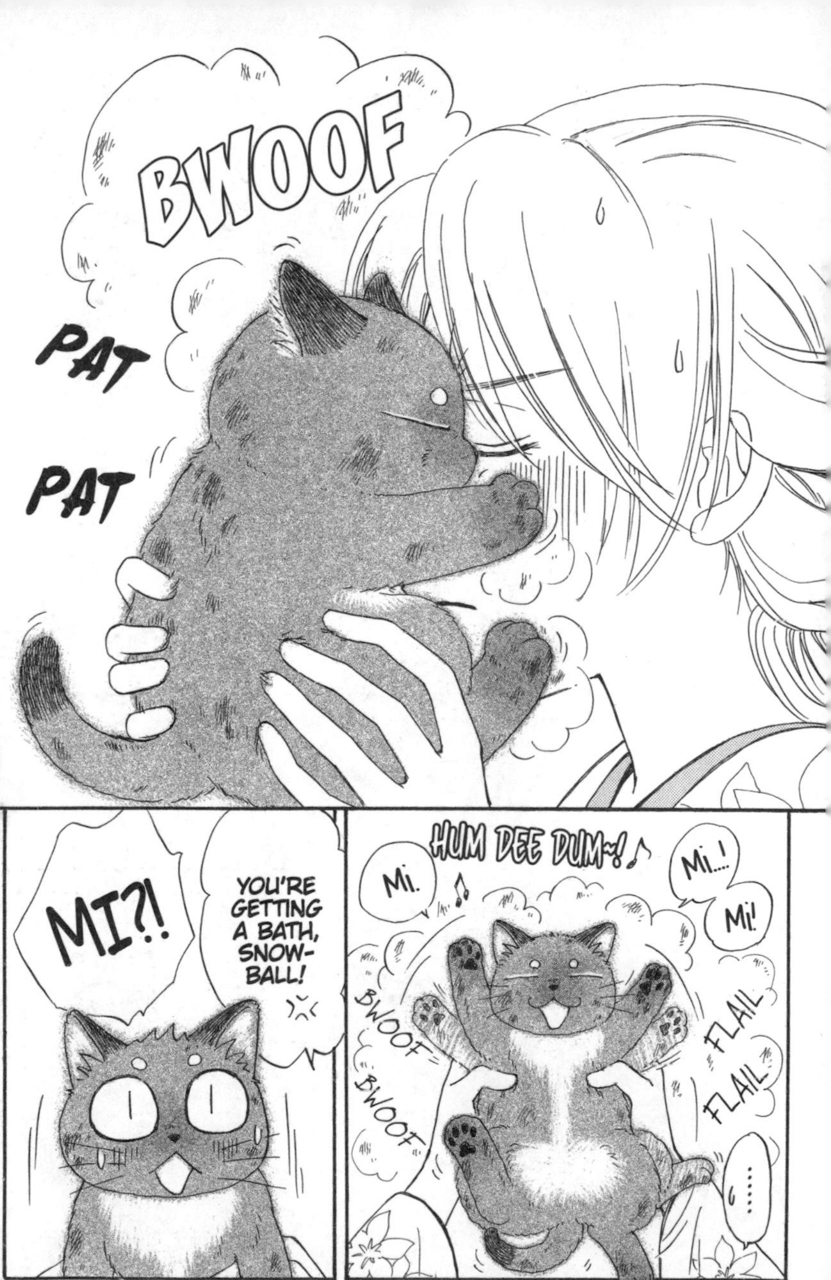
BWOOF
PAT
PAT
HUM DEE DUM~!
Mi...!
Mi!
Mi.
FLAIL
FLAIL
BWOOF
BWOOF
......
YOU'RE GETTING A BATH, SNOW-BALL!
MI?!

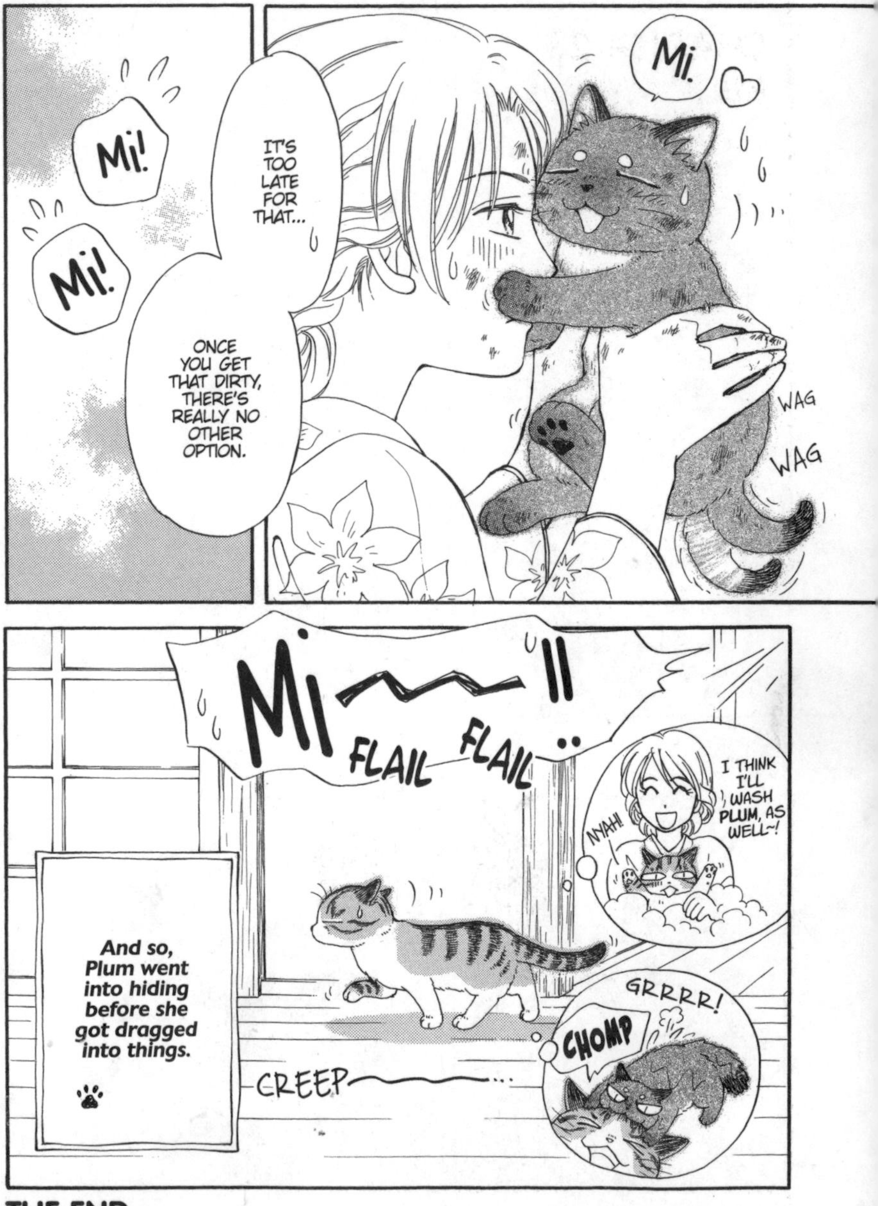
Mi.
IT'S TOO LATE FOR THAT...
ONCE YOU GET THAT DIRTY, THERE'S REALLY NO OTHER OPTION.
WAG
WAG
Mi!
Mi!
Mi~~!!
FLAIL FLAIL
I THINK I'LL WASH PLUM, AS WELL~!
NYAH!
GRRRR!
CHOMP
CREEP...
And so, Plum went into hiding before she got dragged into things.

THE END

CHAPTER 23
Buck's Choice

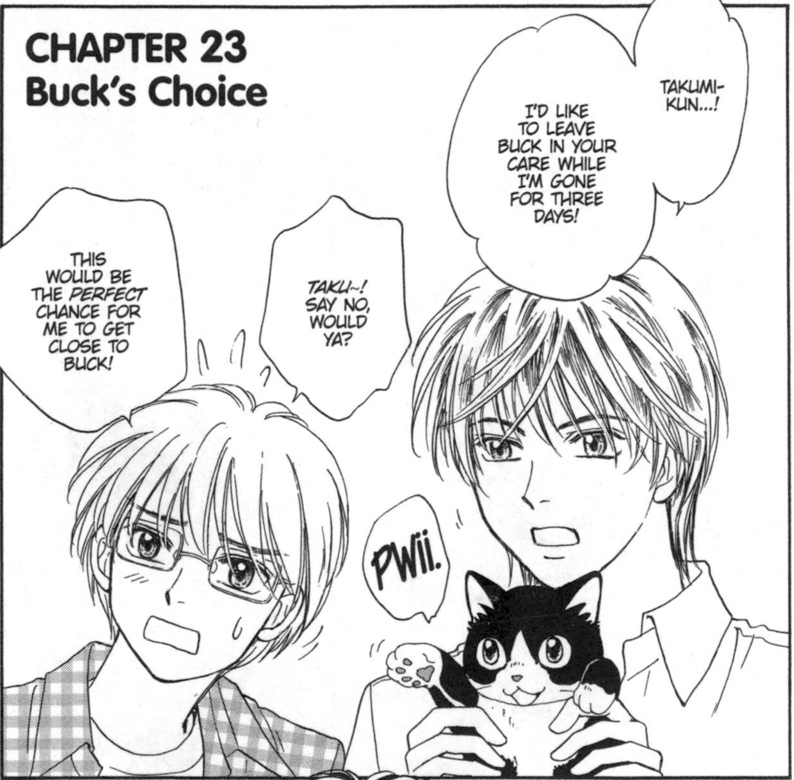
TAKUMI-KUN...!
I'D LIKE TO LEAVE BUCK IN YOUR CARE WHILE I'M GONE FOR THREE DAYS!
PWii.
TAKU~! SAY NO, WOULD YA?
THIS WOULD BE THE *PERFECT* CHANCE FOR ME TO GET CLOSE TO BUCK!

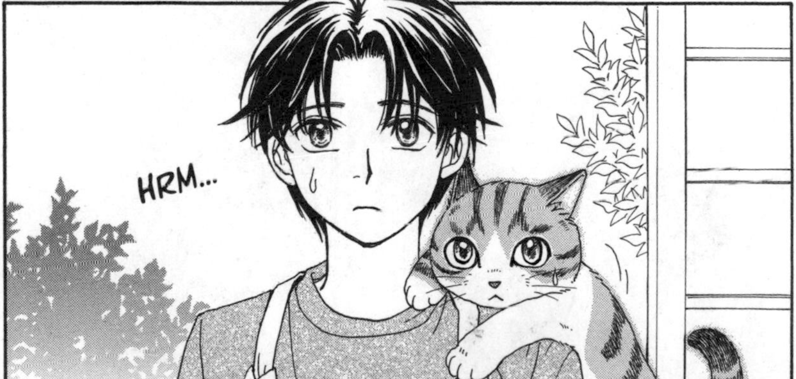
HRM...

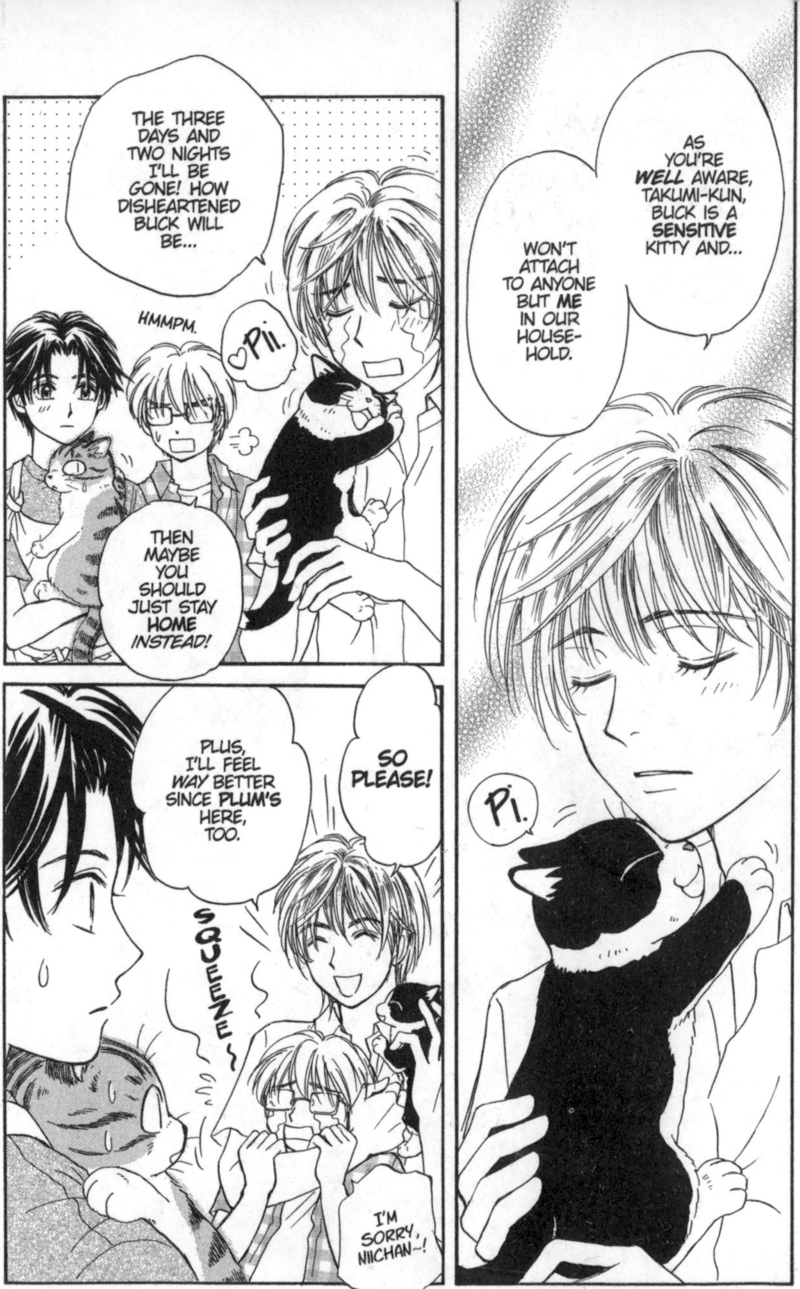
AS YOU'RE WELL AWARE, TAKUMI-KUN, BUCK IS A SENSITIVE KITTY AND...
WON'T ATTACH TO ANYONE BUT ME IN OUR HOUSE-HOLD.
Pi.
THE THREE DAYS AND TWO NIGHTS I'LL BE GONE! HOW DISHEARTENED BUCK WILL BE...
Pii.
HMMPM.
THEN MAYBE YOU SHOULD JUST STAY HOME INSTEAD!
SO PLEASE!
PLUS, I'LL FEEL WAY BETTER SINCE PLUM'S HERE, TOO.
SQUEEZE~
I'M SORRY, NIICHAN~!

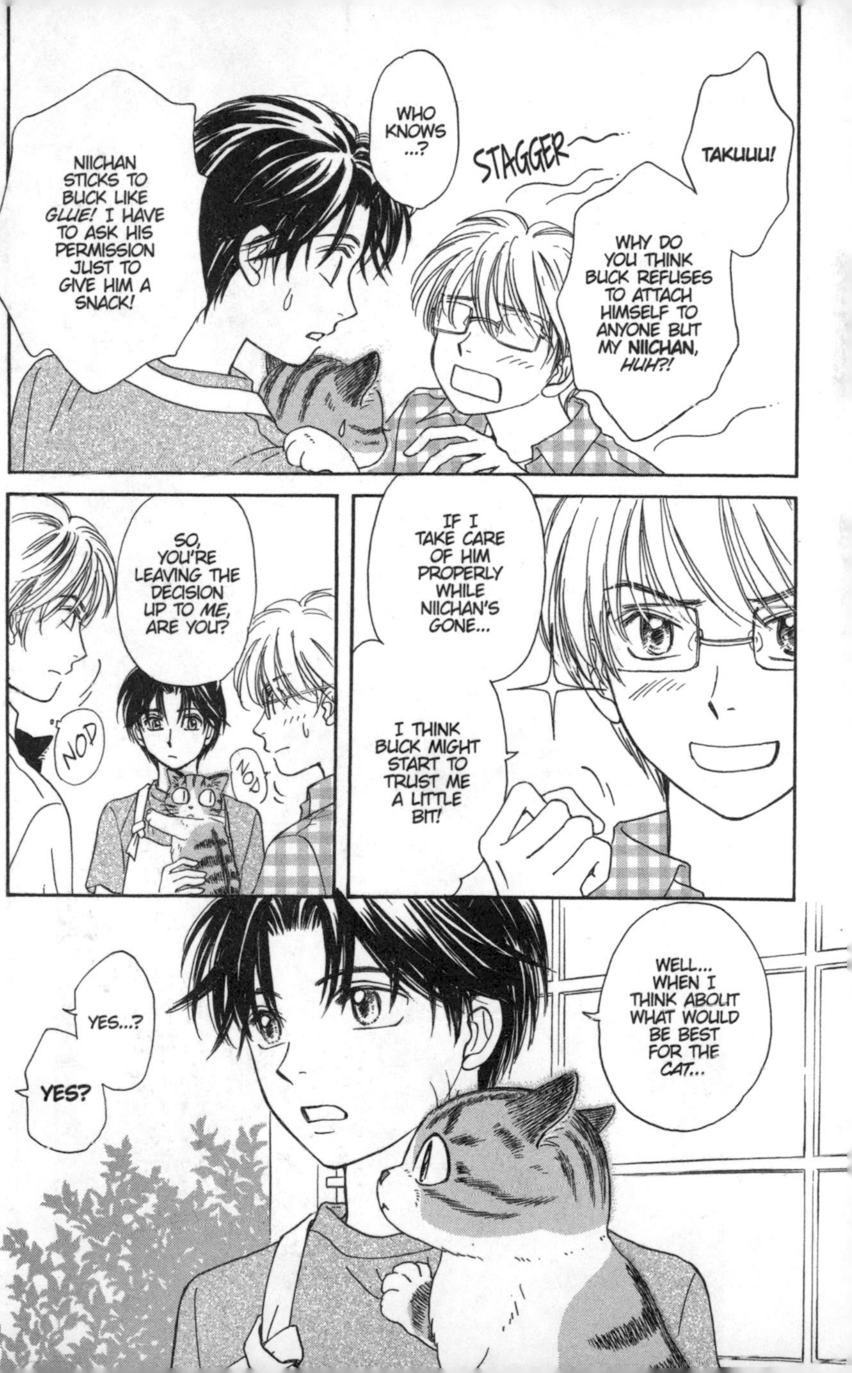
TAKUUU!
WHY DO YOU THINK BUCK REFUSES TO ATTACH HIMSELF TO ANYONE BUT MY NIICHAN, HUH?!
STAGGER
WHO KNOWS ...?
NIICHAN STICKS TO BUCK LIKE GLUE! I HAVE TO ASK HIS PERMISSION JUST TO GIVE HIM A SNACK!
IF I TAKE CARE OF HIM PROPERLY WHILE NIICHAN'S GONE...
I THINK BUCK MIGHT START TO TRUST ME A LITTLE BIT!
SO, YOU'RE LEAVING THE DECISION UP TO ME, ARE YOU?
NOD
NOD
WELL... WHEN I THINK ABOUT WHAT WOULD BE BEST FOR THE CAT...
YES...?
YES?

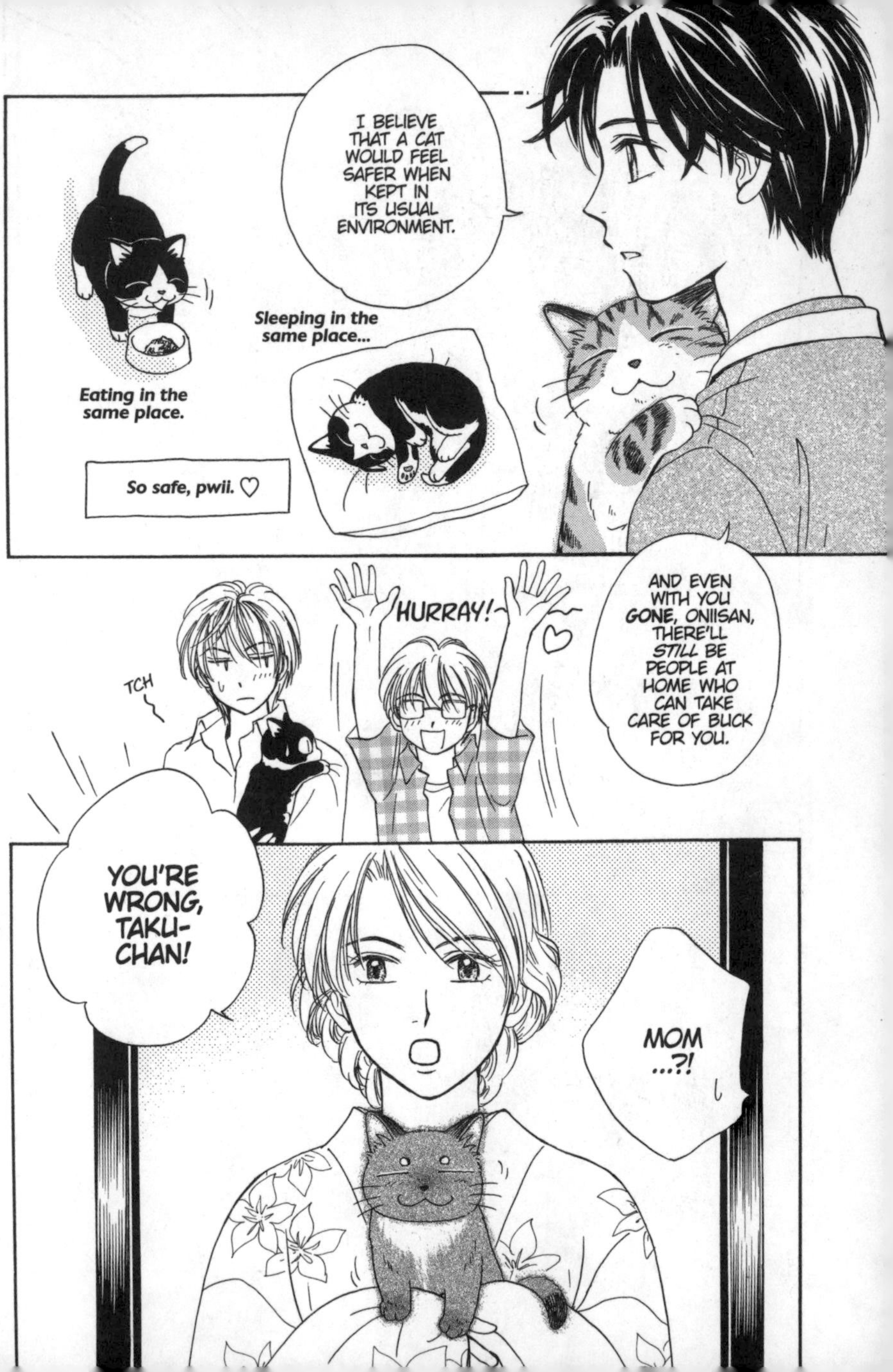
I BELIEVE THAT A CAT WOULD FEEL SAFER WHEN KEPT IN ITS USUAL ENVIRONMENT.
Sleeping in the same place...
Eating in the same place.
So safe, pwii. ♡
AND EVEN WITH YOU GONE, ONIISAN, THERE'LL STILL BE PEOPLE AT HOME WHO CAN TAKE CARE OF BUCK FOR YOU.
HURRAY!
TCH
YOU'RE WRONG, TAKU-CHAN!
MOM ...?!

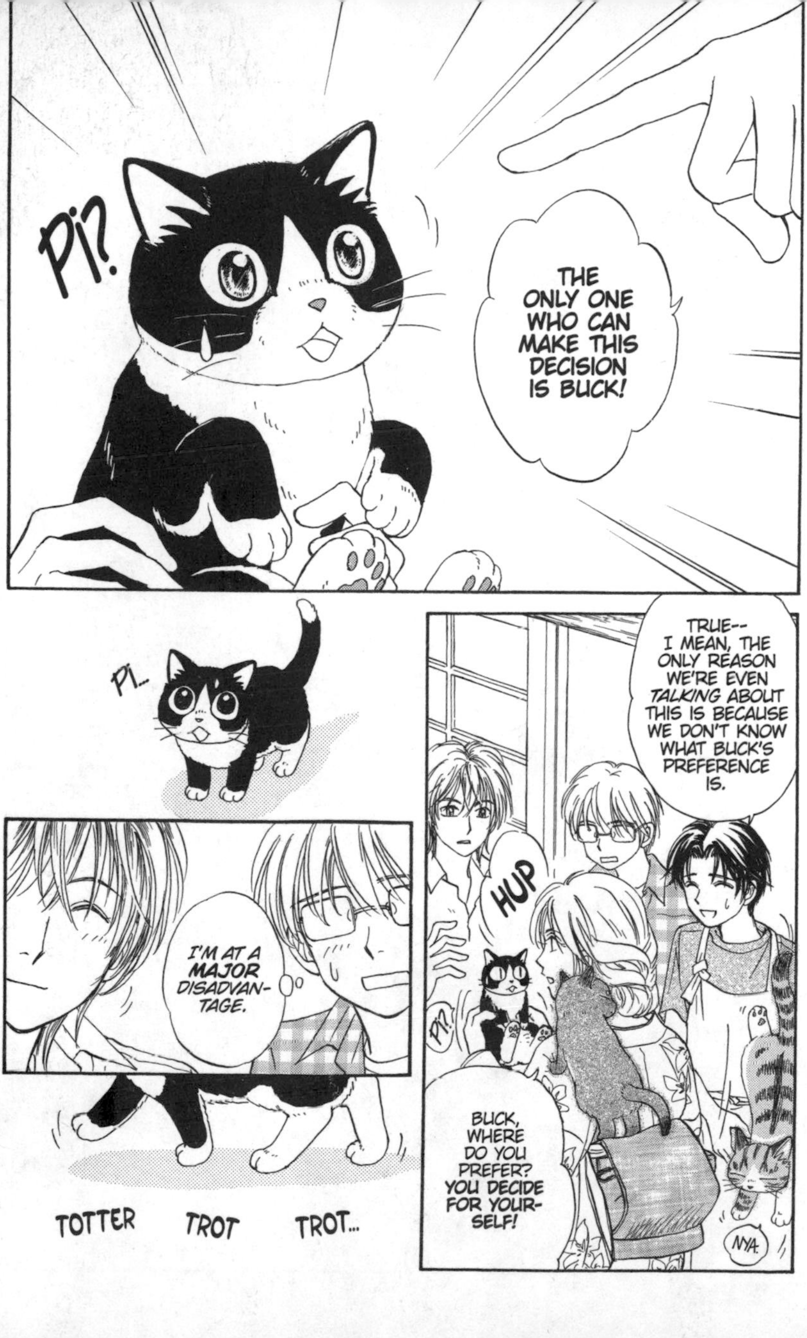
THE ONLY ONE WHO CAN MAKE THIS DECISION IS BUCK!
Pi?
TRUE-- I MEAN, THE ONLY REASON WE'RE EVEN *TALKING* ABOUT THIS IS BECAUSE WE DON'T KNOW WHAT BUCK'S PREFERENCE IS.
HUP
Pi?
BUCK, WHERE DO YOU PREFER? YOU DECIDE FOR YOURSELF!
NYA.
Pi...
I'M AT A MAJOR DISADVANTAGE.
TOTTER TROT TROT...

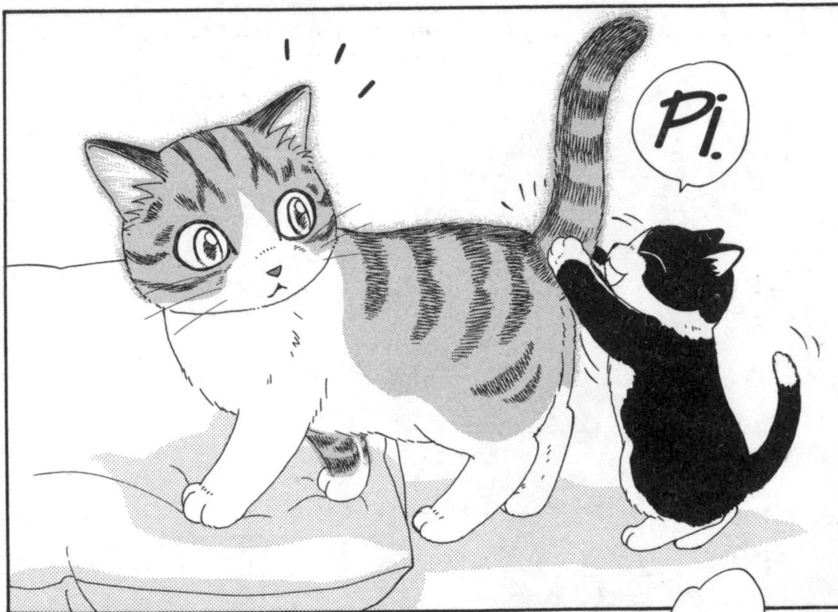
Pi.

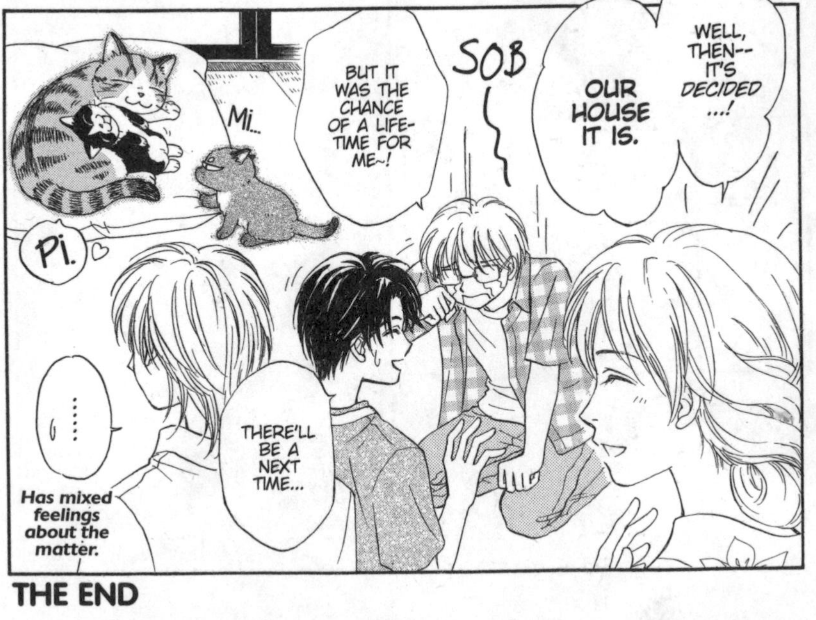
WELL, THEN-- IT'S DECIDED ...!
OUR HOUSE IT IS.
SOB
BUT IT WAS THE CHANCE OF A LIFE-TIME FOR ME~!
Mi...
Pi.
......
THERE'LL BE A NEXT TIME...
Has mixed feelings about the matter.

THE END

Hurry up and notice already!

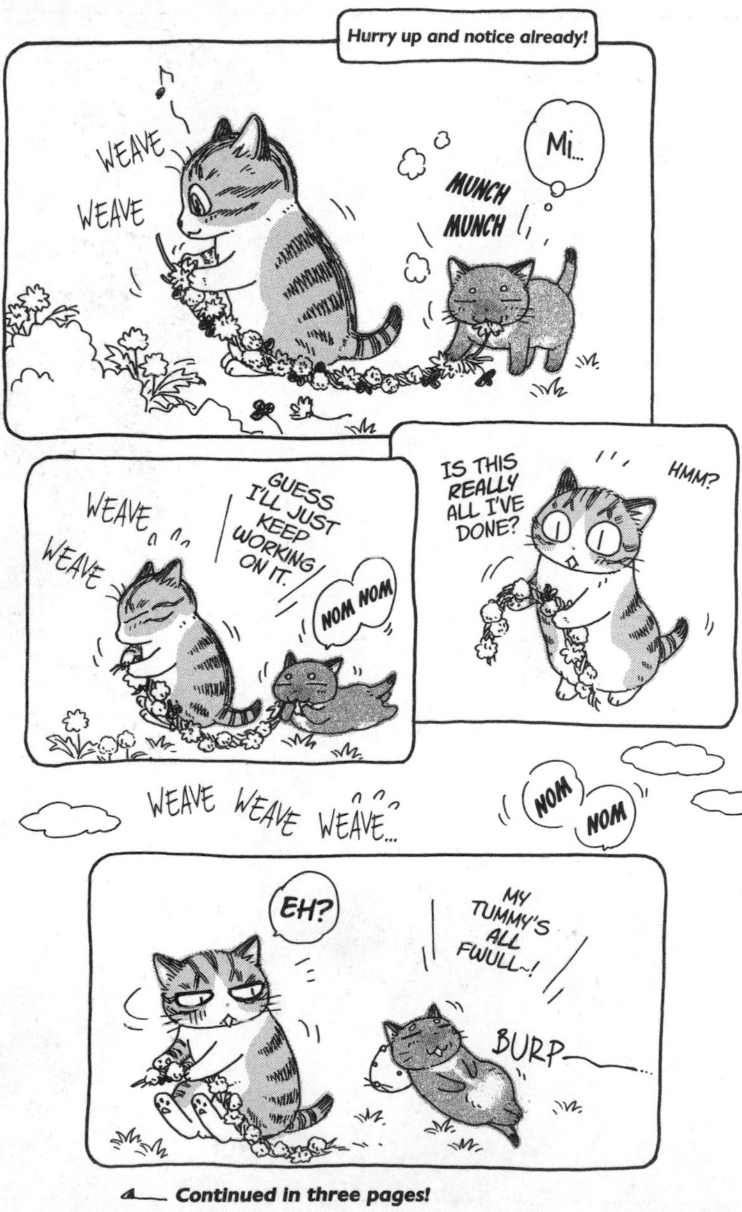

Mi...
MUNCH
MUNCH
WEAVE
WEAVE
HMM?
IS THIS REALLY ALL I'VE DONE?
NOM NOM
GUESS I'LL JUST KEEP WORKING ON IT.
WEAVE
WEAVE
NOM
NOM
WEAVE WEAVE WEAVE...
MY TUMMY'S ALL FWULL~!
BURP...
EH?

Continued in three pages!

SHORT .18
Christmas at Princess' House

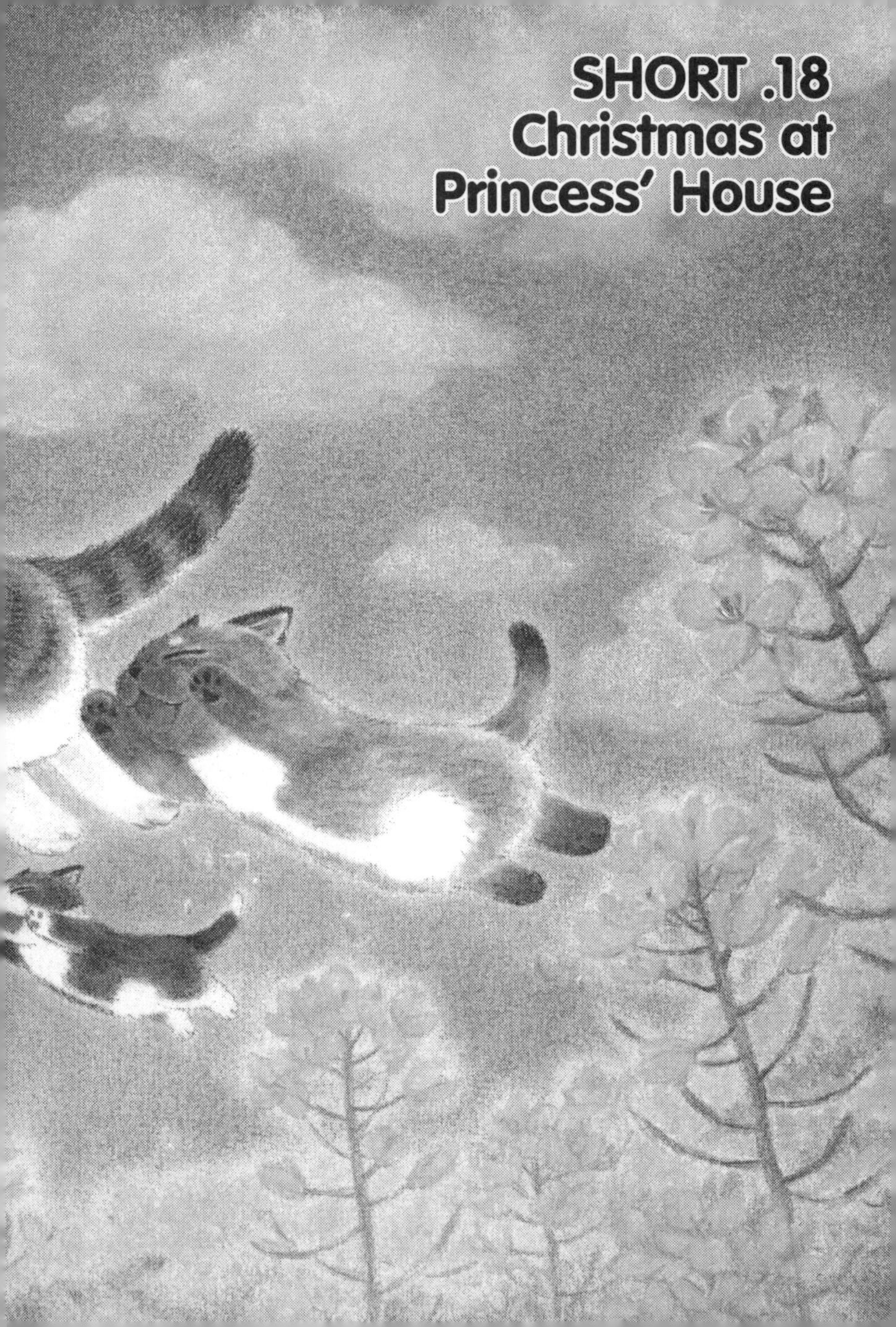

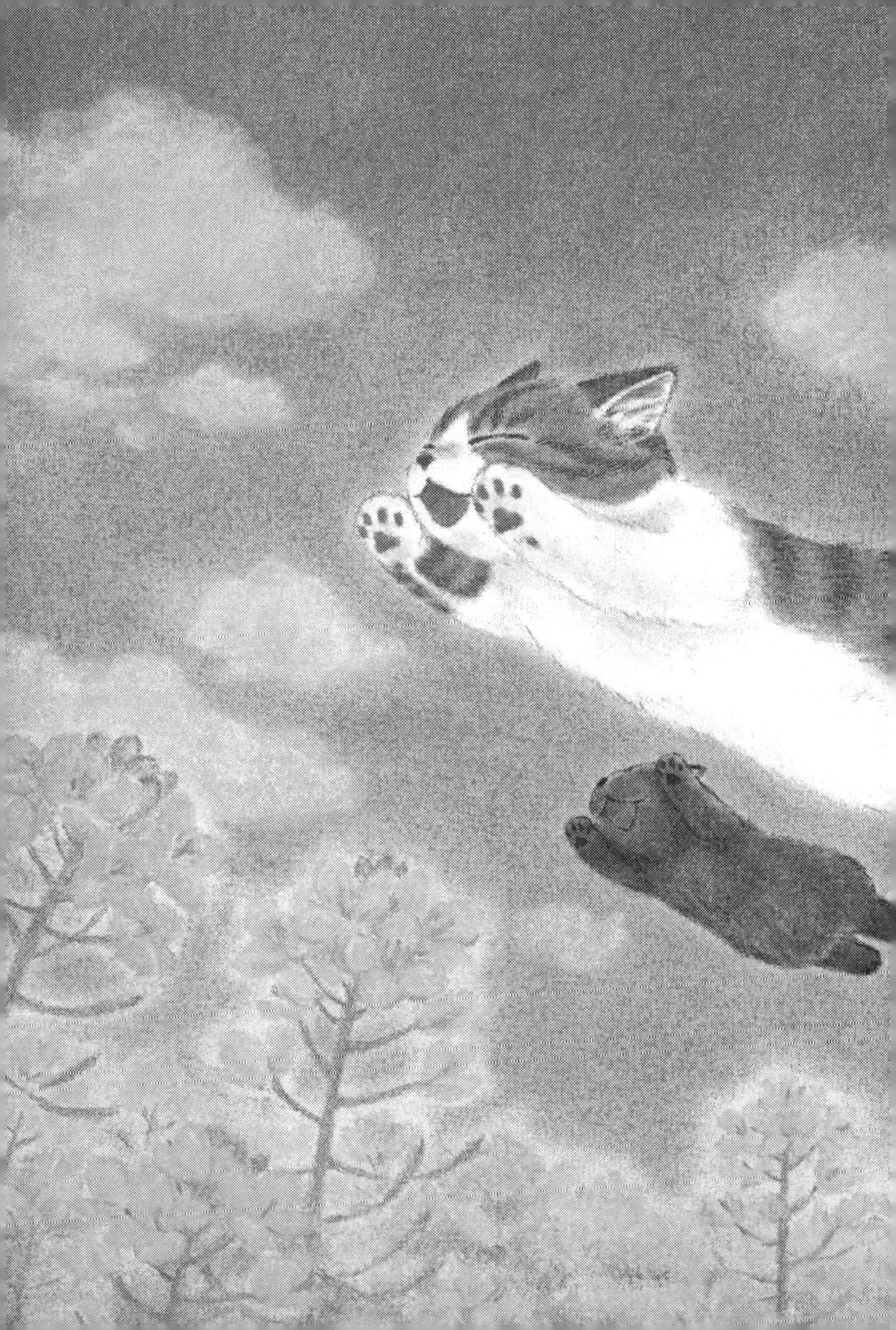

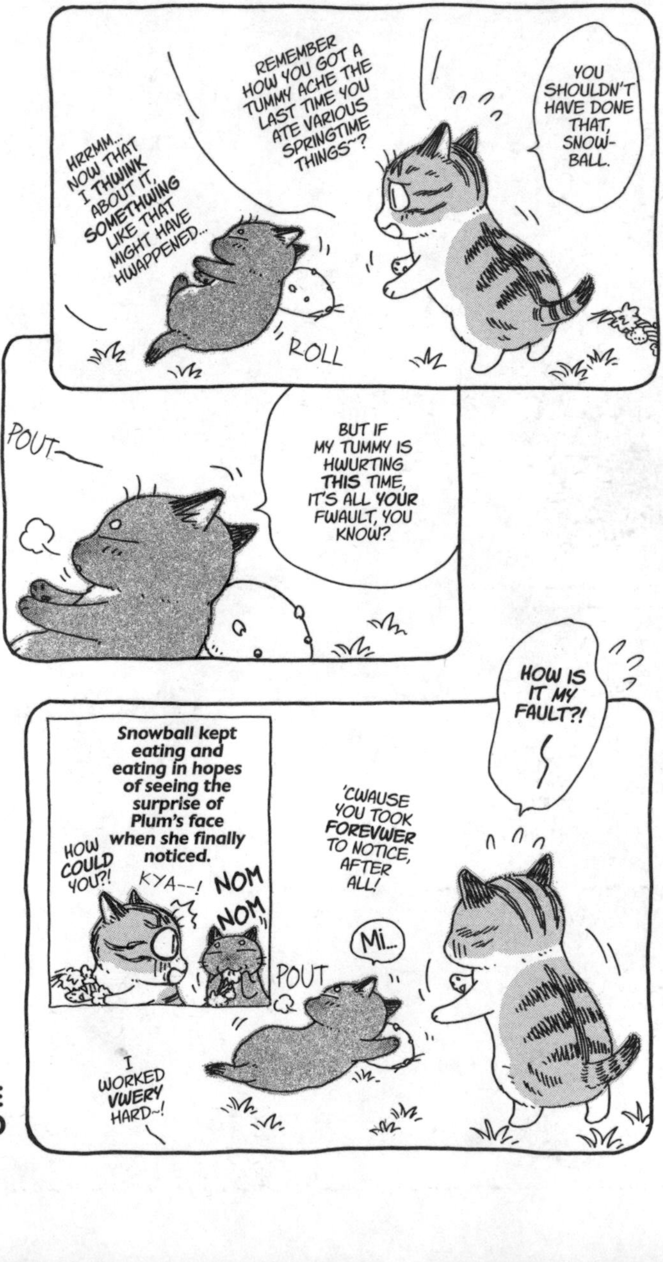
YOU SHOULDN'T HAVE DONE THAT, SNOWBALL.
REMEMBER HOW YOU GOT A TUMMY ACHE THE LAST TIME YOU ATE VARIOUS SPRINGTIME THINGS~?
HRRMM... NOW THAT I THWINK ABOUT IT, SOMETHWING LIKE THAT MIGHT HAVE HWAPPENED...
ROLL
BUT IF MY TUMMY IS HWURTING THIS TIME, IT'S ALL YOUR FWAULT, YOU KNOW?
POUT
HOW IS IT MY FAULT?!
'CWAUSE YOU TOOK FOREVWER TO NOTICE, AFTER ALL!
Mi...
POUT
I WORKED VWERY HARD~!
Snowball kept eating and eating in hopes of seeing the surprise of Plum's face when she finally noticed.
NOM NOM
KYA--!
HOW COULD YOU?!

THE END

SHORT.18 "CHRISTMAS AT PRINCESS'S HOUSE"

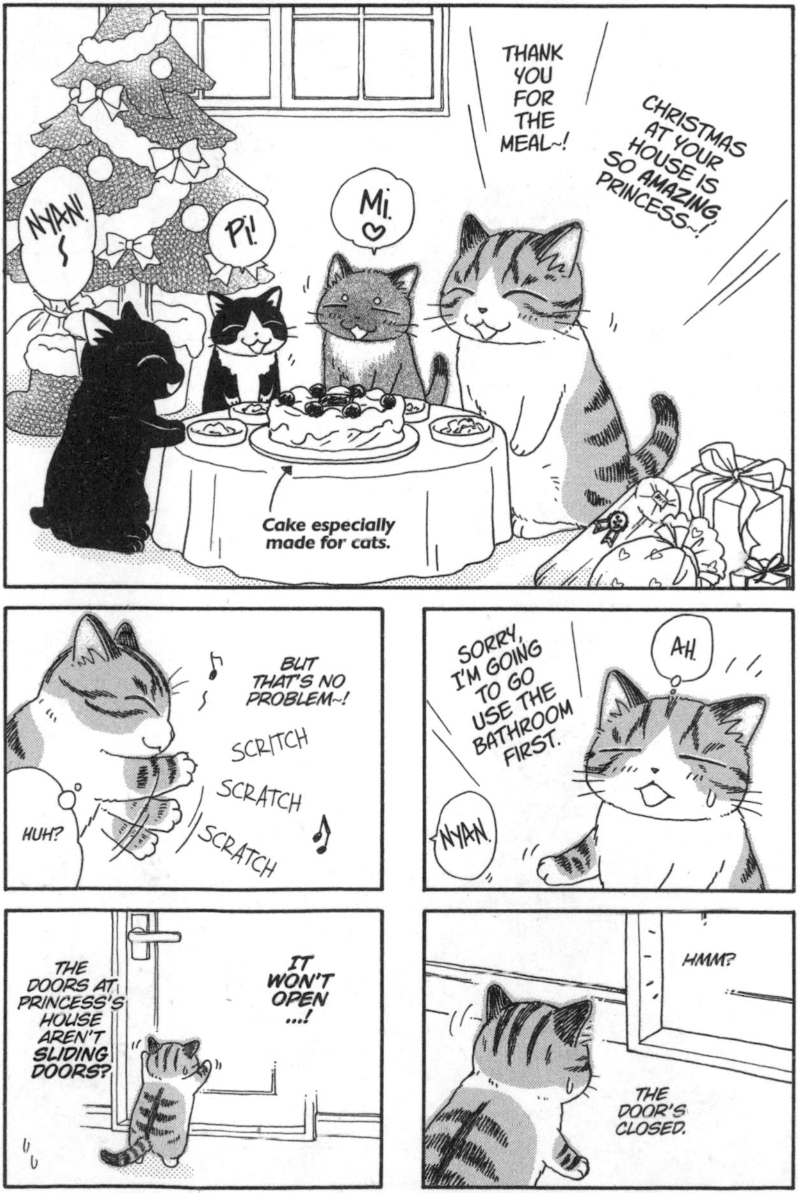
CHRISTMAS AT YOUR HOUSE IS SO AMAZING, PRINCESS~!
THANK YOU FOR THE MEAL~!
Mi. ♡
Pi!
NYAN!
Cake especially made for cats.
AH.
SORRY, I'M GOING TO GO USE THE BATHROOM FIRST.
NYAN.
BUT THAT'S NO PROBLEM~!
SCRITCH
SCRATCH
SCRATCH
HUH?
HMM?
THE DOOR'S CLOSED.
IT WON'T OPEN ...!
THE DOORS AT PRINCESS'S HOUSE AREN'T SLIDING DOORS?

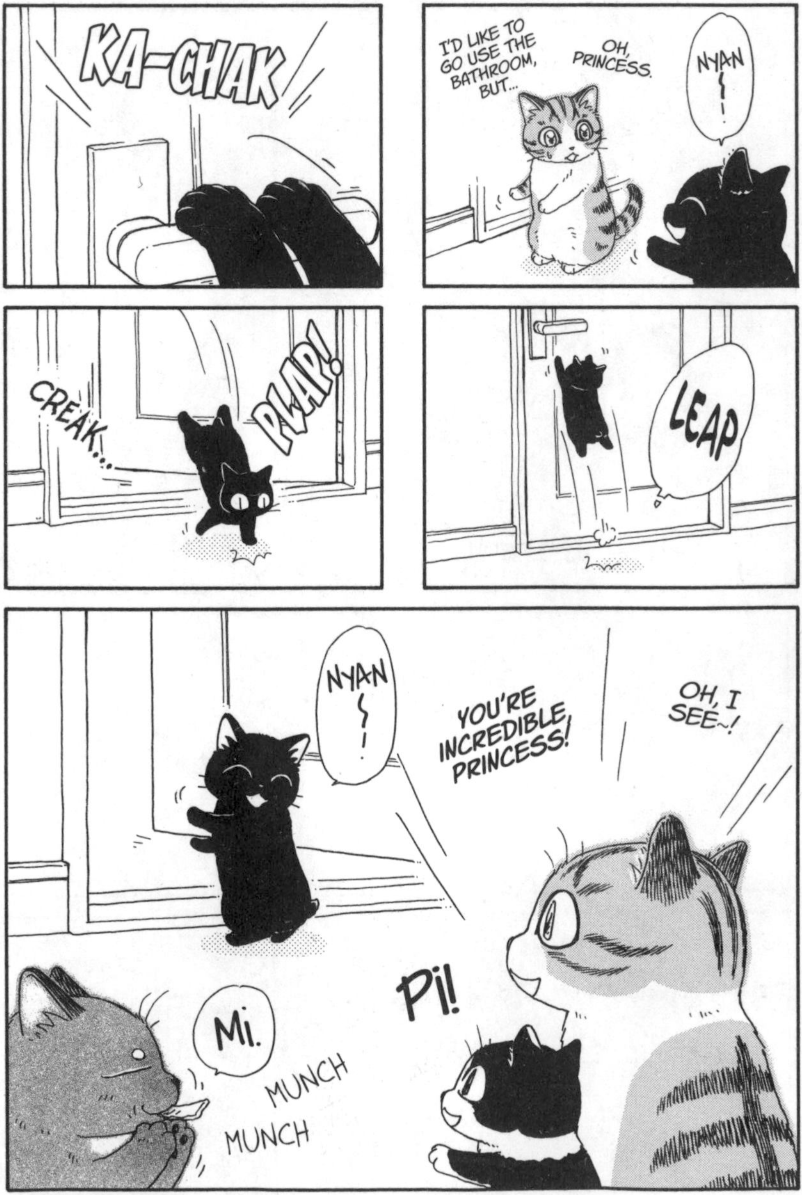
NYAN ~ !
OH, PRINCESS.
I'D LIKE TO GO USE THE BATHROOM, BUT...
KA-CHAK
LEAP
PLAP!
CREAK...
OH, I SEE~!
YOU'RE INCREDIBLE PRINCESS!
NYAN ~ !
Pi!
Mi.
MUNCH
MUNCH

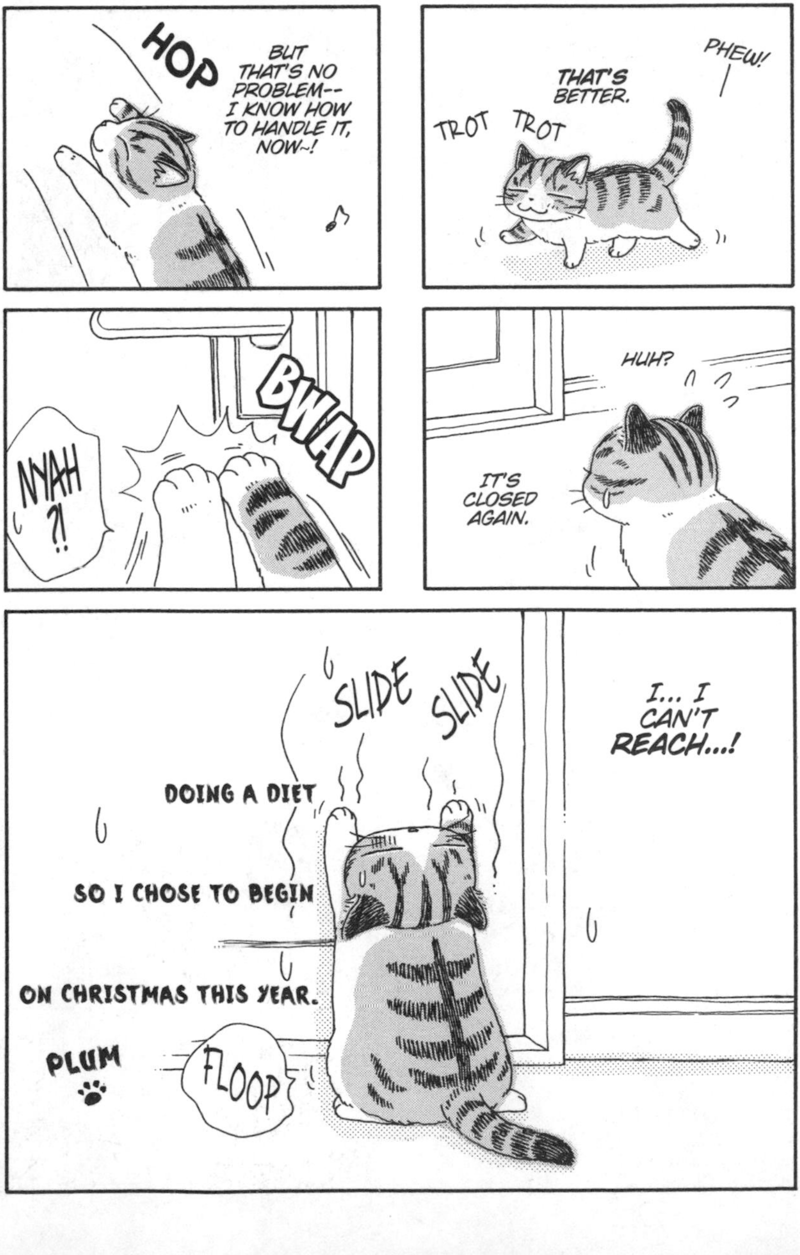
PHEW!
THAT'S BETTER.
TROT TROT
BUT THAT'S NO PROBLEM-- I KNOW HOW TO HANDLE IT, NOW~!
HOP
HUH?
IT'S CLOSED AGAIN.
BWAP
NYAH ?!
I... I CAN'T REACH...!
SLIDE SLIDE
DOING A DIET
SO I CHOSE TO BEGIN
ON CHRISTMAS THIS YEAR.
PLUM
FLOOP

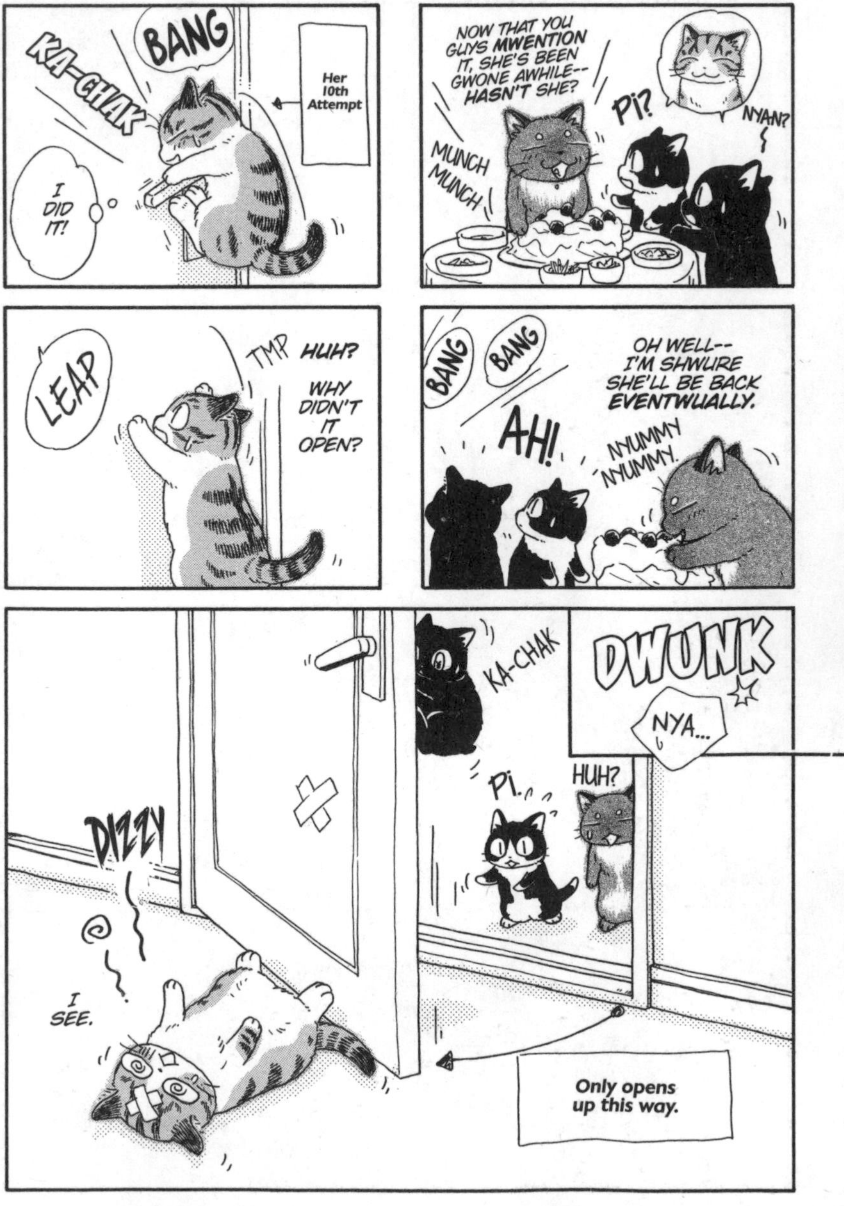
NOW THAT YOU GUYS MWENTION IT, SHE'S BEEN GWONE AWHILE-- HASN'T SHE?
MUNCH MUNCH
Pi?
NYAN?
BANG
KA-CHAK
Her 10th Attempt
I DID IT!
OH WELL-- I'M SHWURE SHE'LL BE BACK EVENTWUALLY.
BANG
BANG
AH!
NYUMMY NYUMMY.
HUH?
WHY DIDN'T IT OPEN?
TMP
LEAP
DWUNK
NYA...
KA-CHAK
HUH?
Pi.
Only opens up this way.
DIZZY
I SEE.

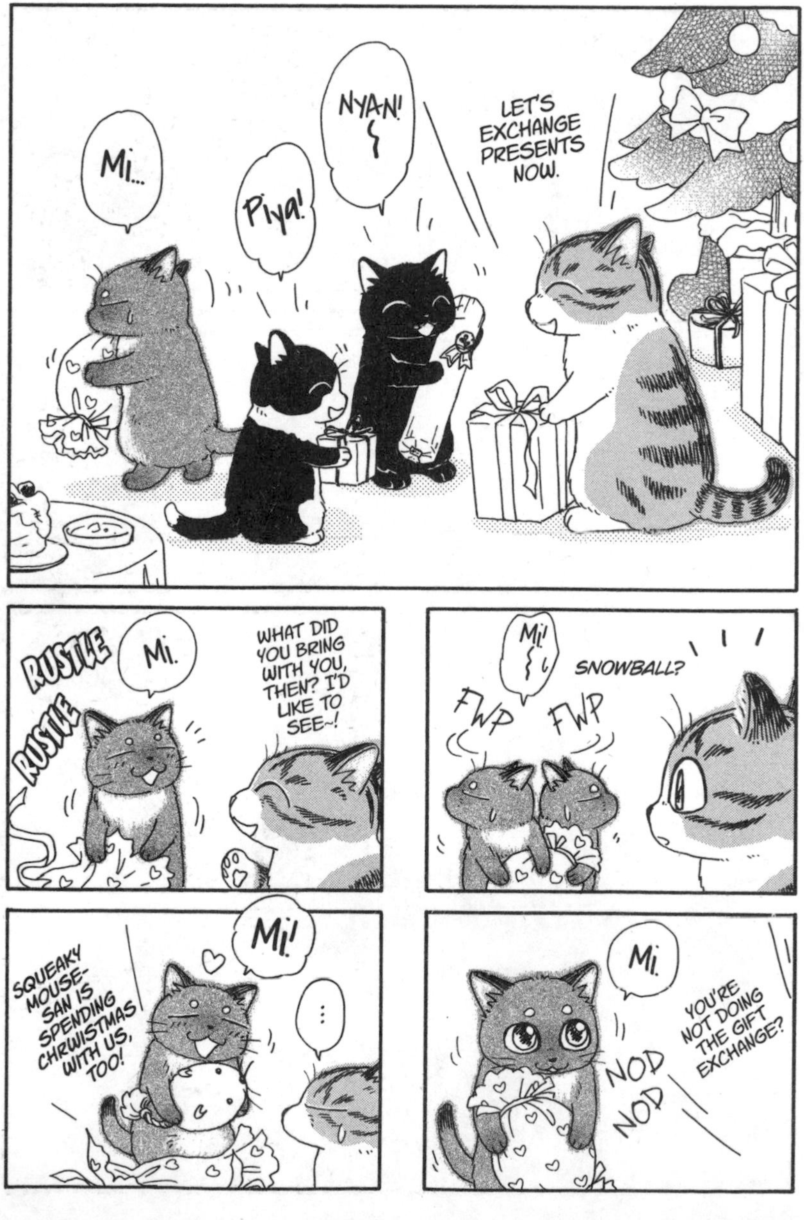

LET'S EXCHANGE PRESENTS NOW.
NYAN!
Piya!
Mi...
SNOWBALL?
Mi!
FWP FWP
WHAT DID YOU BRING WITH YOU, THEN? I'D LIKE TO SEE~!
Mi.
RUSTLE RUSTLE
Mi.
YOU'RE NOT DOING THE GIFT EXCHANGE?
NOD NOD
Mi!
...
SQUEAKY MOUSE-SAN IS SPENDING CHRWISTMAS WITH US, TOO!

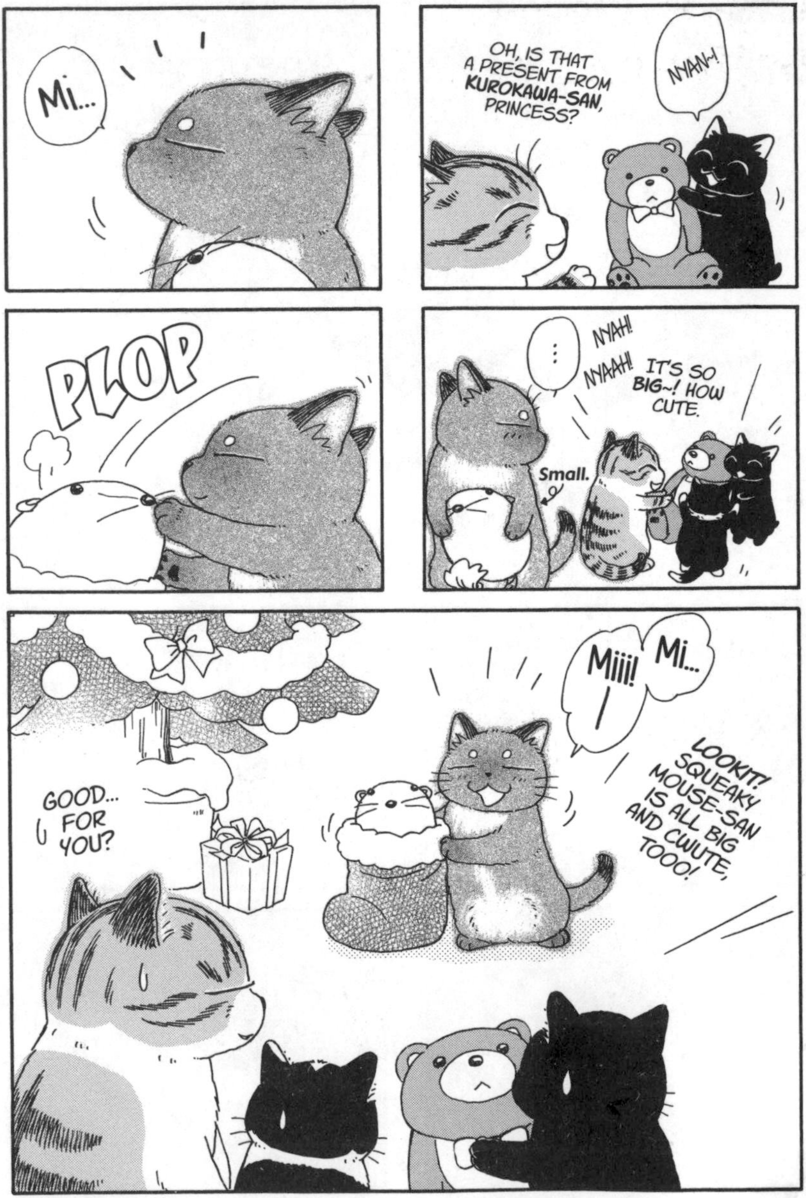
OH, IS THAT A PRESENT FROM KUROKAWA-SAN, PRINCESS?
NYAN~!
Mi...
...
NYAH!
NYAAH!
IT'S SO BIG~! HOW CUTE.
Small.
PLOP
Mi...
Miii!
LOOKIT! SQUEAKY MOUSE-SAN IS ALL BIG AND CWUTE, TOOO!
GOOD... FOR YOU?

THE END

CHAPTER 24
Snowball, At Your Service

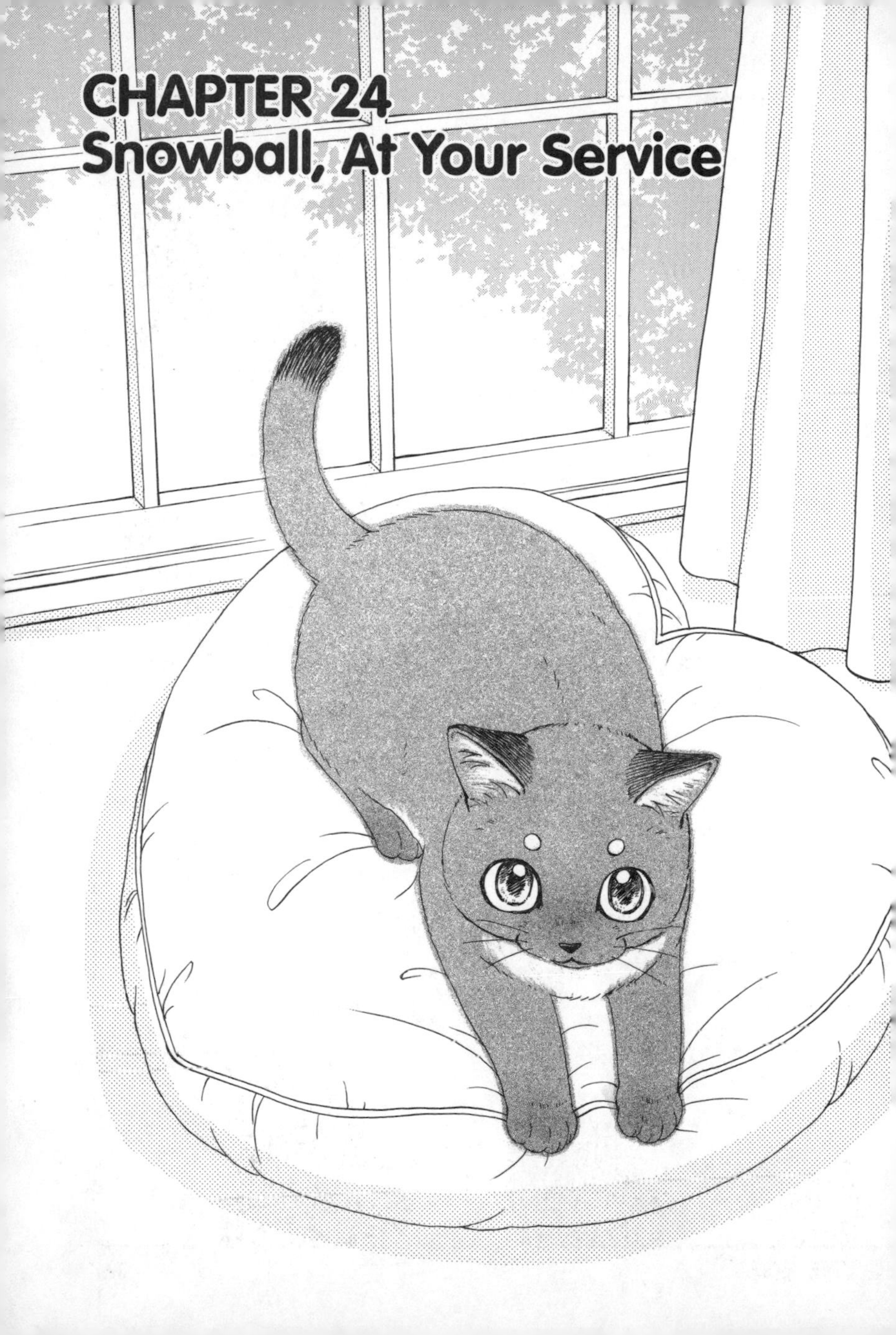

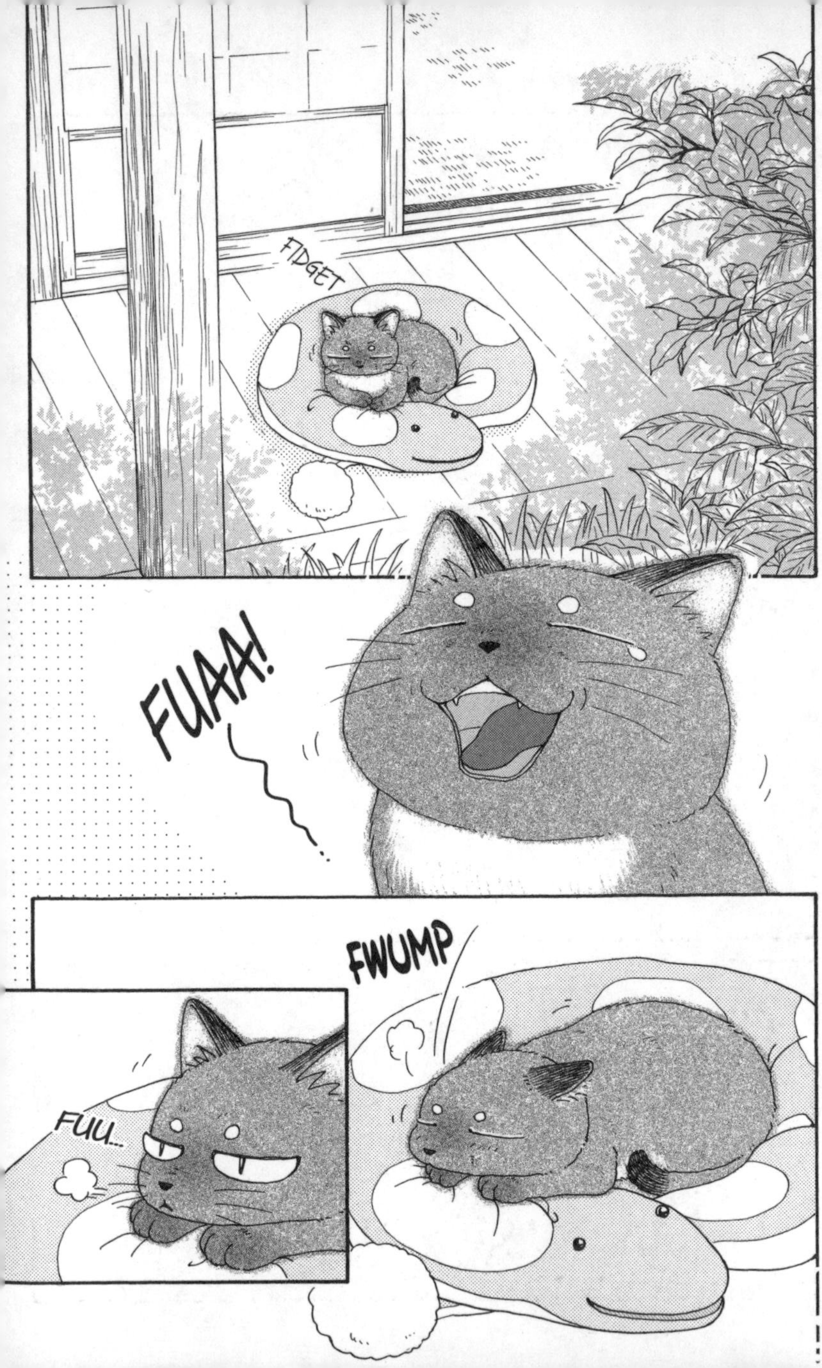
FIDGET
FUAA!
FWUMP
FUU...

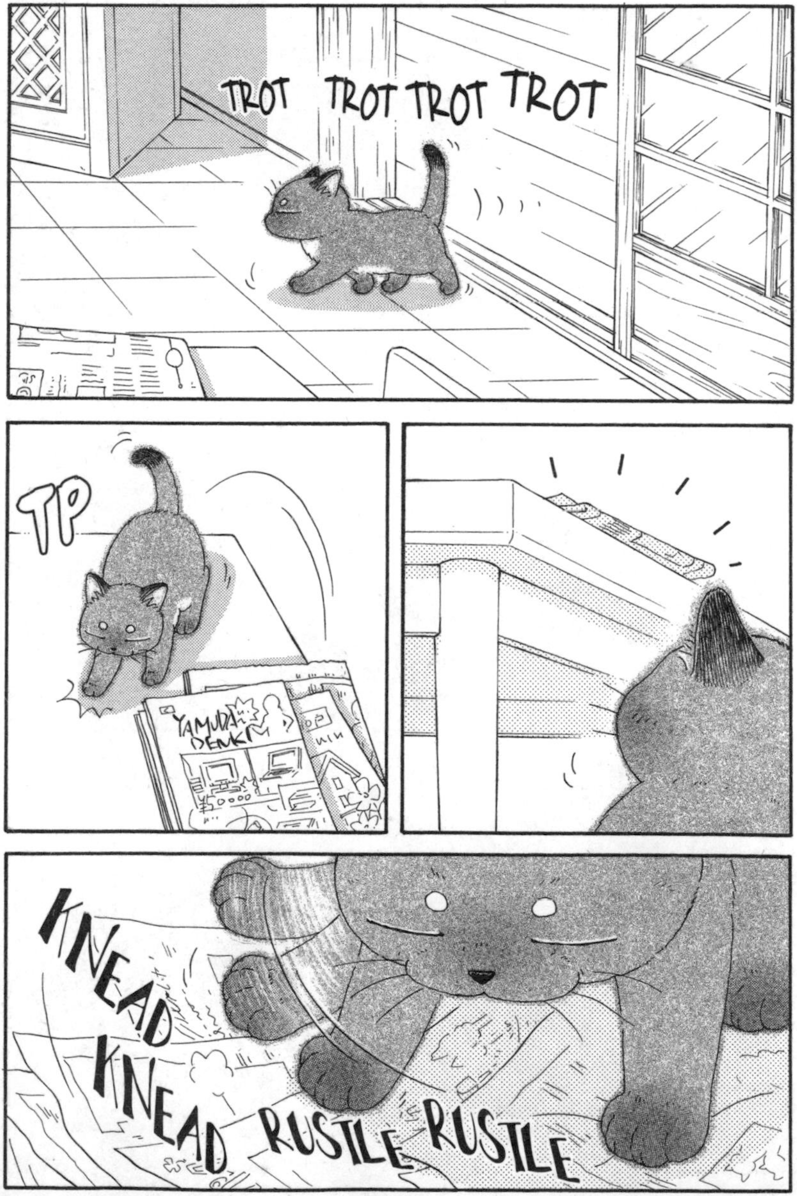
TROT TROT TROT TROT
TP
YAMUDA DENKI
KNEAD KNEAD
RUSTLE RUSTLE

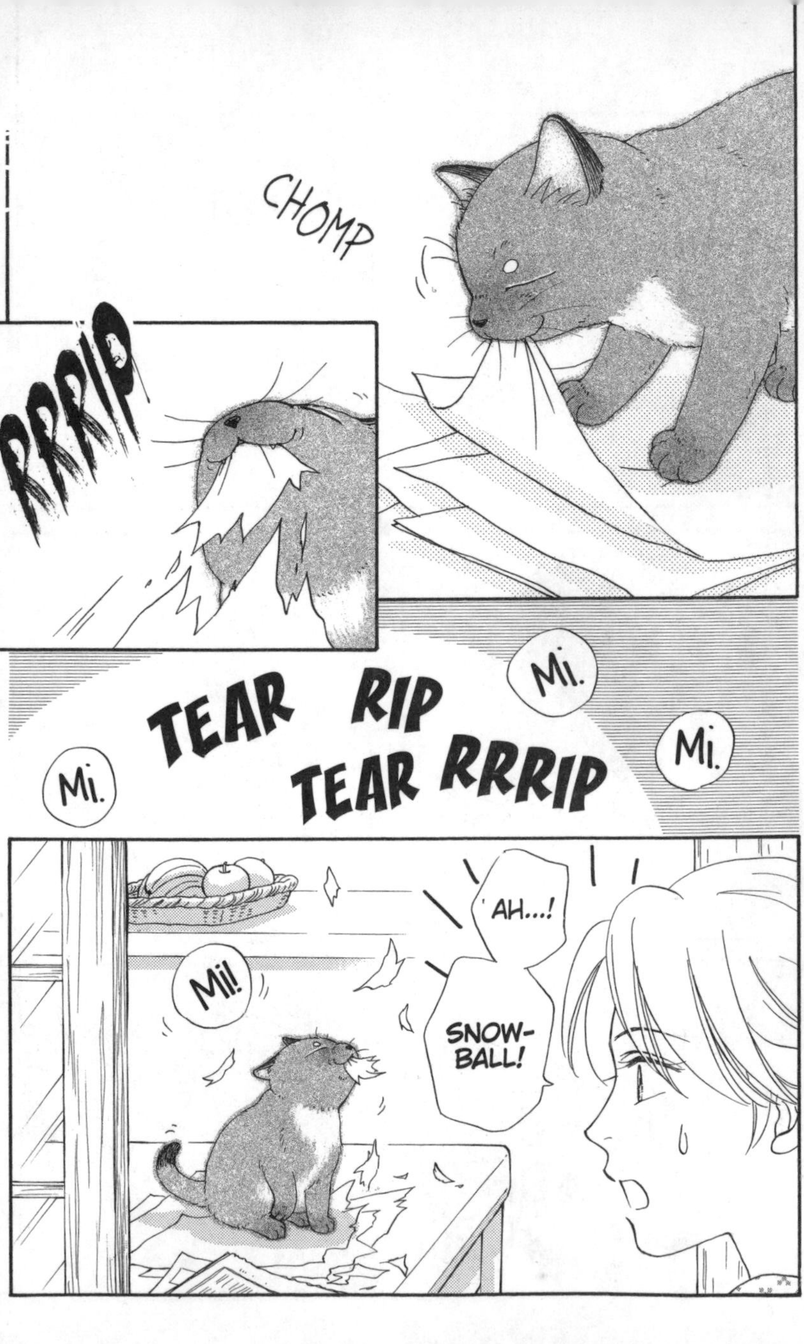
CHOMP
RRRIP
Mi.
Mi.
TEAR RIP
TEAR RRRIP
Mi.
AH...!
SNOW-BALL!
Mi!

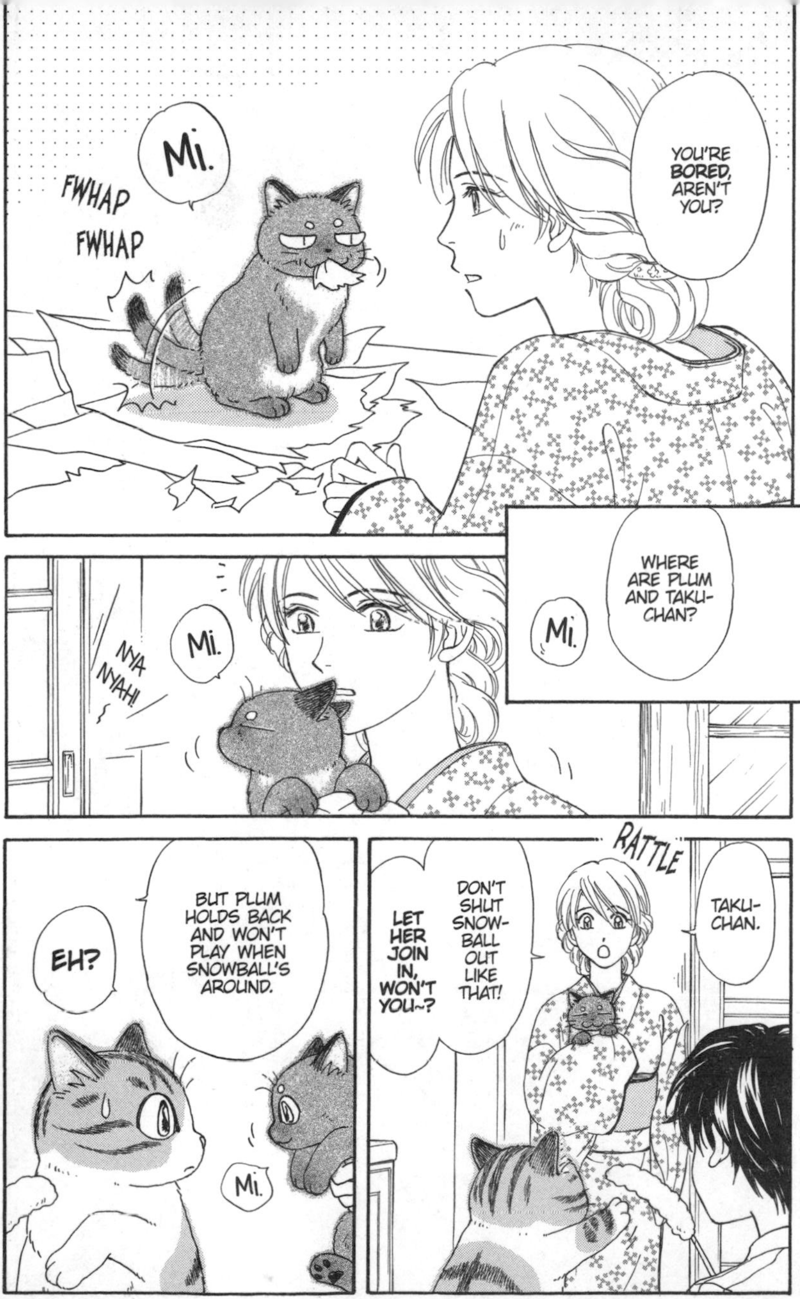
YOU'RE BORED, AREN'T YOU?
Mi.
FWHAP
FWHAP
WHERE ARE PLUM AND TAKU-CHAN?
Mi.
Mi.
NYA NYAH!
RATTLE
TAKU-CHAN.
DON'T SHUT SNOWBALL OUT LIKE THAT!
LET HER JOIN IN, WON'T YOU~?
BUT PLUM HOLDS BACK AND WON'T PLAY WHEN SNOWBALL'S AROUND.
EH?
Mi.

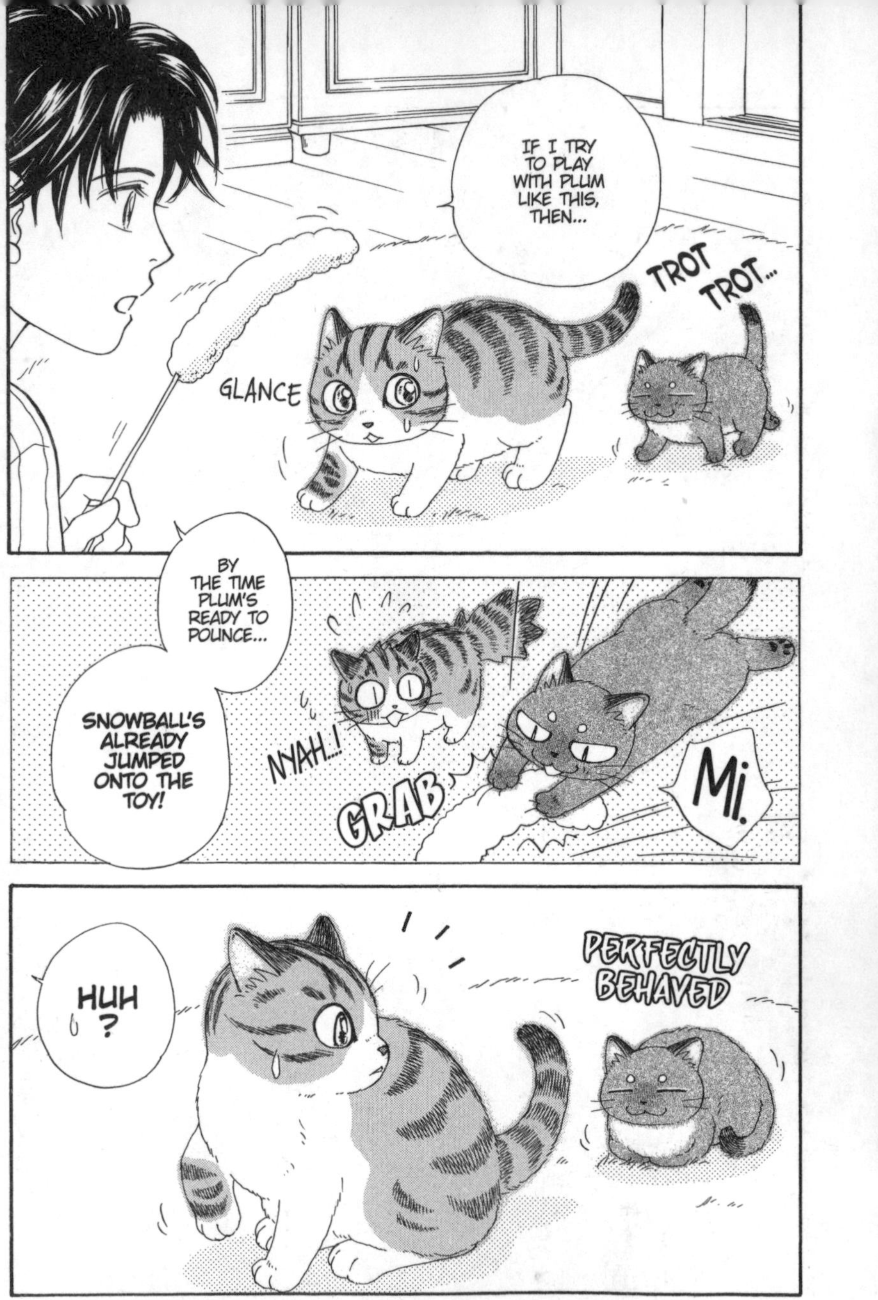
IF I TRY TO PLAY WITH PLUM LIKE THIS, THEN...
TROT TROT...
GLANCE
BY THE TIME PLUM'S READY TO POUNCE...
SNOWBALL'S ALREADY JUMPED ONTO THE TOY!
NYAH..!
GRAB
Mi.
PERFECTLY BEHAVED
HUH?

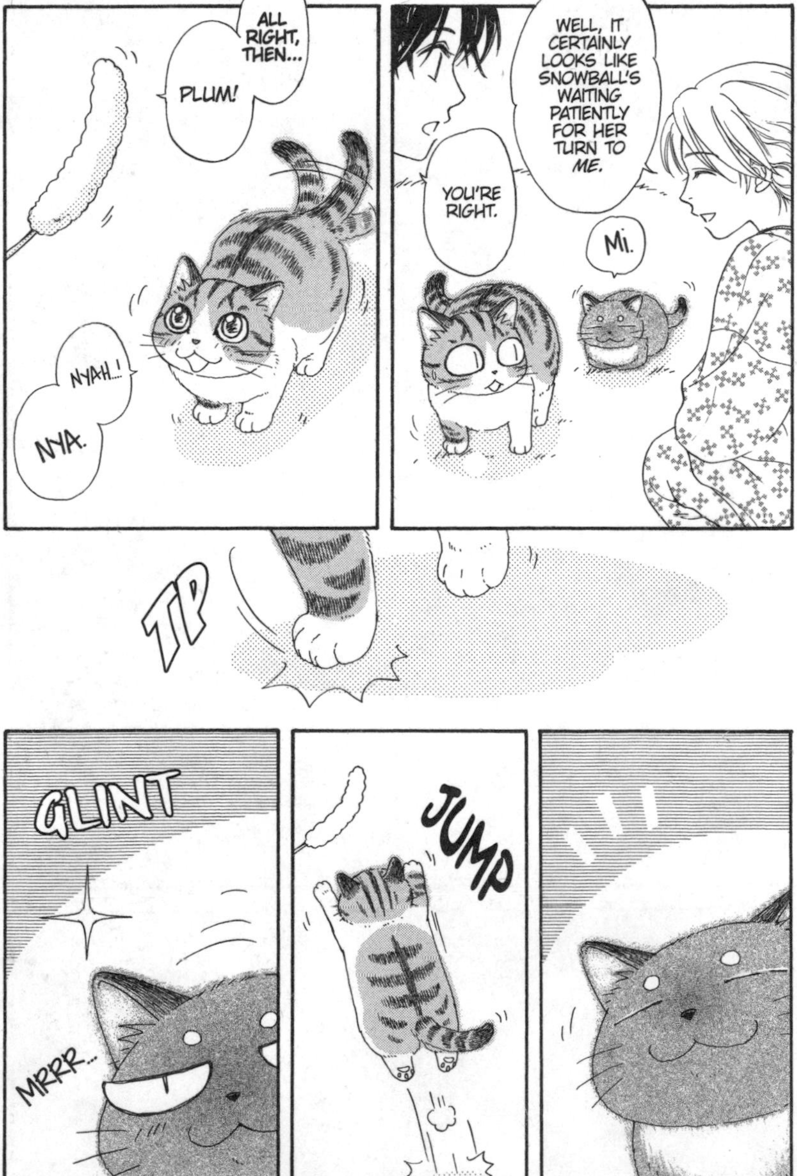
WELL, IT CERTAINLY LOOKS LIKE SNOWBALL'S WAITING PATIENTLY FOR HER TURN TO ME.
YOU'RE RIGHT.
MI.
ALL RIGHT, THEN...
PLUM!
NYAH..!
NYA.
TIP
JUMP
GLINT
MRRR...

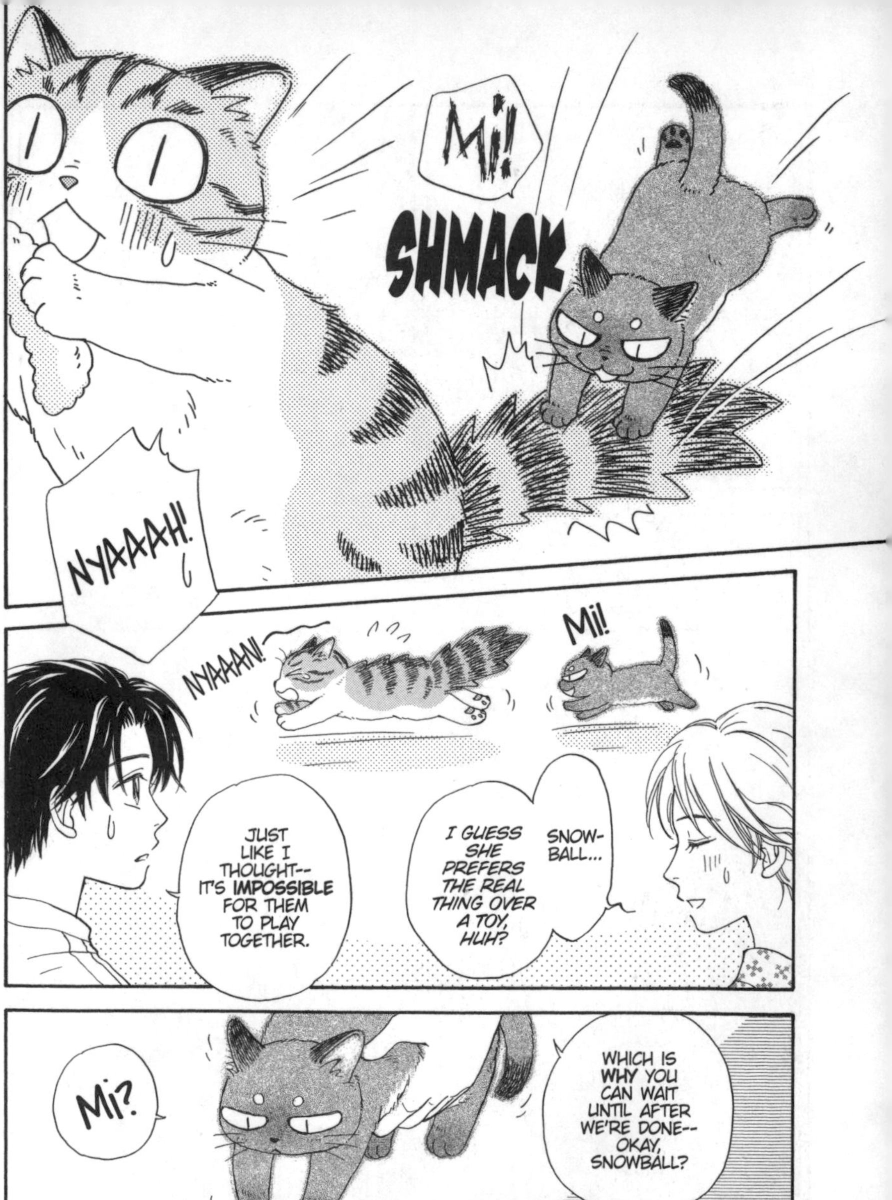
Mi!
SHMACK
NYAAAH!
Mi!
NYAAAN!
SNOW-BALL...
I GUESS SHE PREFERS THE REAL THING OVER A TOY, HUH?
JUST LIKE I THOUGHT-- IT'S **IMPOSSIBLE** FOR THEM TO PLAY TOGETHER.
WHICH IS **WHY** YOU CAN WAIT UNTIL AFTER WE'RE DONE-- OKAY, SNOWBALL?
Mi?

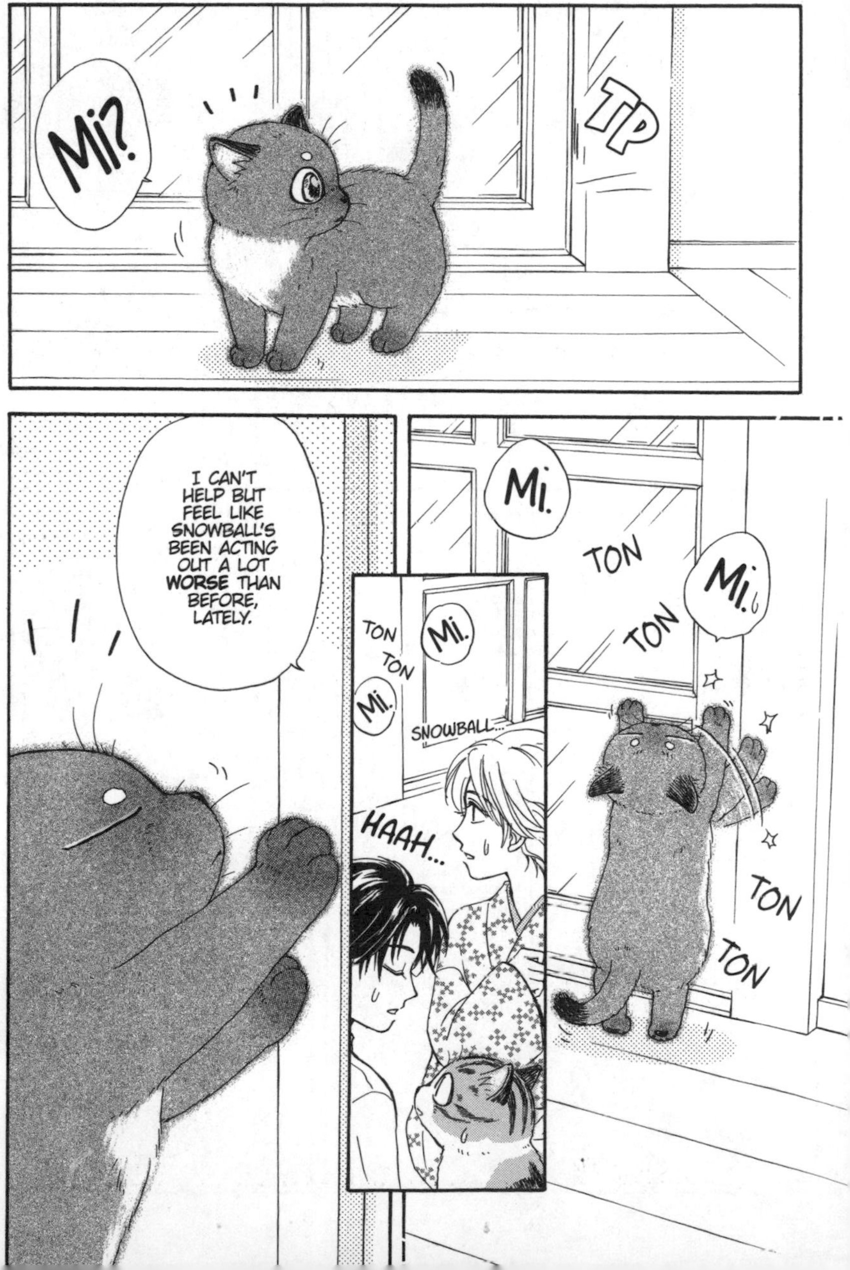
TP
Mi?
Mi.
TON
Mi.
TON
TON
TON
TON
TON
Mi.
Mi.
SNOWBALL...
HAAH...
I CAN'T HELP BUT FEEL LIKE SNOWBALL'S BEEN ACTING OUT A LOT **WORSE** THAN BEFORE, LATELY.

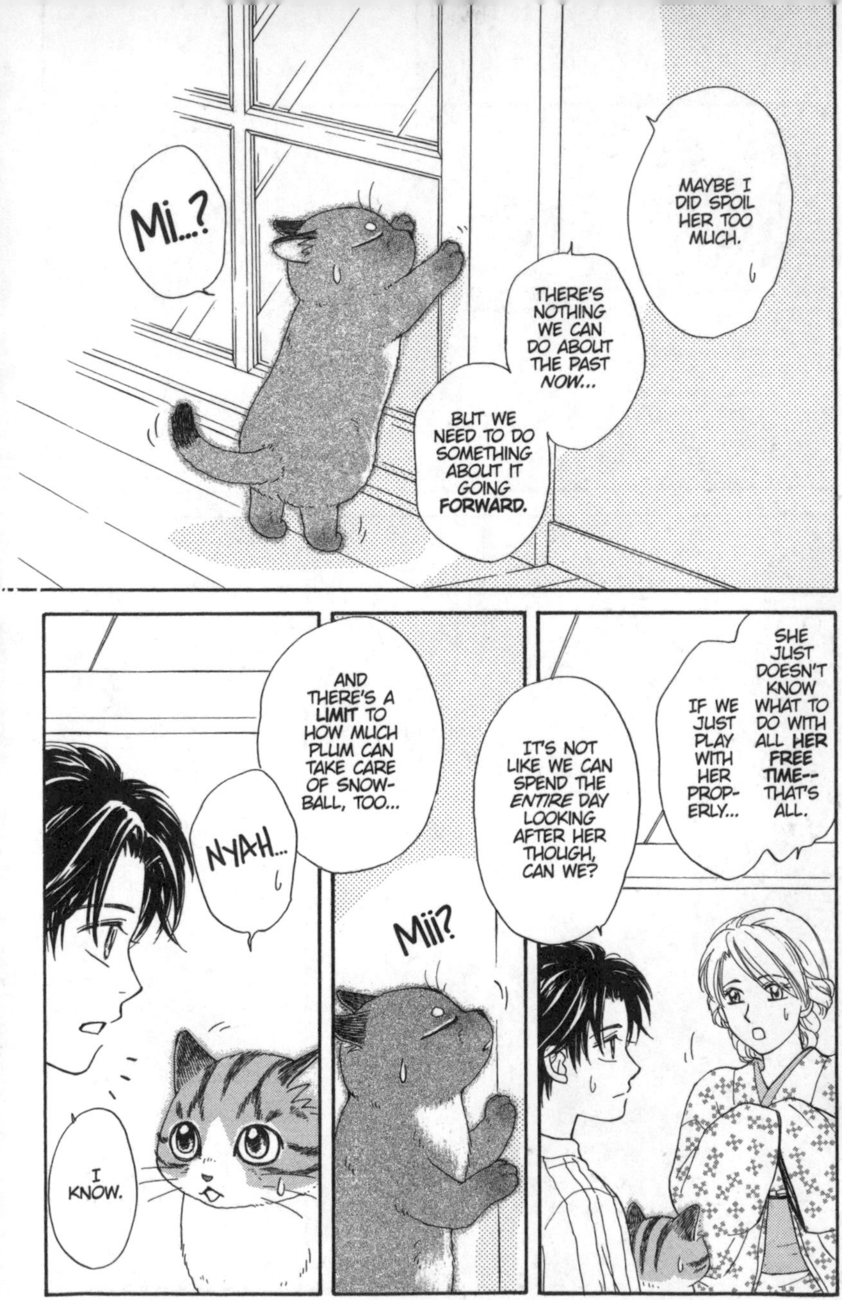
MAYBE I DID SPOIL HER TOO MUCH.
THERE'S NOTHING WE CAN DO ABOUT THE PAST *NOW*...
BUT WE NEED TO DO SOMETHING ABOUT IT GOING **FORWARD.**
Mi..?
SHE JUST DOESN'T KNOW WHAT TO DO WITH ALL **HER FREE TIME**--THAT'S ALL.
IF WE JUST PLAY WITH HER PROPERLY...
IT'S NOT LIKE WE CAN SPEND THE *ENTIRE* DAY LOOKING AFTER HER THOUGH, CAN WE?
AND THERE'S A **LIMIT** TO HOW MUCH PLUM CAN TAKE CARE OF SNOW-BALL, TOO...
Mii?
NYAH...
I KNOW.

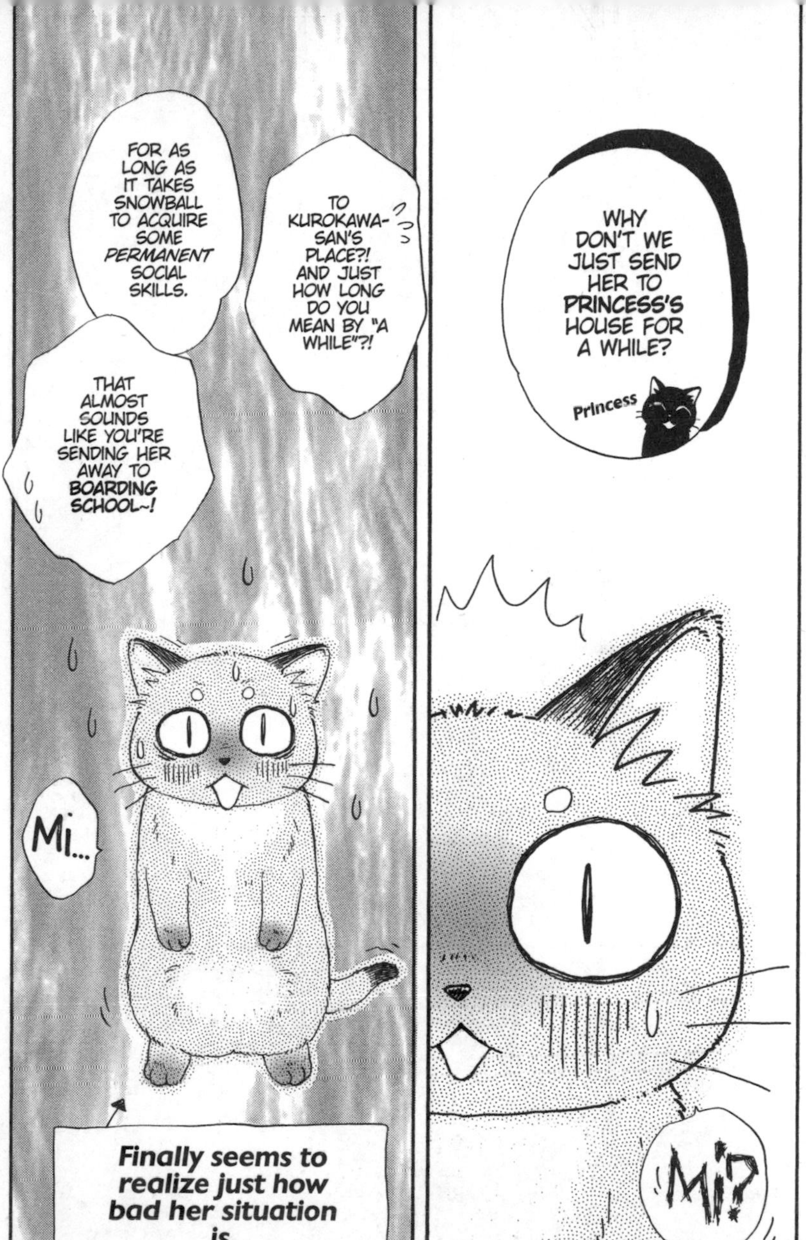
WHY DON'T WE JUST SEND HER TO PRINCESS'S HOUSE FOR A WHILE?
Princess
MI?
TO KUROKAWA-SAN'S PLACE?! AND JUST HOW LONG DO YOU MEAN BY "A WHILE"?!
FOR AS LONG AS IT TAKES SNOWBALL TO ACQUIRE SOME PERMANENT SOCIAL SKILLS.
THAT ALMOST SOUNDS LIKE YOU'RE SENDING HER AWAY TO BOARDING SCHOOL~!
Mi...
Finally seems to realize just how bad her situation is.

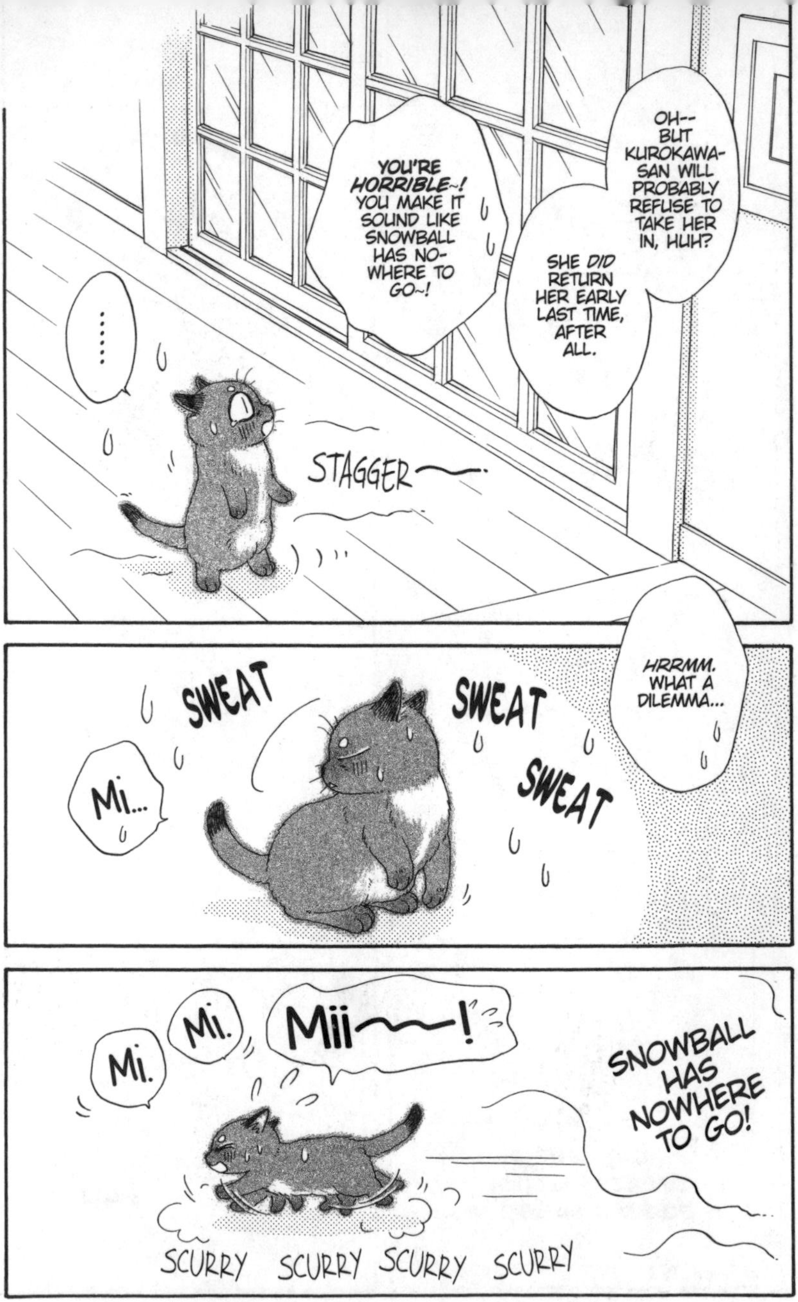
OH-- BUT KUROKAWA-SAN WILL PROBABLY REFUSE TO TAKE HER IN, HUH?
SHE *DID* RETURN HER EARLY LAST TIME, AFTER ALL.
YOU'RE *HORRIBLE*~! YOU MAKE IT SOUND LIKE SNOWBALL HAS NO-WHERE TO GO~!
......
STAGGER
HRRMM. WHAT A DILEMMA...
SWEAT
SWEAT
SWEAT
Mi...
SNOWBALL HAS NOWHERE TO GO!
Mii~~!
Mi.
Mi.
SCURRY SCURRY SCURRY SCURRY

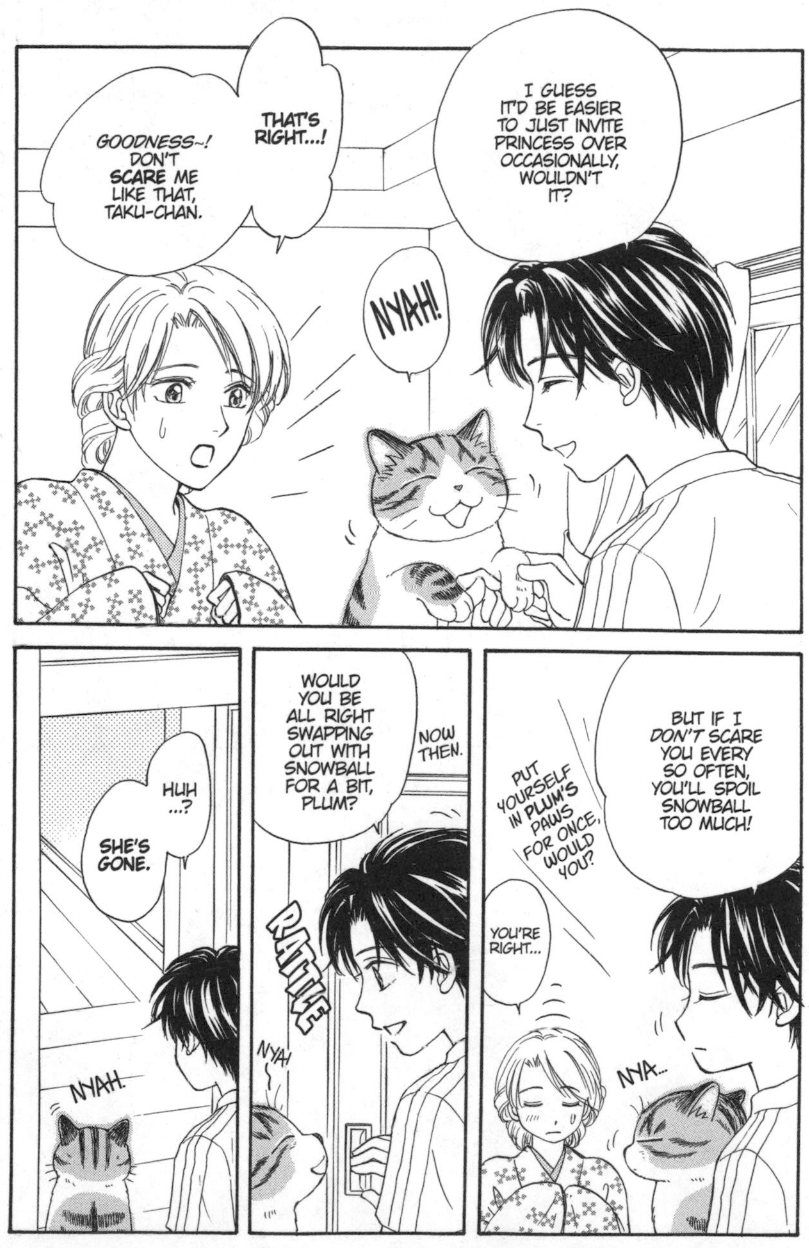
I GUESS IT'D BE EASIER TO JUST INVITE PRINCESS OVER OCCASIONALLY, WOULDN'T IT?
THAT'S RIGHT...!
GOODNESS~! DON'T SCARE ME LIKE THAT, TAKU-CHAN.
NYAH!
BUT IF I DON'T SCARE YOU EVERY SO OFTEN, YOU'LL SPOIL SNOWBALL TOO MUCH!
PUT YOURSELF IN PLUM'S PAWS FOR ONCE, WOULD YOU?
YOU'RE RIGHT...
NYA..
NOW THEN.
WOULD YOU BE ALL RIGHT SWAPPING OUT WITH SNOWBALL FOR A BIT, PLUM?
RATTLE
NYA!
HUH ...?
SHE'S GONE.
NYAH.

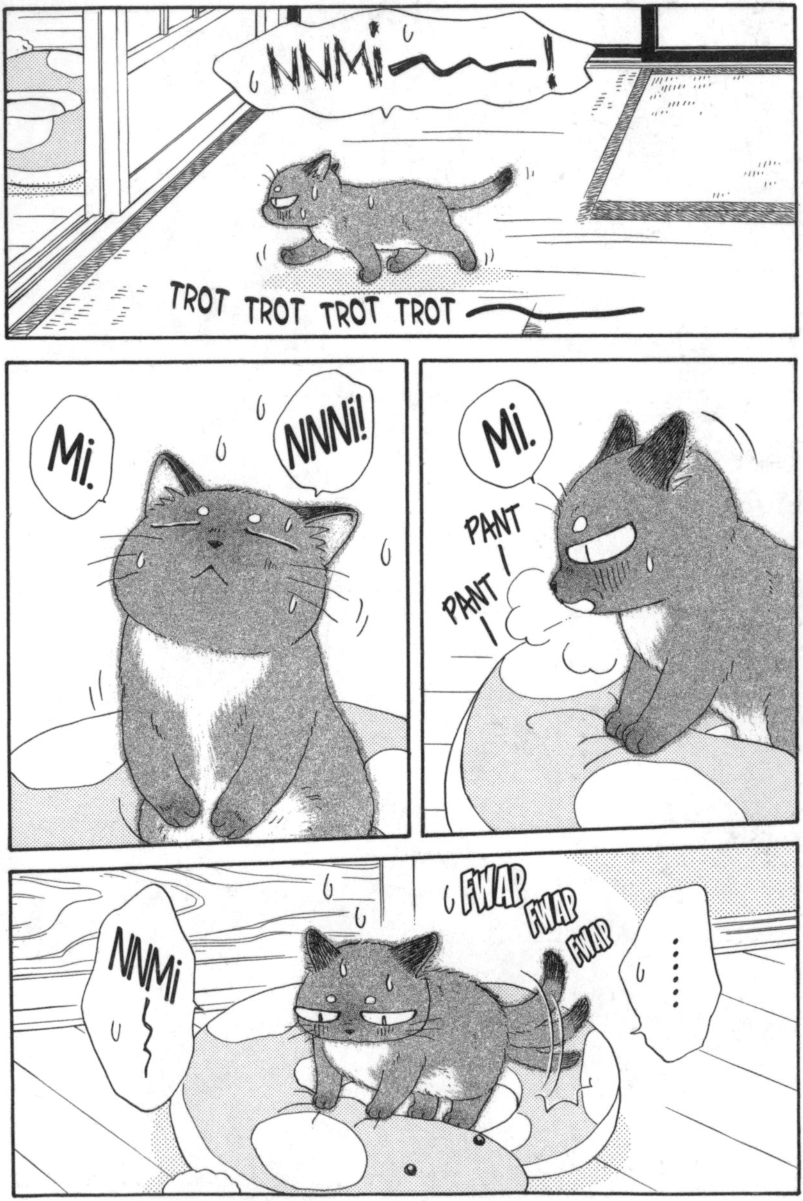
NNMi~~~!
TROT TROT TROT TROT
Mi.
PANT PANT
NNNi!
Mi.
......
FWAP FWAP FWAP
NNMi

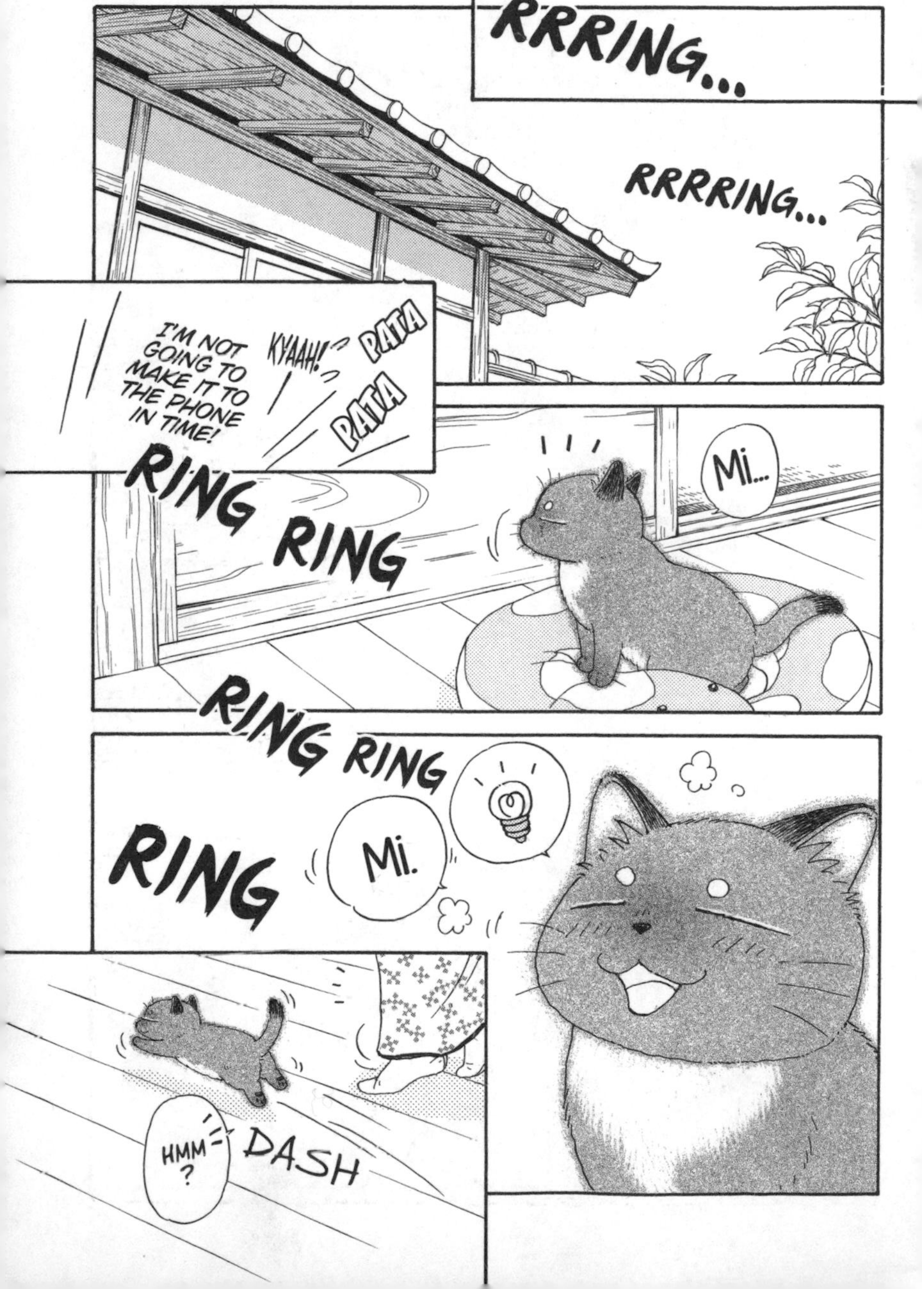

RRRING...
RRRRING...
PATA
PATA
KYAAH!
I'M NOT GOING TO MAKE IT TO THE PHONE IN TIME!
Mi...
RING RING
RING RING
Mi.
RING
DASH
HMM?

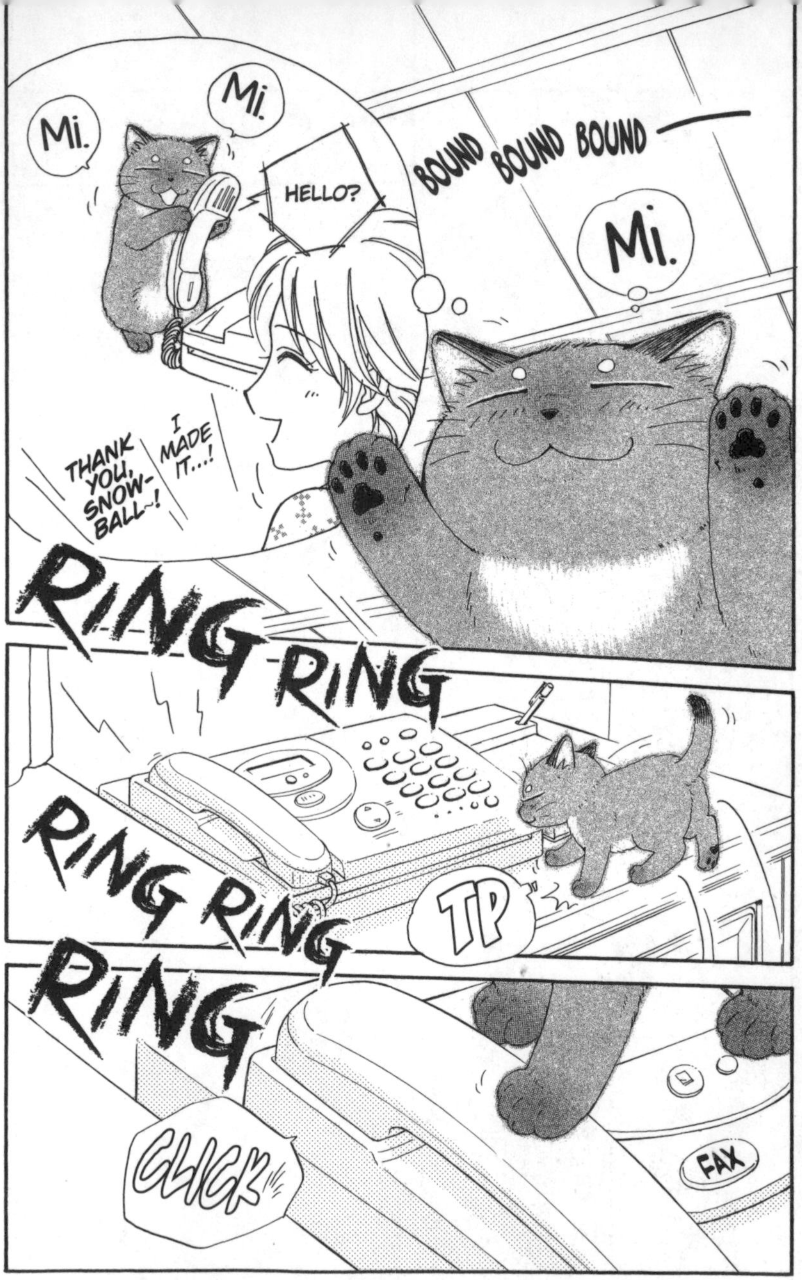
BOUND BOUND BOUND—
Mi.
Mi.
Mi.
HELLO?
I MADE IT...!
THANK YOU, SNOW-BALL~!
RING RING
RING RING
TP
RING
FAX
CLICK

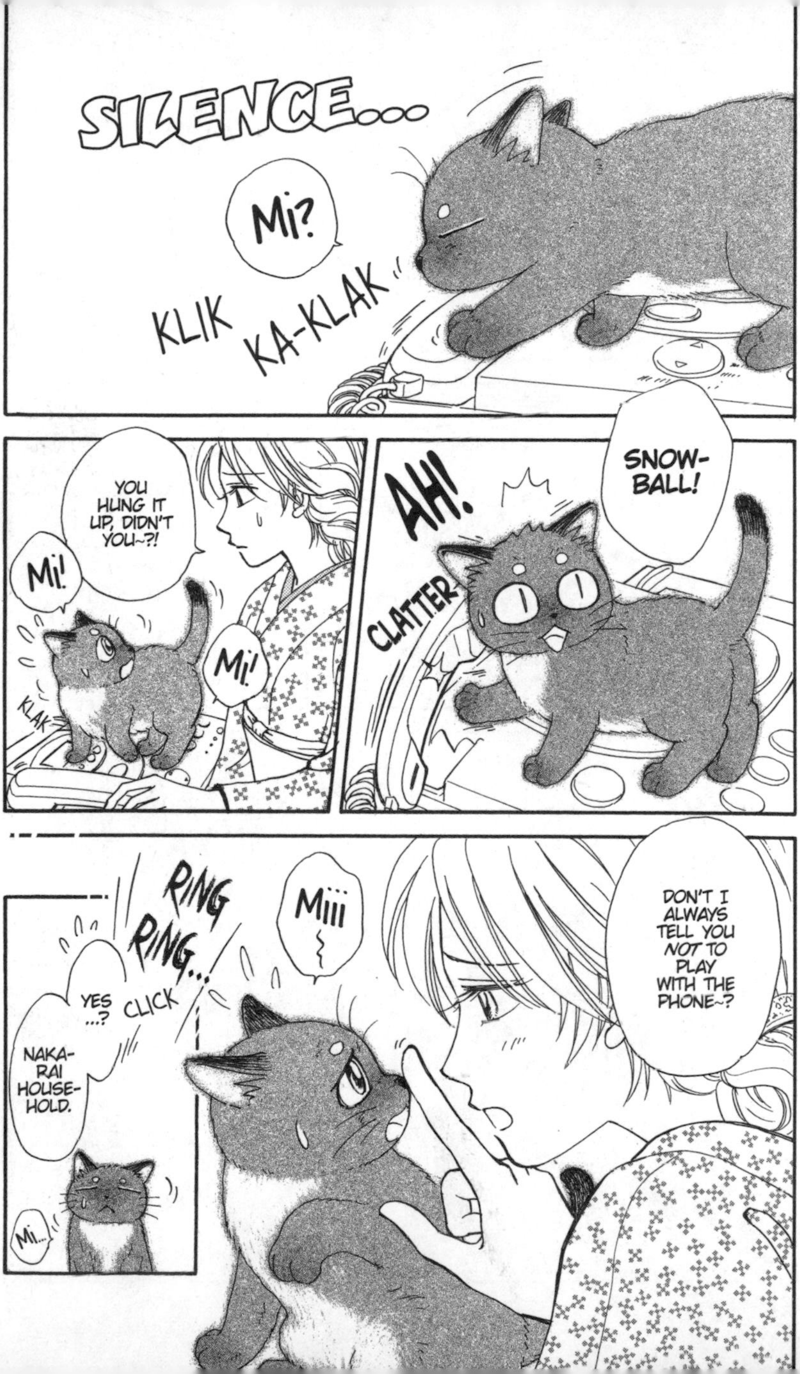
SILENCE...
Mi?
KLIK KA-KLAK
SNOW-BALL!
AH!
CLATTER
YOU HUNG IT UP, DIDN'T YOU~?!
Mi!
Mi!
KLAK
DON'T I ALWAYS TELL YOU *NOT* TO PLAY WITH THE PHONE~?
Miii
RING RING...
YES ...?
CLICK
NAKA-RAI HOUSE-HOLD.
Mi...

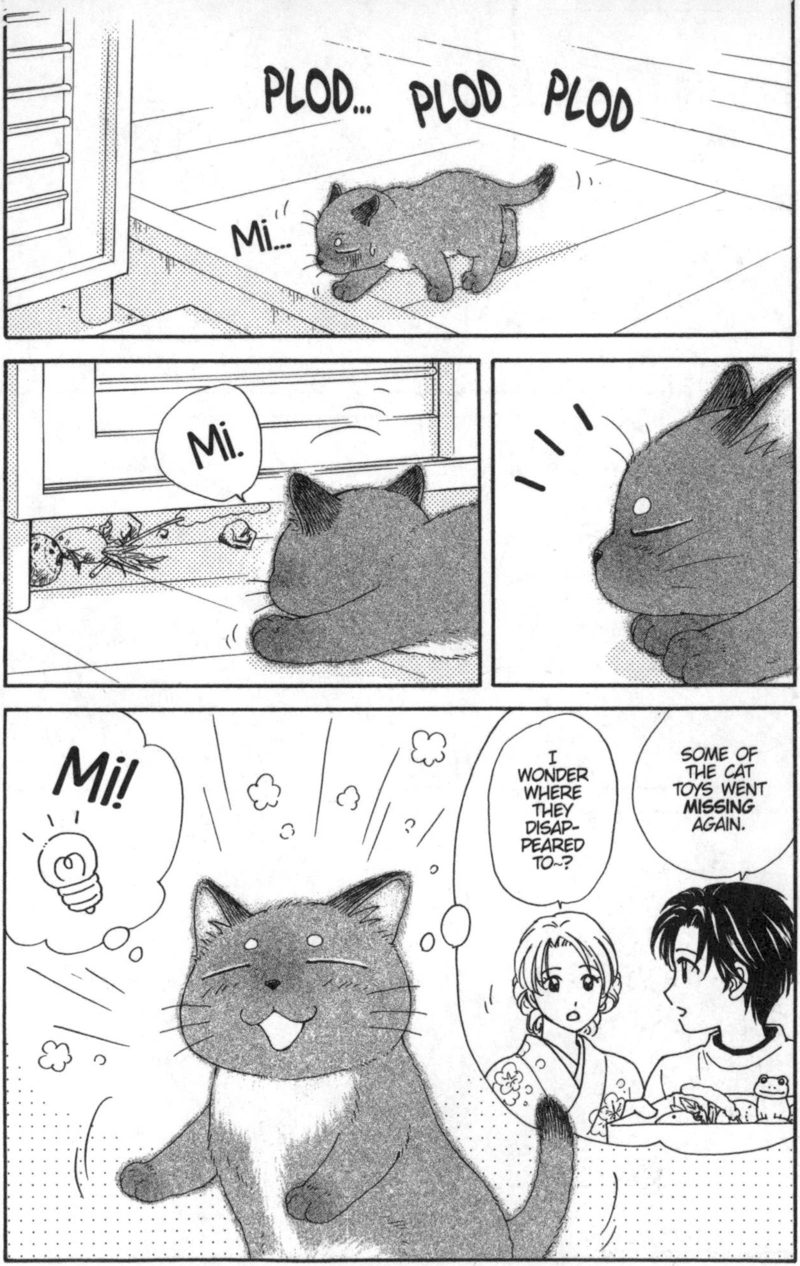
PLOD... PLOD PLOD
Mi...
Mi.
SOME OF THE CAT TOYS WENT MISSING AGAIN.
I WONDER WHERE THEY DISAP-PEARED TO~?
Mi!

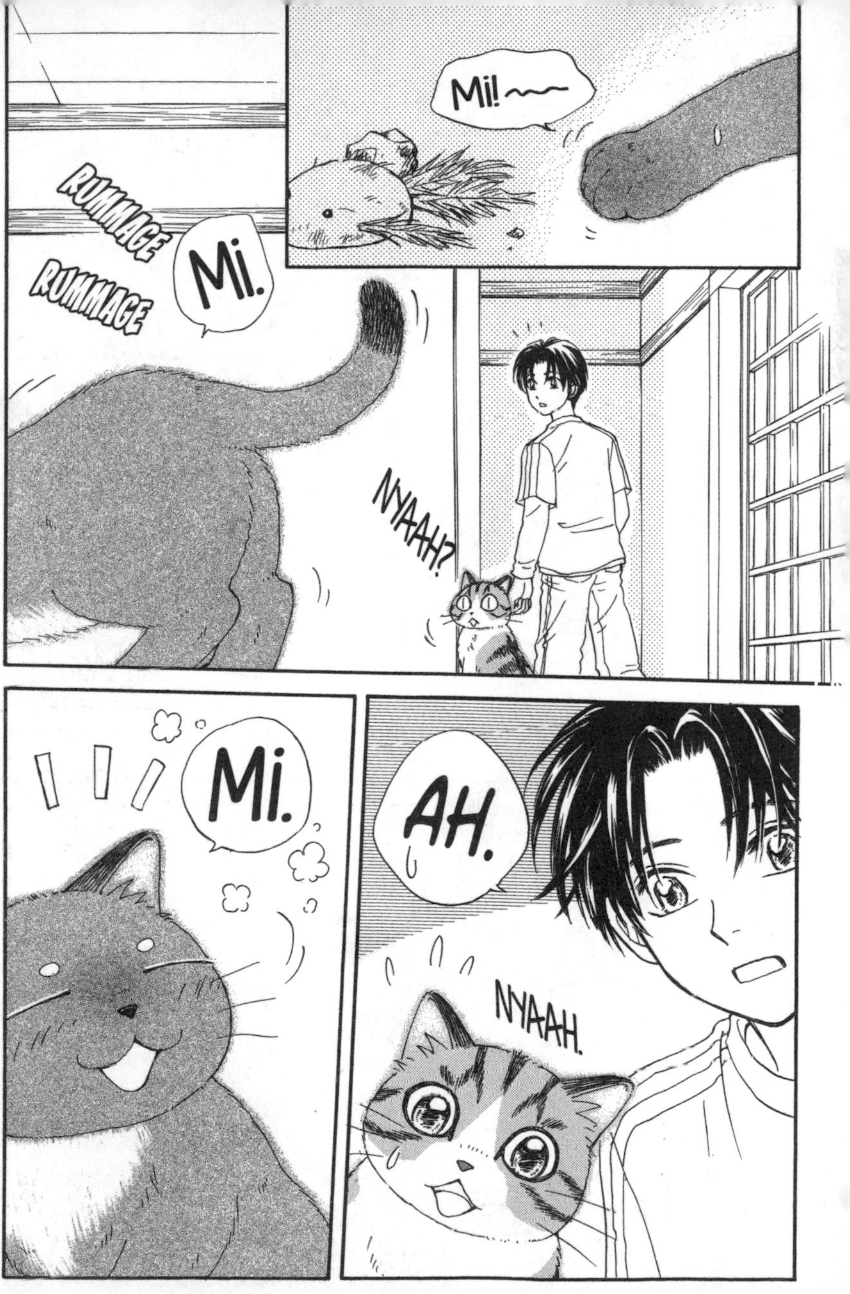

Mi! ~~~
RUMMAGE
RUMMAGE
Mi.
NYAAH?
AH.
NYAAH.
Mi.

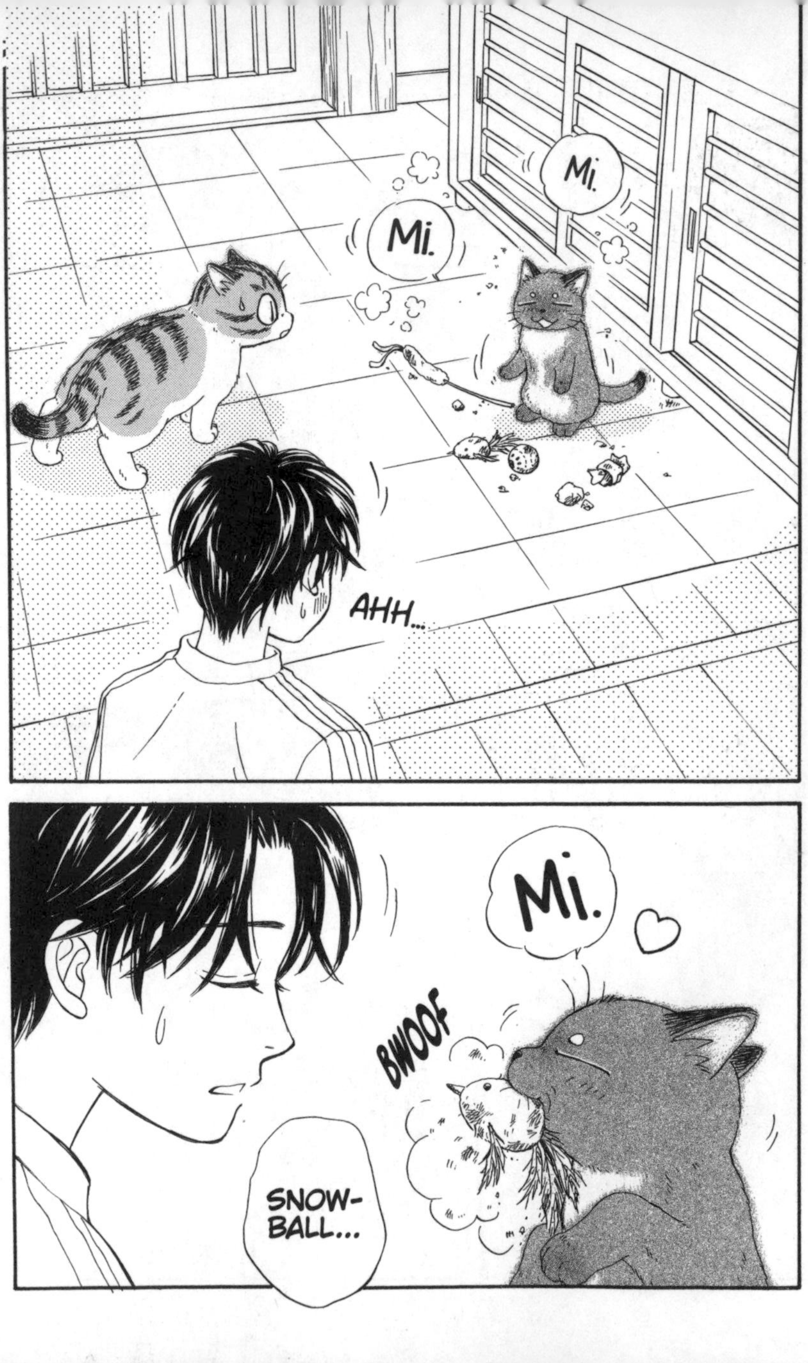
Mi.
Mi.
AHH...
Mi.
BWOOF
SNOW-BALL...

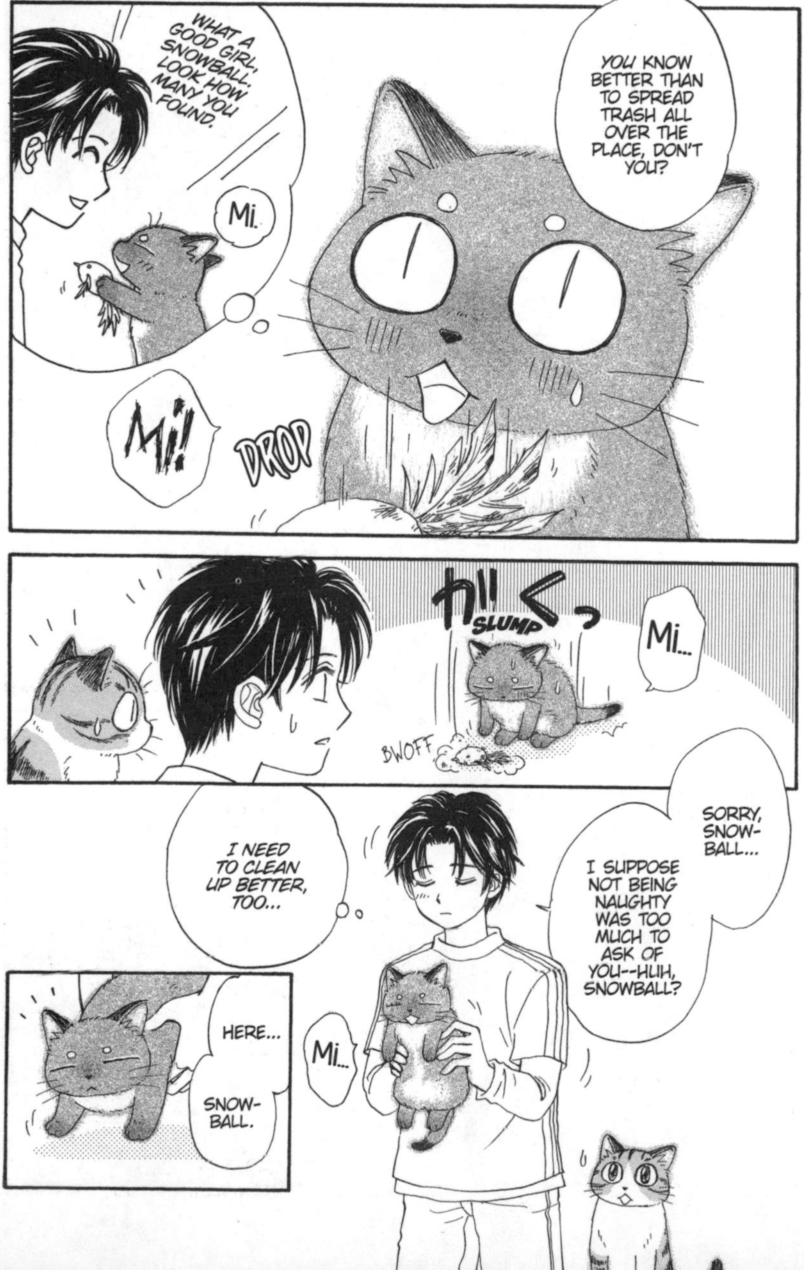
YOU KNOW BETTER THAN TO SPREAD TRASH ALL OVER THE PLACE, DON'T YOU?
WHAT A GOOD GIRL, SNOWBALL. LOOK HOW MANY YOU FOUND.
Mi.
DROP
Mi!
Mi...
かくっ
SLUMP
BWOFF
SORRY, SNOW-BALL...
I SUPPOSE NOT BEING NAUGHTY WAS TOO MUCH TO ASK OF YOU--HUH, SNOWBALL?
I NEED TO CLEAN UP BETTER, TOO...
Mi...
HERE...
SNOW-BALL.

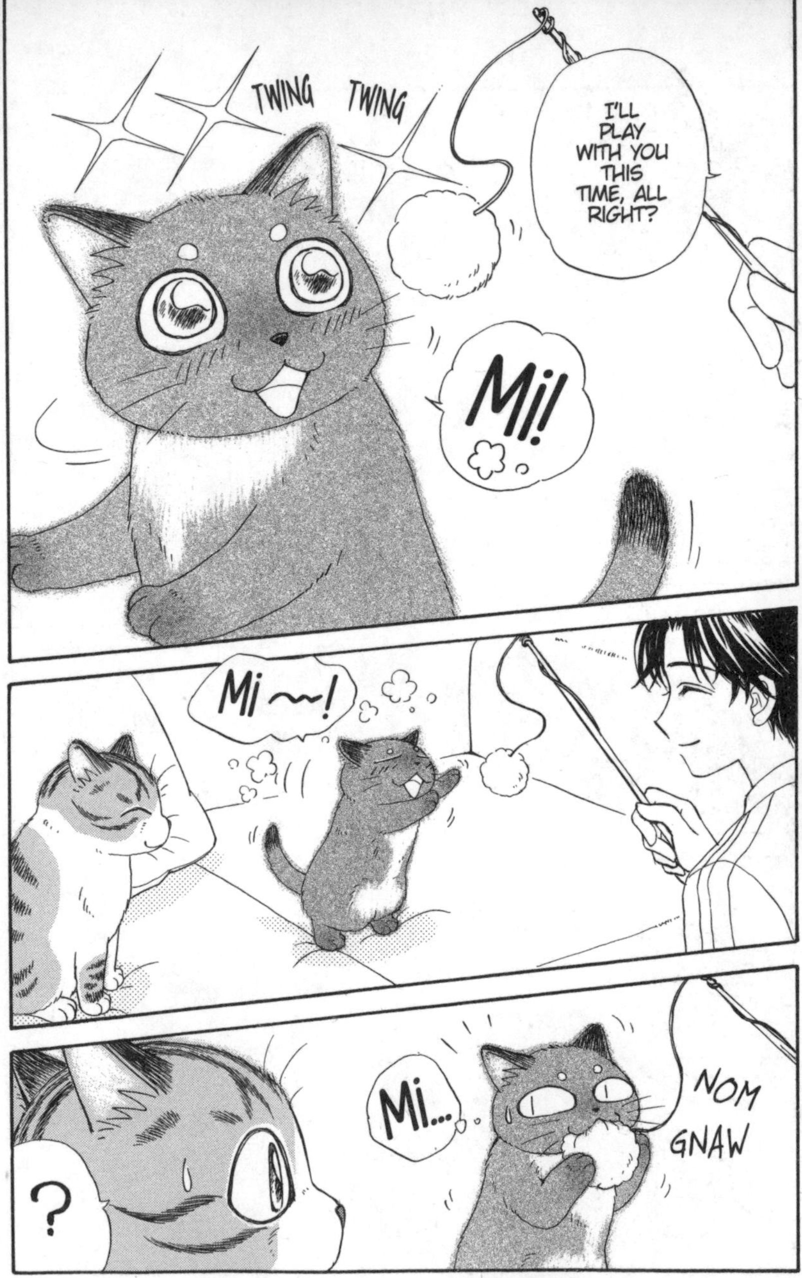
I'LL PLAY WITH YOU THIS TIME, ALL RIGHT?
TWING TWING
Mi!
Mi~~!
NOM GNAW
Mi...
?

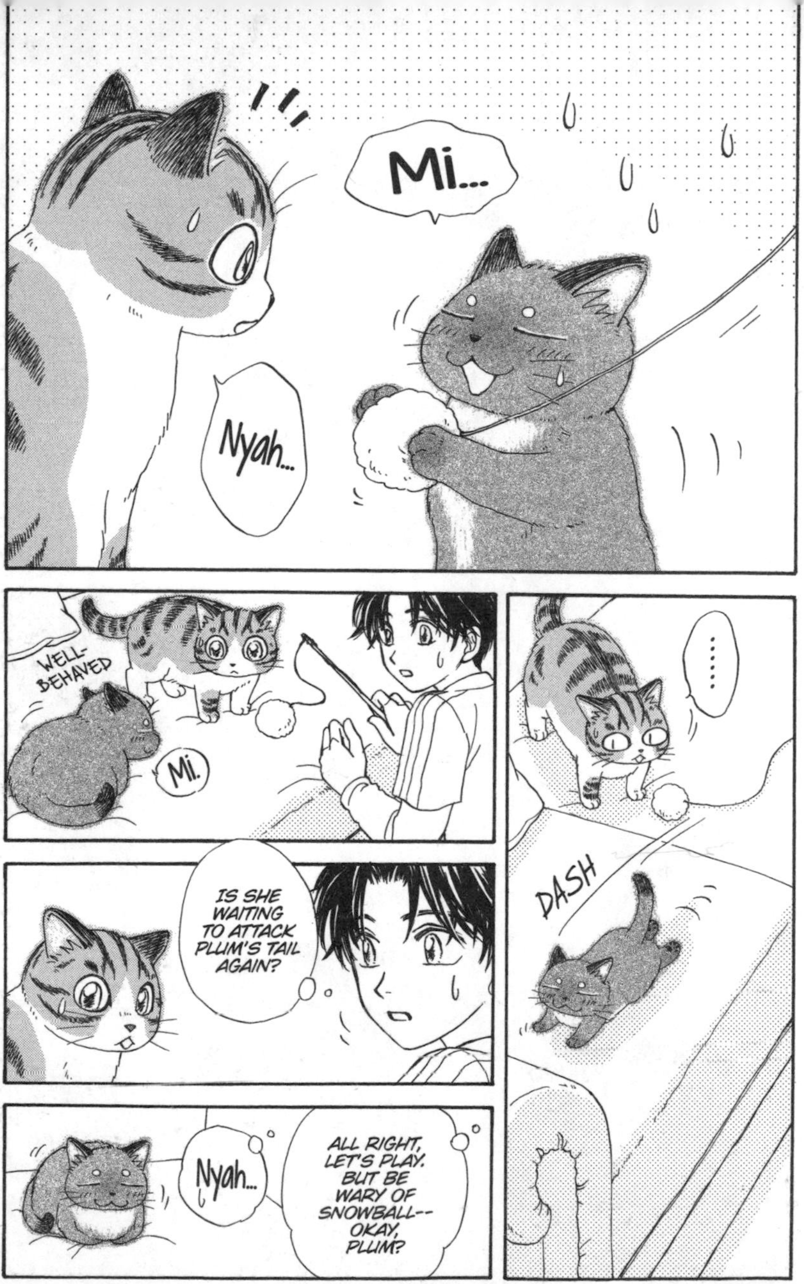
Mi...
Nyah...
......
DASH
WELL-BEHAVED
Mi.
IS SHE WAITING TO ATTACK PLUM'S TAIL AGAIN?
ALL RIGHT, LET'S PLAY. BUT BE WARY OF SNOWBALL--OKAY, PLUM?
Nyah...

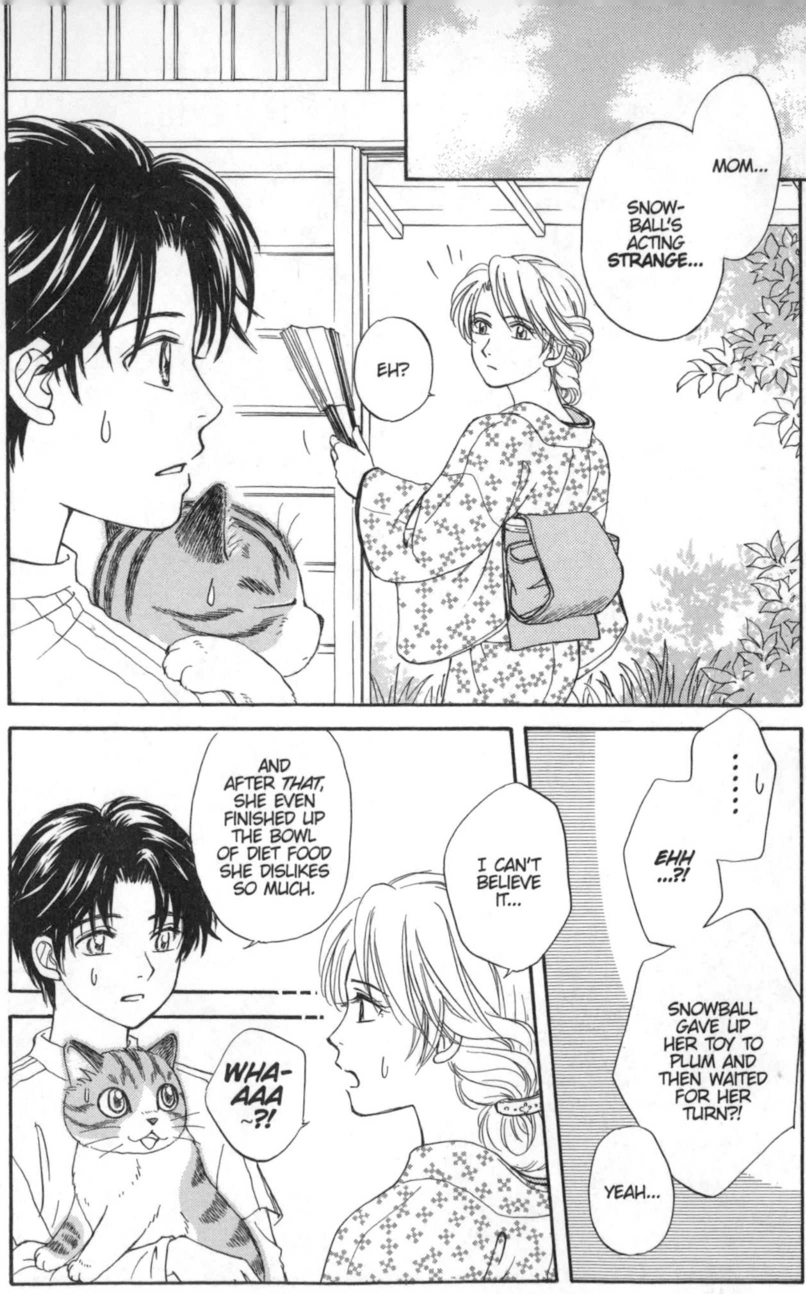
MOM...
SNOW-BALL'S ACTING STRANGE...
EH?
......
EHH ...?!
SNOWBALL GAVE UP HER TOY TO PLUM AND THEN WAITED FOR HER TURN?!
YEAH...
AND AFTER *THAT*, SHE EVEN FINISHED UP THE BOWL OF DIET FOOD SHE DISLIKES SO MUCH.
I CAN'T BELIEVE IT...
WHA-AAA ~?!

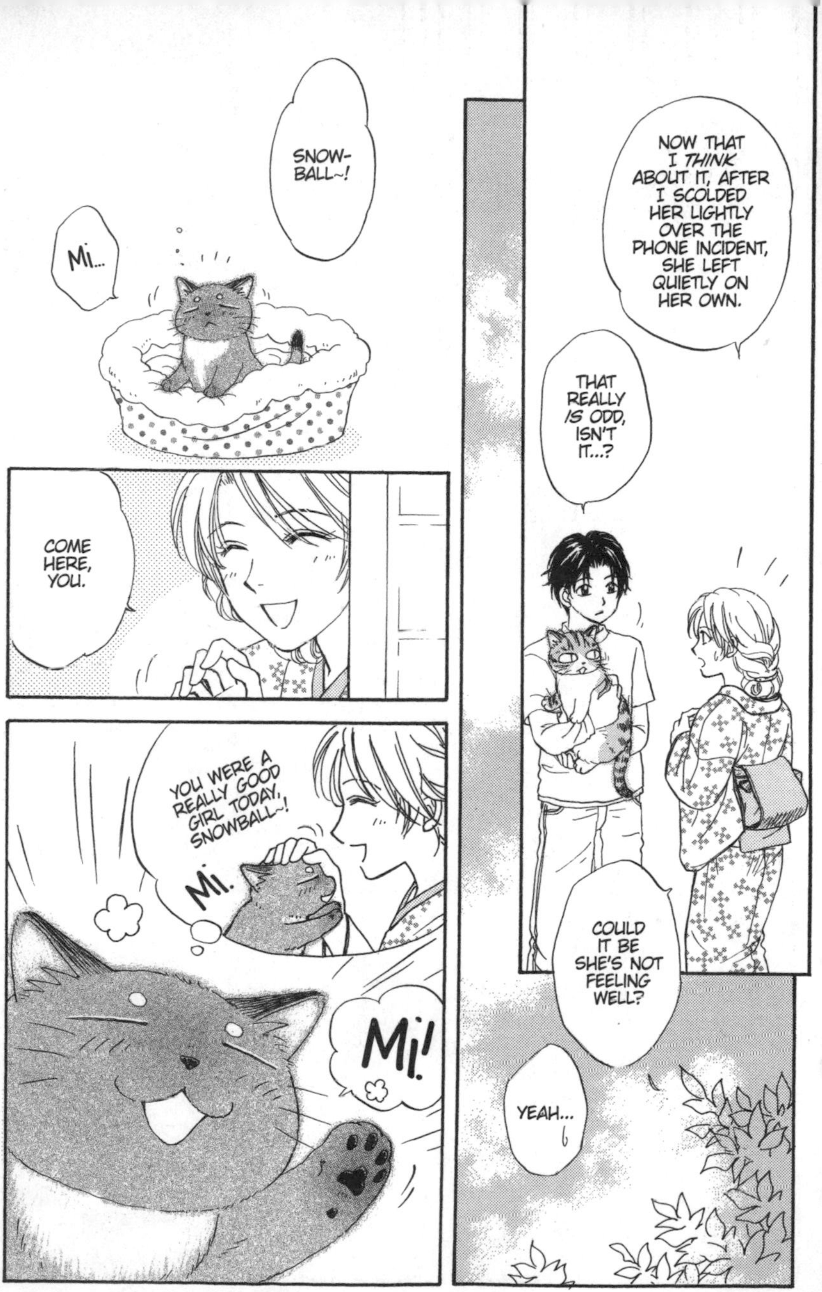
NOW THAT I *THINK* ABOUT IT, AFTER I SCOLDED HER LIGHTLY OVER THE PHONE INCIDENT, SHE LEFT QUIETLY ON HER OWN.
THAT REALLY *IS* ODD, ISN'T IT...?
COULD IT BE SHE'S NOT FEELING WELL?
YEAH...
SNOW-BALL~!
Mi...
COME HERE, YOU.
YOU WERE A REALLY GOOD GIRL TODAY, SNOWBALL~!
Mi.
Mi!

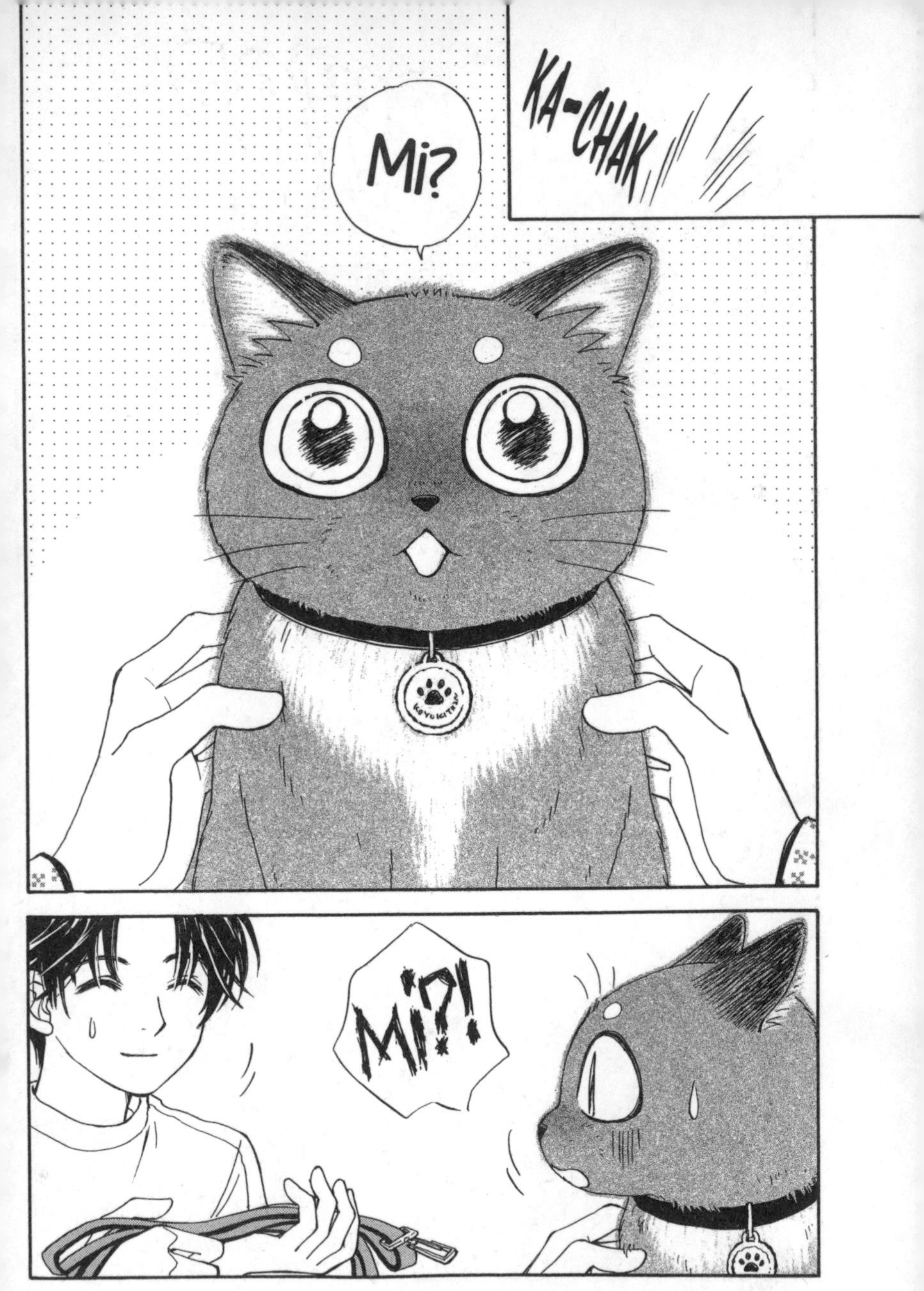
KA-CHAK
Mi?
Mi?!

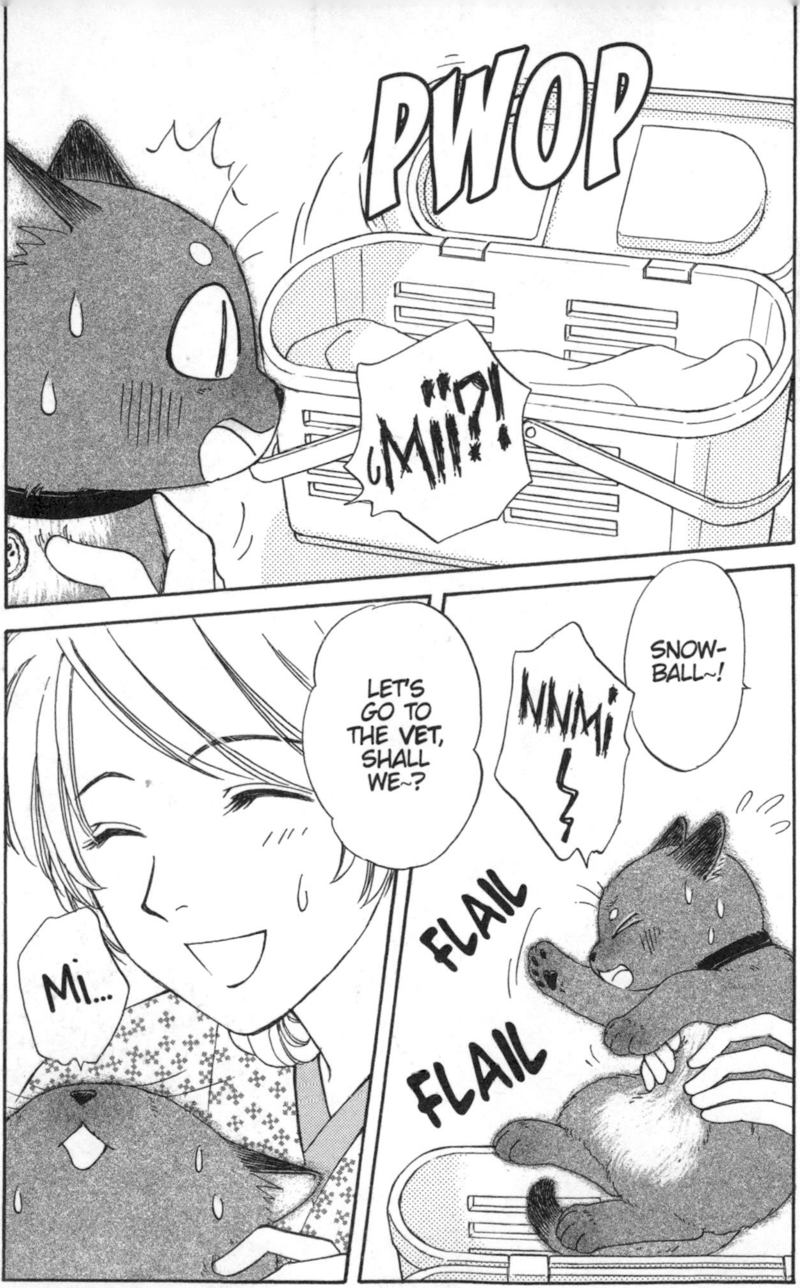
PWOP
¿Mii?!
SNOW-BALL~!
NNMi!
FLAIL
FLAIL
LET'S GO TO THE VET, SHALL WE~?
Mi...

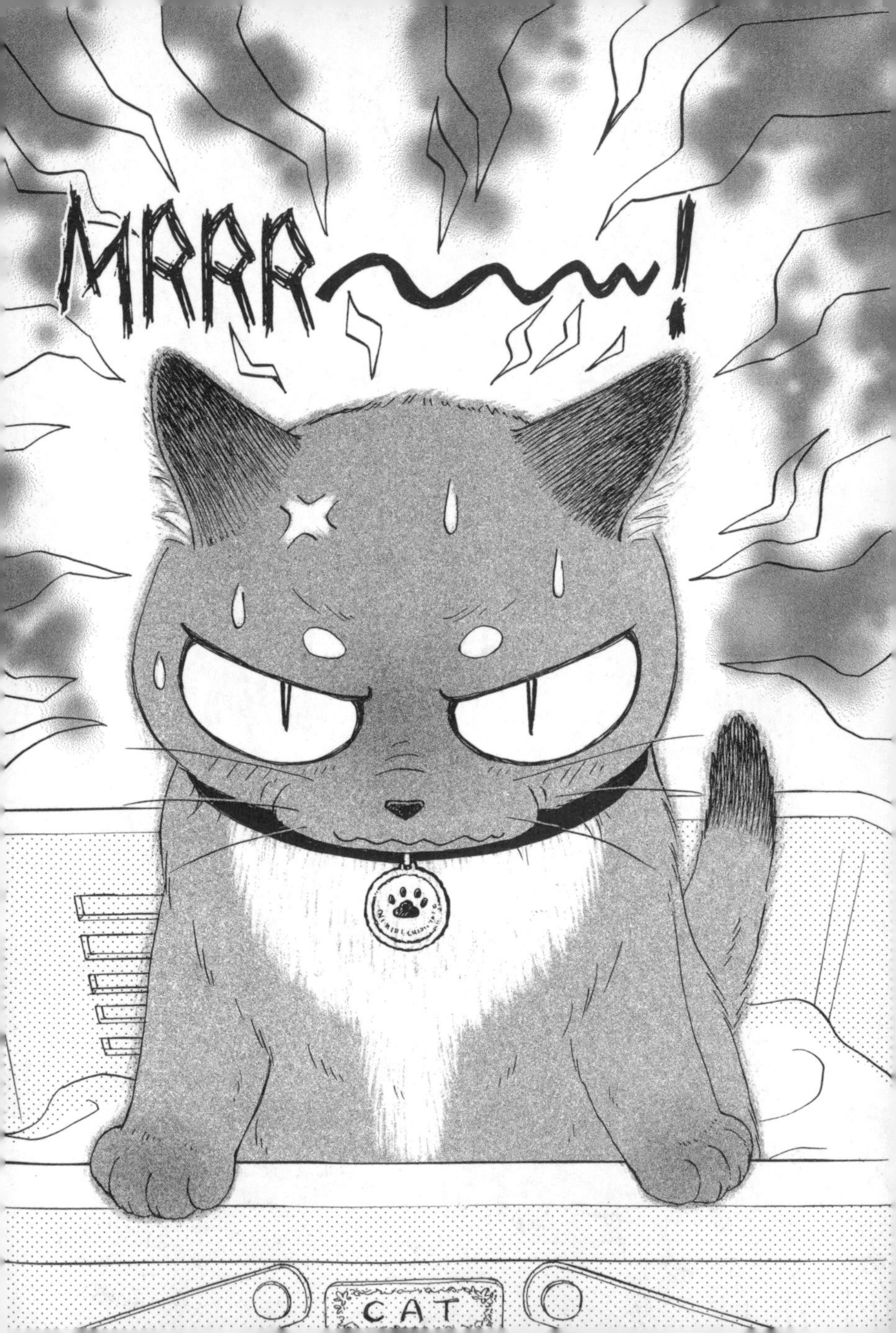

MRRR~!
CAT

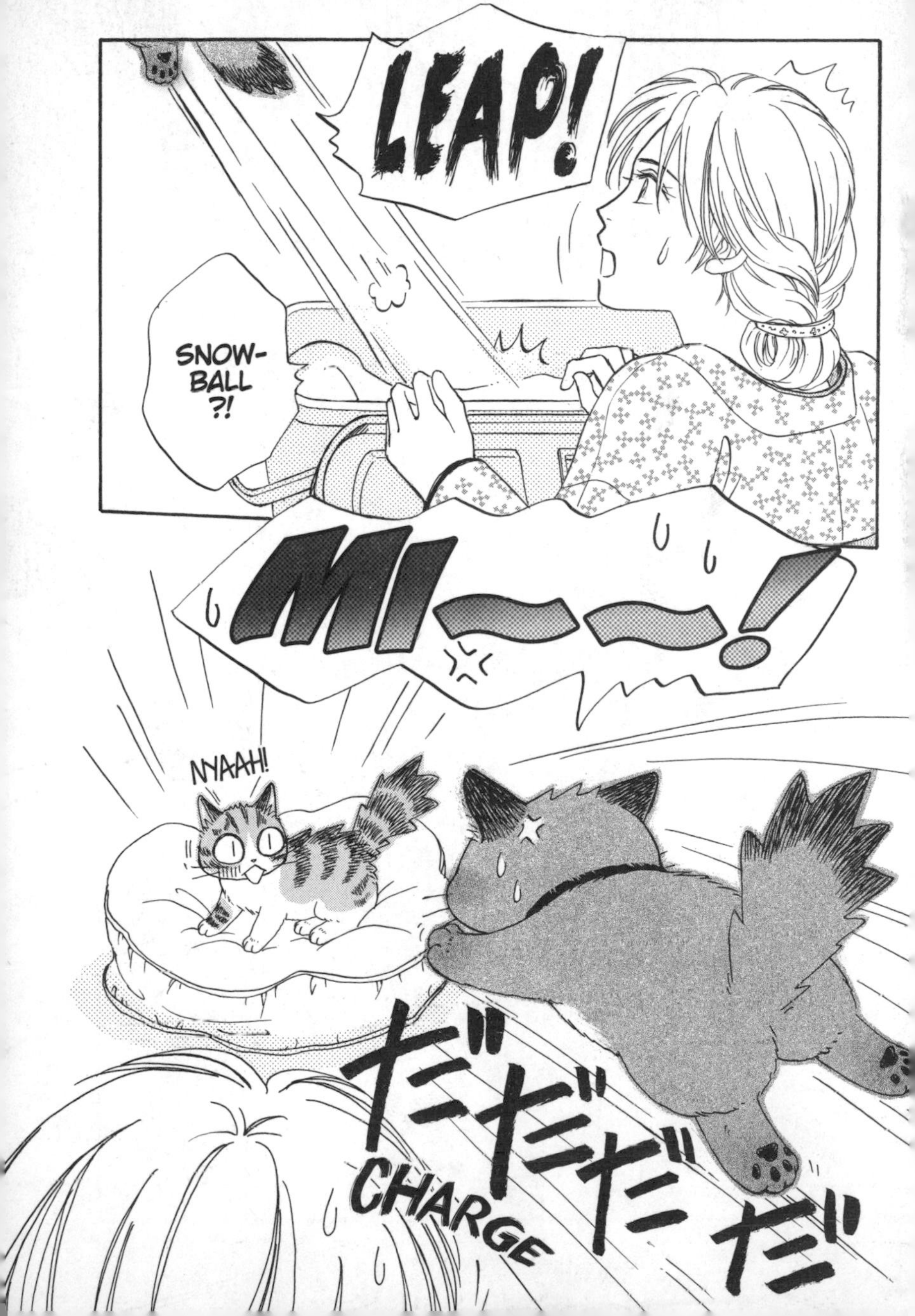
LEAP!
SNOW-BALL?!
MI~~~!
NYAAH!
だだだだだ
CHARGE

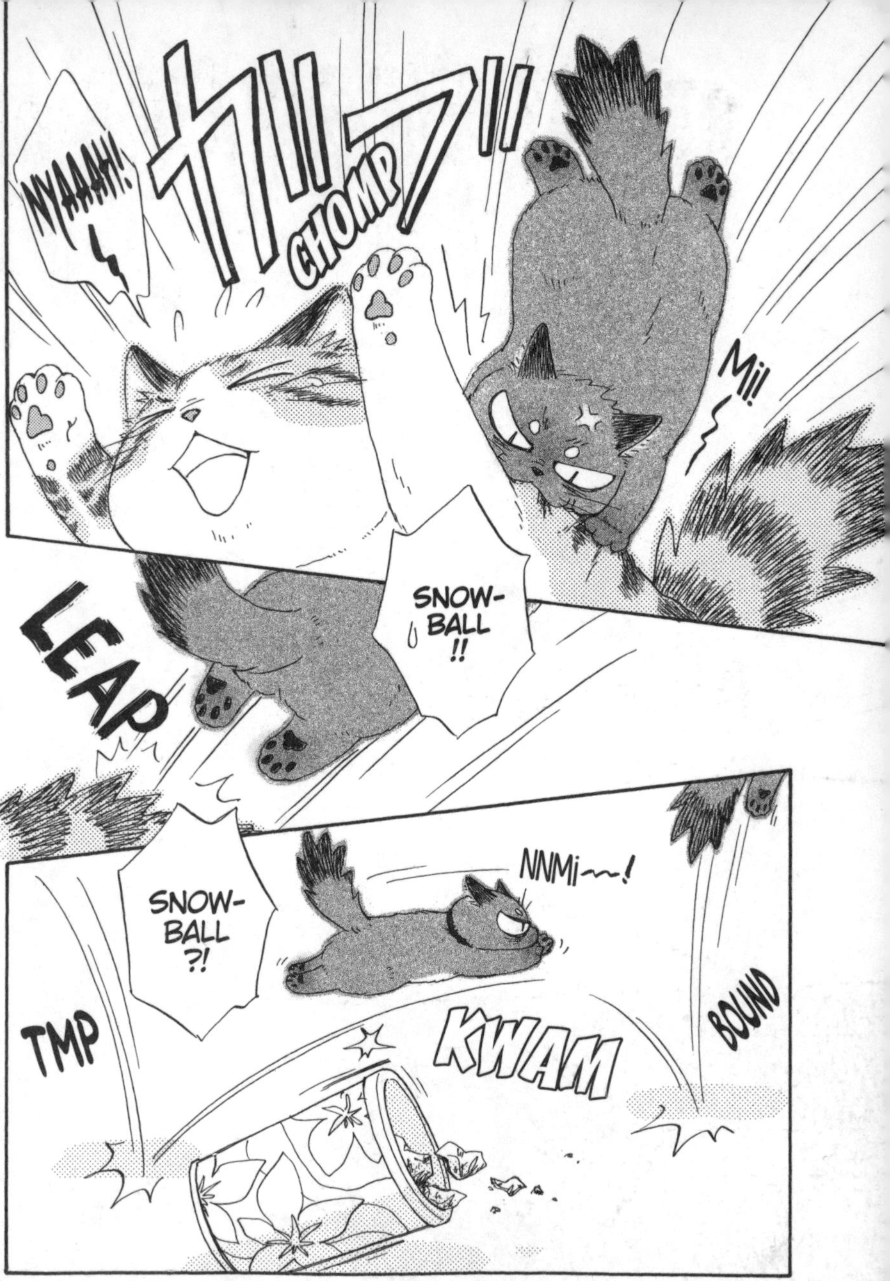
CHOMP
NYAAAH!
Mi!!
SNOW-BALL!!
LEAP
NNMi~~!
SNOW-BALL?!
BOUND
KWAM
TMP

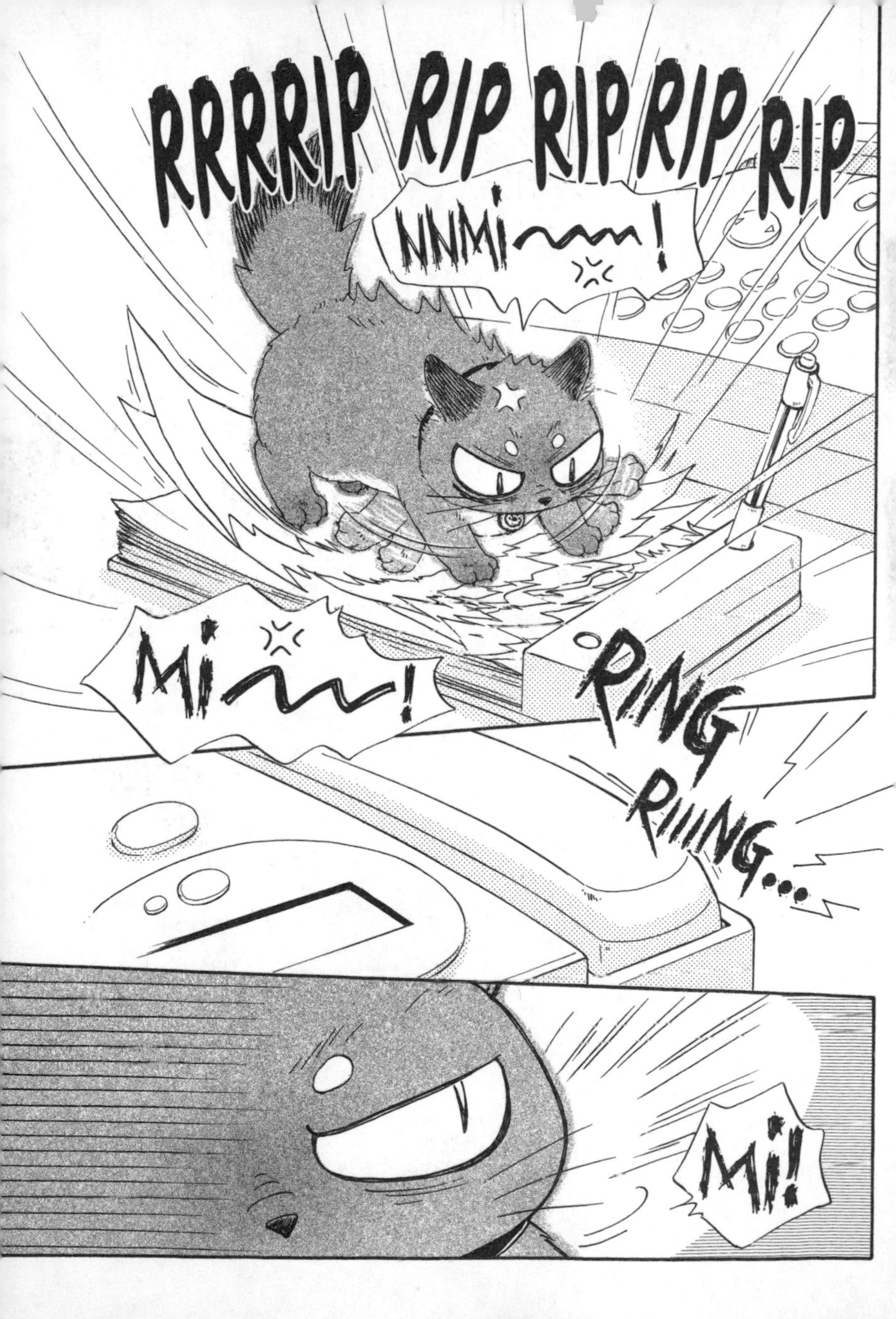
RRRRIP RIP RIP RIP RIP
NNMi~~~!
Mi~~!
RING RIING...
Mi!

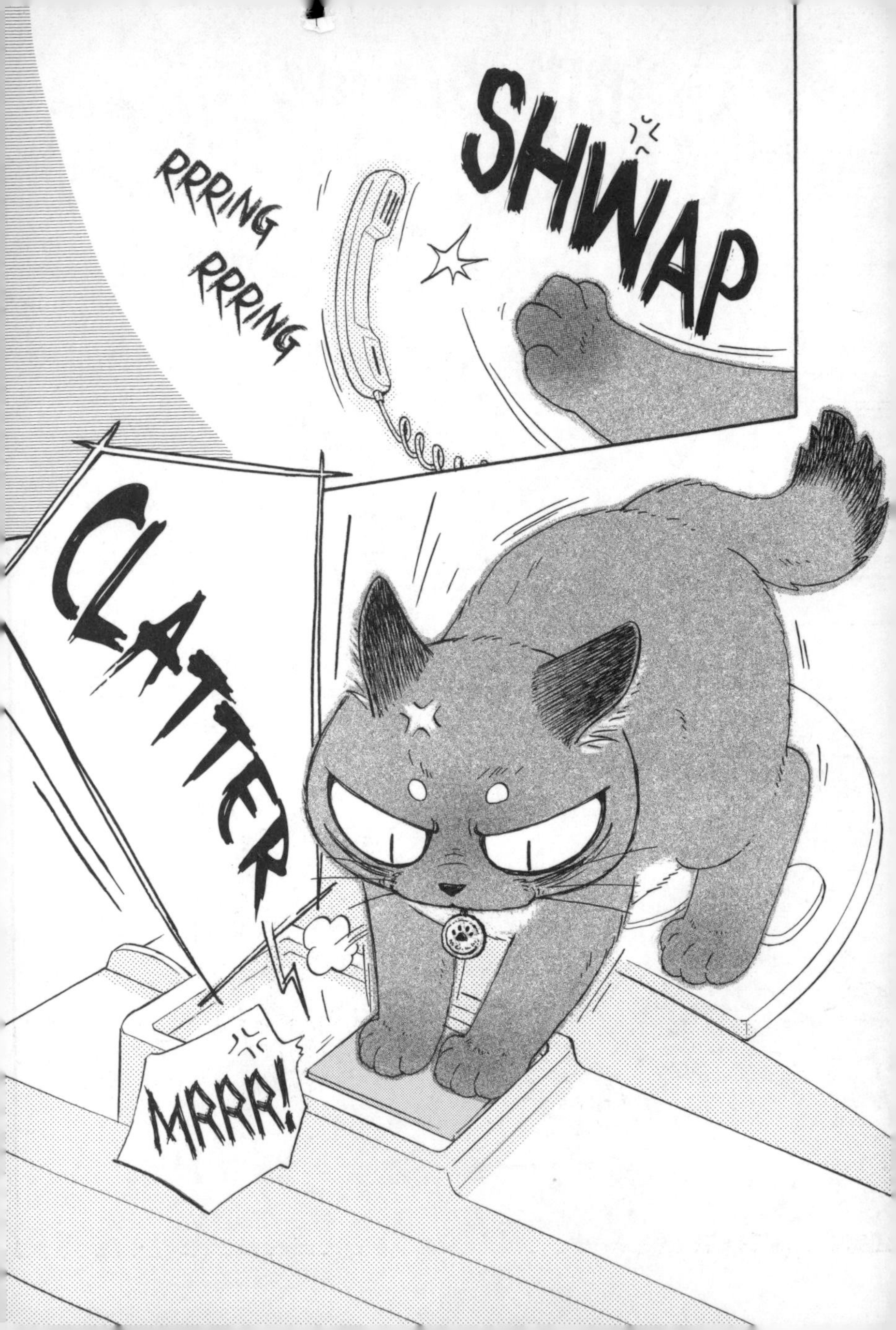
SHWAP
RRRING
RRRING
CLATTER
MRRR!

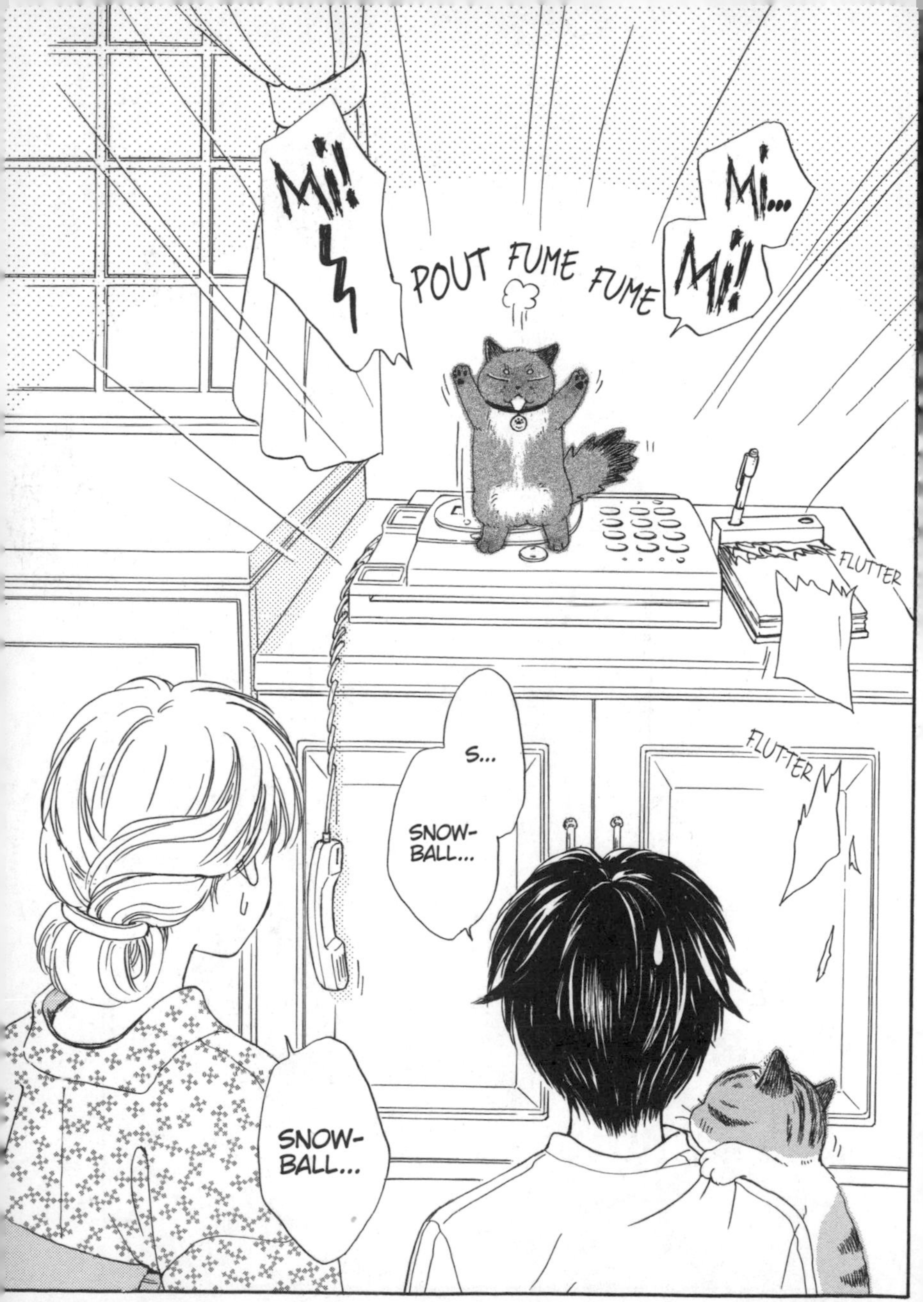
Mi... Mi!
POUT FUME FUME
Mi!
FLUTTER
FLUTTER
S... SNOW-BALL...
SNOW-BALL...

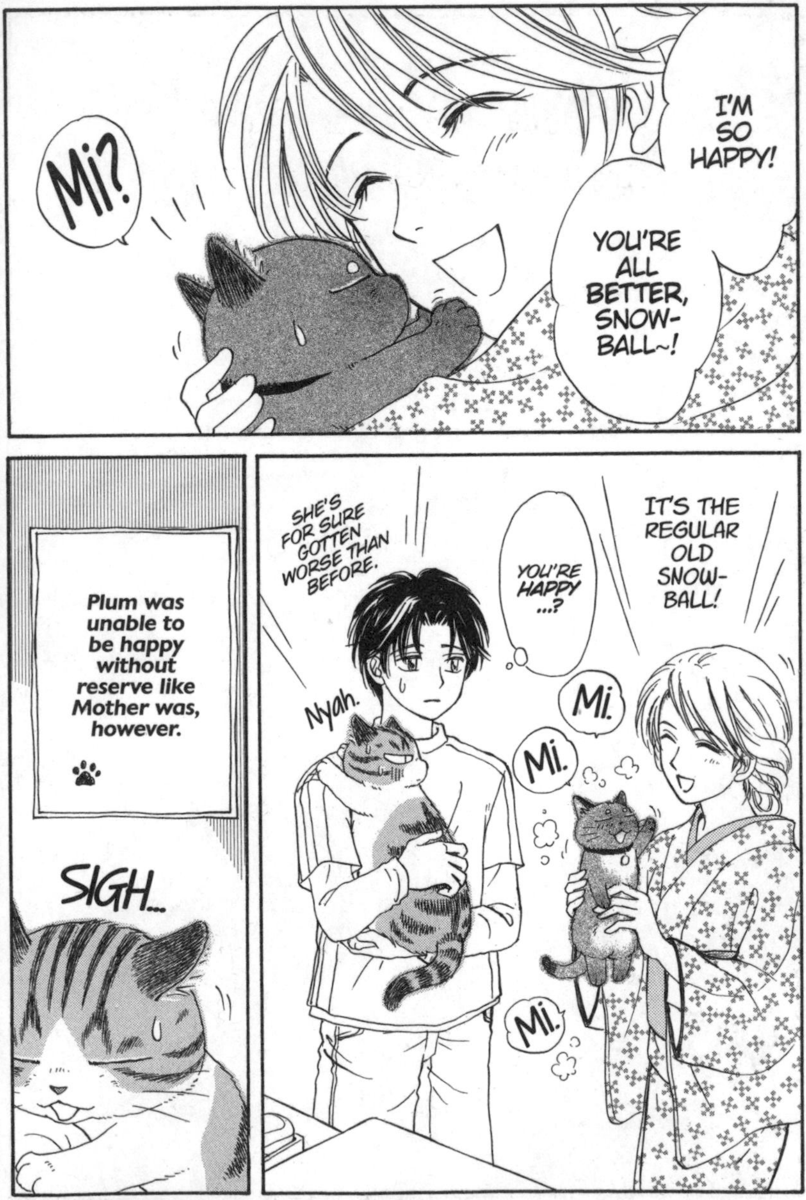
I'M SO HAPPY!
YOU'RE ALL BETTER, SNOW-BALL~!
Mi?
IT'S THE REGULAR OLD SNOW-BALL!
YOU'RE HAPPY ...?
SHE'S FOR SURE GOTTEN WORSE THAN BEFORE.
Mi.
Mi.
Nyah.
Mi.
Plum was unable to be happy without reserve like Mother was, however.
SIGH...

THE END

SHORT.19

New Year's With Squeaky Mouse-san

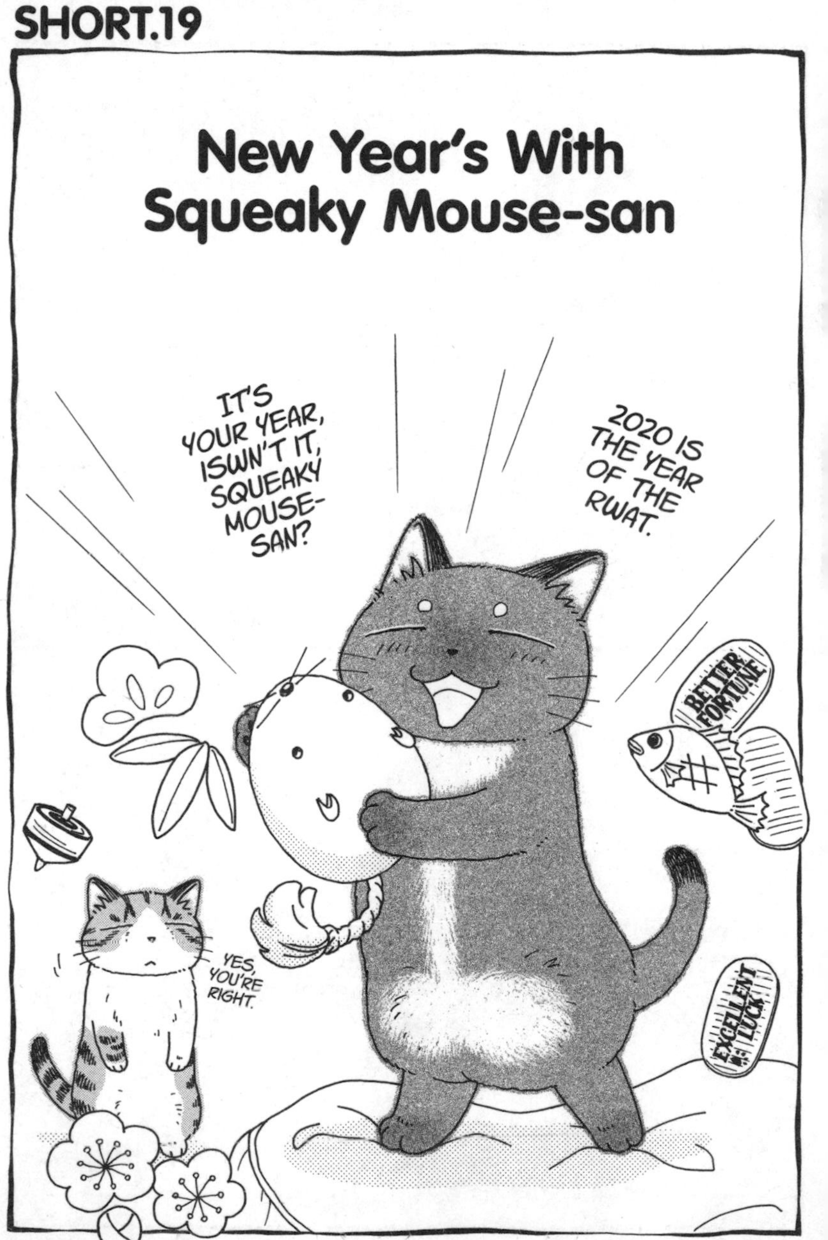
2020 IS THE YEAR OF THE RWAT.
IT'S YOUR YEAR, ISWN'T IT, SQUEAKY MOUSE-SAN?
BETTER FORTUNE
EXCELLENT LUCK
YES, YOU'RE RIGHT.

Are You Standing Out?

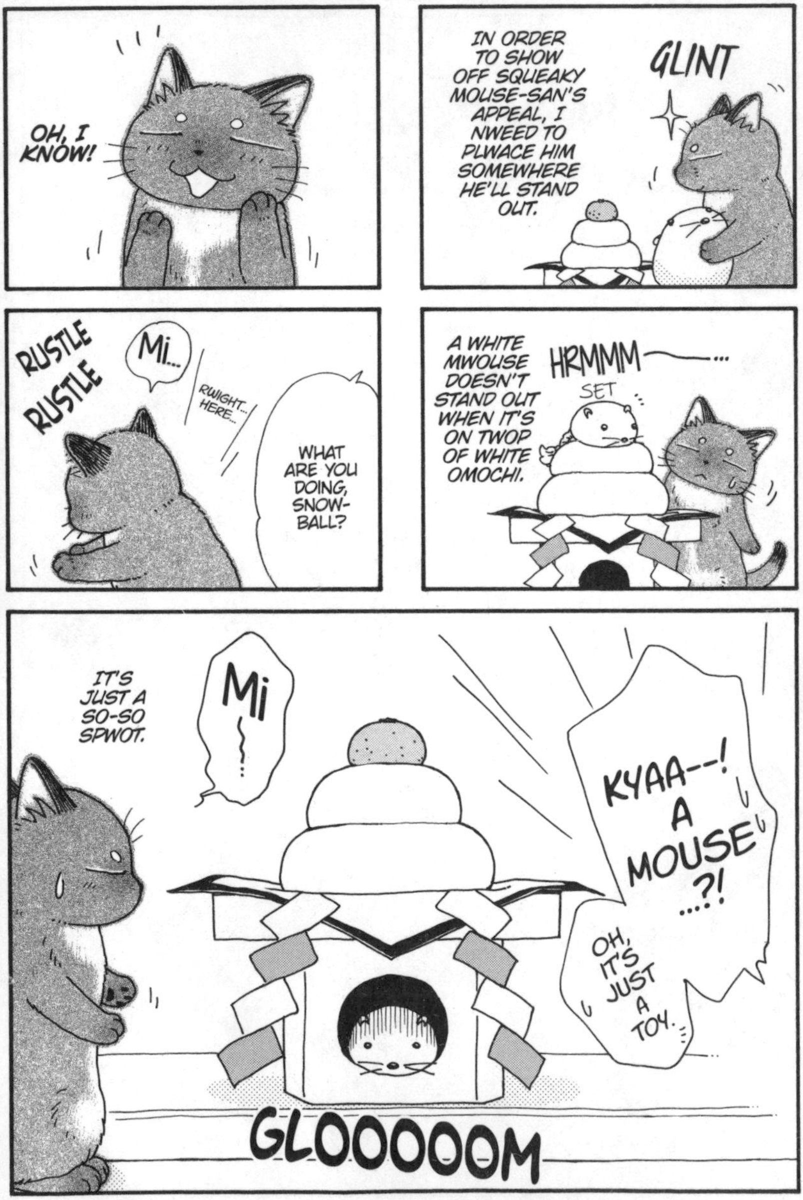
OH, I KNOW!
IN ORDER TO SHOW OFF SQUEAKY MOUSE-SAN'S APPEAL, I NWEED TO PLWACE HIM SOMEWHERE HE'LL STAND OUT.
GLINT
RUSTLE RUSTLE
Mi...
RWIGHT... HERE...
WHAT ARE YOU DOING, SNOW-BALL?
A WHITE MWOUSE DOESN'T STAND OUT WHEN IT'S ON TWOP OF WHITE OMOCHI.
HRMMM——...
SET
IT'S JUST A SO-SO SPWOT.
Mi ~...
KYAA--! A MOUSE ...?!
OH, IT'S JUST A TOY...
GLOOOOOM

Don't Feel Down About Yourself

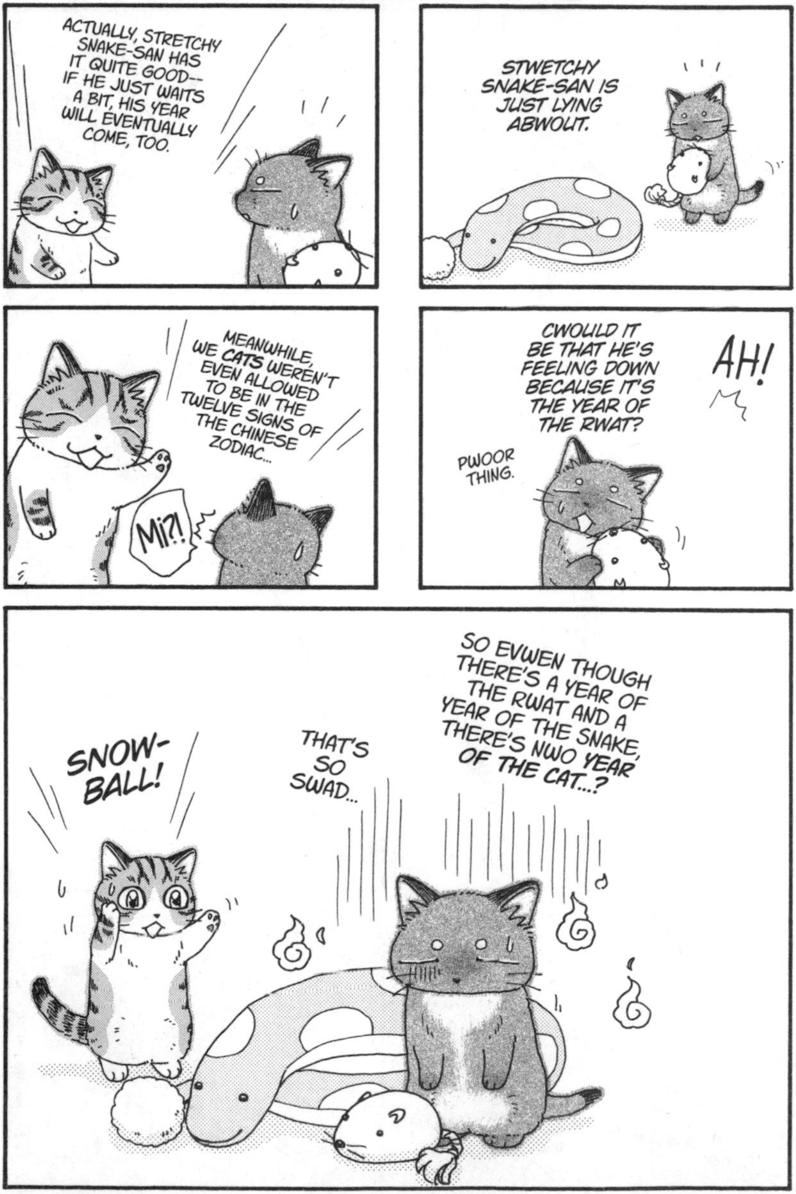
STWETCHY SNAKE-SAN IS JUST LYING ABWOUT.
ACTUALLY, STRETCHY SNAKE-SAN HAS IT QUITE GOOD-- IF HE JUST WAITS A BIT, HIS YEAR WILL EVENTUALLY COME, TOO.
AH!
CWOULD IT BE THAT HE'S FEELING DOWN BECAUSE IT'S THE YEAR OF THE RWAT?
PWOOR THING.
MEANWHILE, WE CATS WEREN'T EVEN ALLOWED TO BE IN THE TWELVE SIGNS OF THE CHINESE ZODIAC...
Mi?!
SO EVWEN THOUGH THERE'S A YEAR OF THE RWAT AND A YEAR OF THE SNAKE, THERE'S NWO YEAR OF THE CAT...?
THAT'S SO SWAD...
SNOW-BALL!

The Search for Snowball's Zodiac Sign

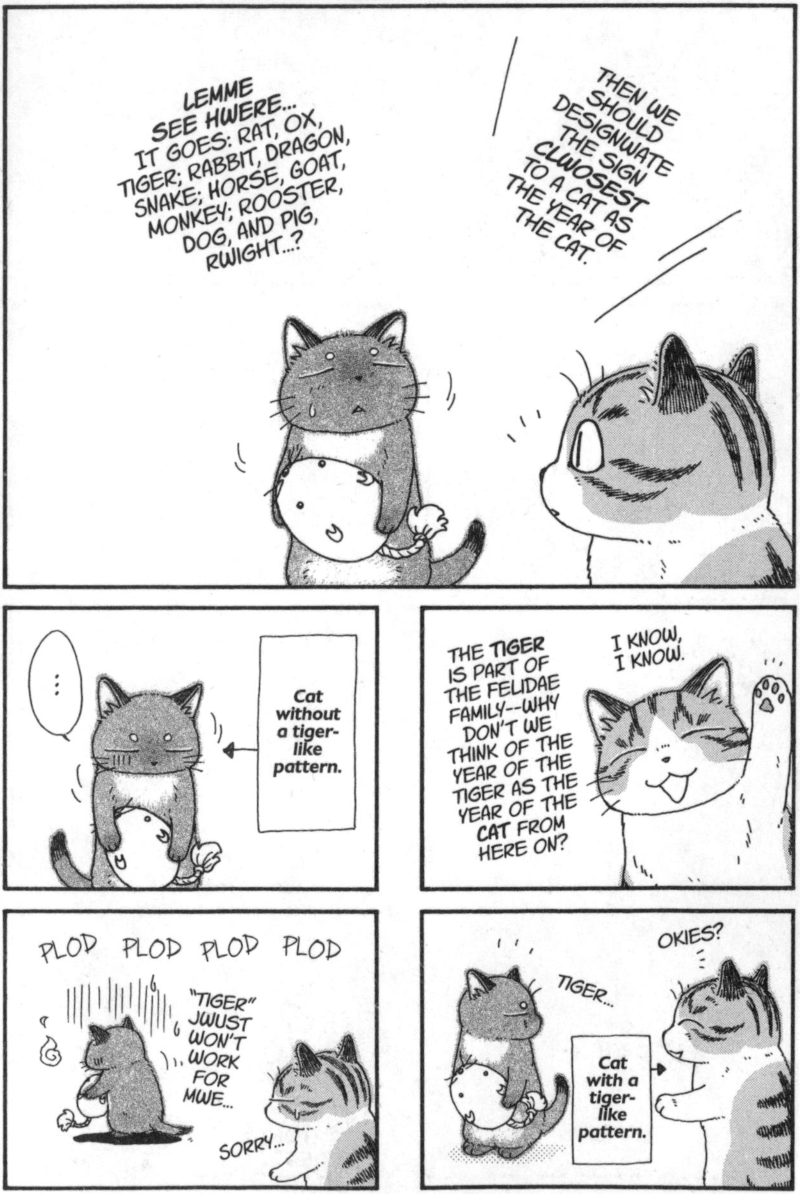

THEN WE SHOULD DESIGNWATE THE SIGN CLWOSEST TO A CAT AS THE YEAR OF THE CAT.
LEMME SEE HWERE... IT GOES: RAT, OX, TIGER; RABBIT, DRAGON, SNAKE; HORSE, GOAT, MONKEY; ROOSTER, DOG, AND PIG, RWIGHT...?
I KNOW, I KNOW.
THE TIGER IS PART OF THE FELIDAE FAMILY--WHY DON'T WE THINK OF THE YEAR OF THE TIGER AS THE YEAR OF THE CAT FROM HERE ON?
Cat without a tiger-like pattern.
...
OKIES?
TIGER...
Cat with a tiger-like pattern.
PLOD PLOD PLOD PLOD
"TIGER" JWUST WON'T WORK FOR MWE...
SORRY...

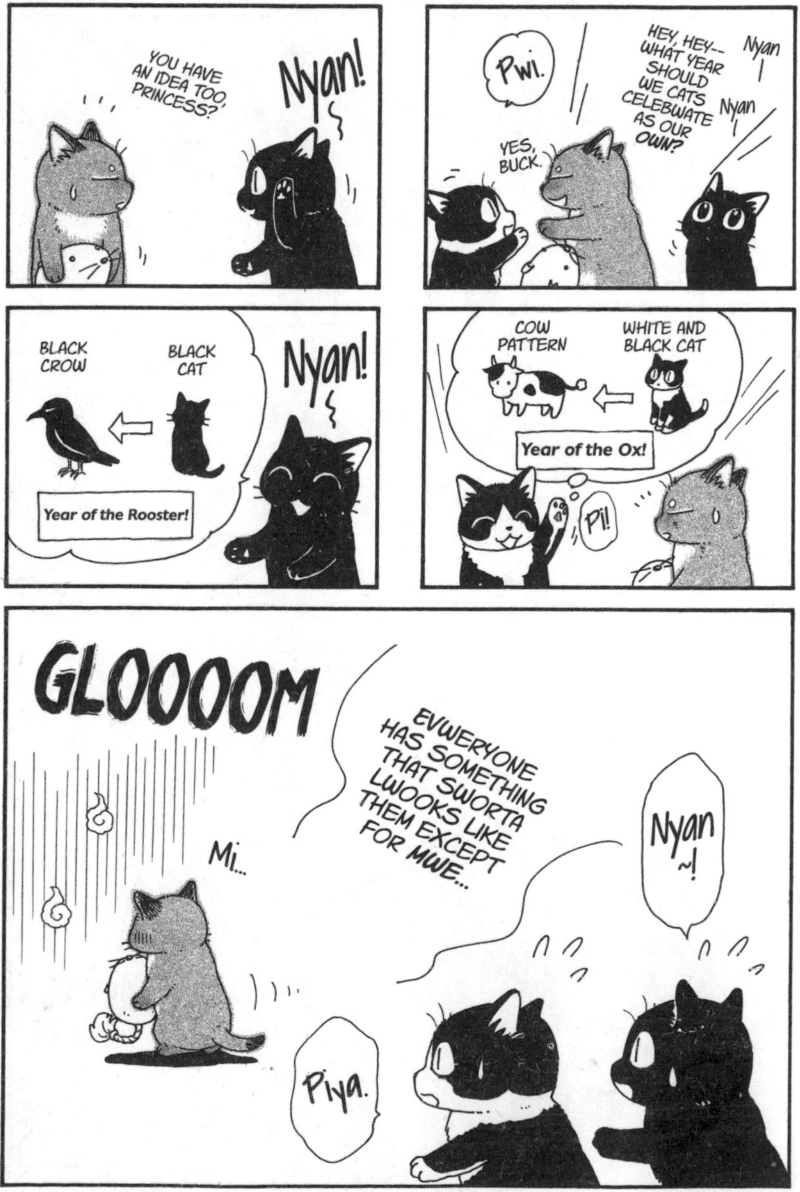
Nyan
Nyan
HEY, HEY-- WHAT YEAR SHOULD WE CATS CELEBWATE AS OUR OWN?
Pwi.
YES, BUCK.
Nyan!
YOU HAVE AN IDEA TOO, PRINCESS?
WHITE AND BLACK CAT
COW PATTERN
Year of the Ox!
Pi!
Nyan!
BLACK CAT
BLACK CROW
Year of the Rooster!
Nyan ~!
EVWERYONE HAS SOMETHING THAT SWORTA LWOOKS LIKE THEM EXCEPT FOR MWE...
GLOOOOM
Mi...
Piya.

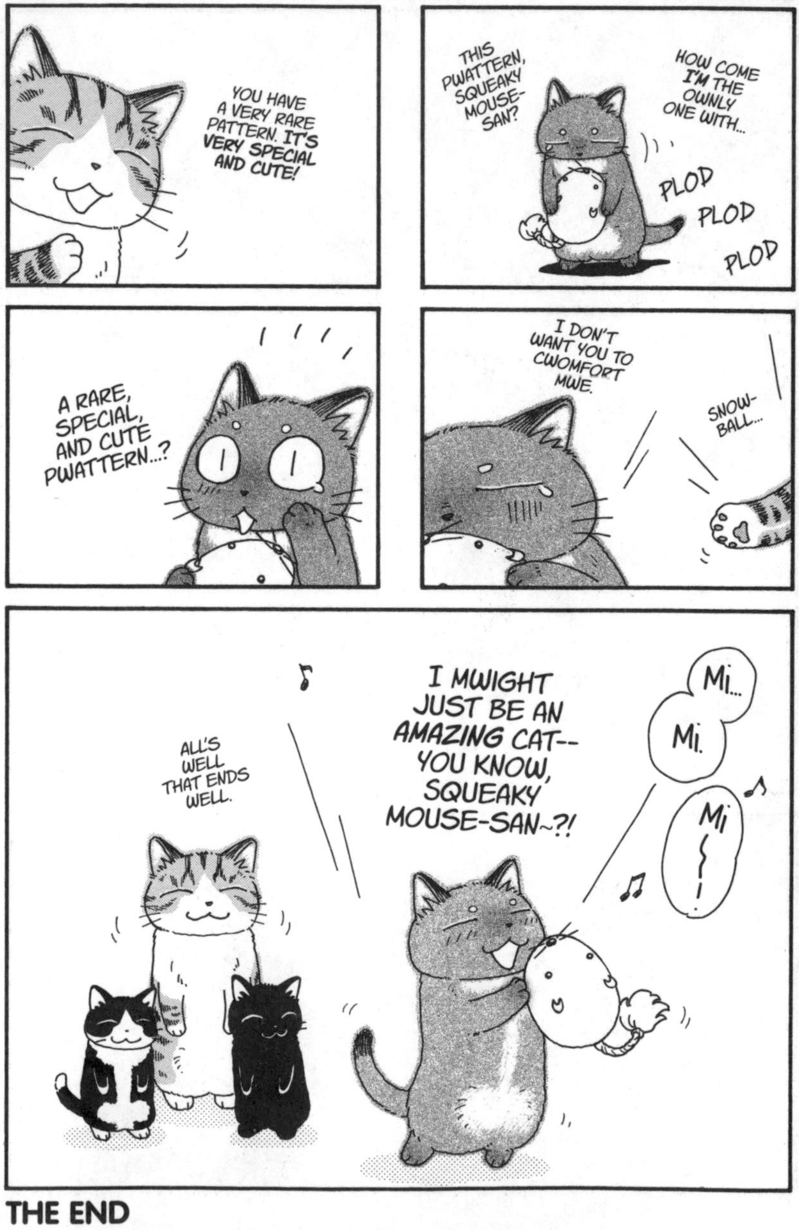
HOW COME I'M THE OWNLY ONE WITH...
THIS PWATTERN, SQUEAKY MOUSE-SAN?
PLOD
PLOD
PLOD
YOU HAVE A VERY RARE PATTERN. IT'S VERY SPECIAL AND CUTE!
SNOW-BALL...
I DON'T WANT YOU TO CWOMFORT MWE.
A RARE, SPECIAL, AND CUTE PWATTERN...?
Mi...
Mi.
Mi~!
I MWIGHT JUST BE AN AMAZING CAT-- YOU KNOW, SQUEAKY MOUSE-SAN~?!
ALL'S WELL THAT ENDS WELL.

THE END

SHORT.20

"The First Dream of the New Year"

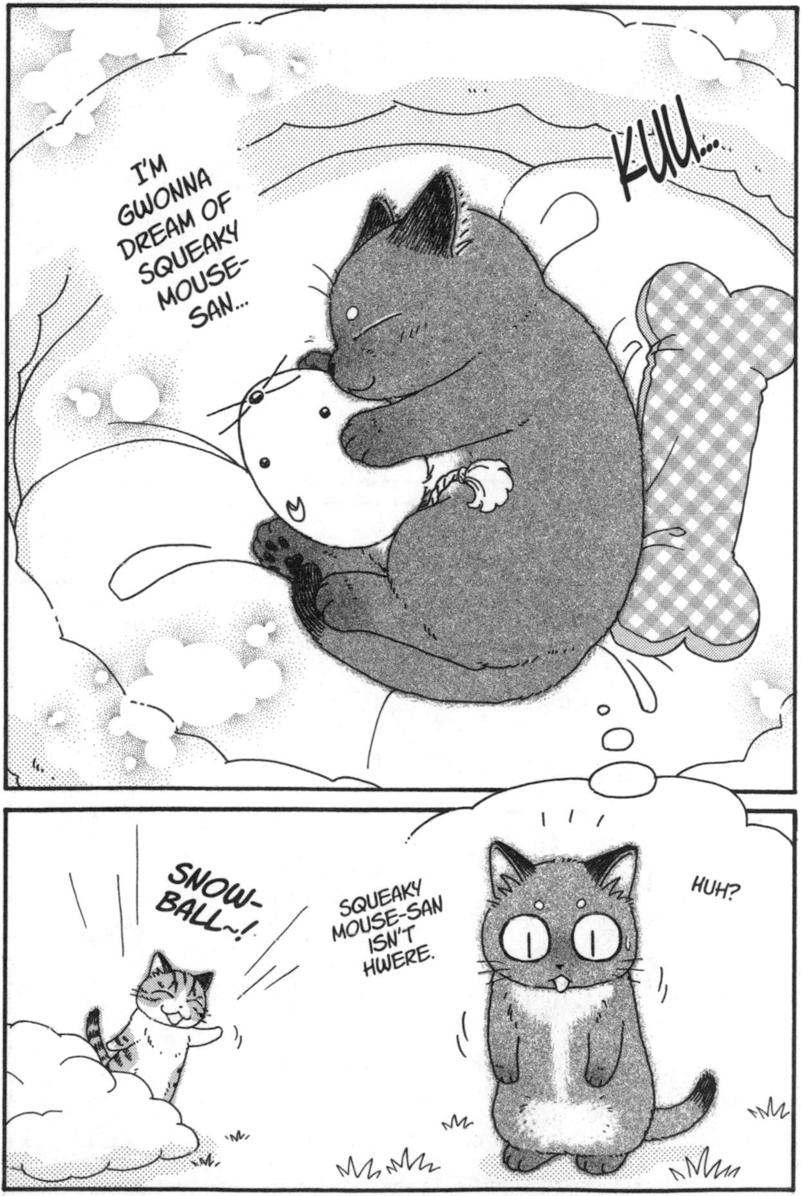

KUU...
I'M GWONNA DREAM OF SQUEAKY MOUSE-SAN...
HUH?
SQUEAKY MOUSE-SAN ISN'T HWERE.
SNOW-BALL~!

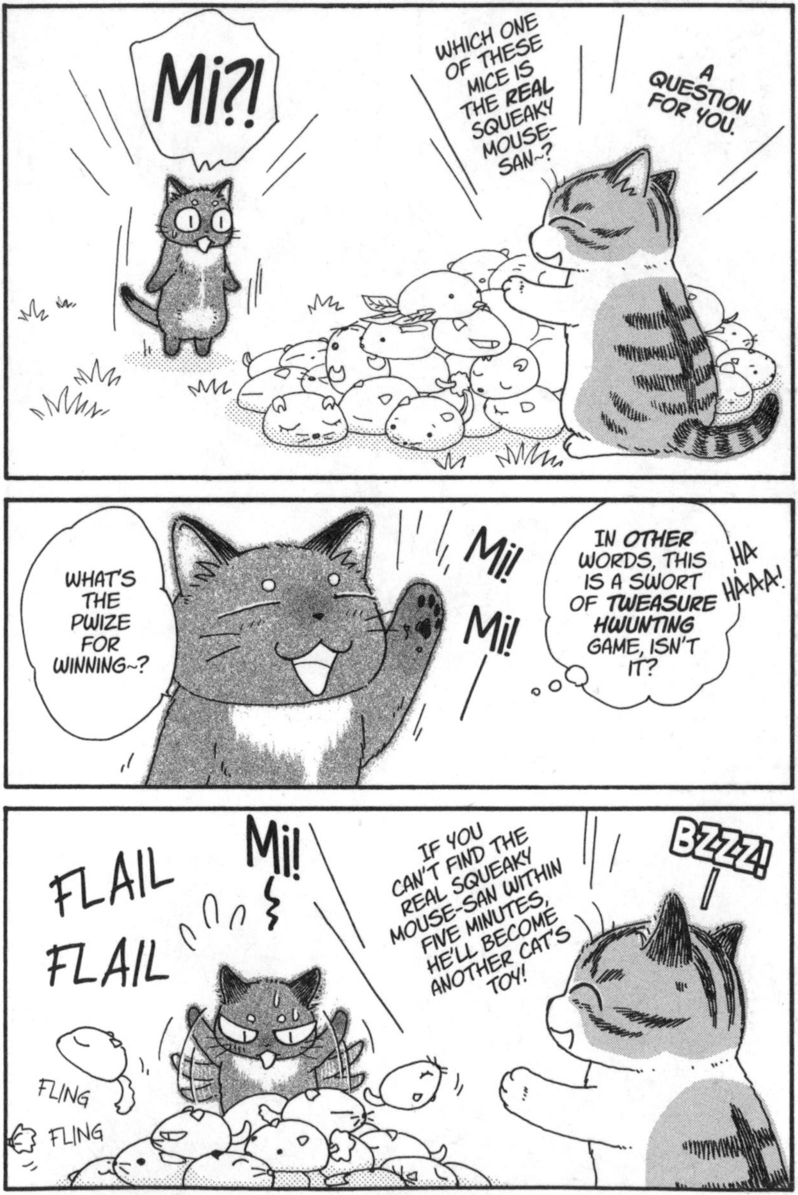
A QUESTION FOR YOU.
WHICH ONE OF THESE MICE IS THE REAL SQUEAKY MOUSE-SAN~?
Mi?!
HA HAAA!
IN OTHER WORDS, THIS IS A SWORT OF TWEASURE HWUNTING GAME, ISN'T IT?
Mi!
Mi!
WHAT'S THE PWIZE FOR WINNING~?
BZZZ!
IF YOU CAN'T FIND THE REAL SQUEAKY MOUSE-SAN WITHIN FIVE MINUTES, HE'LL BECOME ANOTHER CAT'S TOY!
Mi!
FLAIL
FLAIL
FLING
FLING

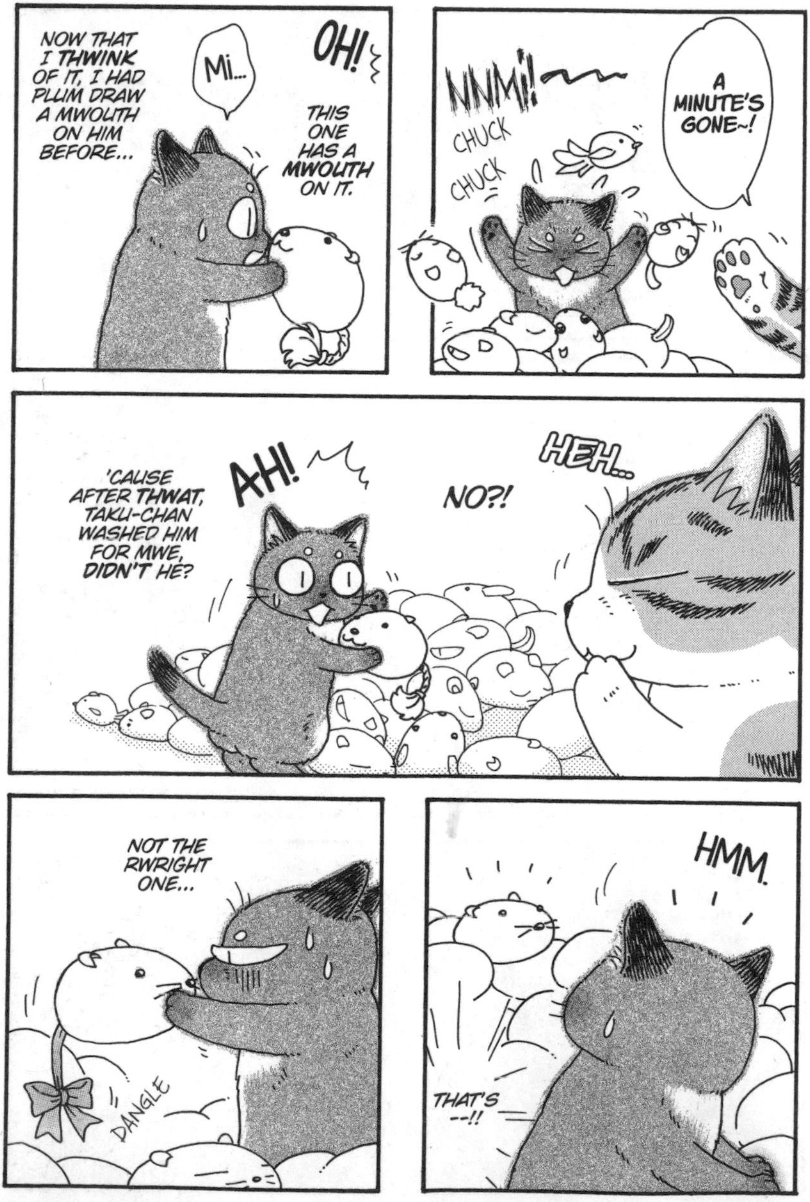
A MINUTE'S GONE~!
NNMI!
CHUCK
CHUCK
OH!
Mi...
NOW THAT I THWINK OF IT, I HAD PLUM DRAW A MWOUTH ON HIM BEFORE...
THIS ONE HAS A MWOUTH ON IT.
HEH...
NO?!
AH!
'CAUSE AFTER THWAT, TAKU-CHAN WASHED HIM FOR MWE, DIDN'T HE?
HMM.
THAT'S --!!
NOT THE RWRIGHT ONE...
DANGLE

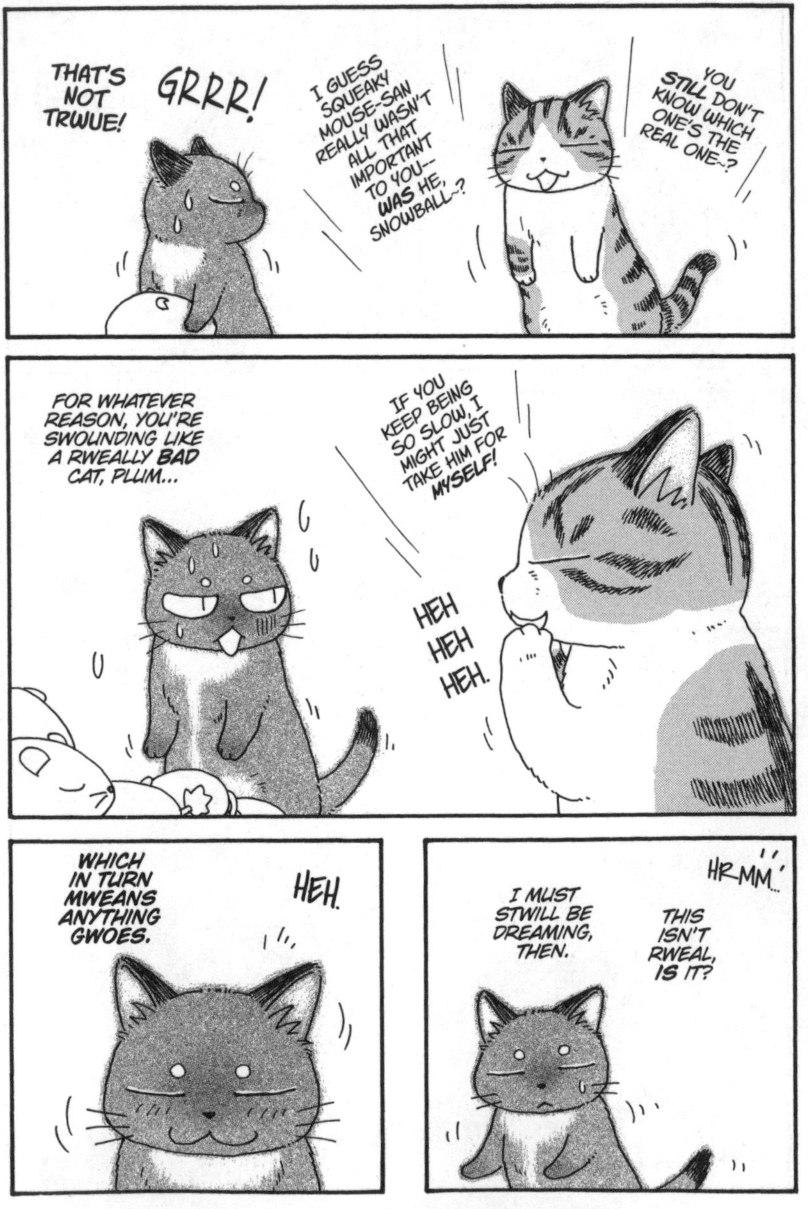
YOU STILL DON'T KNOW WHICH ONE'S THE REAL ONE~?
I GUESS SQUEAKY MOUSE-SAN REALLY WASN'T ALL THAT IMPORTANT TO YOU— WAS HE, SNOWBALL~?
GRRR!
THAT'S NOT TRWUE!
IF YOU KEEP BEING SO SLOW, I MIGHT JUST TAKE HIM FOR MYSELF!
HEH HEH HEH.
FOR WHATEVER REASON, YOU'RE SWOUNDING LIKE A RWEALLY BAD CAT, PLUM...
HRMM...
THIS ISN'T RWEAL, IS IT?
I MUST STWILL BE DREAMING, THEN.
HEH.
WHICH IN TURN MWEANS ANYTHING GWOES.

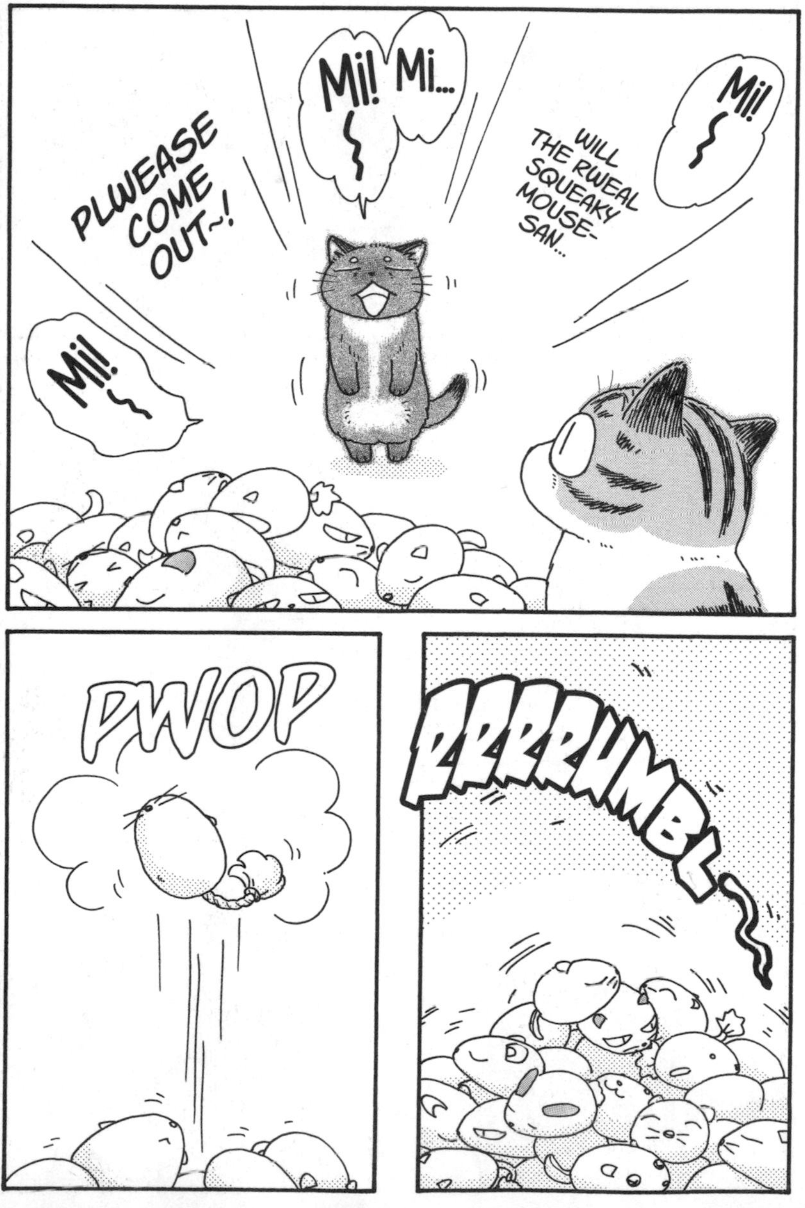
Mi!
WILL THE RWEAL SQUEAKY MOUSE-SAN...
Mi...
Mi!
PLWEASE COME OUT~!
Mi!
BRRRUMBL~
PWOP

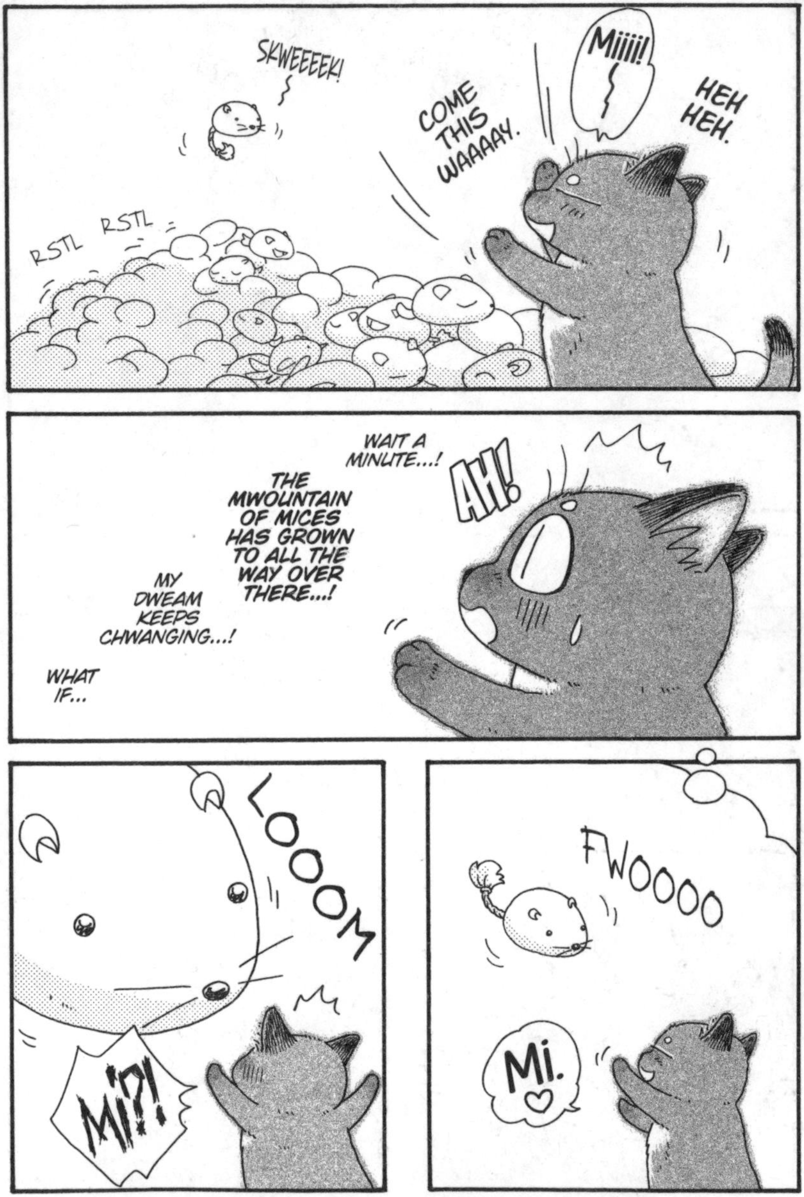
HEH HEH.
Miiii!
COME THIS WAAAAY.
SKWEEEEK!
RSTL RSTL
AH!
WAIT A MINUTE...!
THE MWOUNTAIN OF MICES HAS GROWN TO ALL THE WAY OVER THERE...!
MY DWEAM KEEPS CHWANGING...!
WHAT IF...
FWOOOO
Mi. ♡
LOOOOM
MI?!

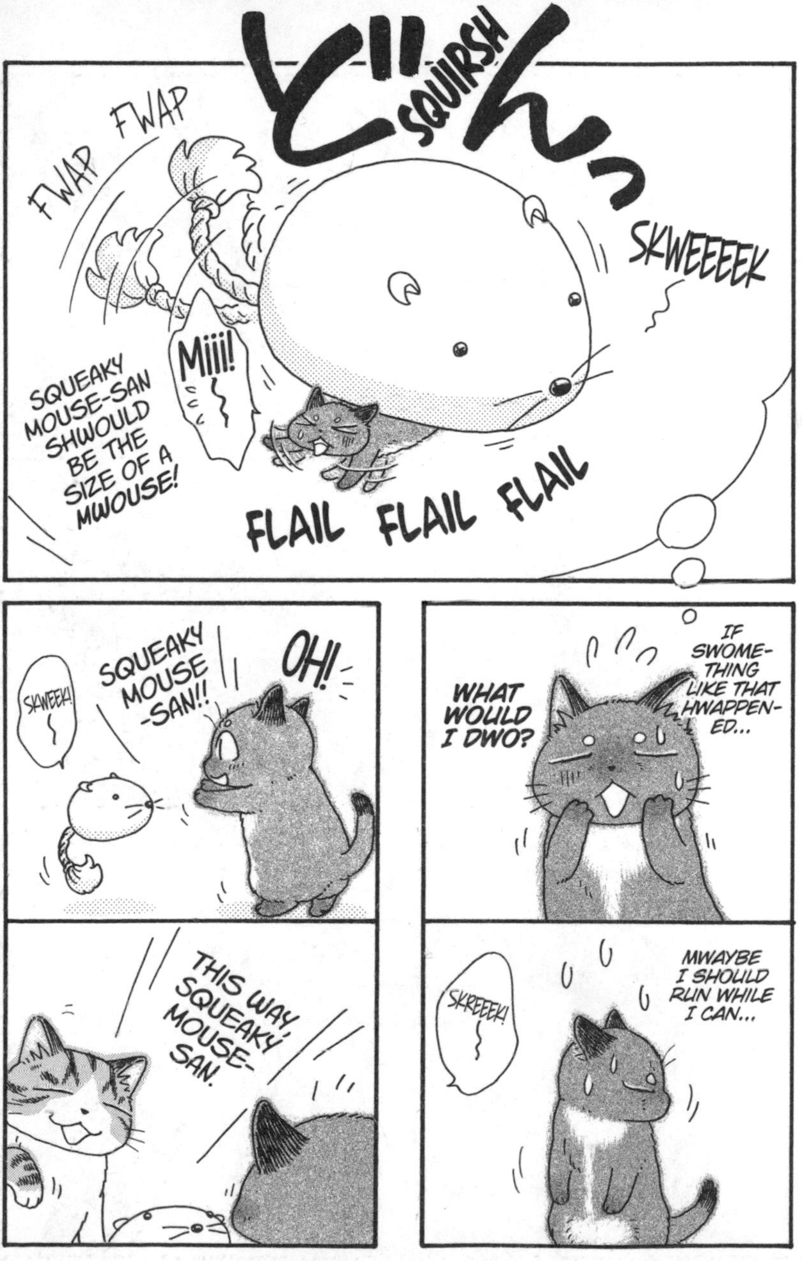
SQUIRSH
SKWEEEEEK
FWAP FWAP FWAP
Miiii!
SQUEAKY MOUSE-SAN SHWOULD BE THE SIZE OF A MWOUSE!
FLAIL FLAIL FLAIL
IF SWOME-THING LIKE THAT HWAPPEN-ED...
WHAT WOULD I DWO?
OH!
SQUEAKY MOUSE -SAN!!
SKWEEK!
MWAYBE I SHOULD RUN WHILE I CAN...
SKREEEK!
THIS WAY, SQUEAKY MOUSE-SAN.

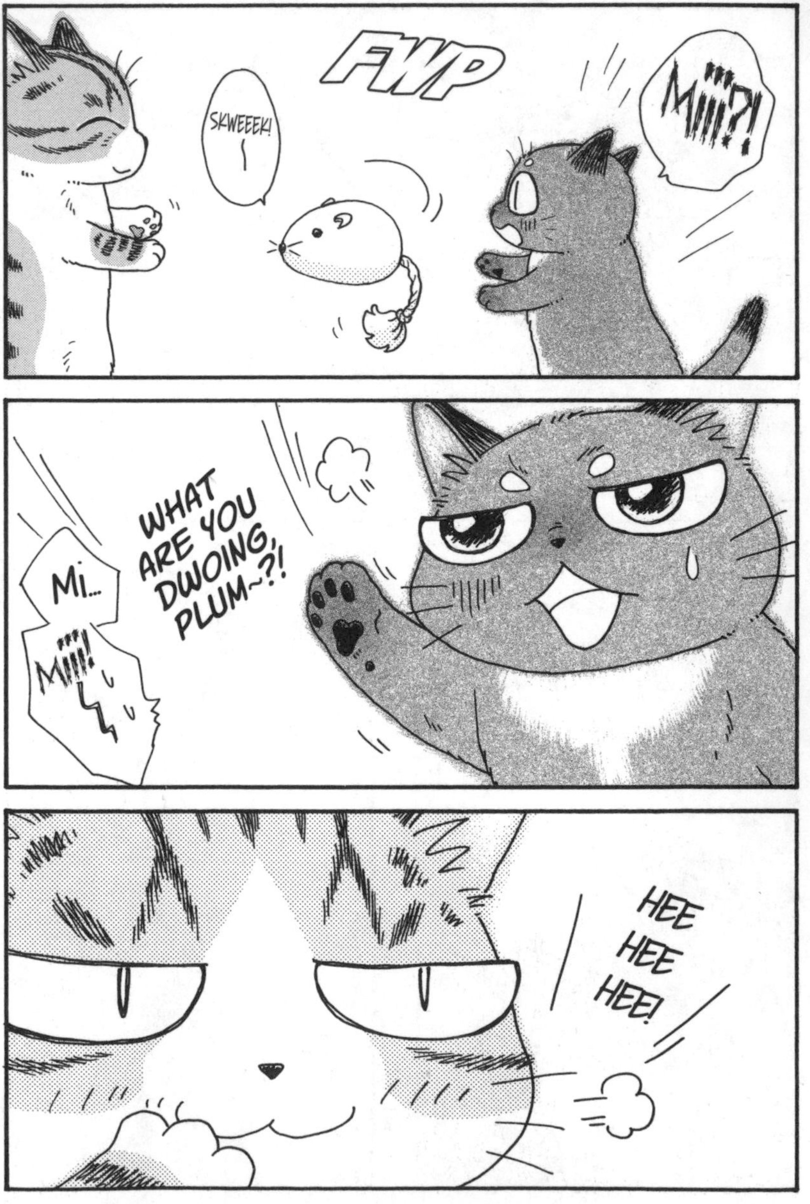
Miii?!
FWP
SKWEEEK!
WHAT ARE YOU DWOING, PLUM~?!
Mi...
Miii!
HEE HEE HEE!

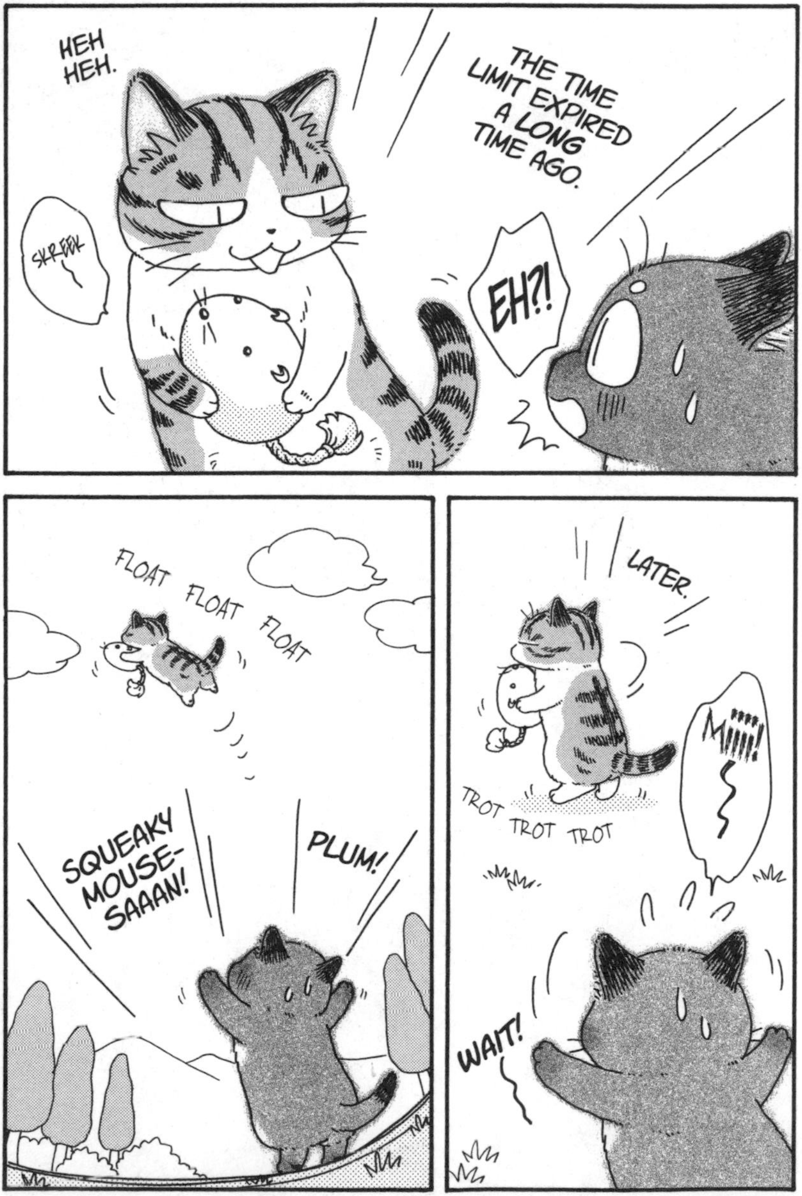
THE TIME LIMIT EXPIRED A LONG TIME AGO.
HEH HEH.
EH?!
SKREEK
LATER.
Miiii!
TROT TROT TROT
WAIT!
FLOAT FLOAT FLOAT
PLUM!
SQUEAKY MOUSE-SAAAN!

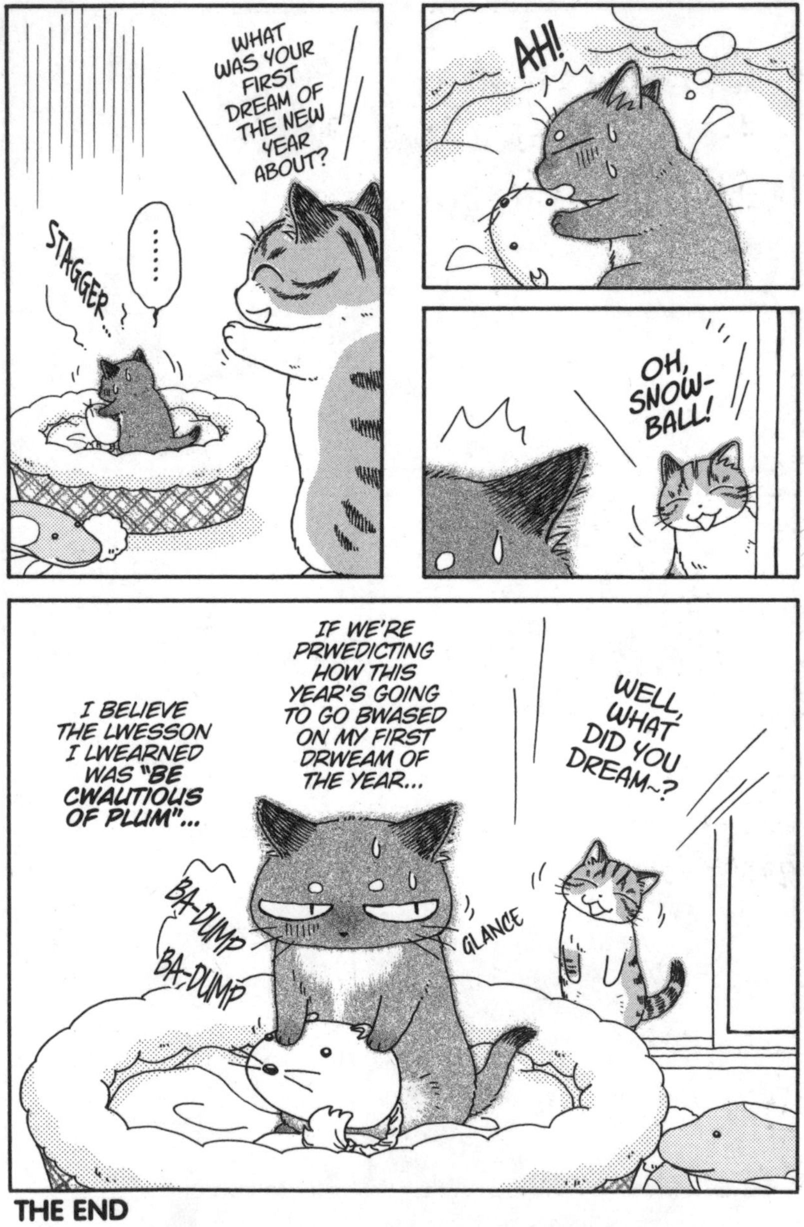
AH!
OH, SNOW-BALL!
WHAT WAS YOUR FIRST DREAM OF THE NEW YEAR ABOUT?
......
STAGGER
WELL, WHAT DID YOU DREAM~?
IF WE'RE PRWEDICTING HOW THIS YEAR'S GOING TO GO BWASED ON MY FIRST DRWEAM OF THE YEAR...
I BELIEVE THE LWESSON I LWEARNED WAS "BE CWAUTIOUS OF PLUM"...
GLANCE
BA-DUMP
BA-DUMP

THE END

CHAPTER 25
An Untearable Paper Sliding Door

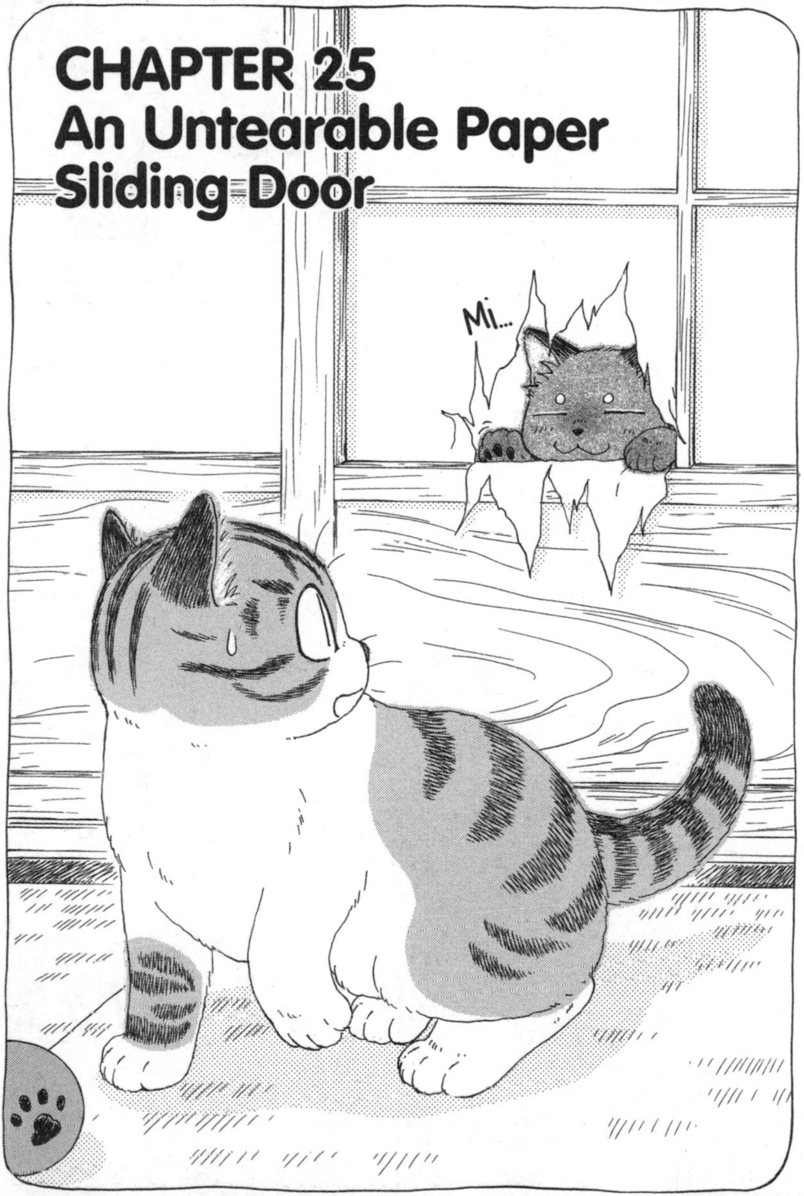
Mi...

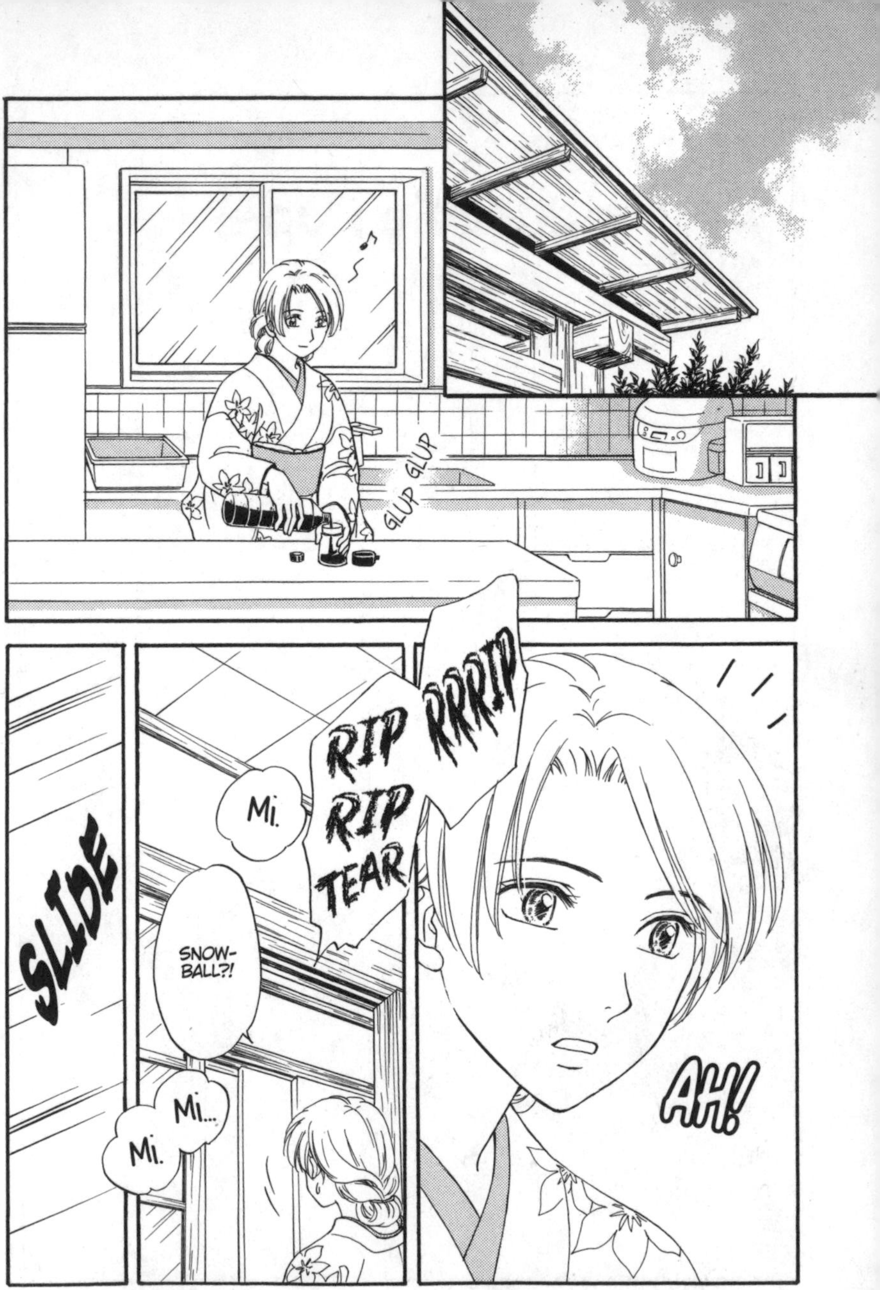
GLUP GLUP
RRRIP
RIP
RIP
TEAR
Mi.
SNOW-BALL?!
SLIDE
Mi...
Mi.
AH!

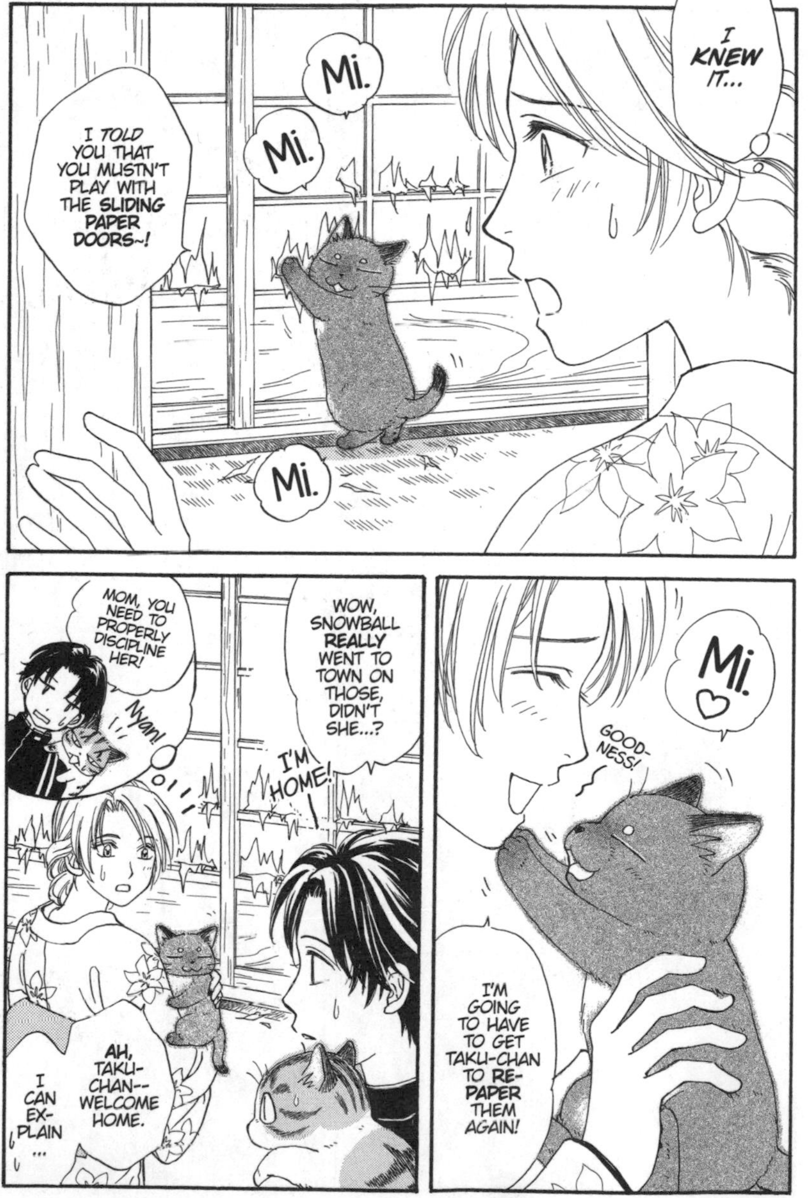
I KNEW IT...
Mi.
Mi.
I TOLD YOU THAT YOU MUSTN'T PLAY WITH THE SLIDING PAPER DOORS~!
Mi.
Mi. ♡
GOODNESS!
I'M GOING TO HAVE TO GET TAKU-CHAN TO RE-PAPER THEM AGAIN!
WOW, SNOWBALL REALLY WENT TO TOWN ON THOSE, DIDN'T SHE...?
MOM, YOU NEED TO PROPERLY DISCIPLINE HER!
Nyan!
I'M HOME!
AH, TAKU-CHAN-- WELCOME HOME.
I CAN EXPLAIN...

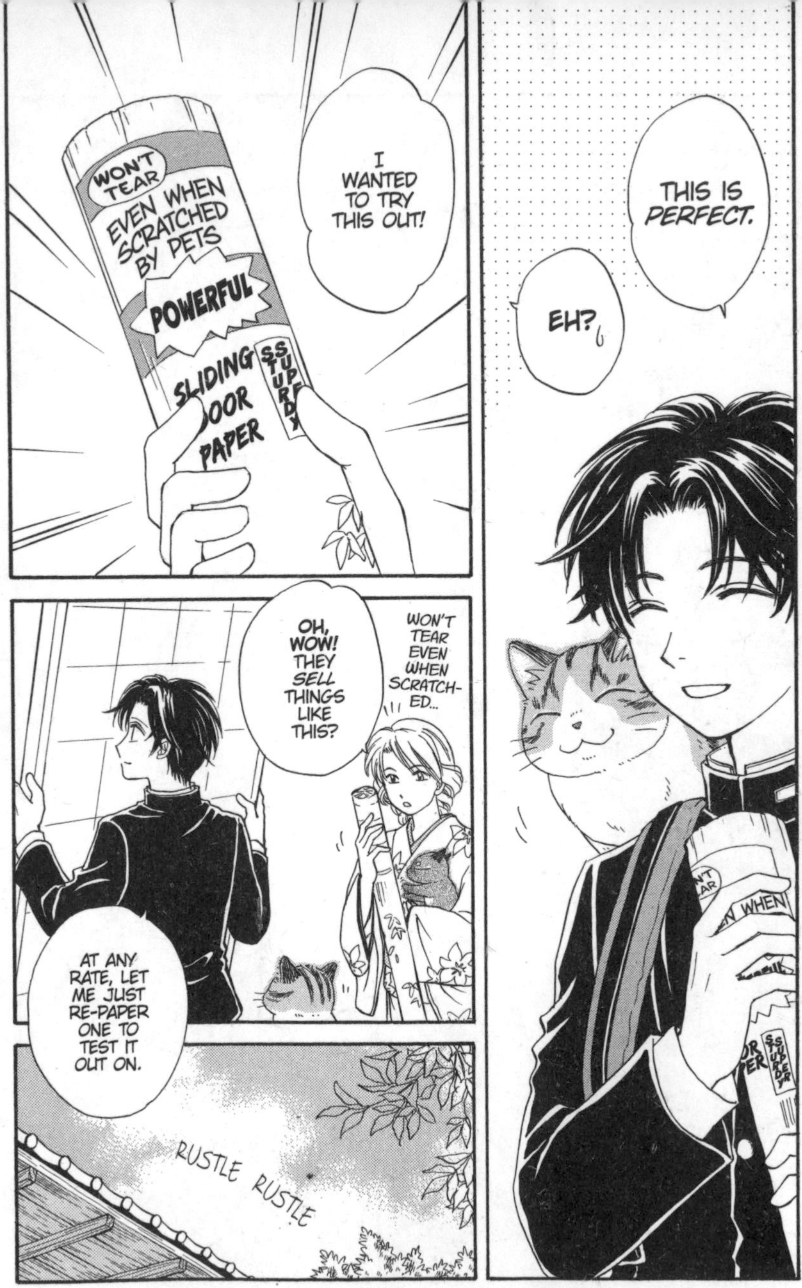
THIS IS PERFECT.
EH?
WON'T TEAR
EVEN WHEN SCRATCHED BY PETS
POWERFUL
SLIDING DOOR PAPER
SUPER STURDY
I WANTED TO TRY THIS OUT!
WON'T TEAR EVEN WHEN SCRATCHED...
OH, WOW! THEY SELL THINGS LIKE THIS?
AT ANY RATE, LET ME JUST RE-PAPER ONE TO TEST IT OUT ON.
RUSTLE RUSTLE

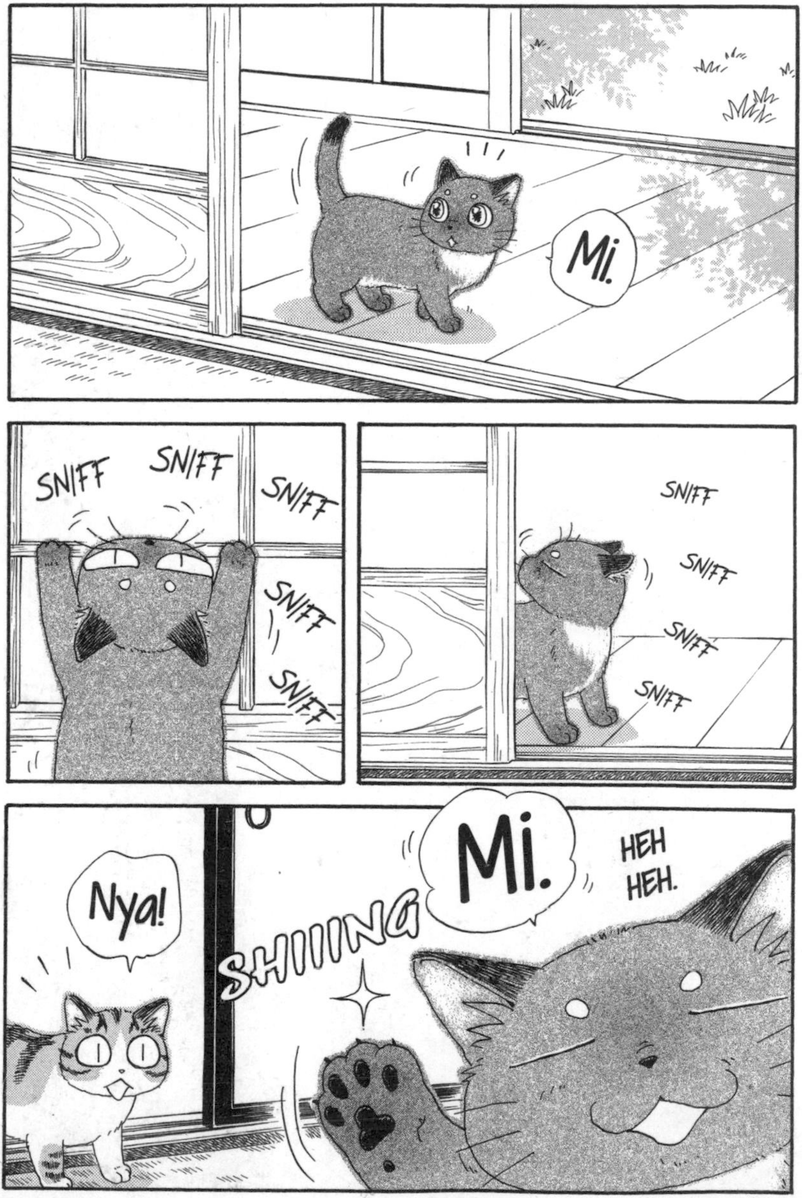
Mi.
SNIFF
SNIFF
SNIFF
SNIFF
SNIFF
SNIFF
SNIFF
SNIFF
SNIFF
HEH
HEH.
Mi.
SHIIING
Nya!

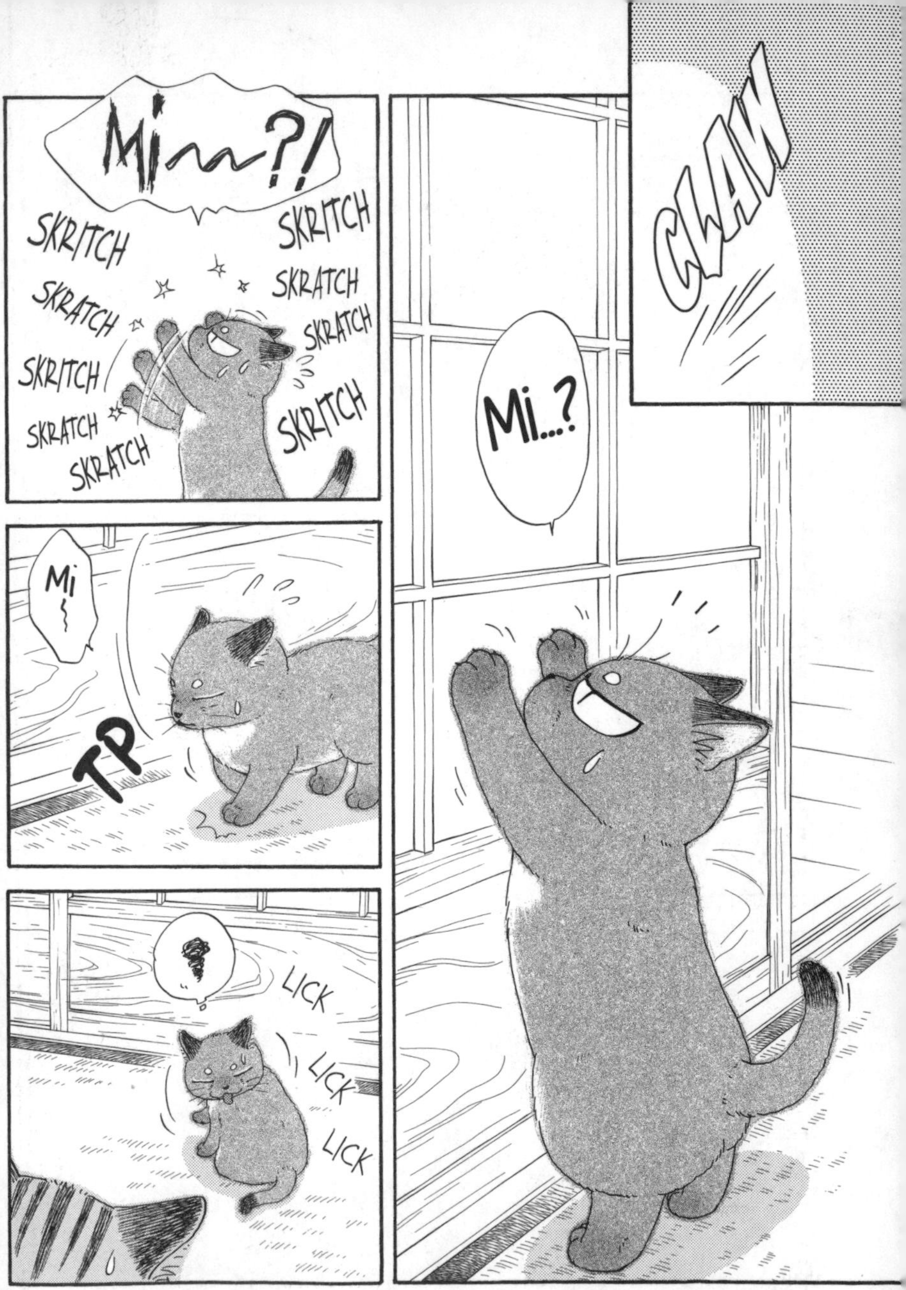
CLAW
Mi...?
Mi~?!
SKRITCH
SKRITCH
SKRATCH
SKRATCH
SKRATCH
SKRITCH
SKRITCH
SKRATCH
SKRATCH
Mi~
TP
LICK
LICK
LICK

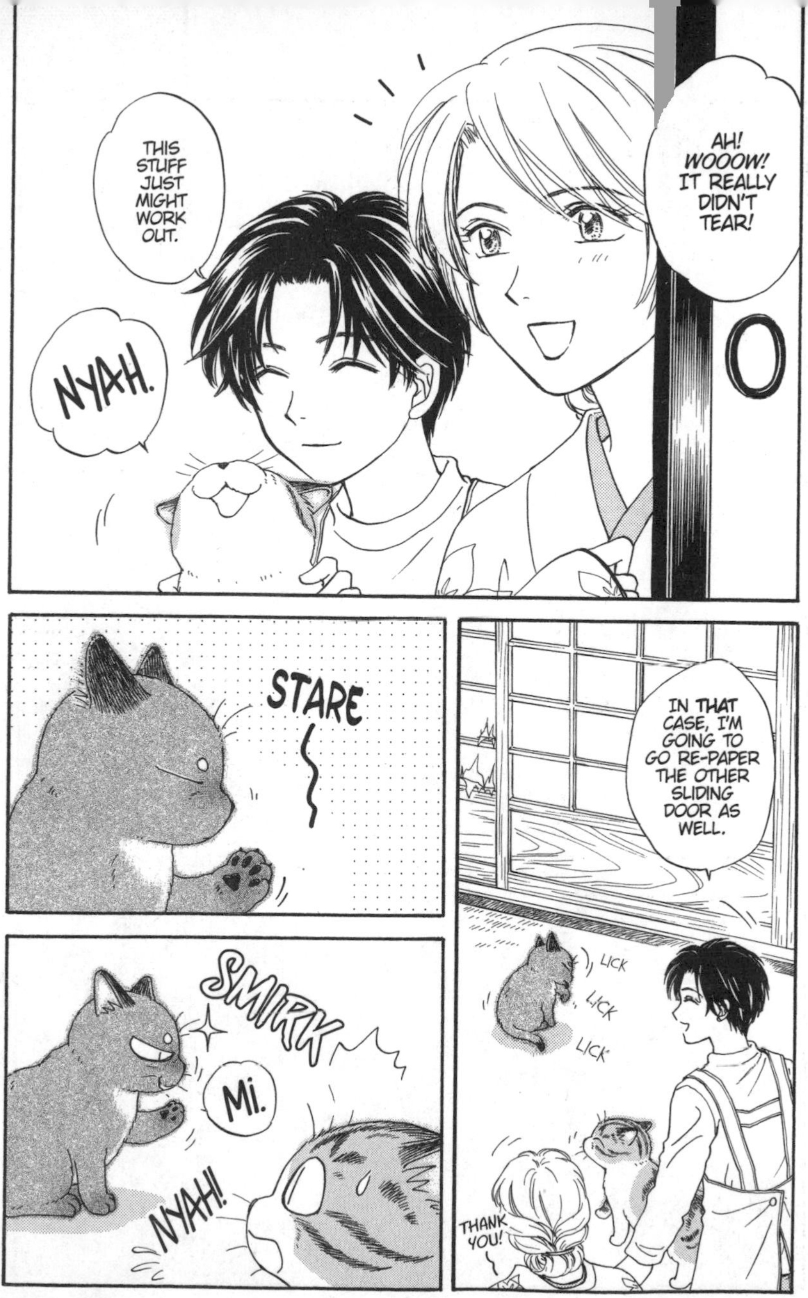
AH! WOOOW! IT REALLY DIDN'T TEAR!
THIS STUFF JUST MIGHT WORK OUT.
NYAH.
IN THAT CASE, I'M GOING TO GO RE-PAPER THE OTHER SLIDING DOOR AS WELL.
LICK
LICK
LICK
THANK YOU!
STARE
SMIRK
Mi.
NYAH!

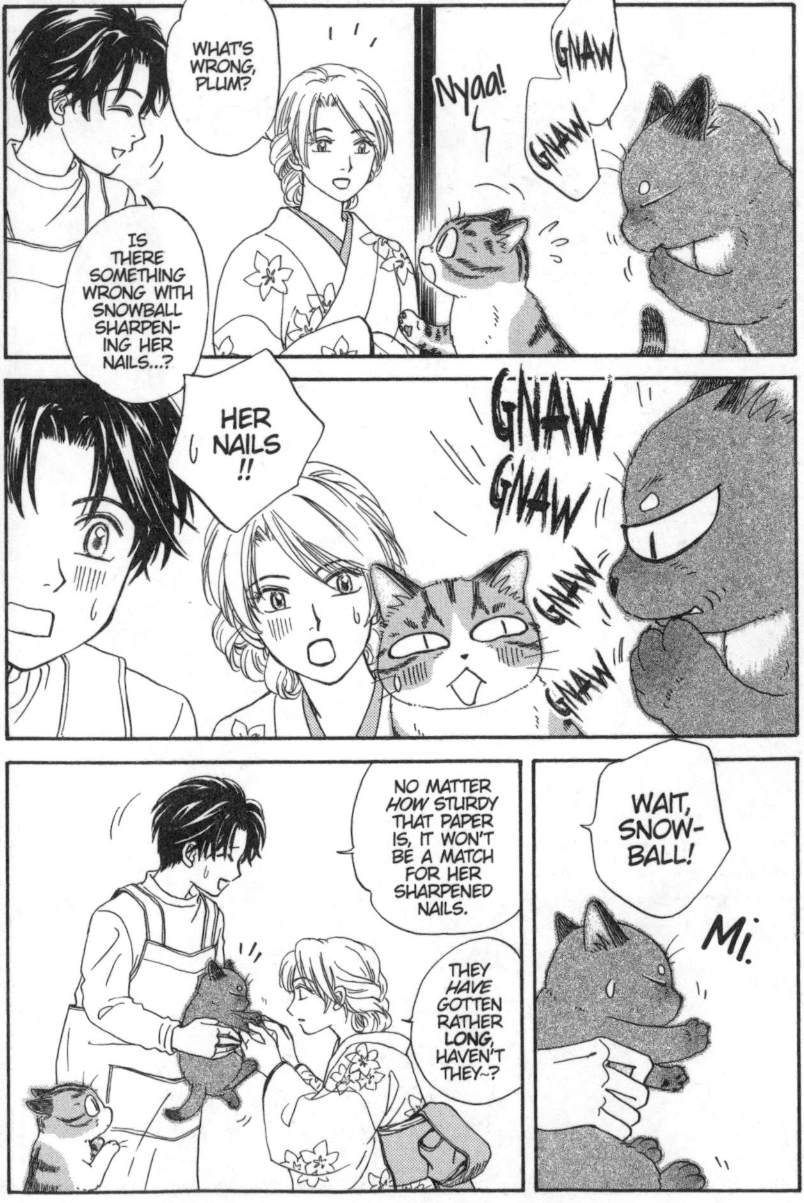
GNAW
GNAW
Nyaa!
WHAT'S WRONG, PLUM?
IS THERE SOMETHING WRONG WITH SNOWBALL SHARPEN-ING HER NAILS...?
GNAW
GNAW
GNAW
GNAW
HER NAILS !!
WAIT, SNOW-BALL!
Mi.
NO MATTER *HOW* STURDY THAT PAPER IS, IT WON'T BE A MATCH FOR HER SHARPENED NAILS.
THEY *HAVE* GOTTEN RATHER **LONG**, HAVEN'T THEY~?

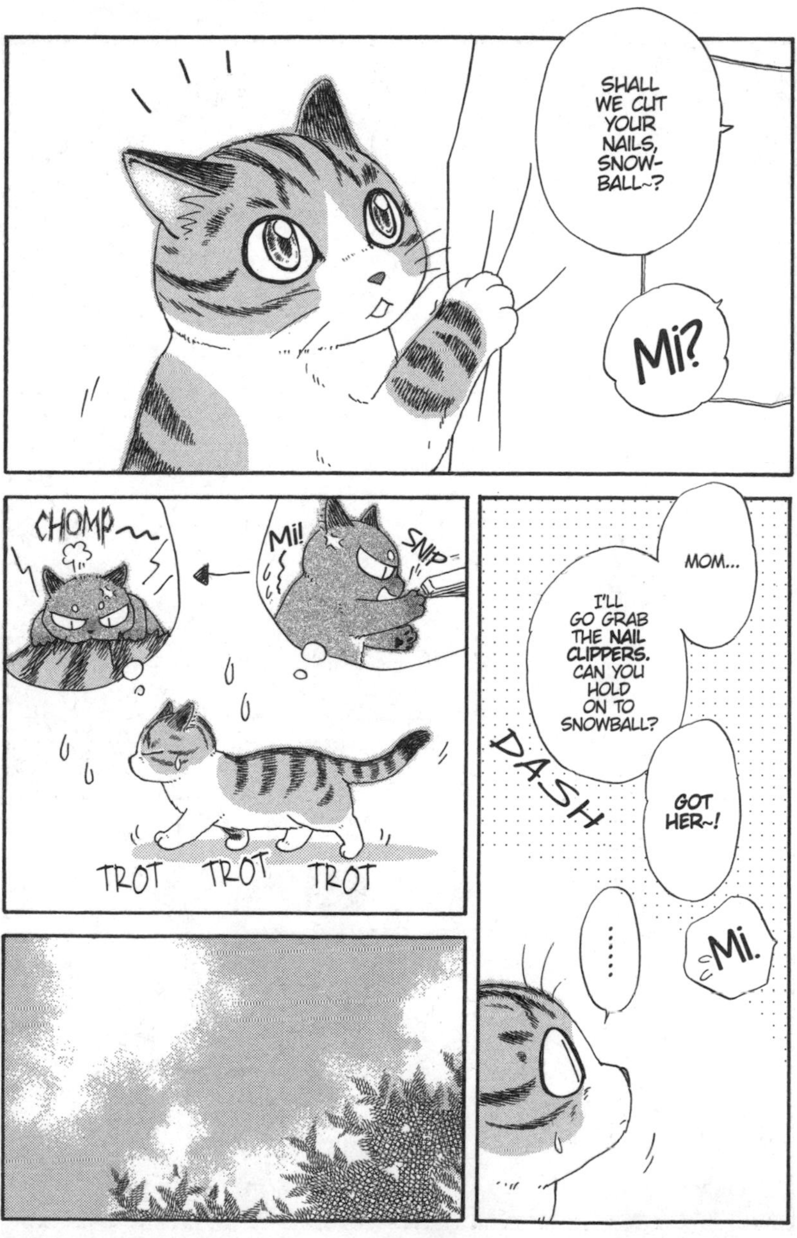
SHALL WE CUT YOUR NAILS, SNOW-BALL~?
Mi?
MOM...
I'LL GO GRAB THE **NAIL CLIPPERS.** CAN YOU HOLD ON TO SNOWBALL?
DASH
GOT HER~!
......
Mi.
Mi!
SNIP
CHOMP~
TROT TROT TROT

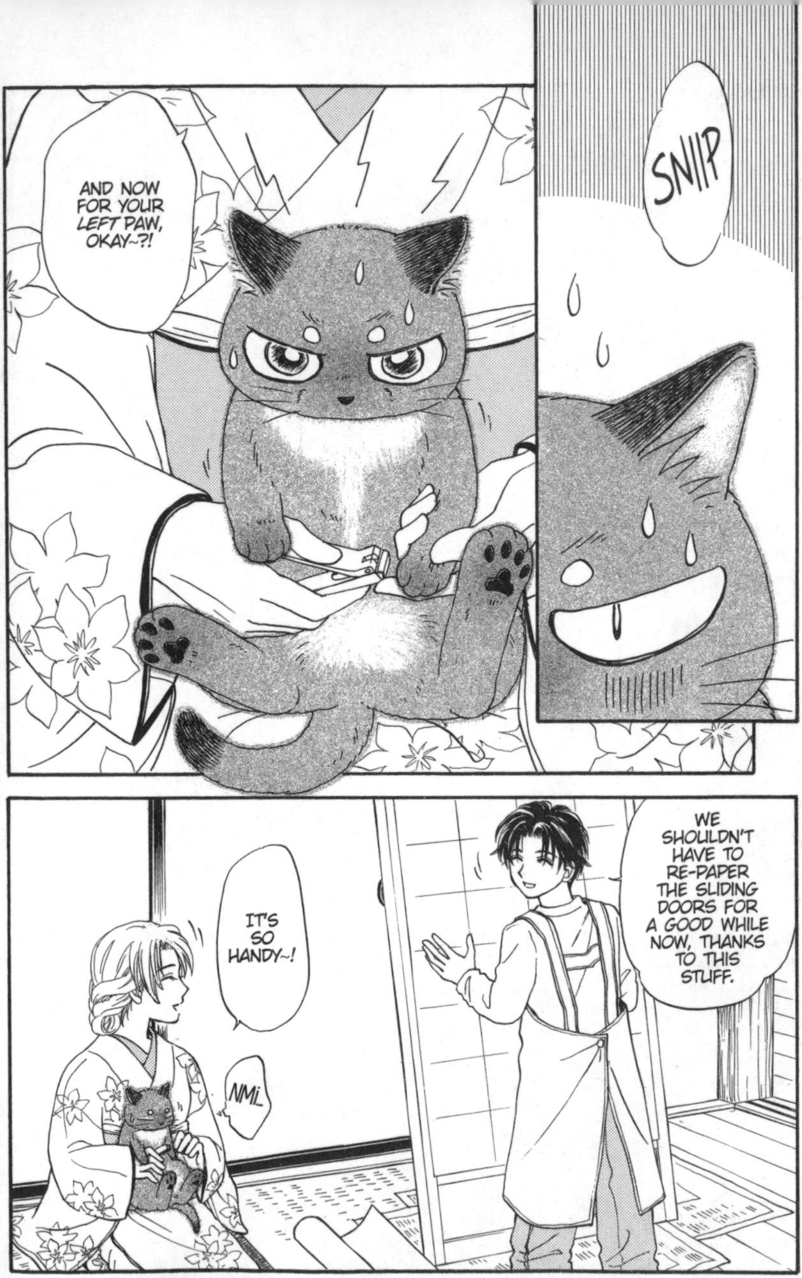
SNIIP
AND NOW FOR YOUR LEFT PAW, OKAY~?!
WE SHOULDN'T HAVE TO RE-PAPER THE SLIDING DOORS FOR A GOOD WHILE NOW, THANKS TO THIS STUFF.
IT'S SO HANDY~!
NMi..

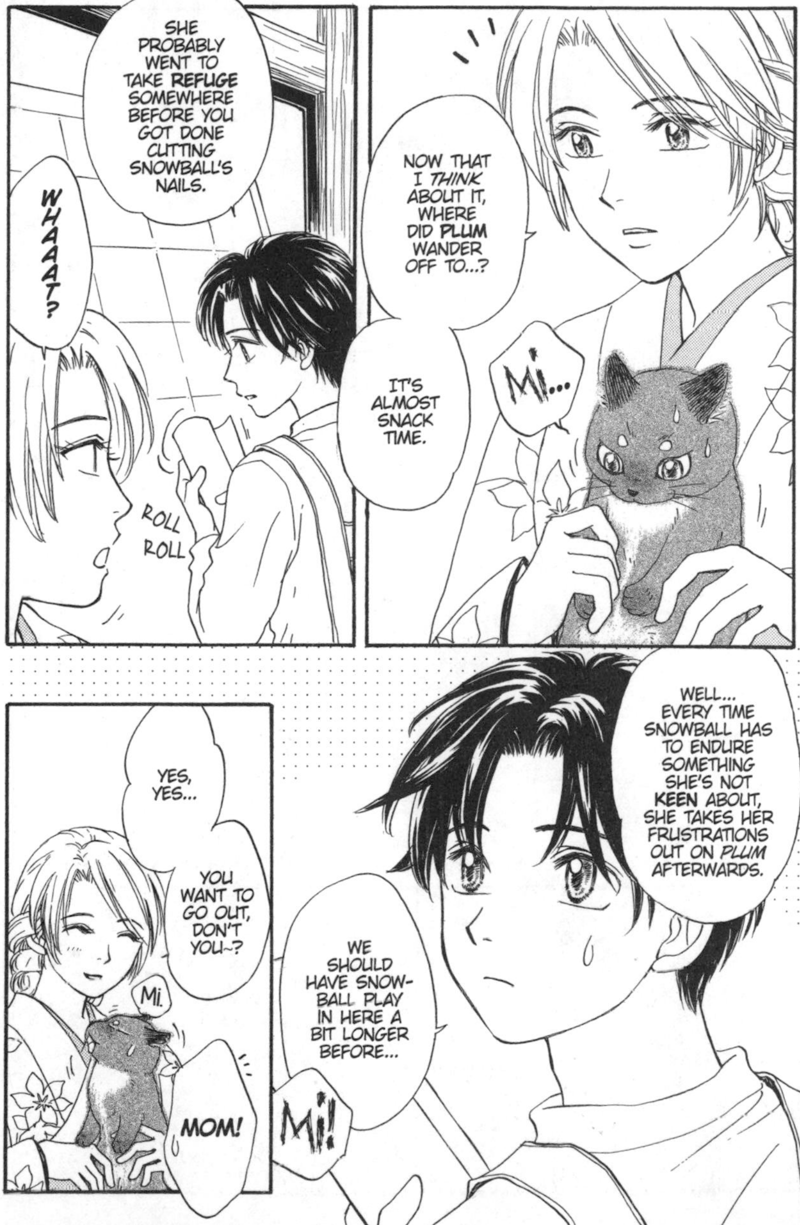
NOW THAT I THINK ABOUT IT, WHERE DID PLUM WANDER OFF TO...?
IT'S ALMOST SNACK TIME.
Mi...
SHE PROBABLY WENT TO TAKE REFUGE SOMEWHERE BEFORE YOU GOT DONE CUTTING SNOWBALL'S NAILS.
WHAAAT?
ROLL ROLL
WELL... EVERY TIME SNOWBALL HAS TO ENDURE SOMETHING SHE'S NOT KEEN ABOUT, SHE TAKES HER FRUSTRATIONS OUT ON PLUM AFTERWARDS.
WE SHOULD HAVE SNOW-BALL PLAY IN HERE A BIT LONGER BEFORE...
Mi!
YES, YES...
YOU WANT TO GO OUT, DON'T YOU~?
Mi.
MOM!

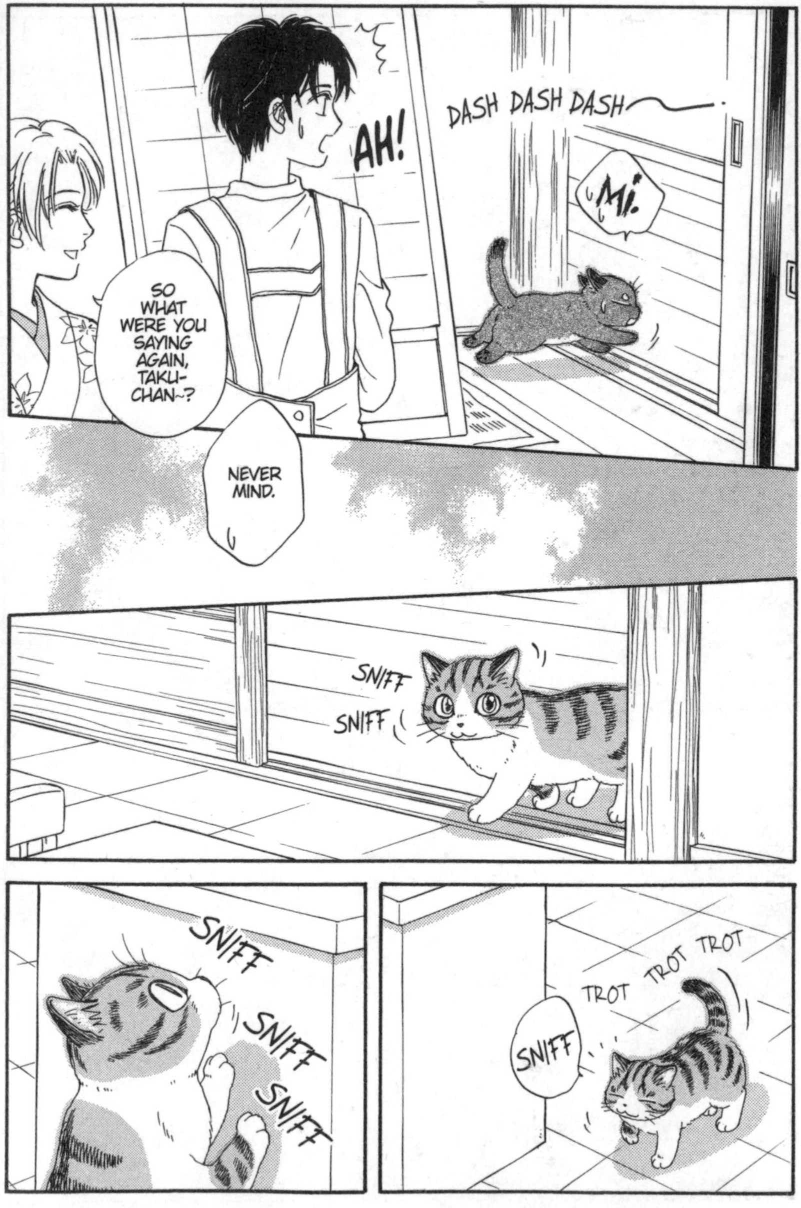
DASH DASH DASH
Mi.
AH!
SO WHAT WERE YOU SAYING AGAIN, TAKU-CHAN~?
NEVER MIND.
SNIFF
SNIFF
TROT TROT TROT
SNIFF
SNIFF
SNIFF
SNIFF

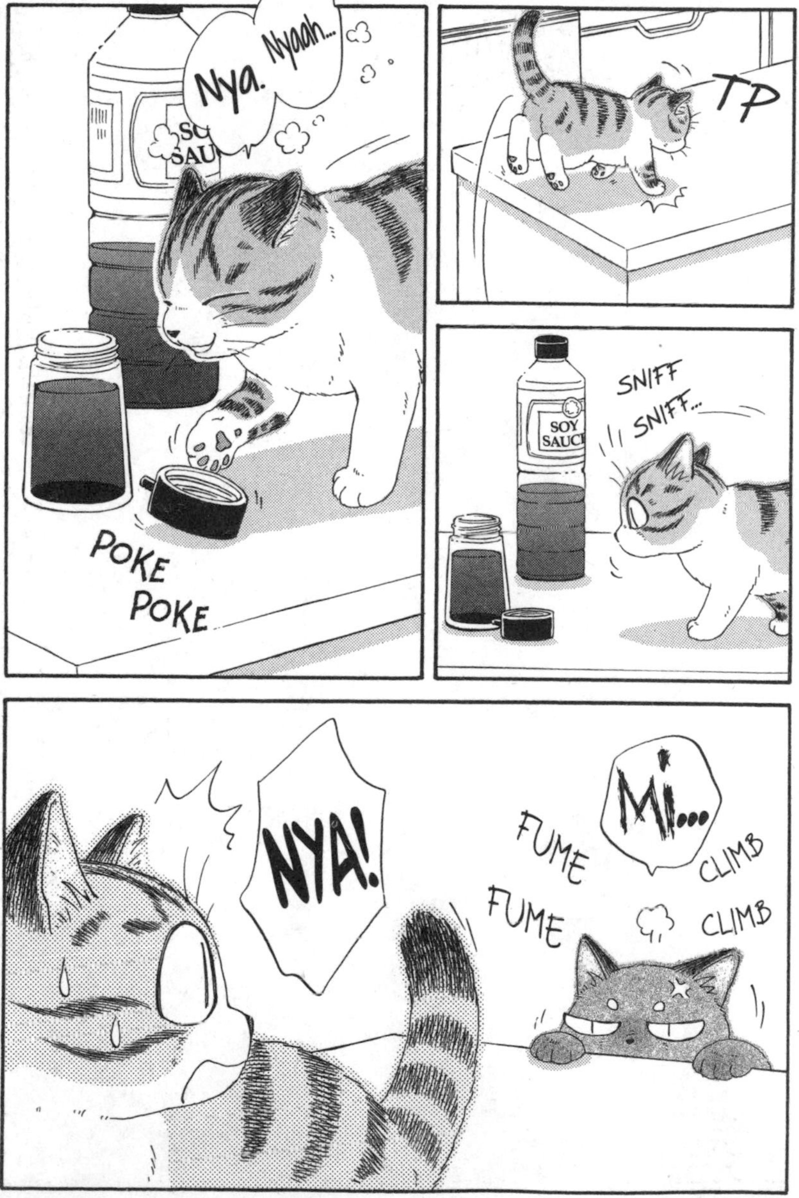
TP
SNIFF SNIFF...
Nya.
Nyaah...
POKE POKE
Mi...
CLIMB CLIMB
FUME FUME
NYA!

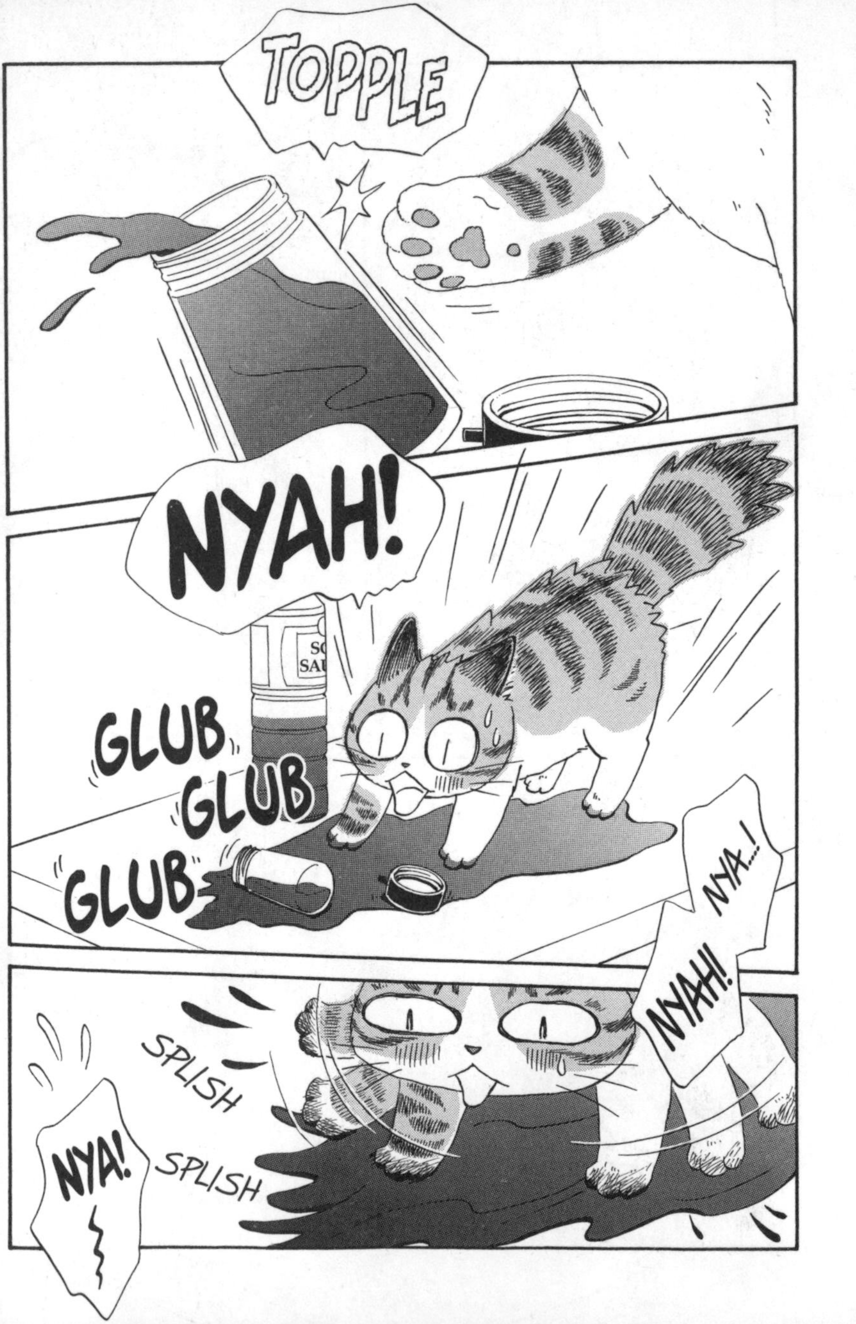
TOPPLE
NYAH!
NYA...!
GLUB
GLUB
GLUB
NYAH!
SPLISH
SPLISH
NYA!

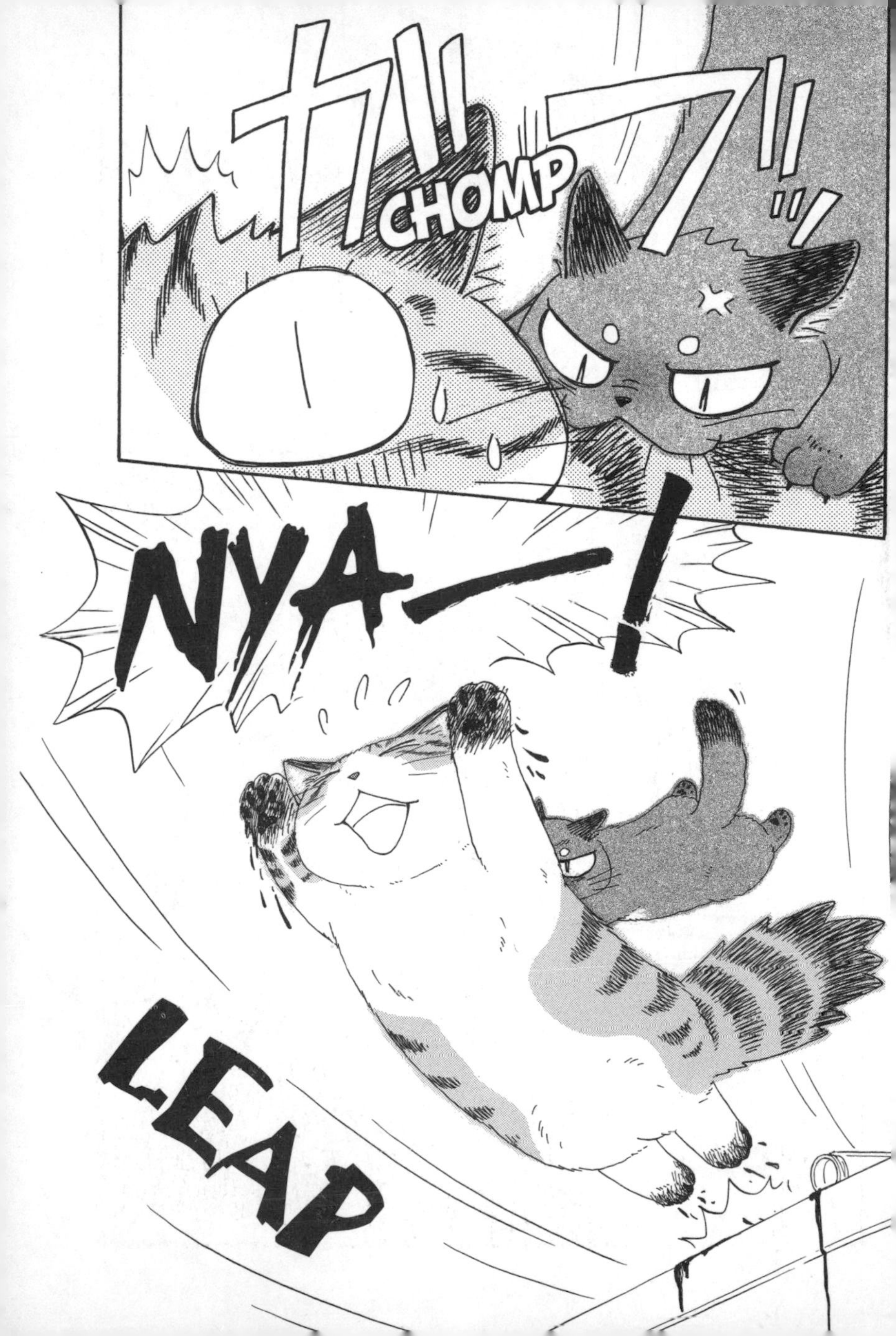
CHOMP
NYA—!
LEAP

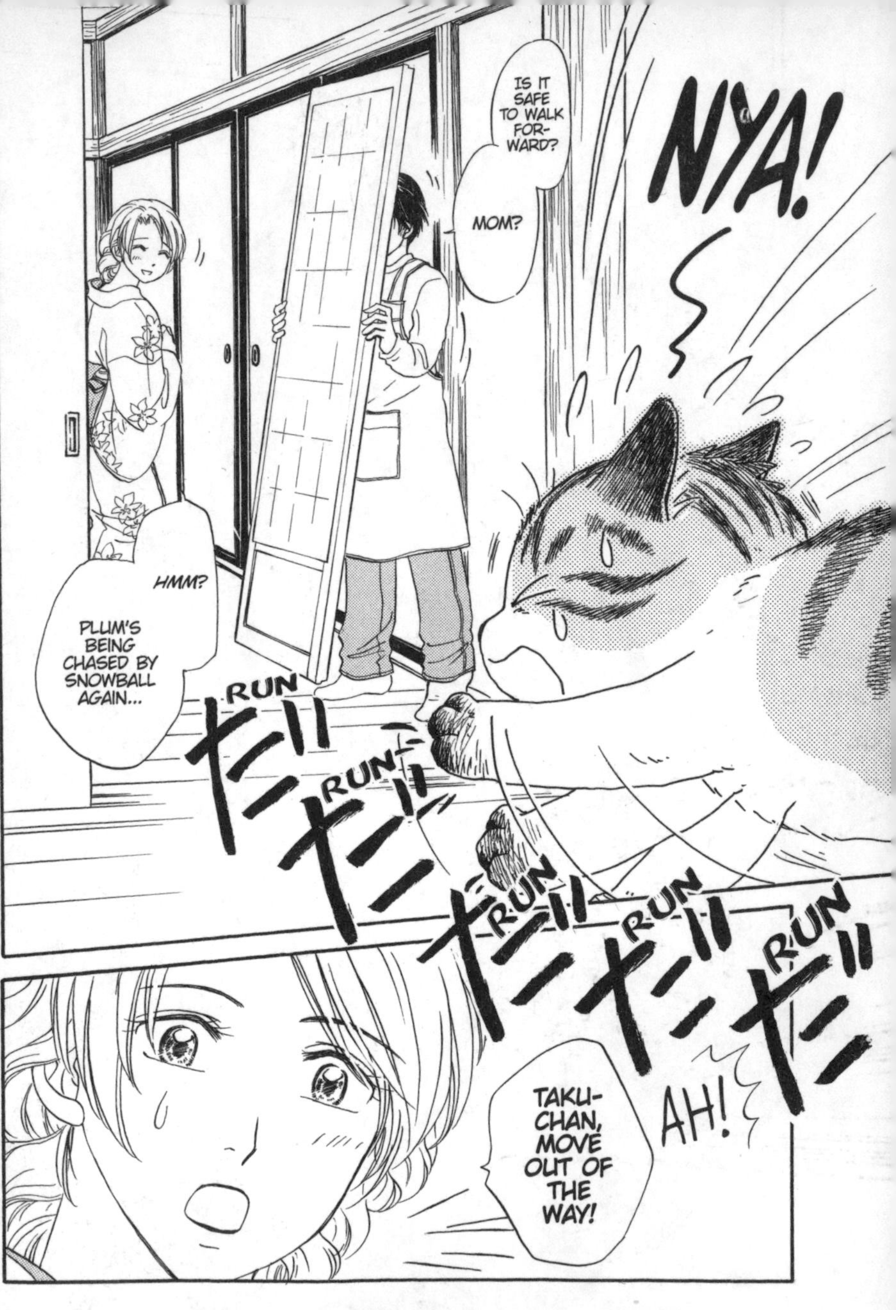
NYA!
IS IT SAFE TO WALK FOR-WARD?
MOM?
HMM?
PLUM'S BEING CHASED BY SNOWBALL AGAIN...
RUN
RUN
RUN
RUN
RUN
AH!
TAKU-CHAN, MOVE OUT OF THE WAY!

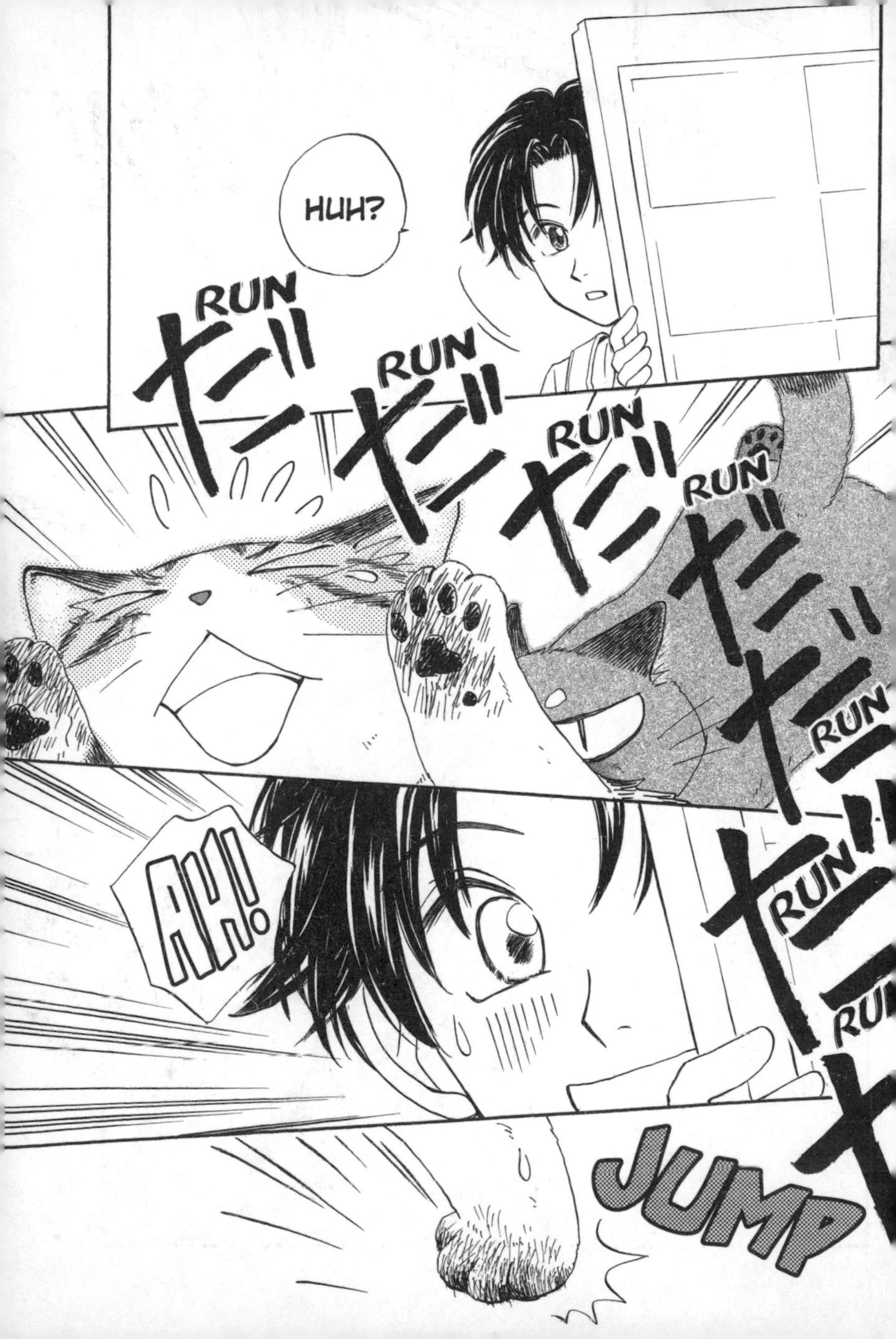
HUH?
RUN
RUN
RUN
RUN
RUN
RUN
RU
AH!
JUMP

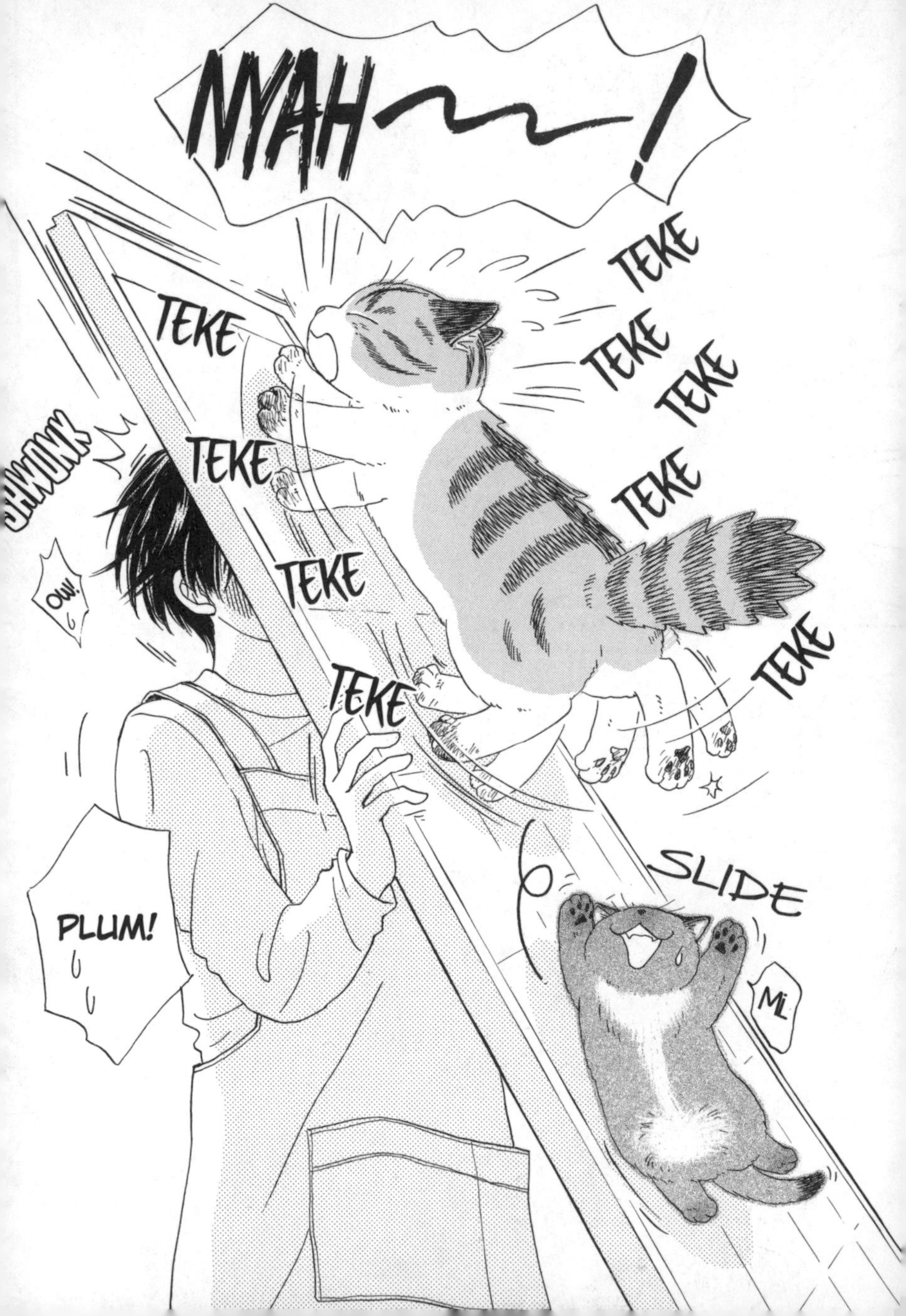
NYAH~~!
TEKE
TEKE
TEKE
TEKE
TEKE
TEKE
TEKE
TEKE
TEKE
SHWONK
OW!
SLIDE
MI
PLUM!

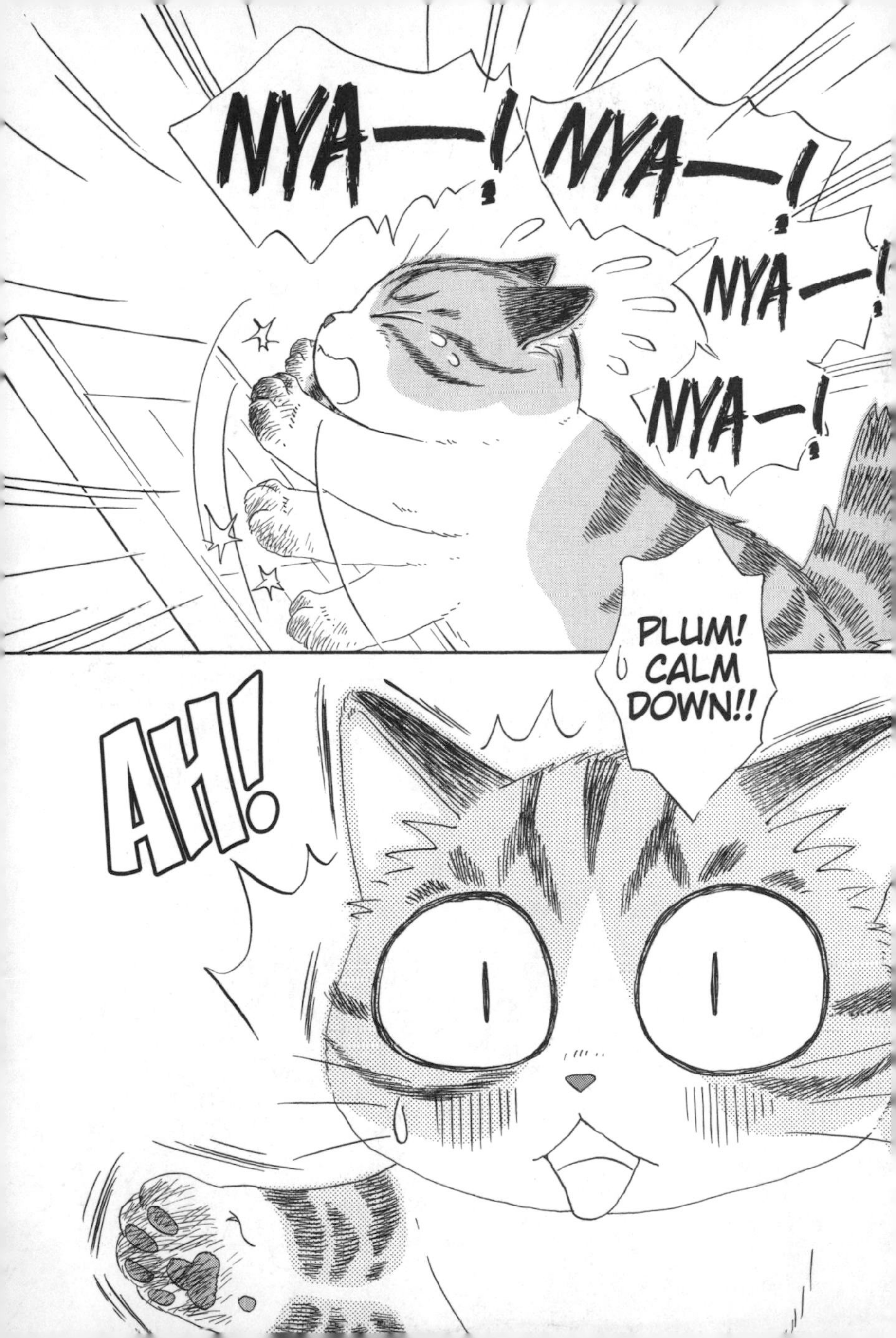
NYA—!
NYA—!
NYA—!
NYA—!
PLUM! CALM DOWN!!
AH!

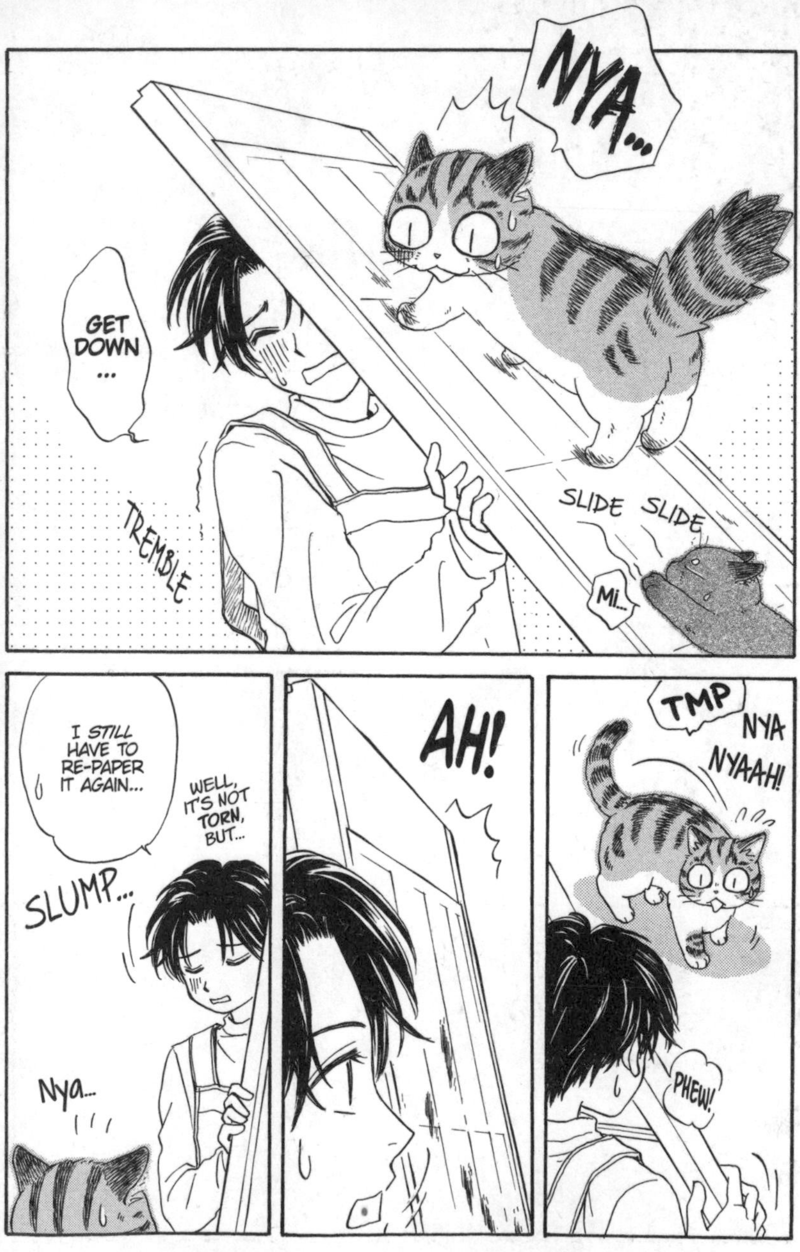
NYA...
GET DOWN ...
SLIDE SLIDE
Mi...
TREMBLE
TMP
NYA NYAAH!
PHEW!
AH!
WELL, IT'S NOT TORN, BUT...
I STILL HAVE TO RE-PAPER IT AGAIN...
SLUMP...
Nya...

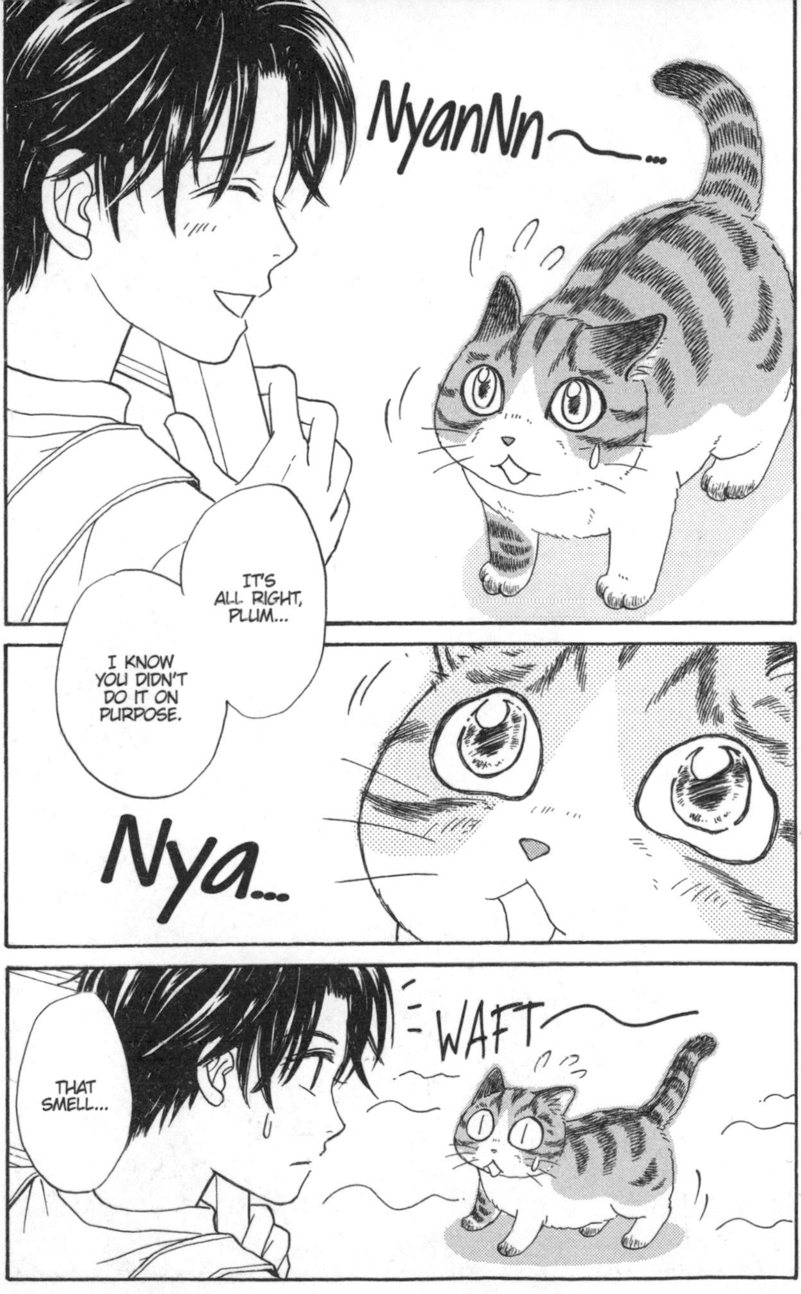
NyanNn~~...
IT'S ALL RIGHT, PLUM...
I KNOW YOU DIDN'T DO IT ON PURPOSE.
Nya...
WAFT
THAT SMELL...

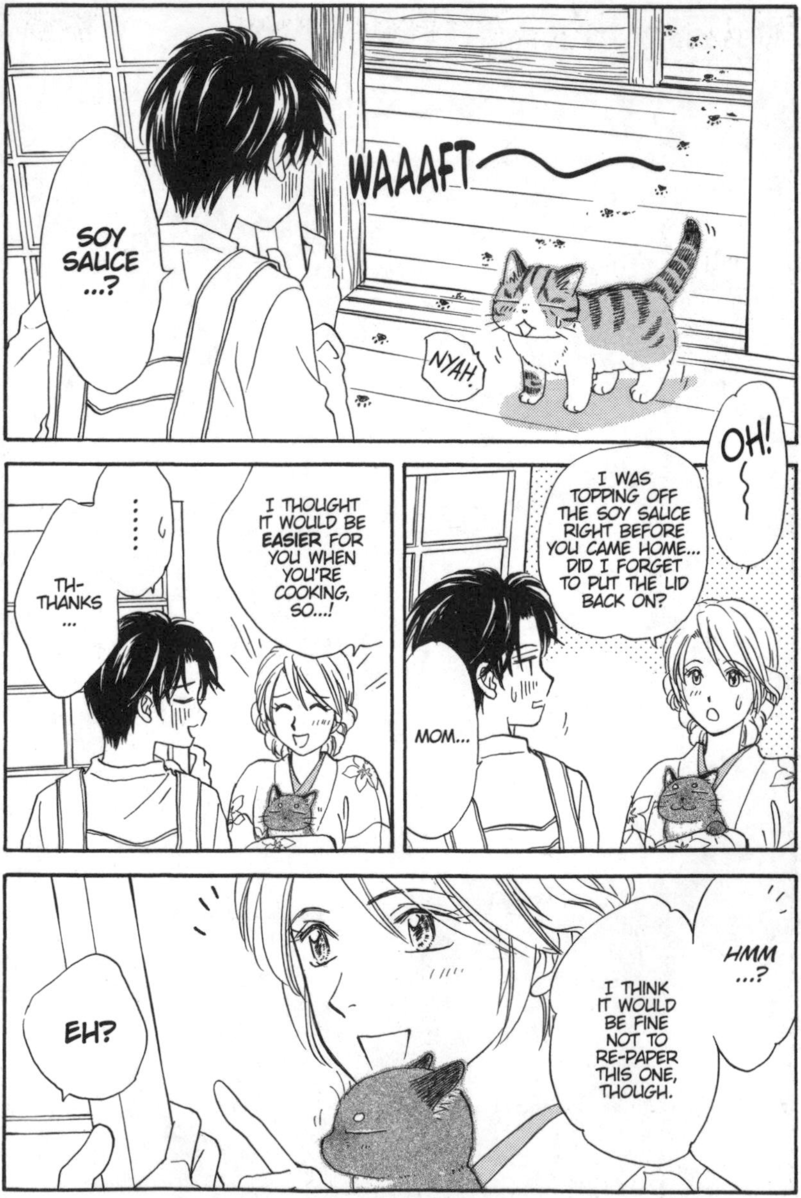
WAAAFT
SOY SAUCE ...?
NYAH!
OH!
I WAS TOPPING OFF THE SOY SAUCE RIGHT BEFORE YOU CAME HOME... DID I FORGET TO PUT THE LID BACK ON?
MOM...
I THOUGHT IT WOULD BE EASIER FOR YOU WHEN YOU'RE COOKING, SO...!
......
TH-THANKS ...
HMM ...?
I THINK IT WOULD BE FINE NOT TO RE-PAPER THIS ONE, THOUGH.
EH?

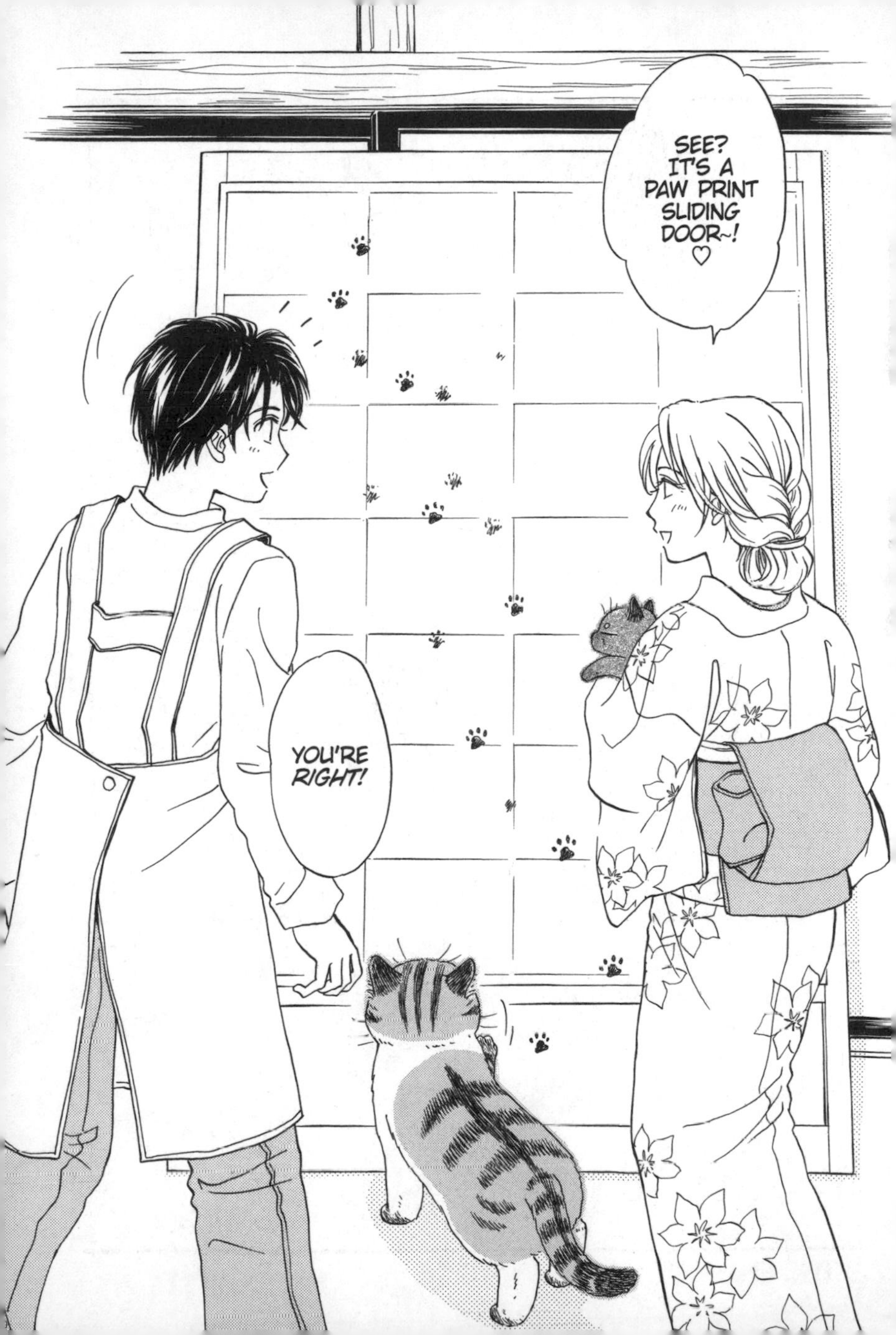
SEE? IT'S A PAW PRINT SLIDING DOOR~! ♡
YOU'RE RIGHT!

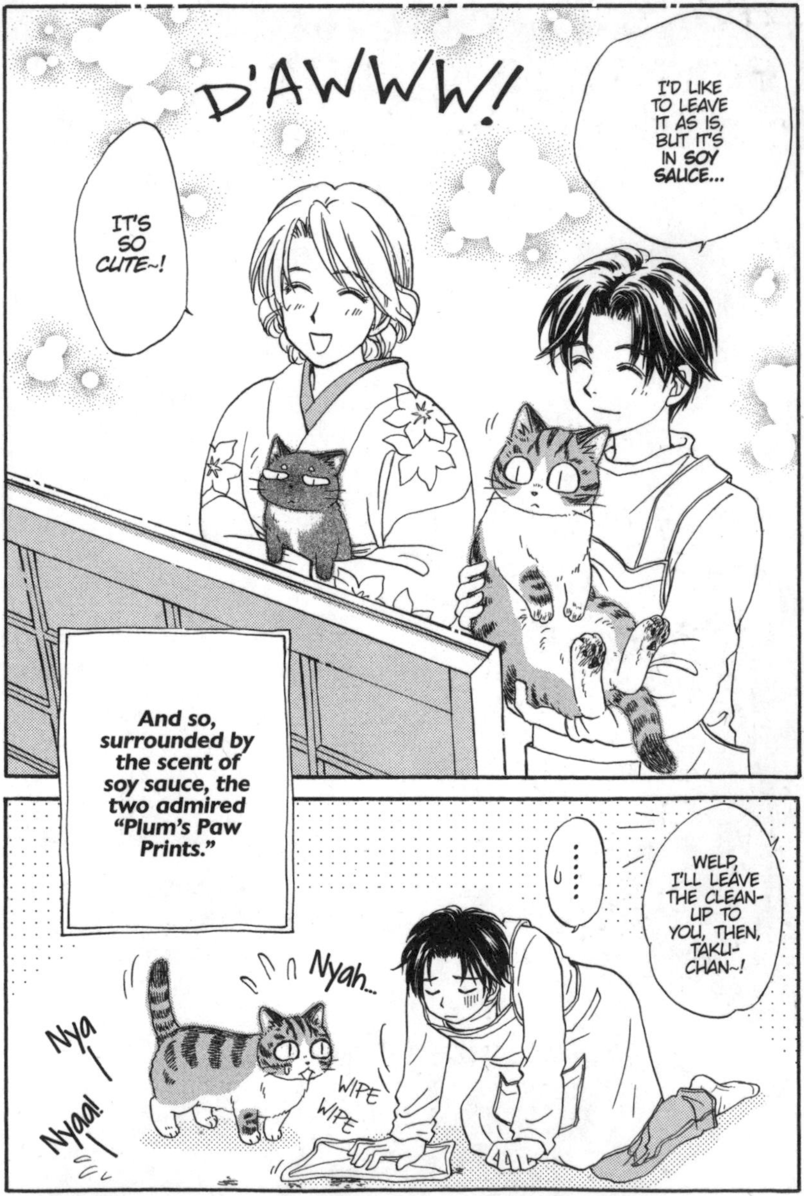
I'D LIKE TO LEAVE IT AS IS, BUT IT'S IN SOY SAUCE...
D'AWWW!
IT'S SO CUTE~!
And so, surrounded by the scent of soy sauce, the two admired "Plum's Paw Prints."
WELP, I'LL LEAVE THE CLEAN-UP TO YOU, THEN, TAKU-CHAN~!
......
Nyah...
Nya
Nyaa!
WIPE WIPE

THE END

SHORT. 21
I Want to Snuggle Up in a Teeny Tiny Space

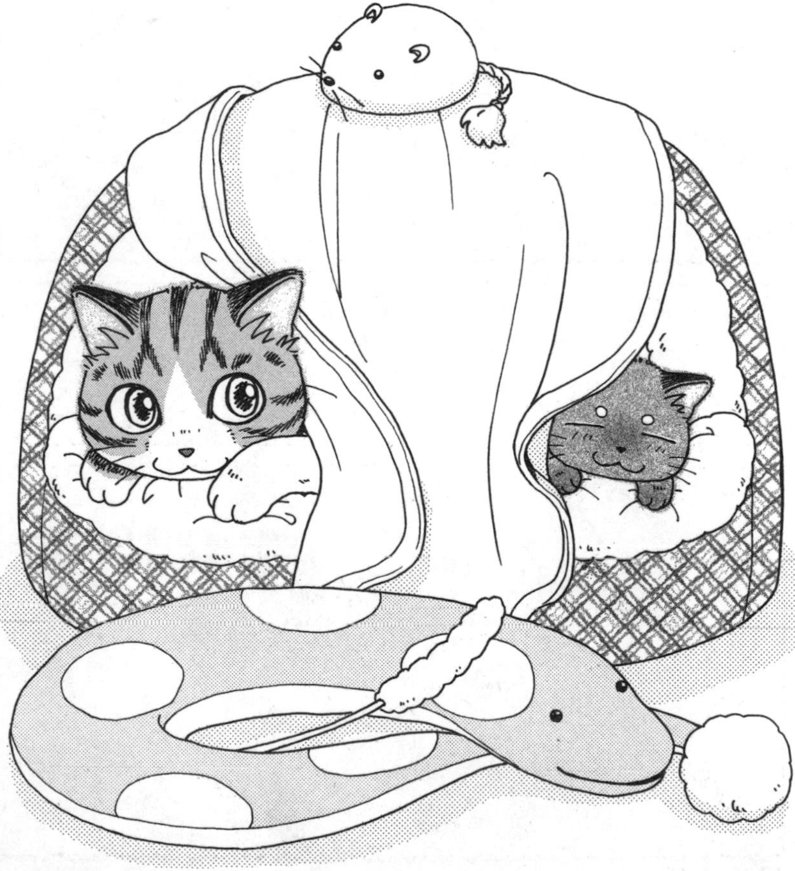

Ecological Cat Bed

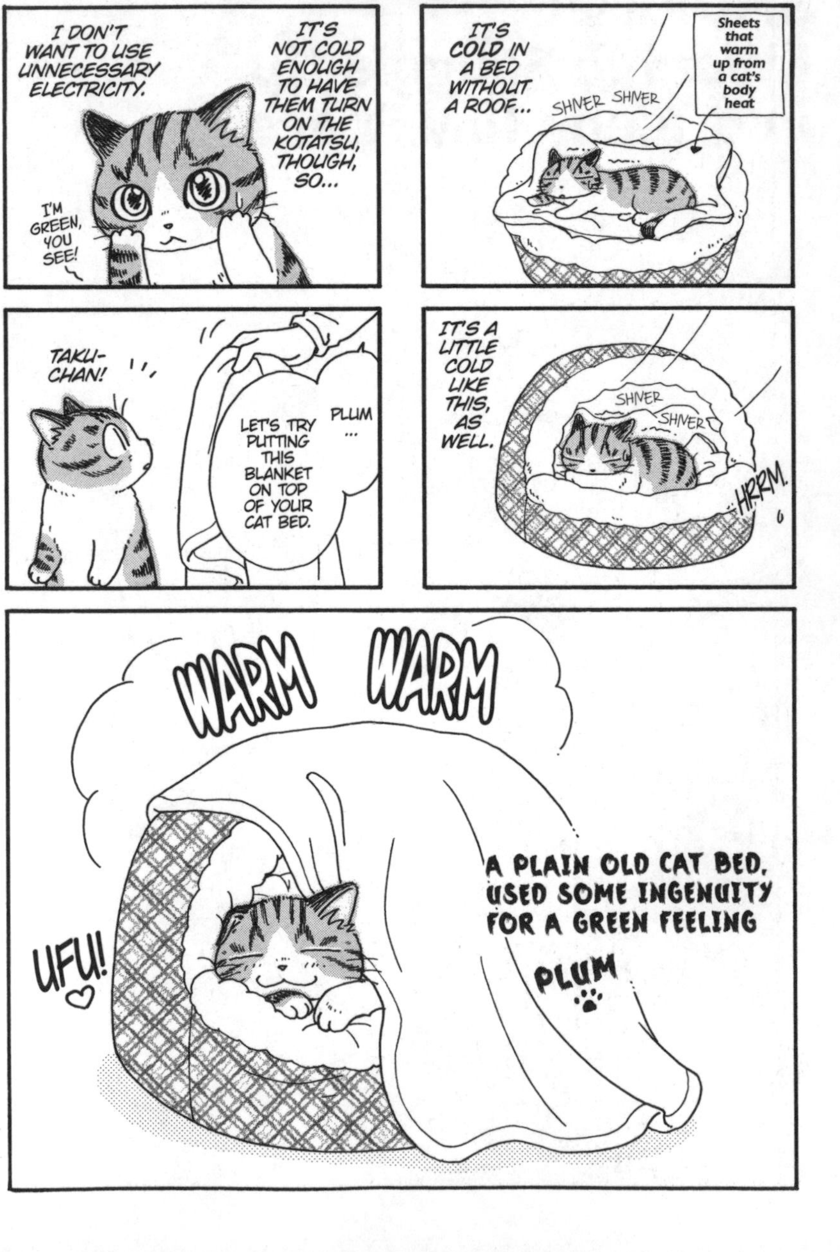
Sheets that warm up from a cat's body heat
IT'S COLD IN A BED WITHOUT A ROOF...
SHIVER SHIVER
IT'S NOT COLD ENOUGH TO HAVE THEM TURN ON THE KOTATSU, THOUGH, SO...
I DON'T WANT TO USE UNNECESSARY ELECTRICITY.
I'M GREEN, YOU SEE!
IT'S A LITTLE COLD LIKE THIS, AS WELL.
SHIVER
SHIVER
HRRM.
PLUM ...
LET'S TRY PUTTING THIS BLANKET ON TOP OF YOUR CAT BED.
TAKU-CHAN!
WARM WARM
A PLAIN OLD CAT BED, USED SOME INGENUITY FOR A GREEN FEELING
PLUM
UFU!

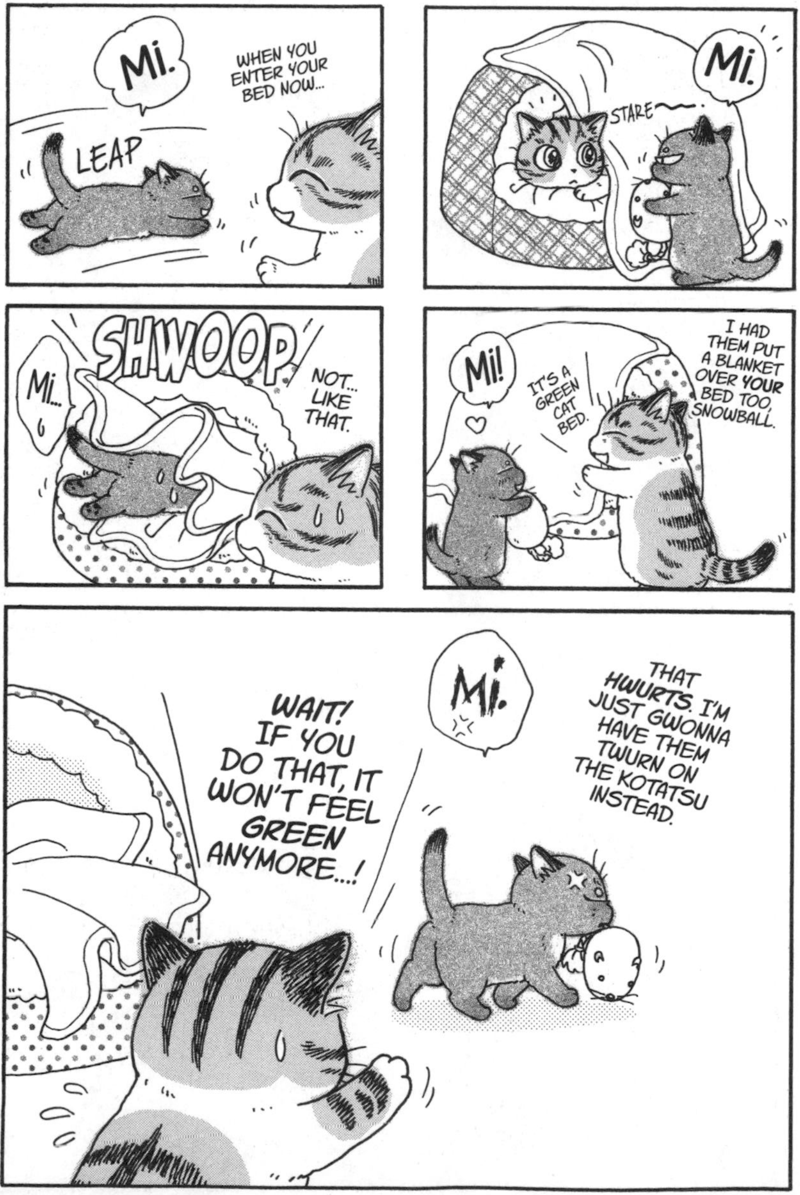
Mi.
STARE~~
Mi.
WHEN YOU ENTER YOUR BED NOW...
LEAP
I HAD THEM PUT A BLANKET OVER **YOUR** BED TOO, SNOWBALL.
IT'S A GREEN CAT BED.
Mi!
SHWOOP
NOT... LIKE THAT.
Mi...
THAT **HWURTS**. I'M JUST GWONNA HAVE THEM TWURN ON THE KOTATSU INSTEAD.
Mi.
WAIT! IF YOU DO THAT, IT WON'T FEEL **GREEN** ANYMORE...!

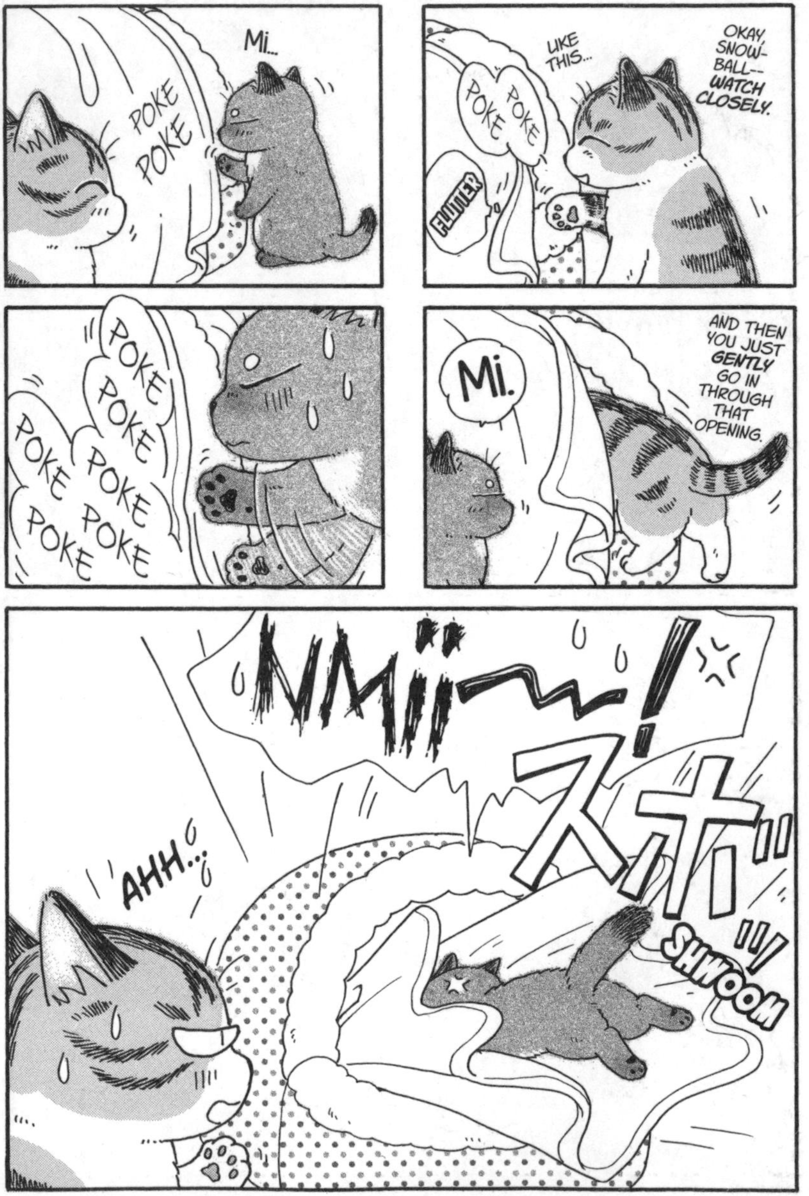
OKAY, SNOW-BALL-- WATCH CLOSELY.
LIKE THIS...
POKE POKE
FLUTTER
Mi...
POKE POKE
AND THEN YOU JUST GENTLY GO IN THROUGH THAT OPENING.
Mi.
POKE POKE POKE POKE POKE POKE
NMii~!
スボ
SHWOOM
AHH...!

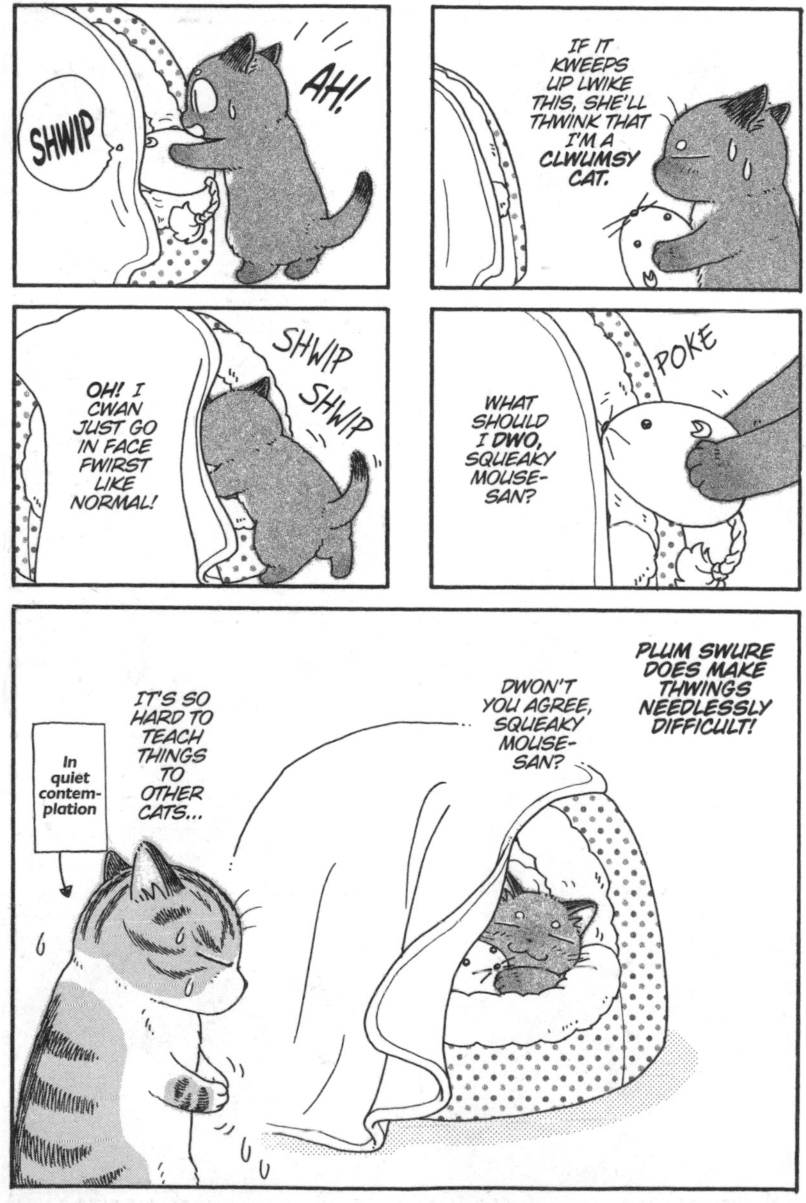
IF IT KWEEPS UP LWIKE THIS, SHE'LL THWINK THAT I'M A CLWUMSY CAT.
AH!
SHWIP
POKE
WHAT SHOULD I DWO, SQUEAKY MOUSE-SAN?
SHWIP SHWIP
OH! I CWAN JUST GO IN FACE FWIRST LIKE NORMAL!
PLUM SWURE DOES MAKE THWINGS NEEDLESSLY DIFFICULT!
DWON'T YOU AGREE, SQUEAKY MOUSE-SAN?
IT'S SO HARD TO TEACH THINGS TO OTHER CATS...
In quiet contemplation

I Want to Snuggle Up in a Teeny Tiny Space

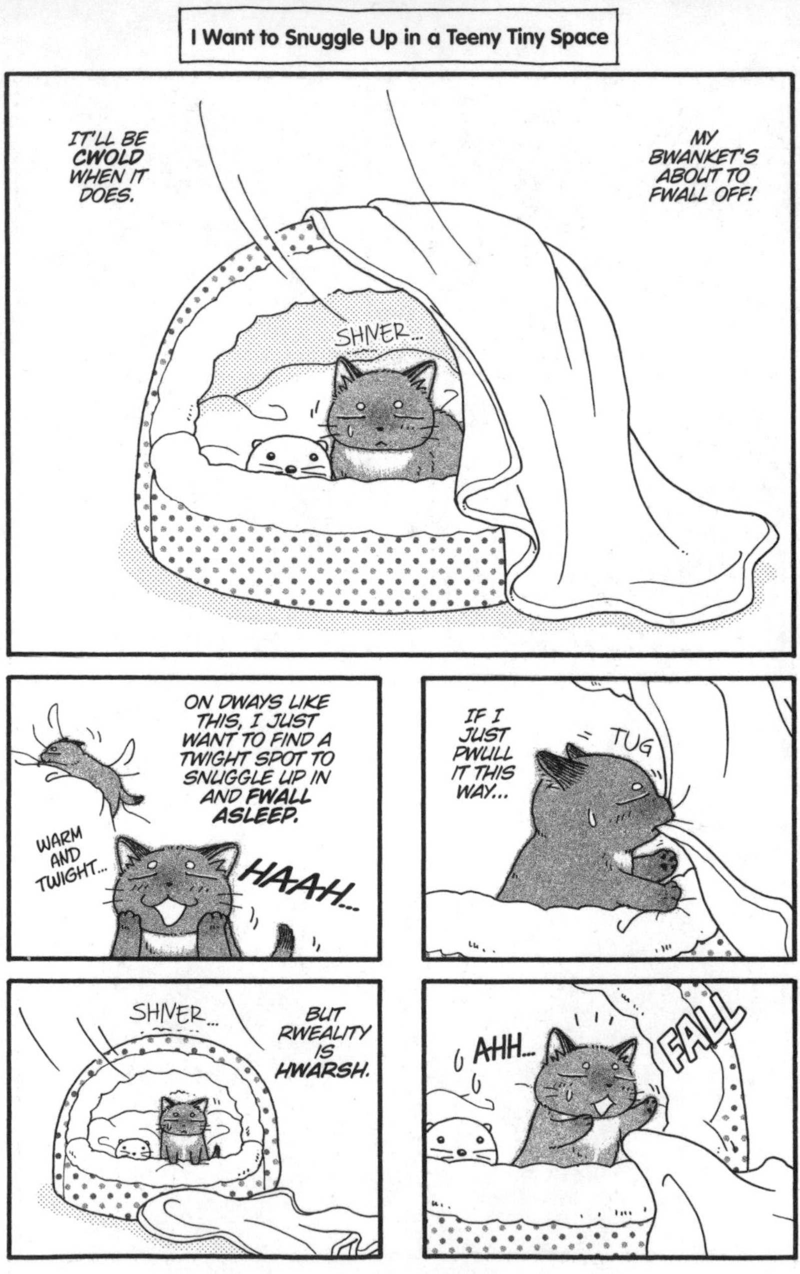
MY BWANKET'S ABOUT TO FWALL OFF!
SHIVER...
IT'LL BE CWOLD WHEN IT DOES.
IF I JUST PWULL IT THIS WAY...
TUG
ON DWAYS LIKE THIS, I JUST WANT TO FIND A TWIGHT SPOT TO SNUGGLE UP IN AND FWALL ASLEEP.
WARM AND TWIGHT...
HAAH...
FALL
AHH...
BUT RWEALITY IS HWARSH.
SHIVER...

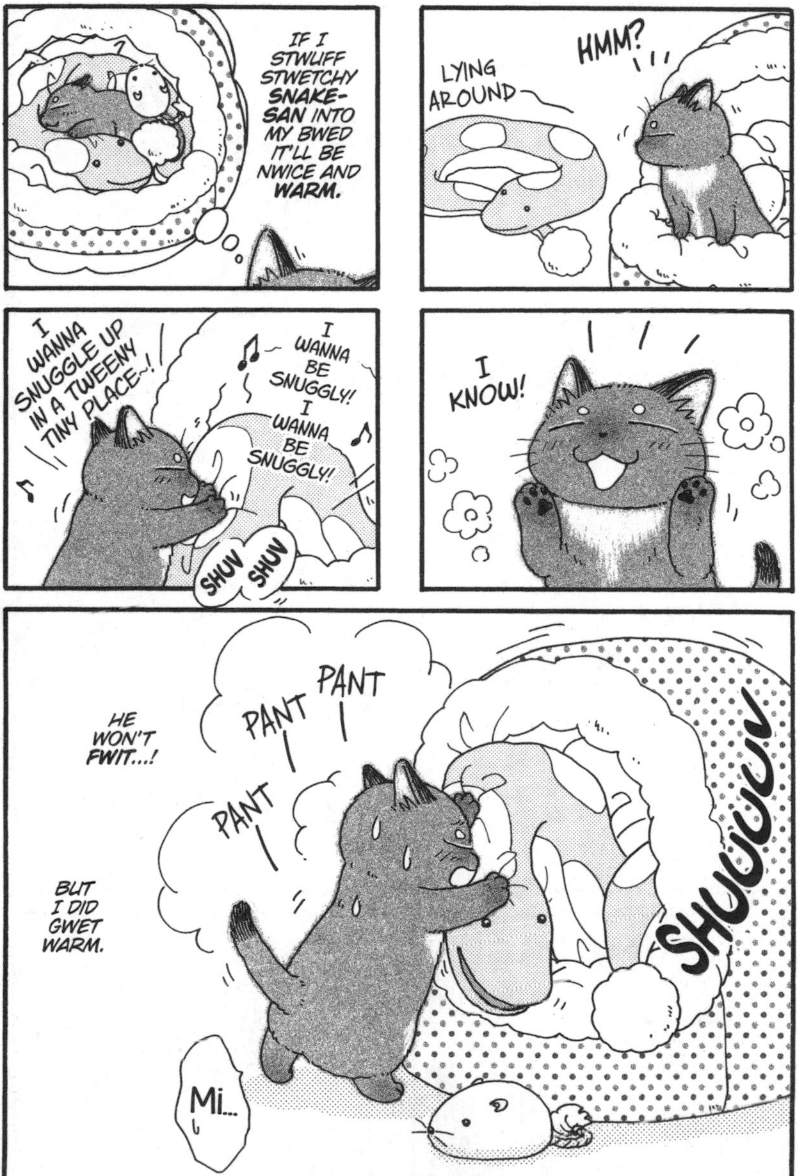
HMM?
LYING AROUND
IF I STWUFF STWETCHY SNAKE-SAN INTO MY BWED IT'LL BE NWICE AND WARM.
I KNOW!
I WANNA BE SNUGGLY! I WANNA BE SNUGGLY!
I WANNA SNUGGLE UP IN A TWEENY TINY PLACE~!
SHUV SHUV
SHUUUUN
PANT PANT
PANT
HE WON'T FWIT...!
BUT I DID GWET WARM.
Mi...

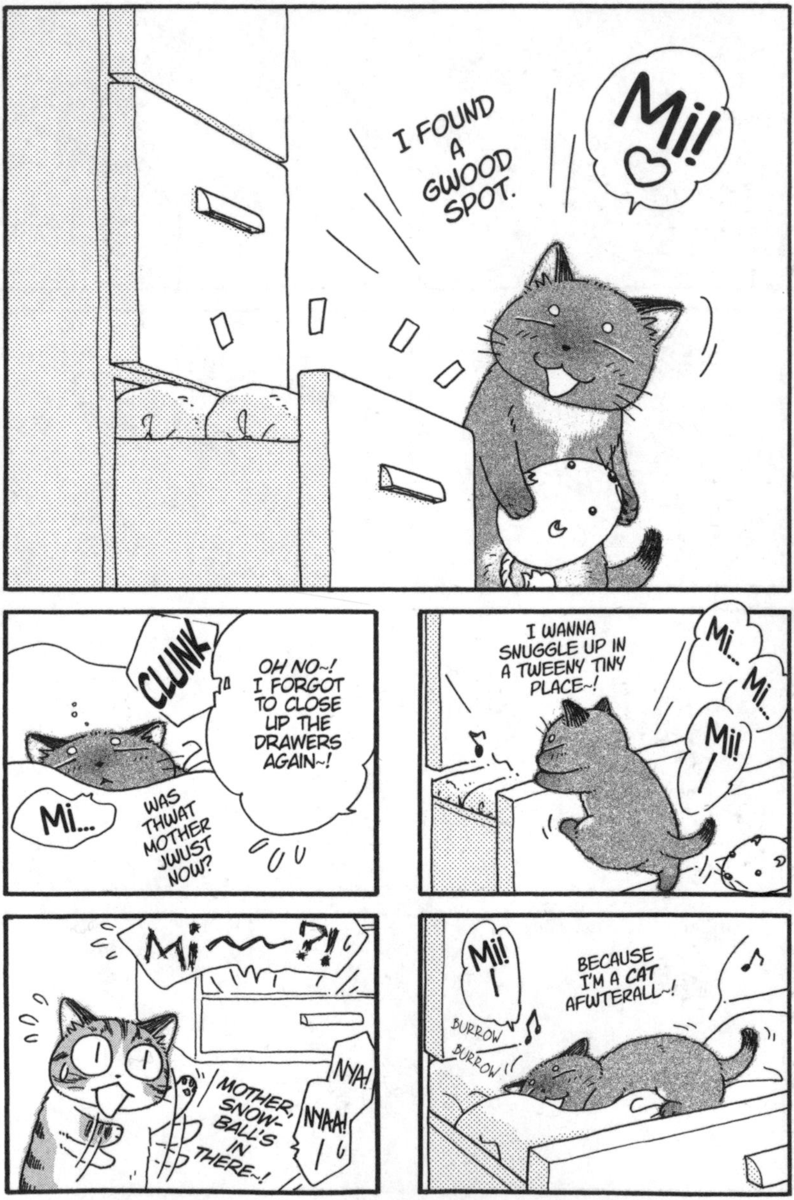
Mi! ♡
I FOUND A GWOOD SPOT.
Mi...
Mi...
Mi!
I WANNA SNUGGLE UP IN A TWEENY TINY PLACE~!
OH NO~! I FORGOT TO CLOSE UP THE DRAWERS AGAIN~!
CLUNK
WAS THWAT MOTHER JWUST NOW?
Mi...
BECAUSE I'M A CAT AFWTERALL~!
Mii!
BURROW
BURROW
NYA!
NYAA!
MOTHER, SNOW-BALL'S IN THERE~!
Mi~~?!

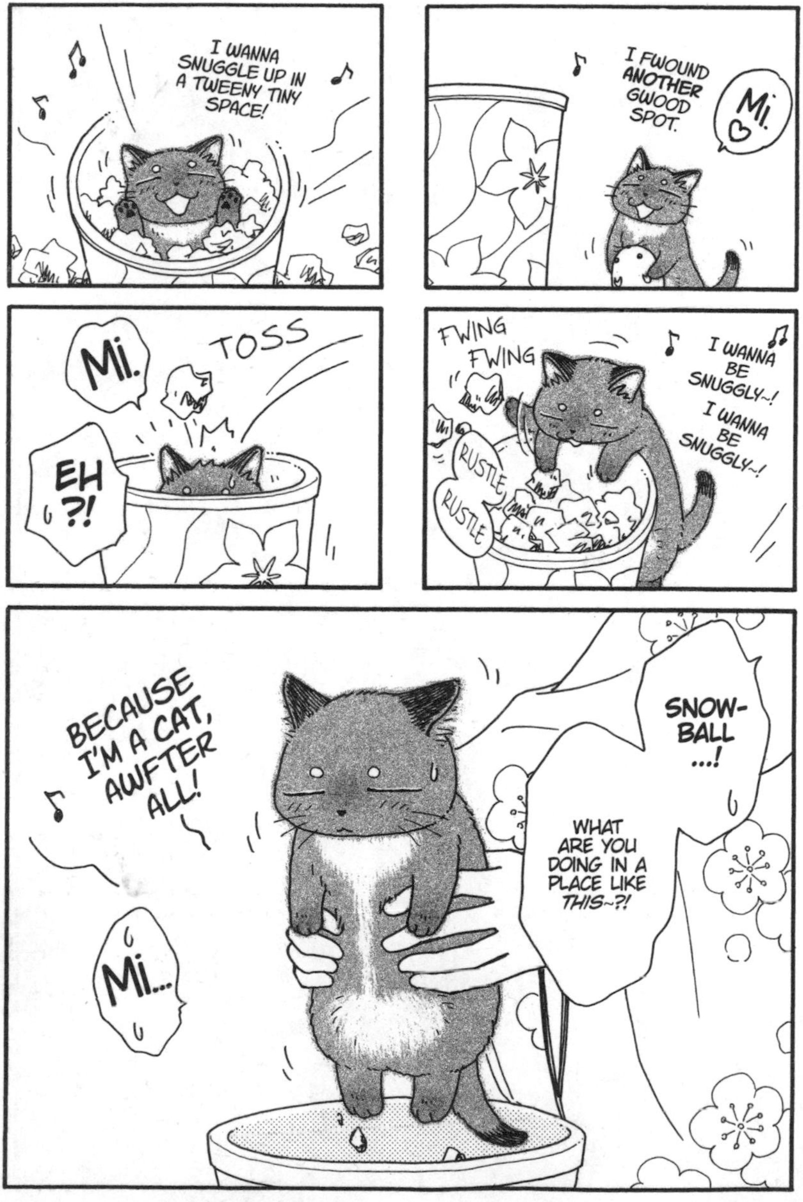
I FWOUND ANOTHER GWOOD SPOT.
Mi. ♡
I WANNA SNUGGLE UP IN A TWEENY TINY SPACE!
I WANNA BE SNUGGLY~! I WANNA BE SNUGGLY~!
FWING FWING
RUSTLE RUSTLE
TOSS
Mi.
EH?!
SNOW-BALL...!
WHAT ARE YOU DOING IN A PLACE LIKE *THIS*~?!
BECAUSE I'M A CAT, AWFTER ALL!
Mi...

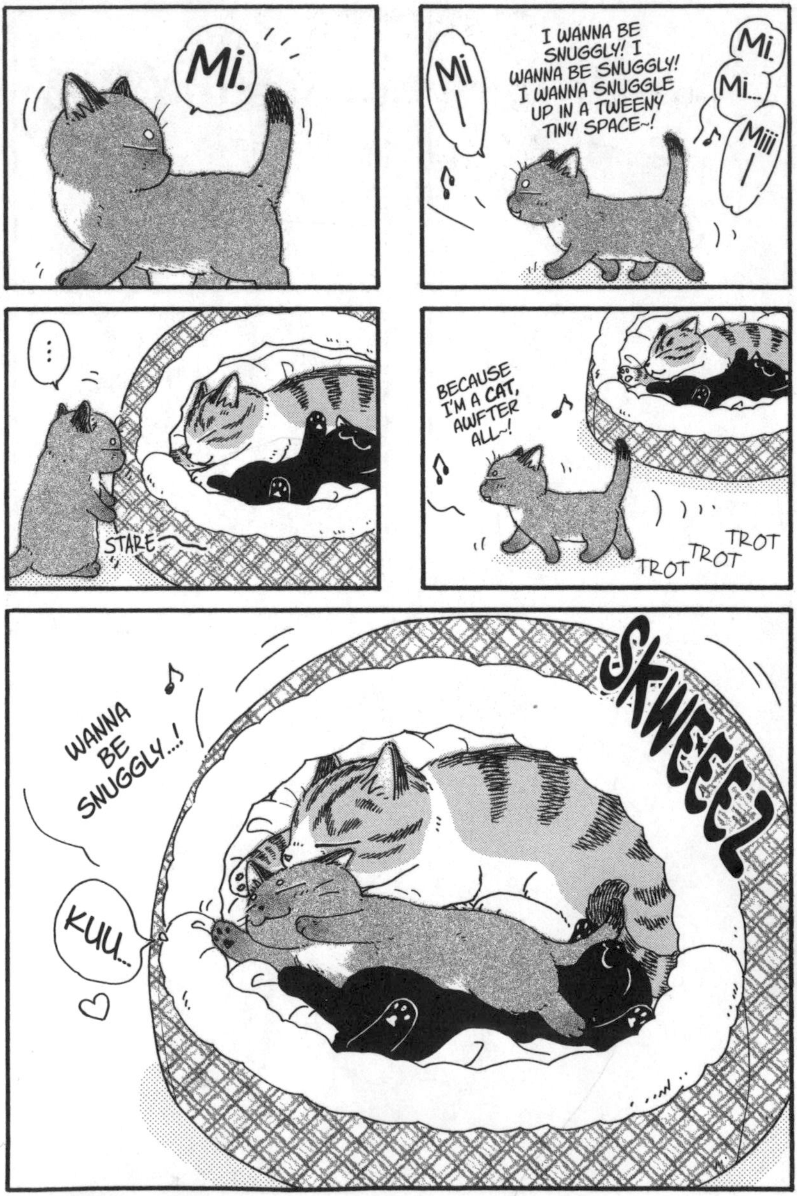
Mi.
Mi...
Miii—
I WANNA BE SNUGGLY! I WANNA BE SNUGGLY! I WANNA SNUGGLE UP IN A TWEENY TINY SPACE~!
Mi—
Mi.
BECAUSE I'M A CAT, AWFTER ALL~!
TROT TROT TROT
...
STARE
SKWEEEZ
WANNA BE SNUGGLY...!
KUU...

THE END

CHAPTER 26
An Unfounded Accusation Against Plum

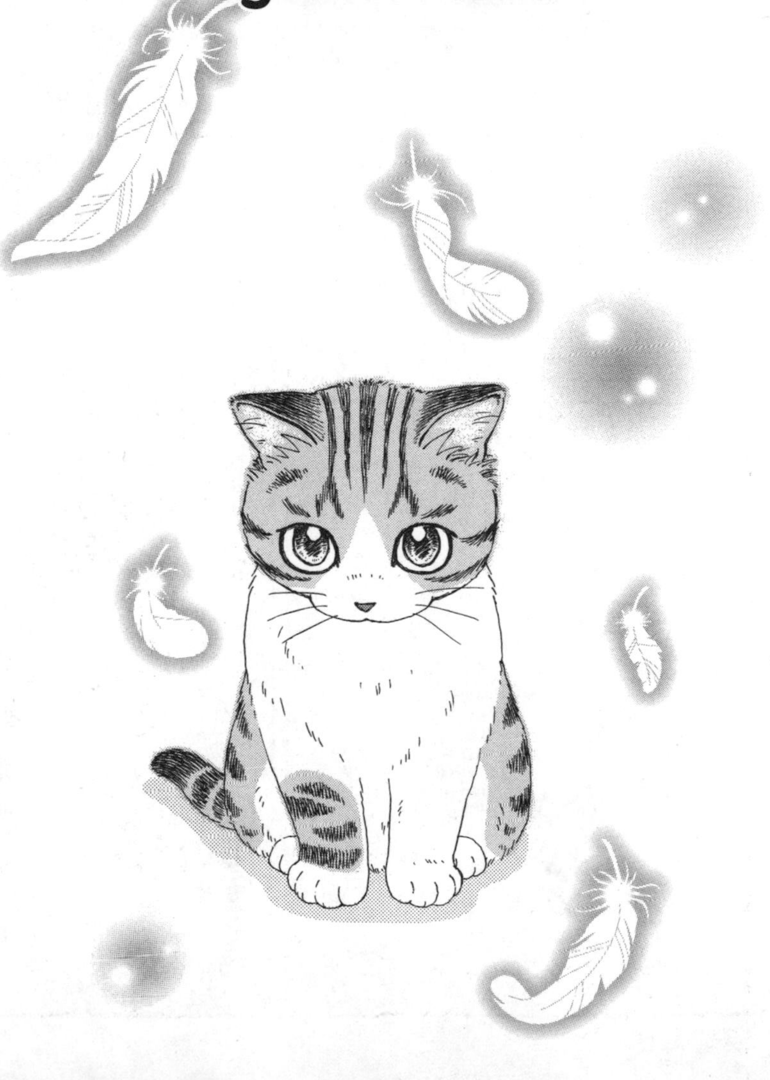

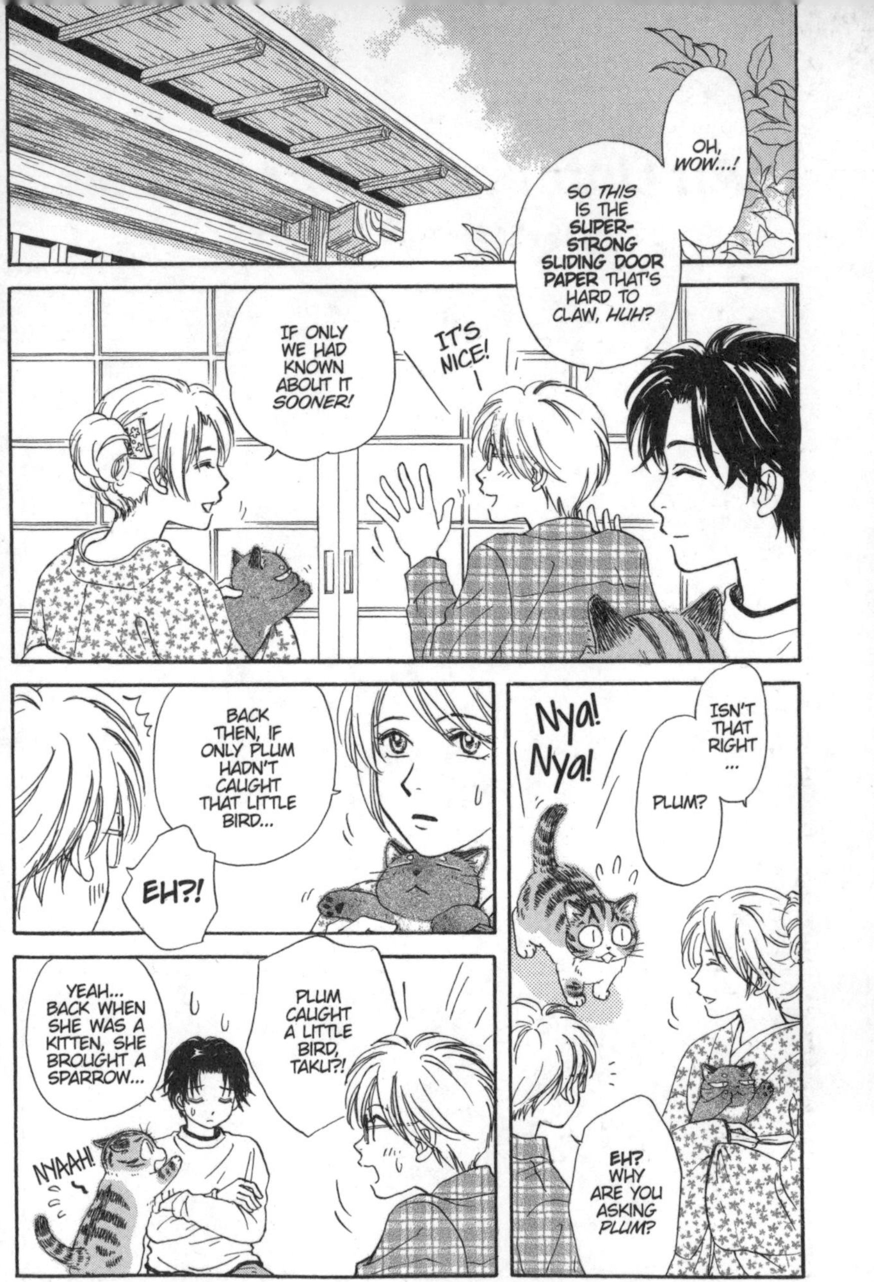

OH, WOW...!
SO THIS IS THE SUPER-STRONG SLIDING DOOR PAPER THAT'S HARD TO CLAW, HUH?
IT'S NICE!
IF ONLY WE HAD KNOWN ABOUT IT SOONER!
Nya! Nya!
ISN'T THAT RIGHT ... PLUM?
EH? WHY ARE YOU ASKING PLUM?
BACK THEN, IF ONLY PLUM HADN'T CAUGHT THAT LITTLE BIRD...
EH?!
PLUM CAUGHT A LITTLE BIRD, TAKU?!
YEAH... BACK WHEN SHE WAS A KITTEN, SHE BROUGHT A SPARROW...
NYAAH!

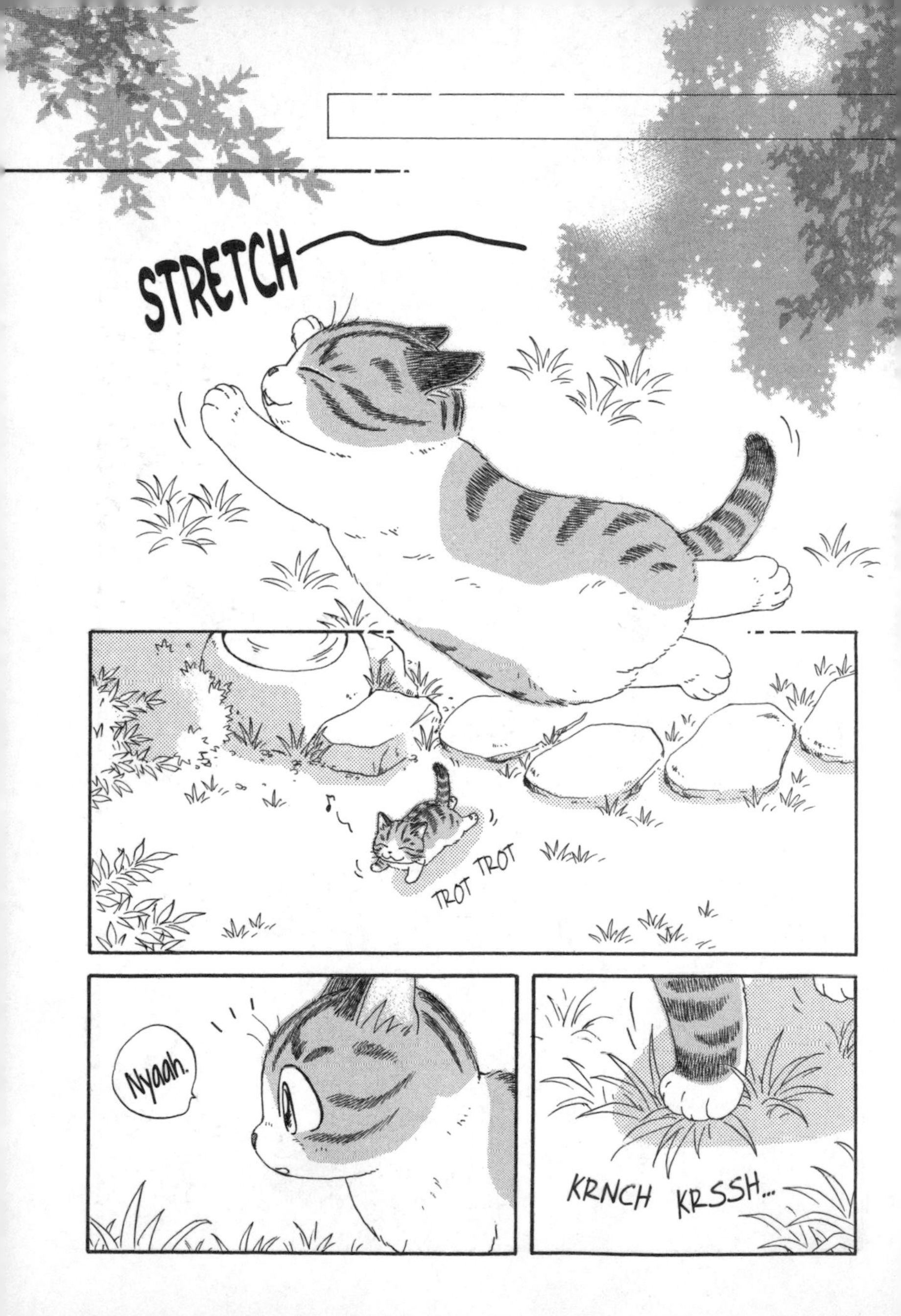
STRETCH
TROT TROT
KRNCH KRSSH...
Nyaah.

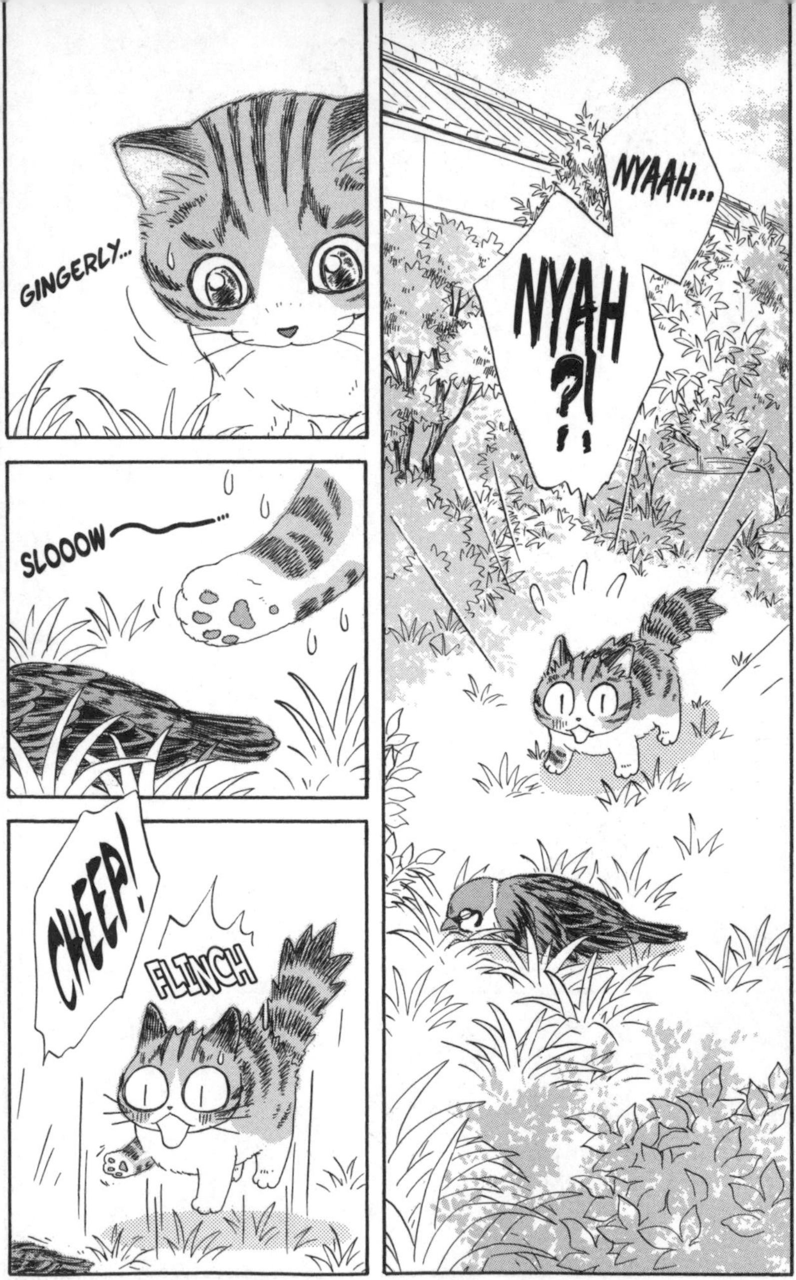
NYAAH...
NYAH ?!!
GINGERLY...
SLOOOW—...
CHEEP!
FLINCH

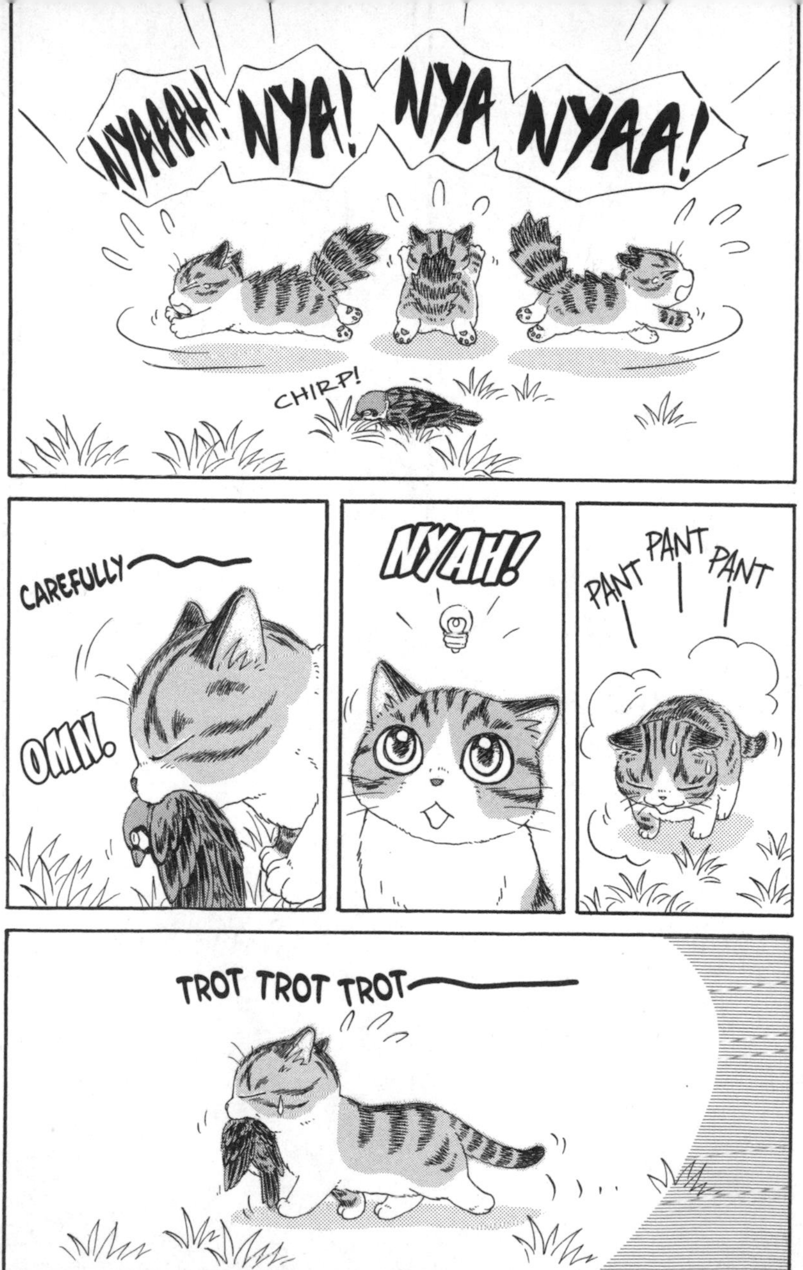
NYAAAH! NYA! NYA NYAA!
CHIRP!
PANT PANT PANT
NYAH!
CAREFULLY
OMN.
TROT TROT TROT

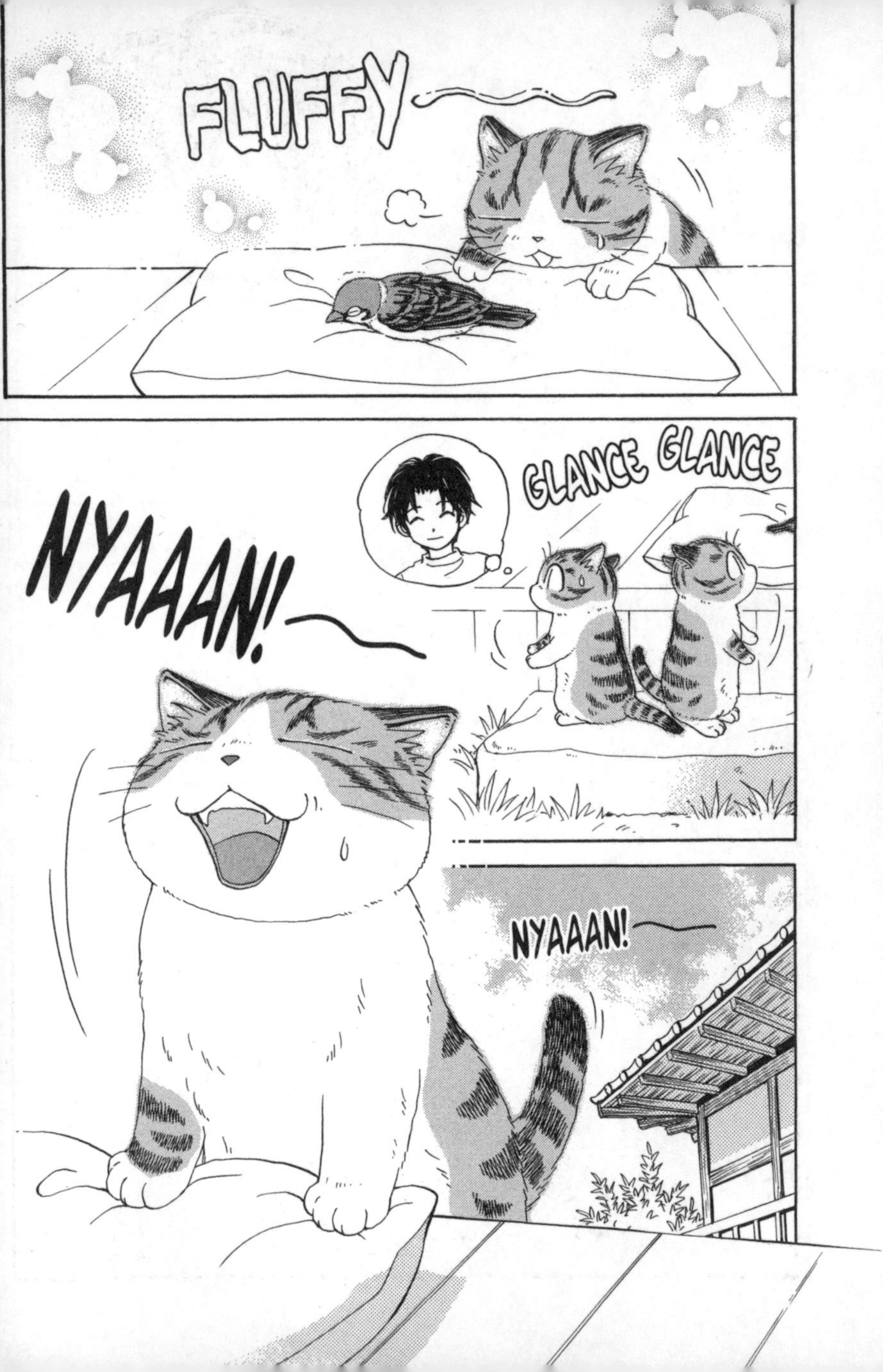
FLUFFY
GLANCE GLANCE
NYAAAN!
NYAAAN!

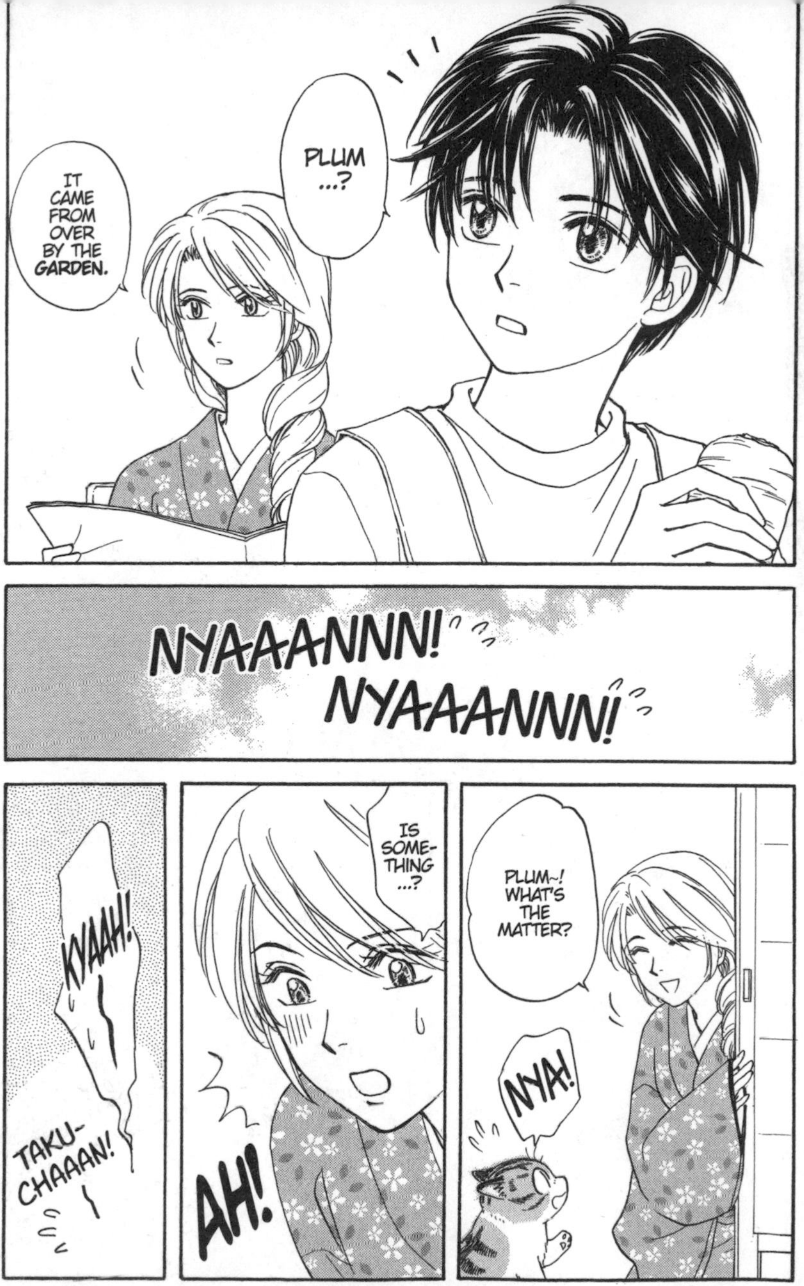
PLUM ...?
IT CAME FROM OVER BY THE GARDEN.
NYAAANNN!
NYAAANNN!
PLUM~! WHAT'S THE MATTER?
NYA!
IS SOME-THING ...?
AH!
KYAAH!
TAKU-CHAAAN!

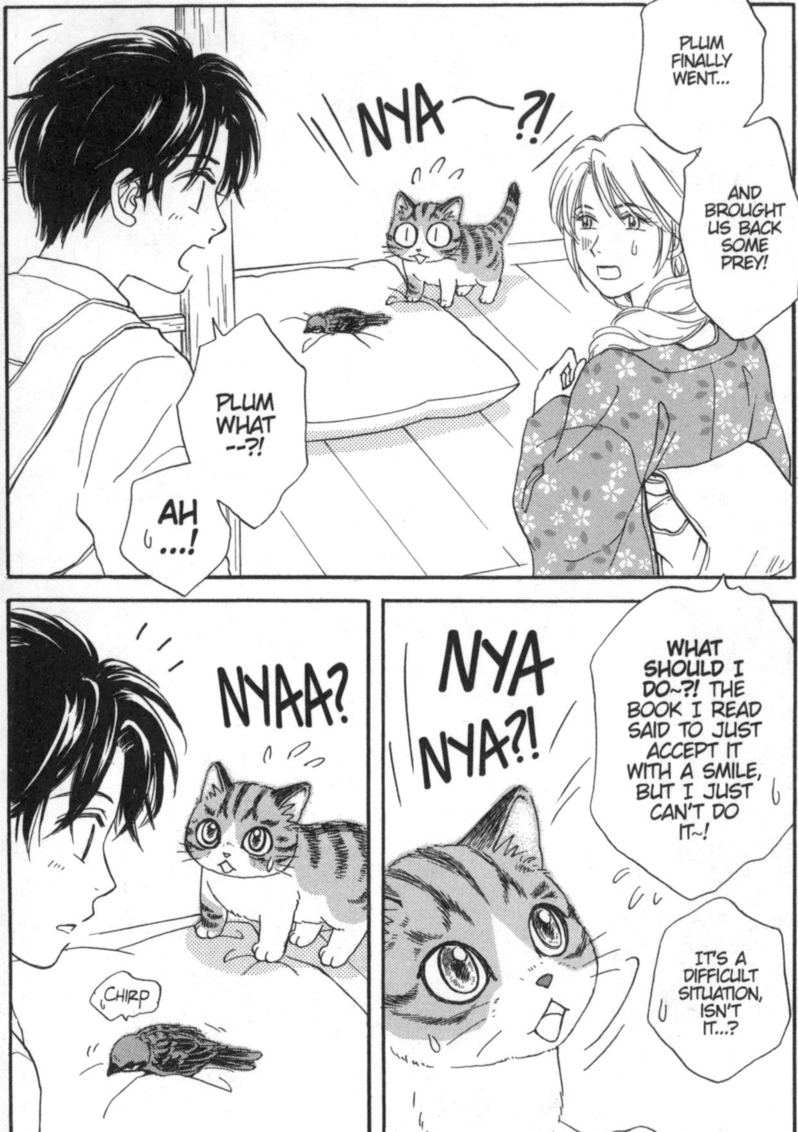
PLUM FINALLY WENT...
AND BROUGHT US BACK SOME PREY!
NYA~~?!
PLUM WHAT--?!
AH...!
WHAT SHOULD I DO~?! THE BOOK I READ SAID TO JUST ACCEPT IT WITH A SMILE, BUT I JUST CAN'T DO IT~!
NYA NYA?!
IT'S A DIFFICULT SITUATION, ISN'T IT...?
NYAA?
CHIRP

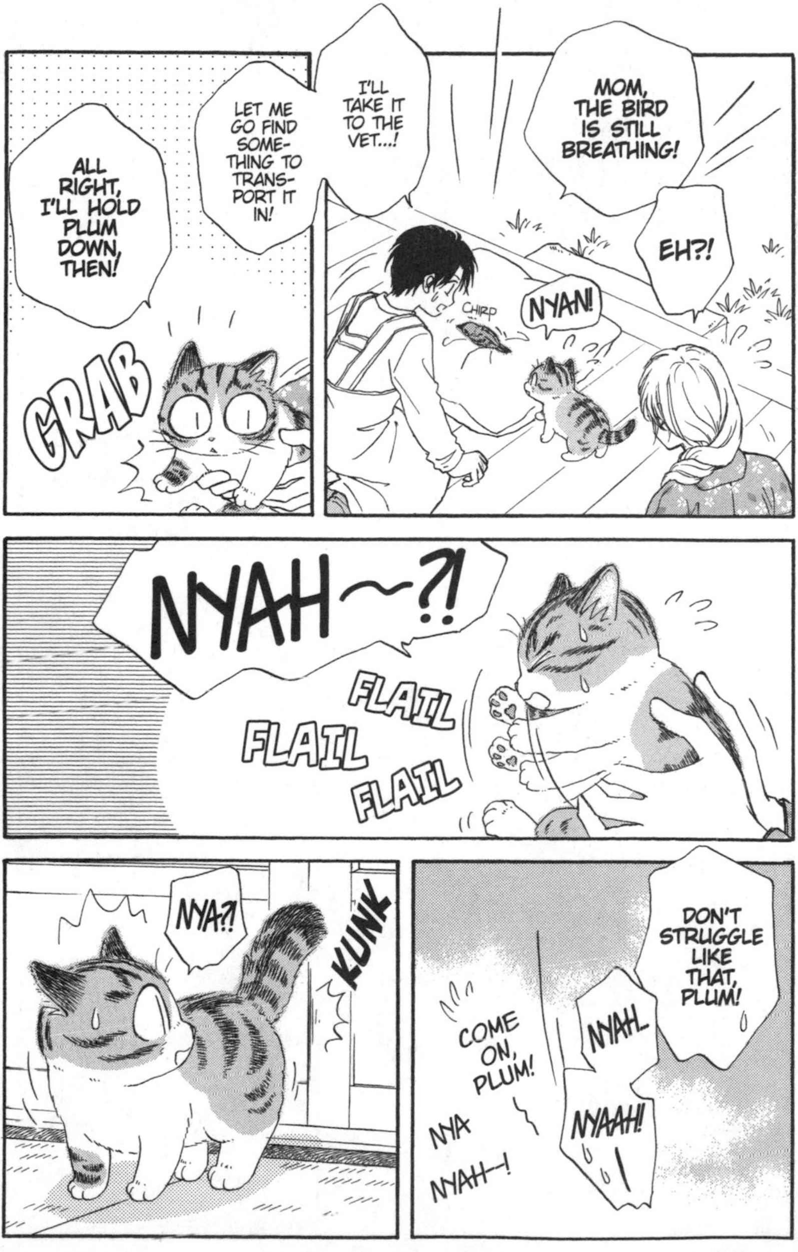
MOM, THE BIRD IS STILL BREATHING!
EH?!
I'LL TAKE IT TO THE VET...!
NYAN!
CHIRP
LET ME GO FIND SOME-THING TO TRANS-PORT IT IN!
ALL RIGHT, I'LL HOLD PLUM DOWN, THEN!
GRAB
NYAH~?!
FLAIL
FLAIL
FLAIL
DON'T STRUGGLE LIKE THAT, PLUM!
NYAH
COME ON, PLUM!
NYAAH!
NYA
NYAH—!
KUNK
NYA?!

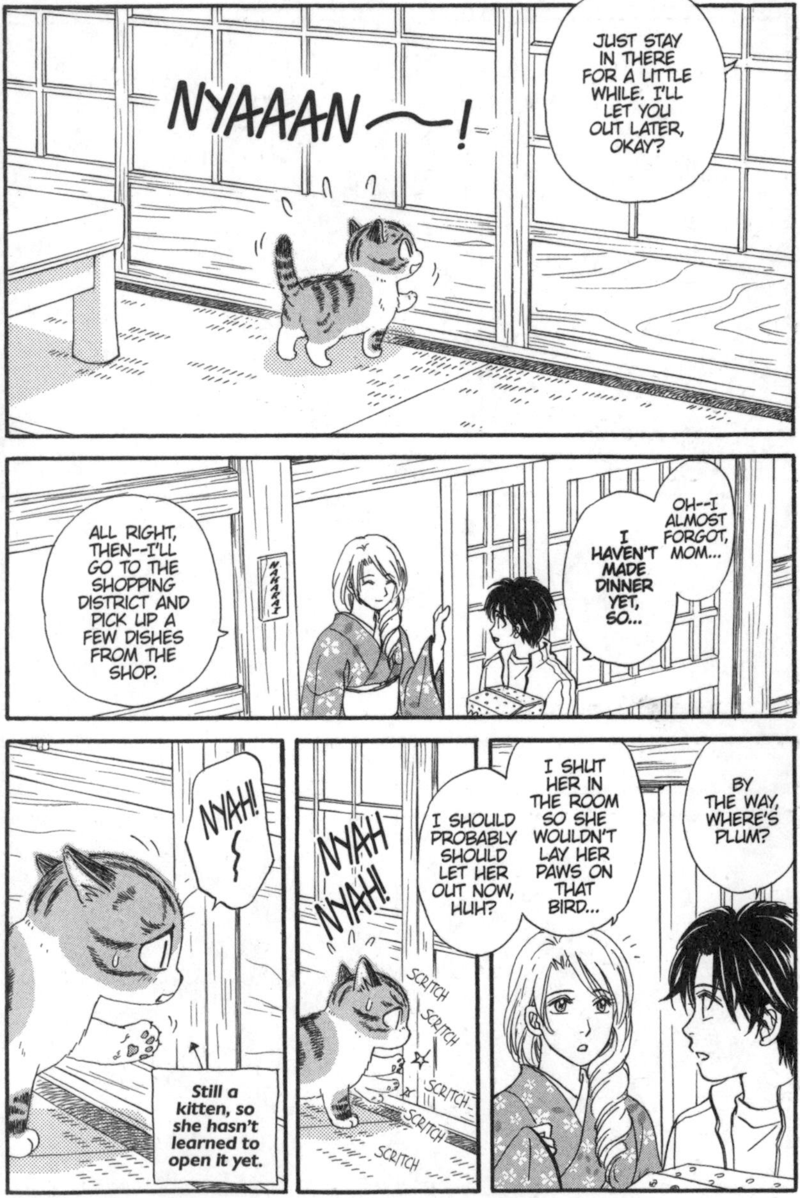
JUST STAY IN THERE FOR A LITTLE WHILE. I'LL LET YOU OUT LATER, OKAY?
NYAAAN~!
OH--I ALMOST FORGOT, MOM...
I HAVEN'T MADE DINNER YET, SO...
ALL RIGHT, THEN--I'LL GO TO THE SHOPPING DISTRICT AND PICK UP A FEW DISHES FROM THE SHOP.
BY THE WAY, WHERE'S PLUM?
I SHUT HER IN THE ROOM SO SHE WOULDN'T LAY HER PAWS ON THAT BIRD...
I SHOULD PROBABLY SHOULD LET HER OUT NOW, HUH?
NYAH NYAH!
SCRITCH
SCRITCH
SCRITCH
SCRITCH
SCRITCH
NYAH!
Still a kitten, so she hasn't learned to open it yet.

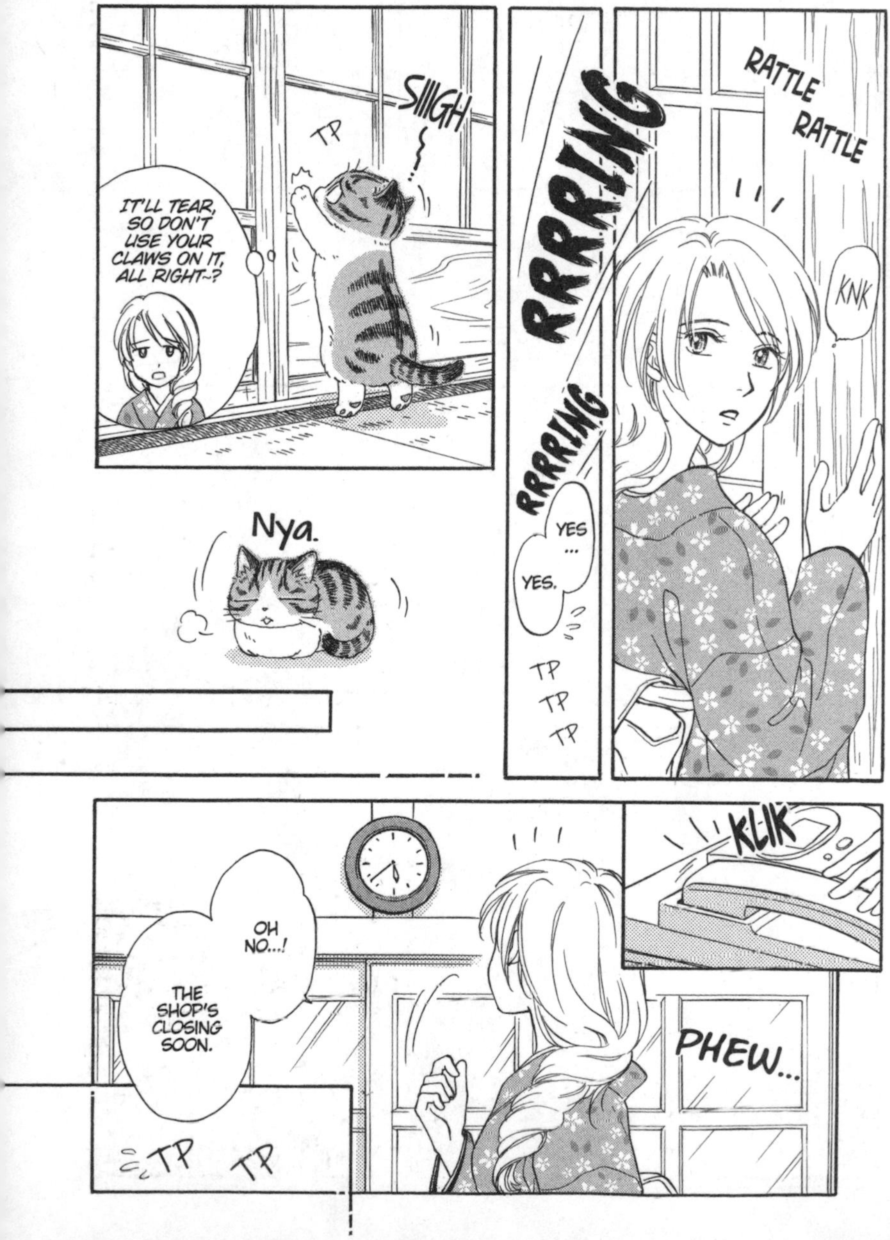
RATTLE RATTLE
KNK
RRRRING
RRRRING
YES...
YES.
TP TP TP
SIIIGH
TP
IT'LL TEAR, SO DON'T USE YOUR CLAWS ON IT, ALL RIGHT~?
Nya.
KLIK
PHEW...
OH NO...!
THE SHOP'S CLOSING SOON.
TP TP

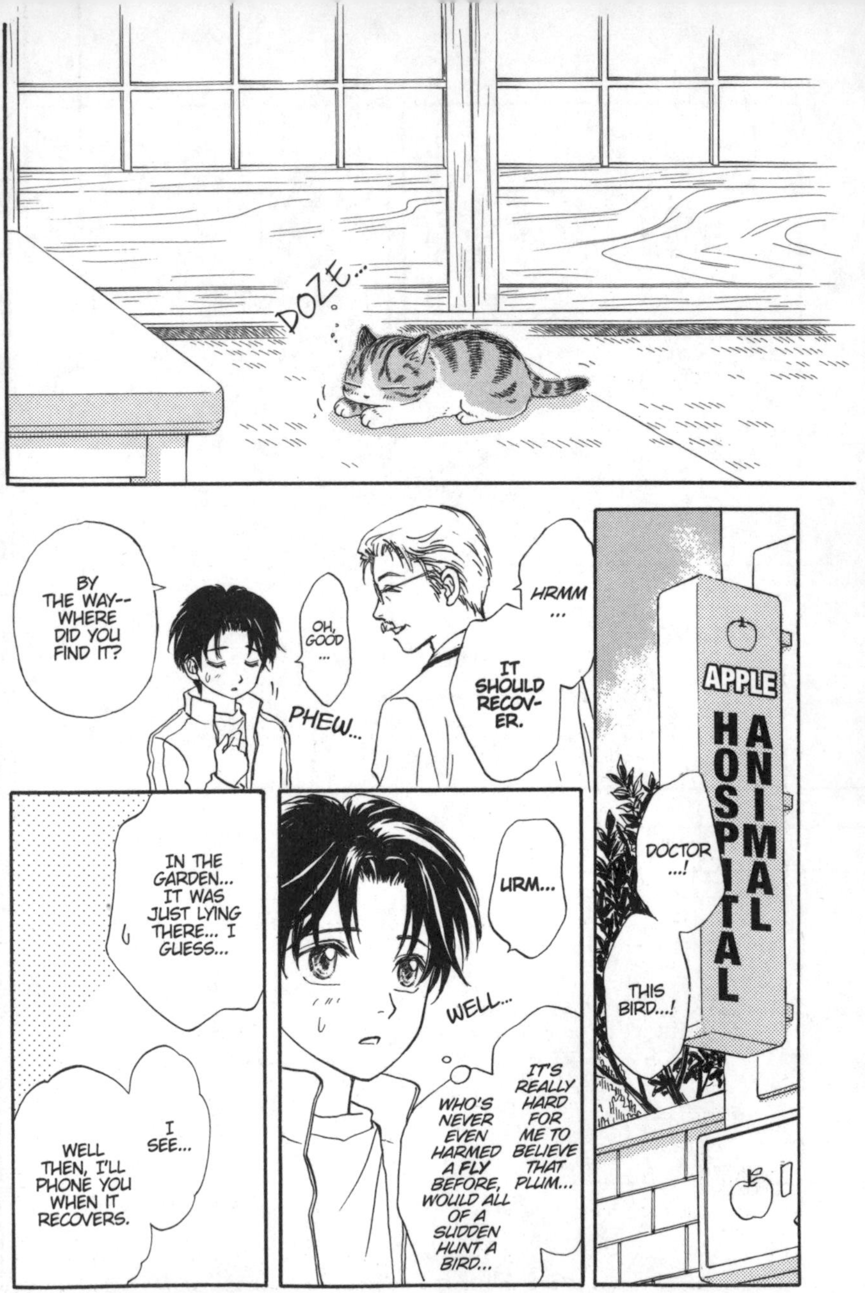
DOZE...
APPLE ANIMAL HOSPITAL
DOCTOR ...!
THIS BIRD...!
HRMM ...
IT SHOULD RECOVER.
OH, GOOD ...
PHEW...
BY THE WAY-- WHERE DID YOU FIND IT?
URM...
WELL...
IT'S REALLY HARD FOR ME TO BELIEVE THAT PLUM...
WHO'S NEVER EVEN HARMED A FLY BEFORE, WOULD ALL OF A SUDDEN HUNT A BIRD...
IN THE GARDEN... IT WAS JUST LYING THERE... I GUESS...
I SEE...
WELL THEN, I'LL PHONE YOU WHEN IT RECOVERS.

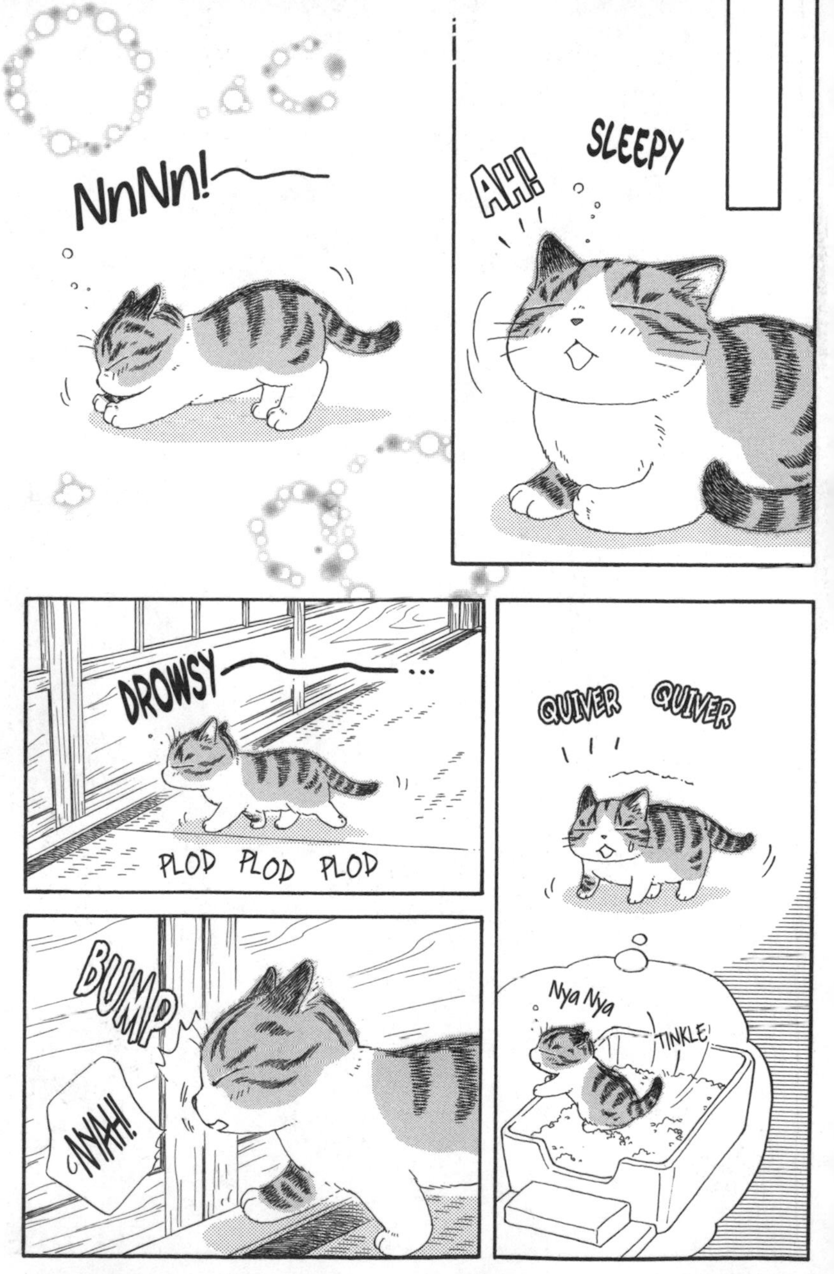
SLEEPY
AH!
NnNn!
QUIVER QUIVER
TINKLE
Nya Nya
DROWSY...
PLOD PLOD PLOD
BUMP
NYAH!

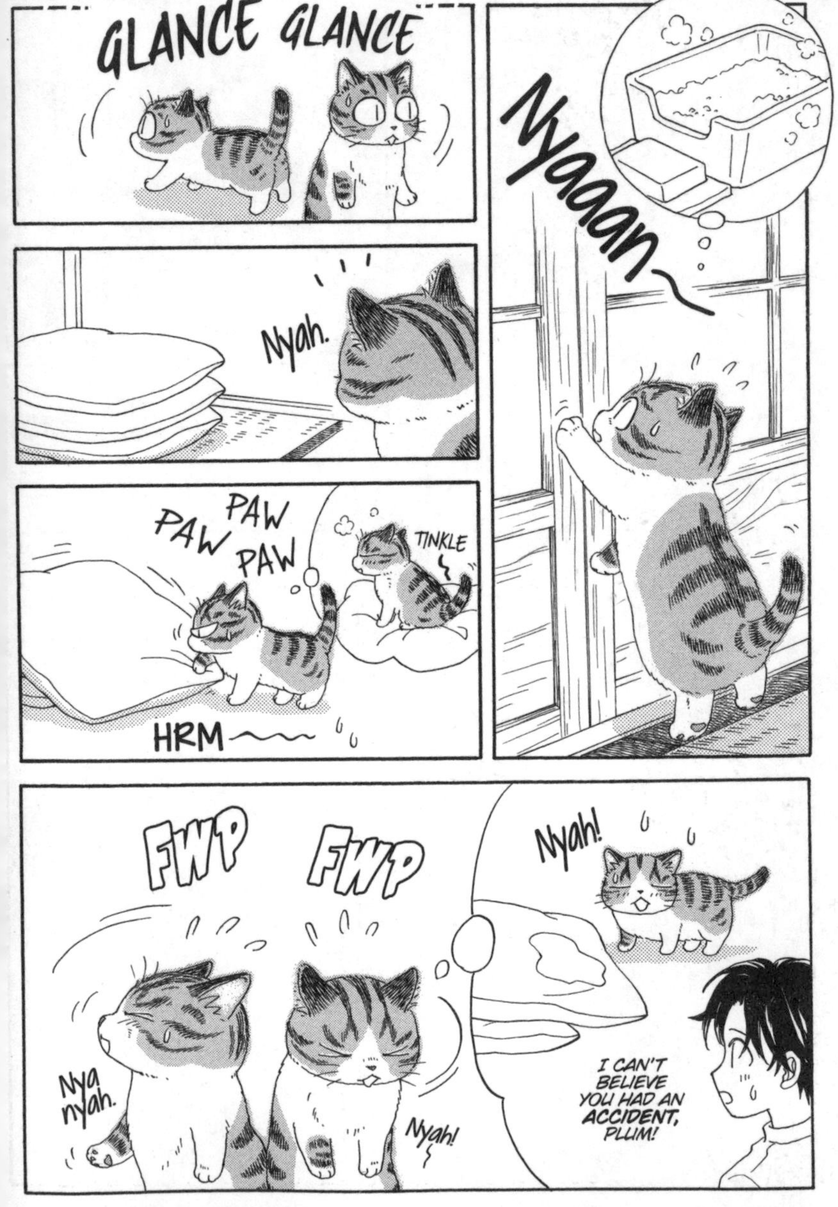
Nyaaan~
GLANCE GLANCE
Nyah.
PAW PAW PAW
TINKLE
HRM
Nyah!
FWP FWP
I CAN'T BELIEVE YOU HAD AN ACCIDENT, PLUM!
Nyah!
Nya nyah.

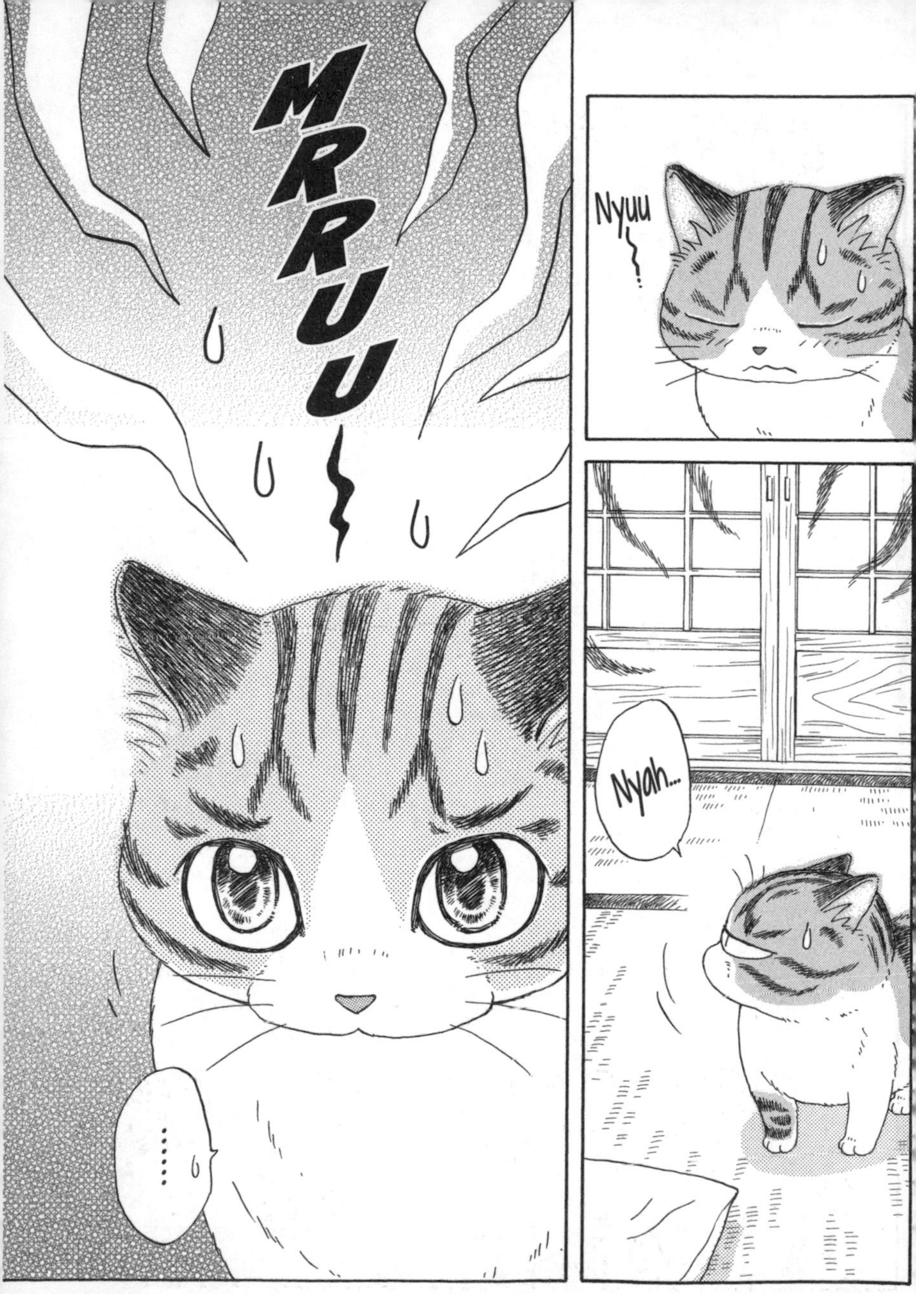
Nyuu
Nyah...
MRRUU
......

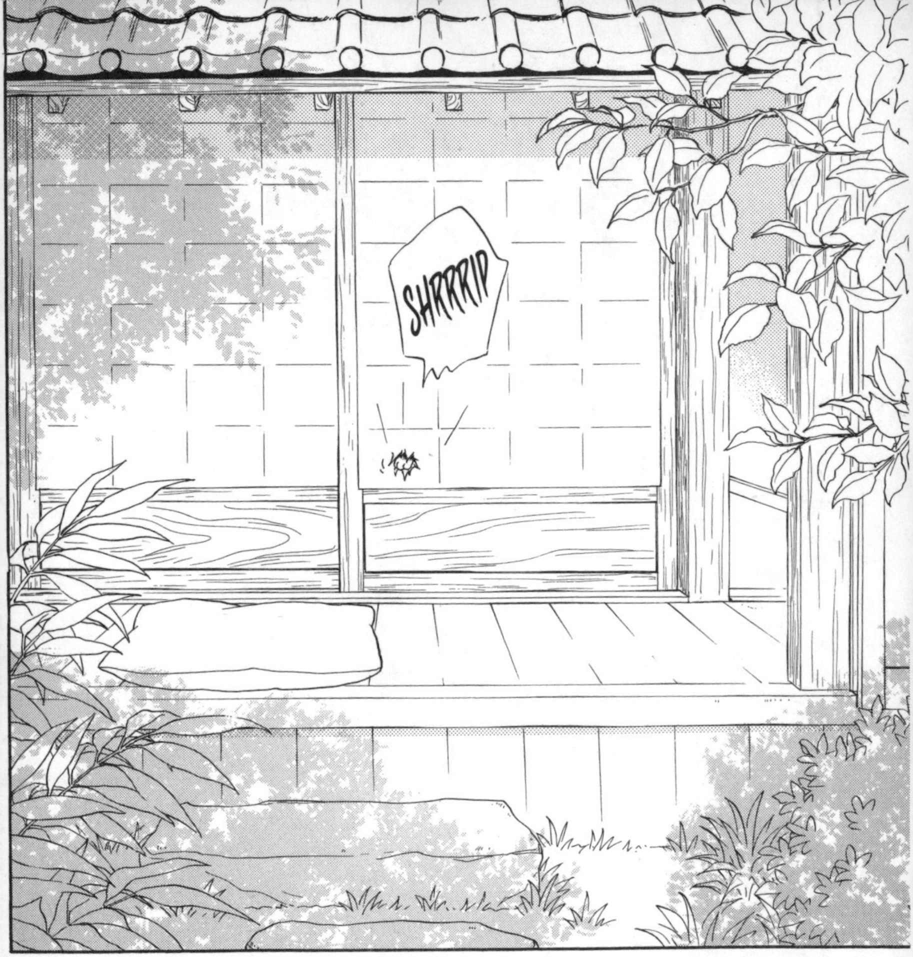
SHRRRIP

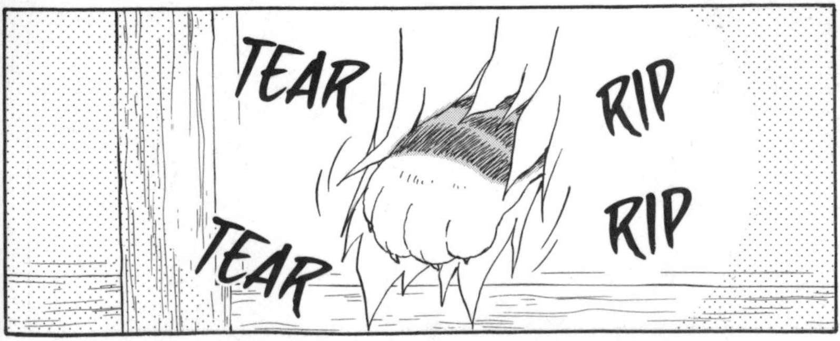
RIP
TEAR
RIP
TEAR

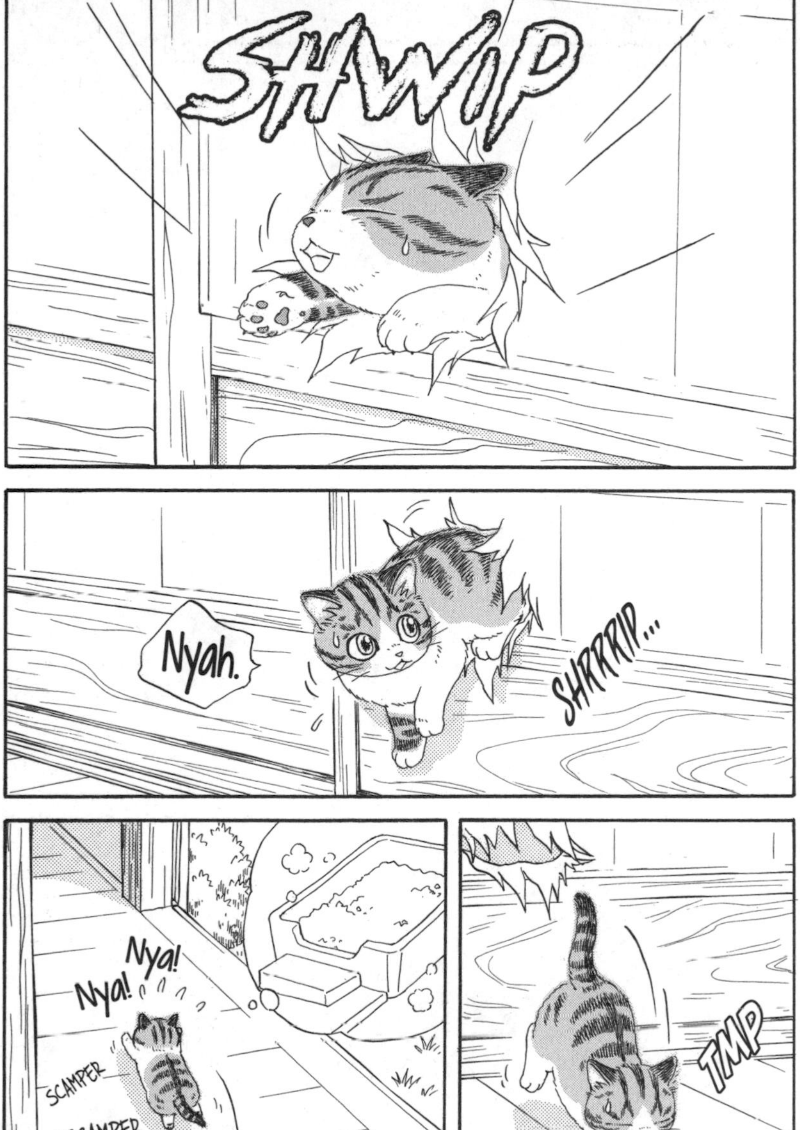
SHWIP
SHRRRIP...
Nyah.
TMP
Nya!
Nya!
SCAMPER
SCAMPER
SCAMPER

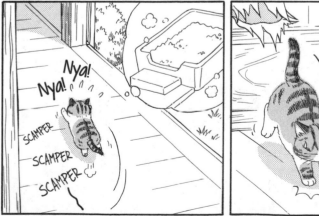

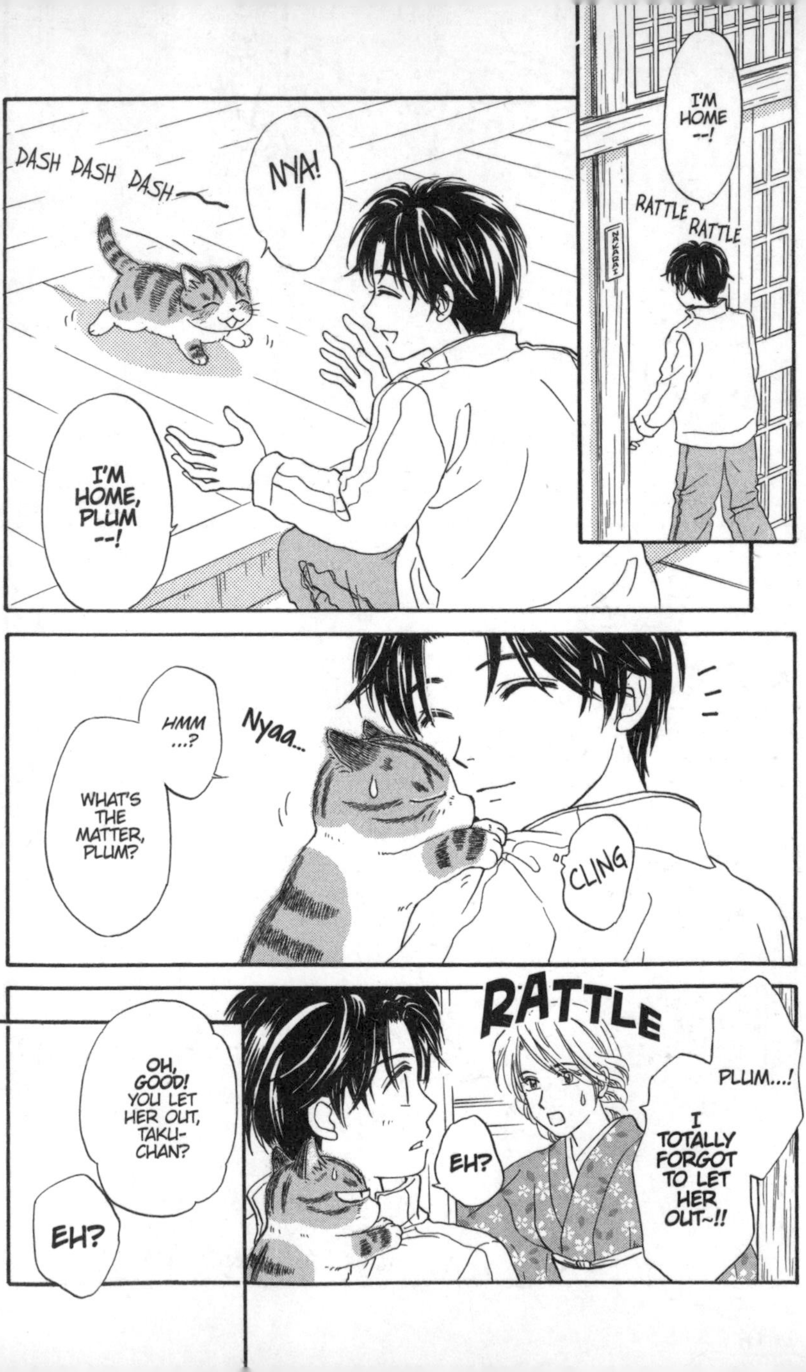
I'M HOME --!
RATTLE RATTLE
NAKARAI
NYA!
DASH DASH DASH
I'M HOME, PLUM --!
Nyaa...
CLING
HMM ...?
WHAT'S THE MATTER, PLUM?
RATTLE
PLUM...!
I TOTALLY FORGOT TO LET HER OUT~!!
EH?
OH, GOOD! YOU LET HER OUT, TAKU-CHAN?
EH?

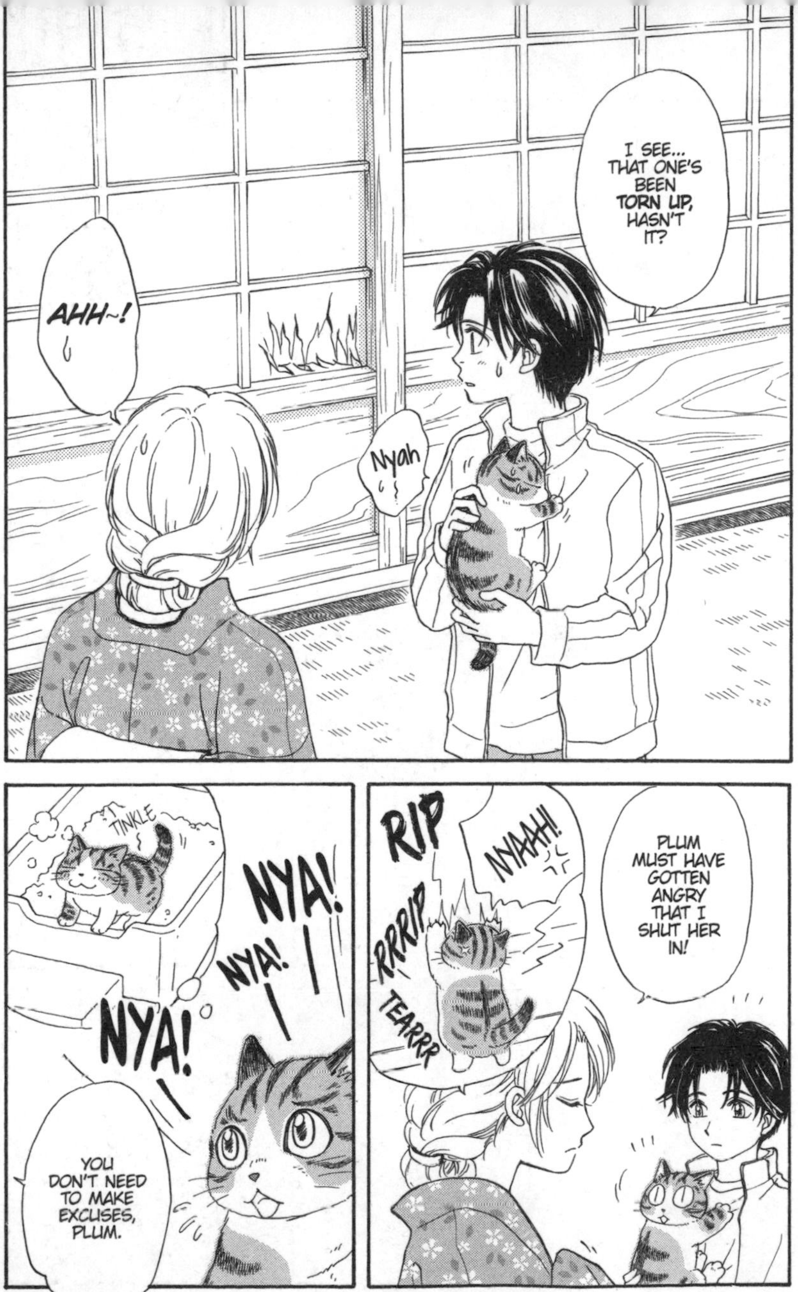
I SEE... THAT ONE'S BEEN TORN UP, HASN'T IT?
AHH~!
Nyah
PLUM MUST HAVE GOTTEN ANGRY THAT I SHUT HER IN!
NYAAH!
RIP
RRRRIP
TEARRR
TINKLE
NYA!
NYA!
NYA!
YOU DON'T NEED TO MAKE EXCUSES, PLUM.

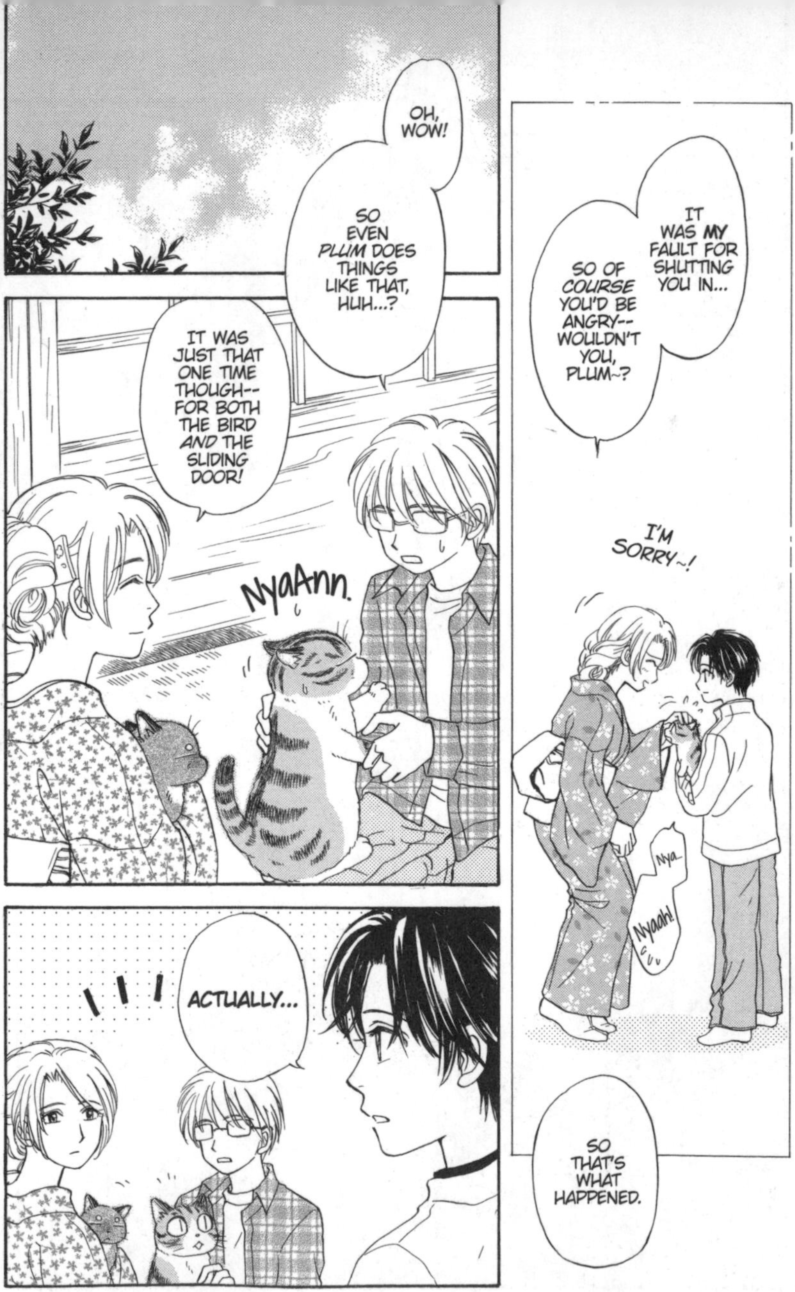
IT WAS MY FAULT FOR SHUTTING YOU IN...
SO OF COURSE YOU'D BE ANGRY-- WOULDN'T YOU, PLUM~?
I'M SORRY~!
Nya...
Nyaah!
SO THAT'S WHAT HAPPENED.
OH, WOW!
SO EVEN PLUM DOES THINGS LIKE THAT, HUH...?
IT WAS JUST THAT ONE TIME THOUGH-- FOR BOTH THE BIRD AND THE SLIDING DOOR!
NyaAnn.
ACTUALLY...

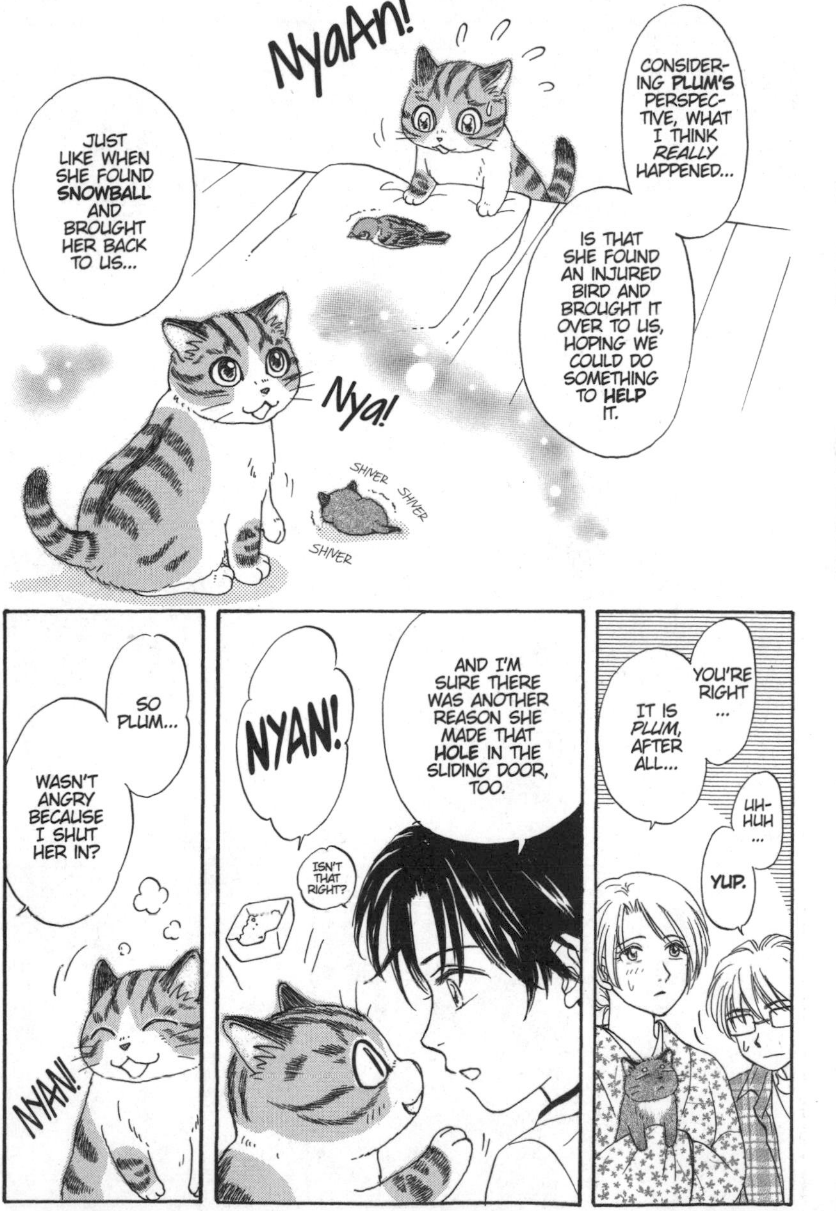
CONSIDERING PLUM'S PERSPECTIVE, WHAT I THINK REALLY HAPPENED...
NyaAn!
IS THAT SHE FOUND AN INJURED BIRD AND BROUGHT IT OVER TO US, HOPING WE COULD DO SOMETHING TO HELP IT.
JUST LIKE WHEN SHE FOUND SNOWBALL AND BROUGHT HER BACK TO US...
Nya!
SHIVER SHIVER
SHIVER
YOU'RE RIGHT ...
IT IS PLUM, AFTER ALL...
UH-HUH ...
YUP.
AND I'M SURE THERE WAS ANOTHER REASON SHE MADE THAT HOLE IN THE SLIDING DOOR, TOO.
NYAN!
ISN'T THAT RIGHT?
SO PLUM...
WASN'T ANGRY BECAUSE I SHUT HER IN?
NYAN!

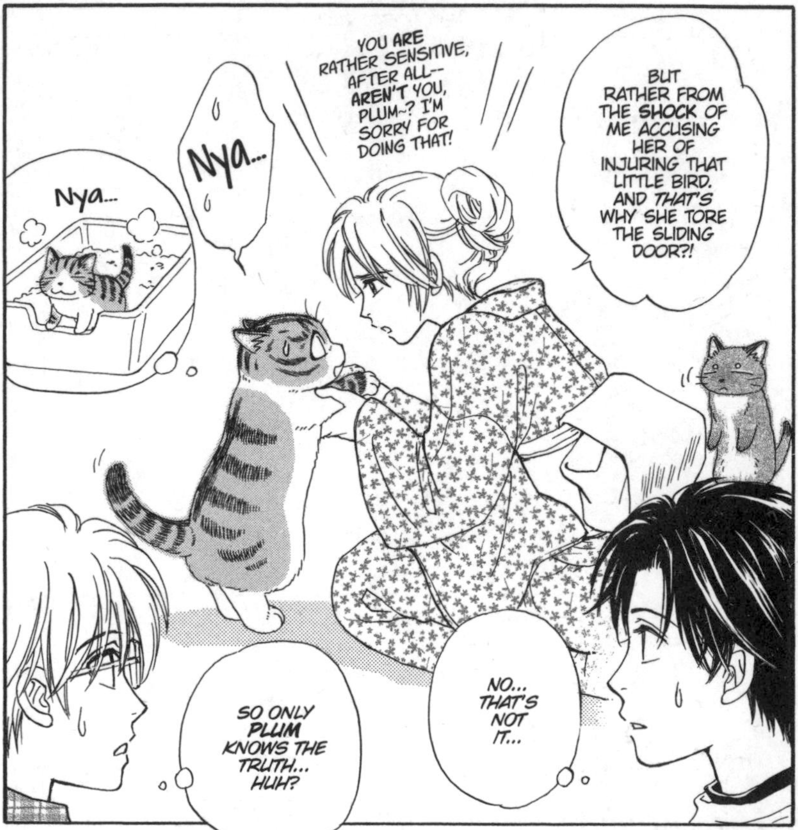
BUT RATHER FROM THE SHOCK OF ME ACCUSING HER OF INJURING THAT LITTLE BIRD. AND THAT'S WHY SHE TORE THE SLIDING DOOR?!
YOU ARE RATHER SENSITIVE, AFTER ALL-- AREN'T YOU, PLUM~? I'M SORRY FOR DOING THAT!
Nya...
Nya...
NO... THAT'S NOT IT...
SO ONLY PLUM KNOWS THE TRUTH... HUH?

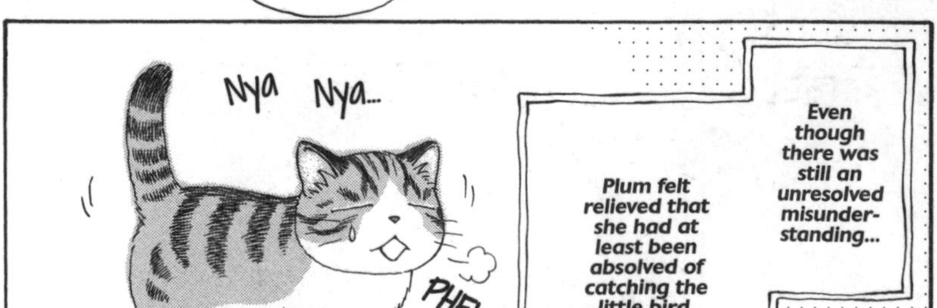
Even though there was still an unresolved misunder-standing...
Plum felt relieved that she had at least been absolved of catching the little bird.
PHEW...
Nya Nya...

THE END

The Untearable Sliding Paper Door

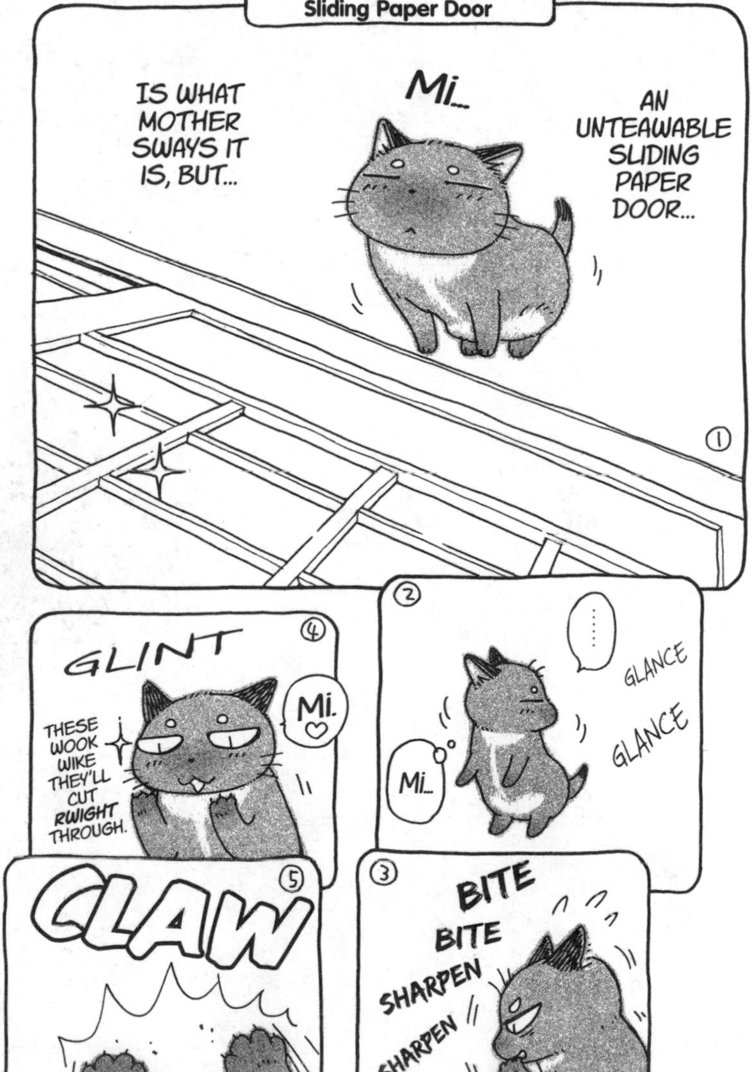
AN UNTEAWABLE SLIDING PAPER DOOR...
Mi...
IS WHAT MOTHER SWAYS IT IS, BUT...
......
GLANCE
GLANCE
Mi...
BITE
BITE
SHARPEN
SHARPEN
Mi. ♡
GLINT
THESE WOOK WIKE THEY'LL CUT RWIGHT THROUGH.
CLAW

Continued in three pages!

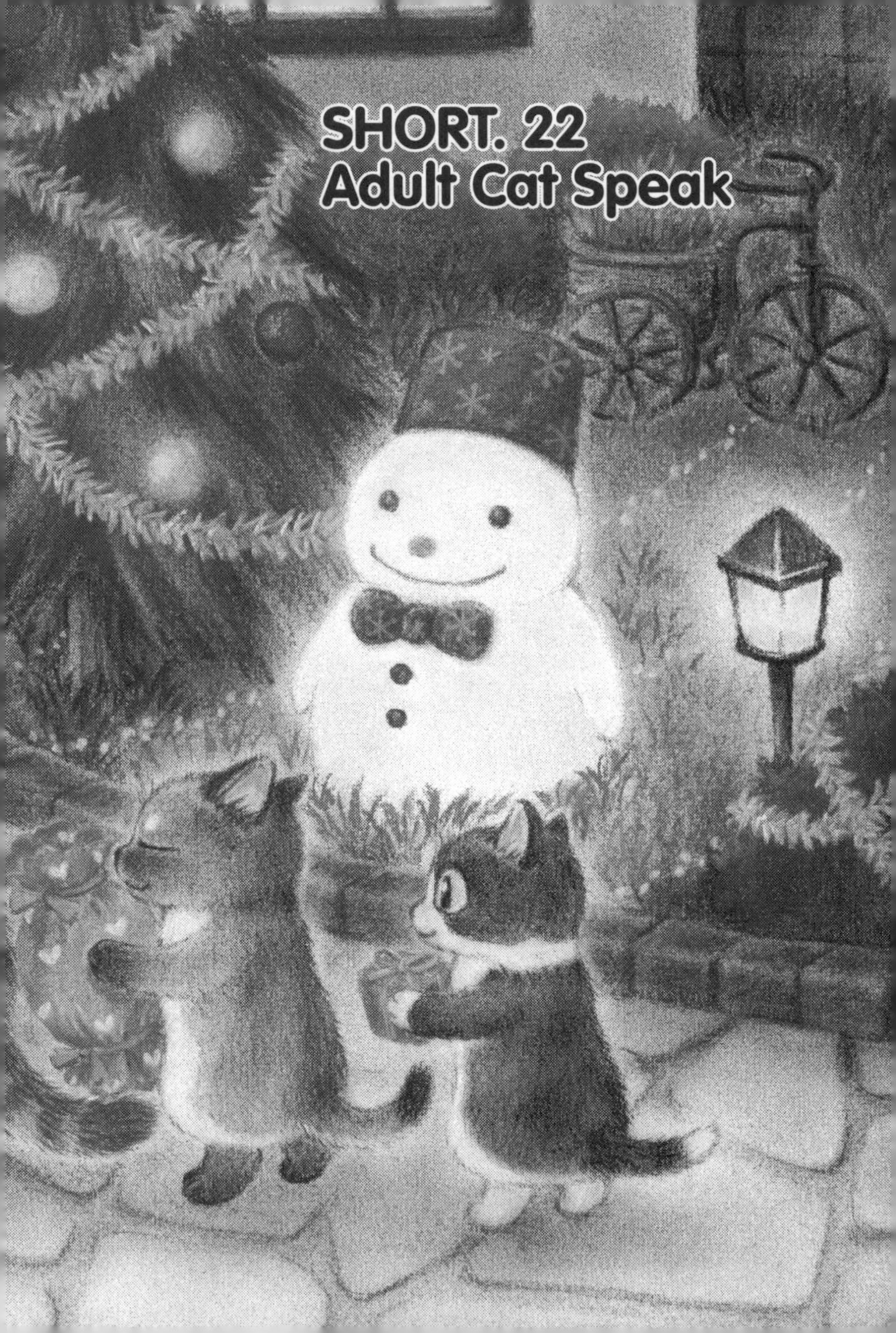
SHORT. 22
Adult Cat Speak

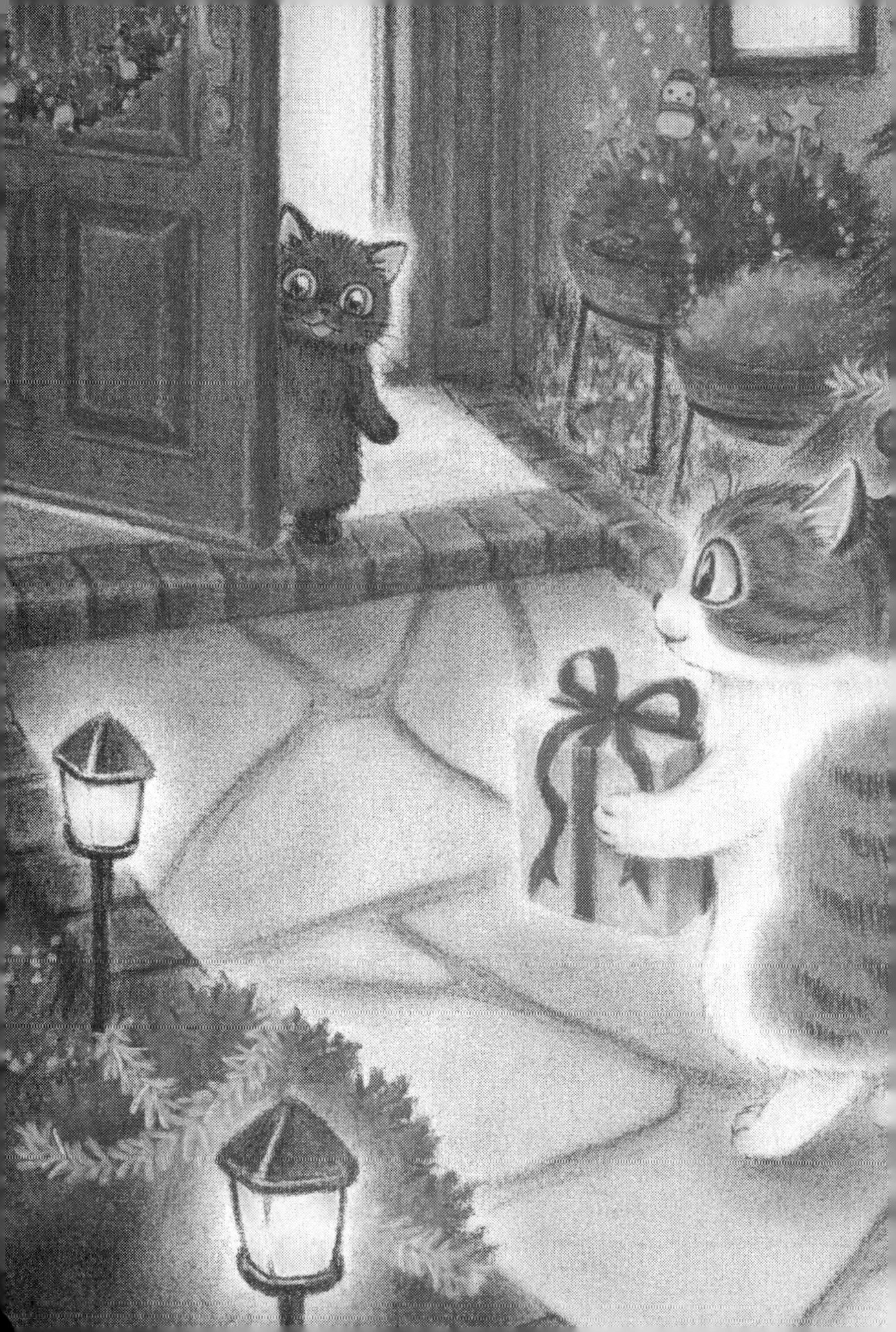

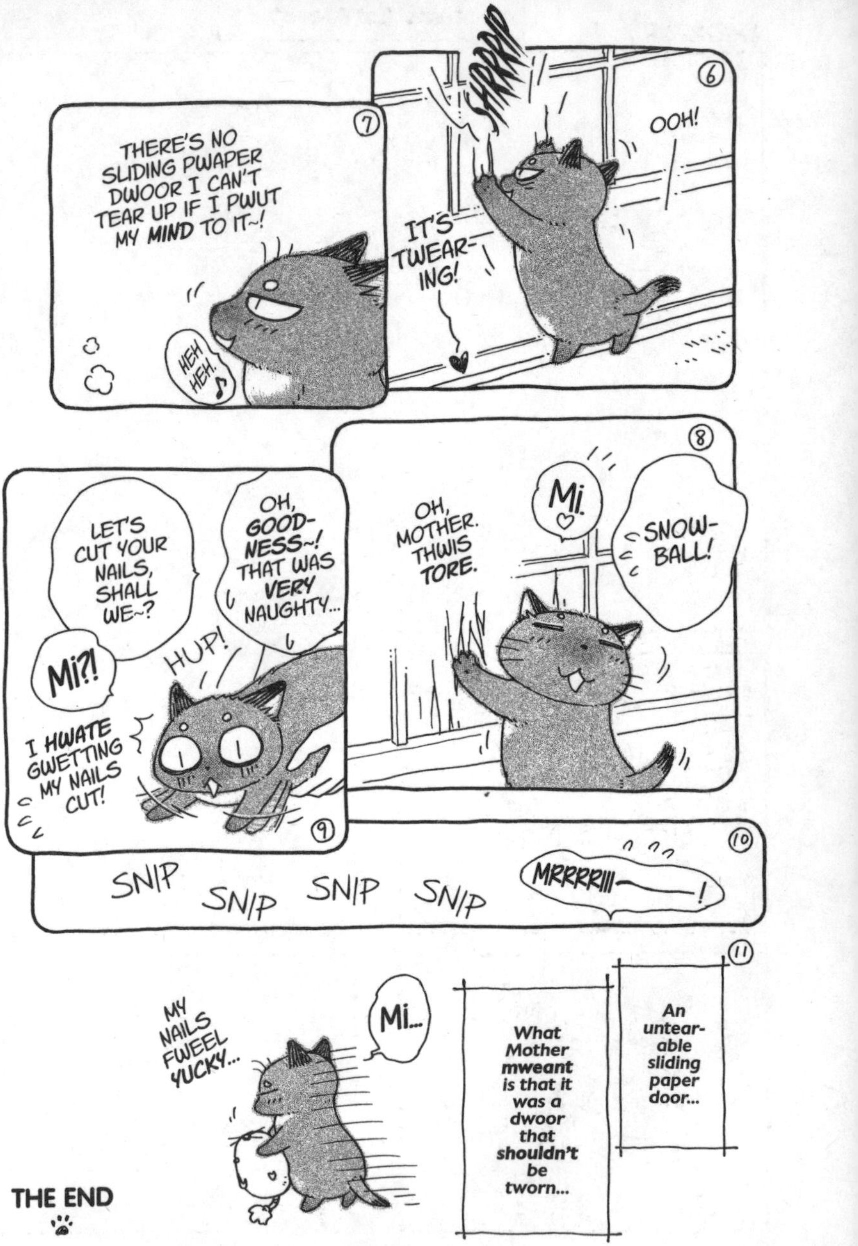
SHRRRP
OOH!
IT'S TWEARING!
THERE'S NO SLIDING PWAPER DWOOR I CAN'T TEAR UP IF I PWUT MY **MIND** TO IT~!
HEH HEH. ♪
SNOWBALL!
Mi. ♡
OH, MOTHER. THWIS **TORE**.
OH, **GOODNESS**~! THAT WAS **VERY** NAUGHTY...
LET'S CUT YOUR NAILS, SHALL WE~?
HUP!
Mi?!
I **HWATE** GWETTING MY NAILS CUT!
MRRRRIII———!
SNIP
SNIP
SNIP
SNIP
An untearable sliding paper door...
What Mother mweant is that it was a dwoor that shouldn't be tworn...
Mi...
MY NAILS FWEEL **YUCKY**...
THE END

SHORT.22

"Adult Cat Speak"

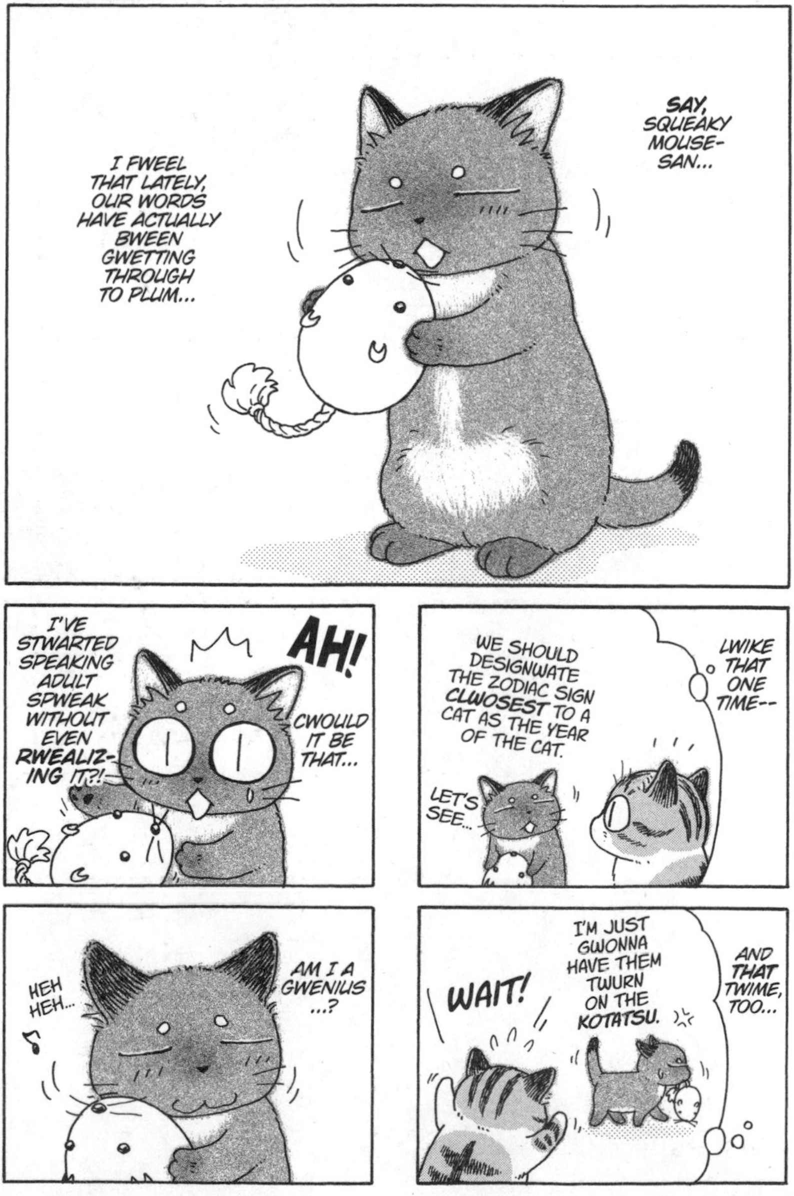
SAY, SQUEAKY MOUSE-SAN...
I FWEEL THAT LATELY, OUR WORDS HAVE ACTUALLY BWEEN GWETTING THROUGH TO PLUM...
LWIKE THAT ONE TIME--
WE SHOULD DESIGNWATE THE ZODIAC SIGN CLWOSEST TO A CAT AS THE YEAR OF THE CAT.
LET'S SEE...
AH!
CWOULD IT BE THAT...
I'VE STWARTED SPEAKING ADULT SPWEAK WITHOUT EVEN RWEALIZING IT?!
AND THAT TWIME, TOO...
I'M JUST GWONNA HAVE THEM TWURN ON THE KOTATSU.
WAIT!
AM I A GWENIUS ...?
HEH HEH...

Snowball-sensei

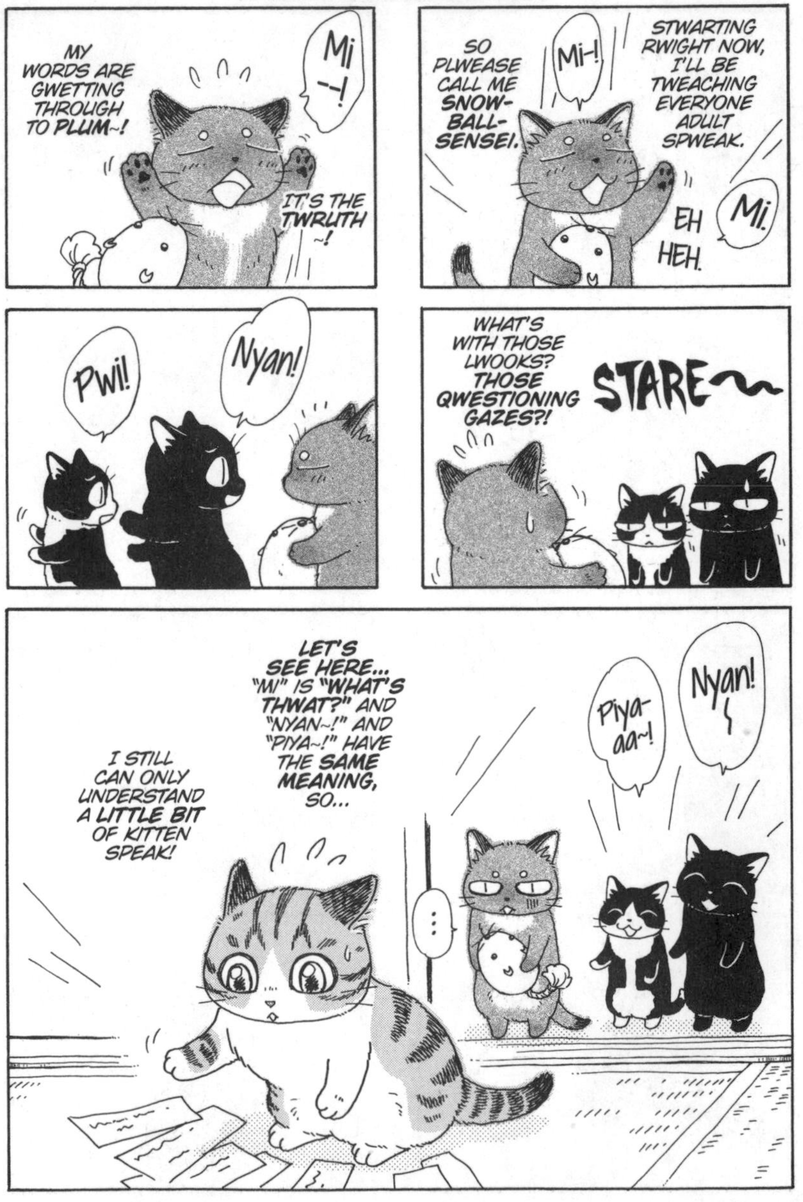
STWARTING RWIGHT NOW, I'LL BE TWEACHING EVERYONE ADULT SPWEAK.
Mi-!
SO PLWEASE CALL ME SNOW-BALL-SENSEI.
Mi.
EH HEH.
Mi --!
MY WORDS ARE GWETTING THROUGH TO PLUM~!
IT'S THE TWRUTH ~!
STARE~
WHAT'S WITH THOSE LWOOKS? THOSE QWESTIONING GAZES?!
Nyan!
Pwi!
Nyan!
Piya-aa~!
LET'S SEE HERE... "MI" IS "WHAT'S THWAT?" AND "NYAN~!" AND "PIYA~!" HAVE THE SAME MEANING, SO...
I STILL CAN ONLY UNDERSTAND A LITTLE BIT OF KITTEN SPEAK!
...

I Will Try My Bwest

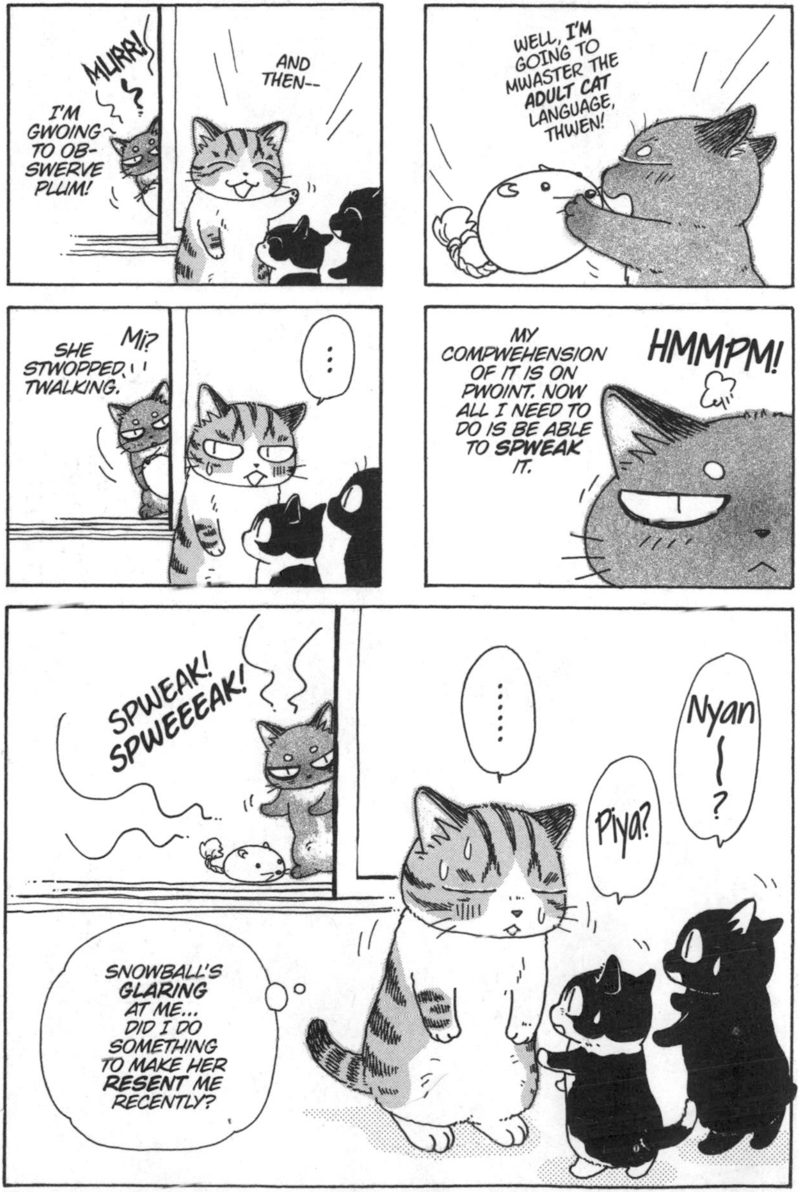
WELL, I'M GOING TO MWASTER THE ADULT CAT LANGUAGE, THWEN!
AND THEN--
MURR!
I'M GWOING TO OB-SWERVE PLUM!
HMMPM!
MY COMPWEHENSION OF IT IS ON PWOINT. NOW ALL I NEED TO DO IS BE ABLE TO SPWEAK IT.
...
Mi?
SHE STWOPPED TWALKING.
Nyan ~ ?
Piya?
......
SPWEAK! SPWEEEAK!
SNOWBALL'S GLARING AT ME... DID I DO SOMETHING TO MAKE HER RESENT ME RECENTLY?

I Will Twy Harder

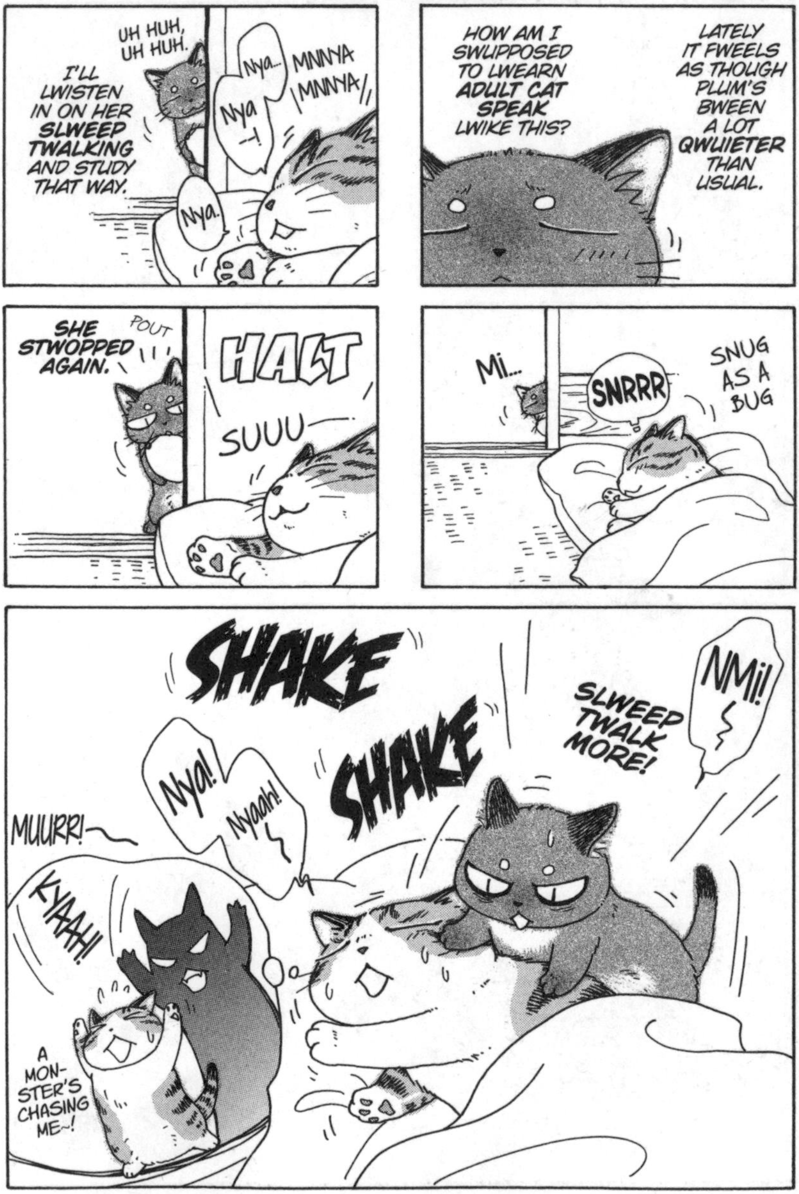

LATELY IT FWEELS AS THOUGH PLUM'S BWEEN A LOT QWUIETER THAN USUAL.
HOW AM I SWUPPOSED TO LWEARN ADULT CAT SPEAK LWIKE THIS?
MNNYA MNNYA
Nya...
Nya —!
UH HUH, UH HUH.
I'LL LWISTEN IN ON HER SLWEEP TWALKING AND STUDY THAT WAY.
Nya.
SNUG AS A BUG
SNRRR
Mi...
HALT
SUUU
POUT
SHE STWOPPED AGAIN.
NMi!
SLWEEP TWALK MORE!
SHAKE
SHAKE
Nya!
Nyaah!
MUURR!
KYAAH!
A MON-STER'S CHASING ME~!

I Will Twy Evwen Harder

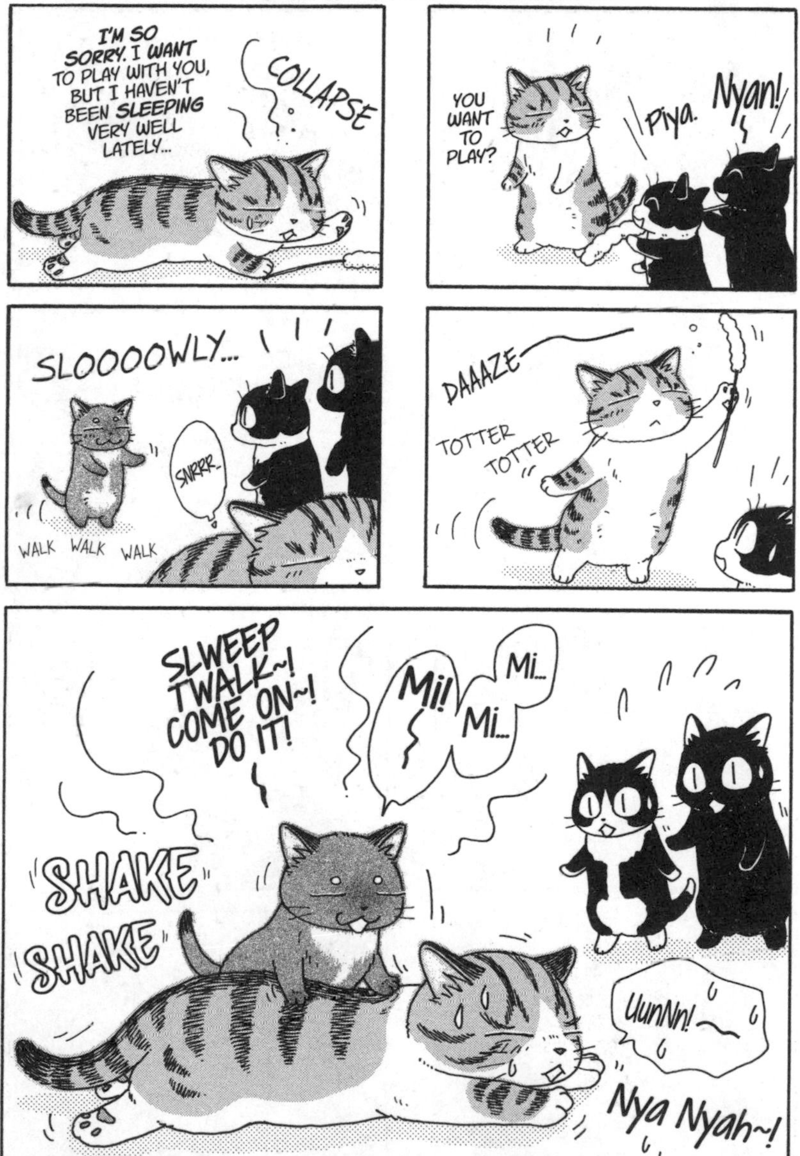
YOU WANT TO PLAY?
Piya.
Nyan!
I'M SO SORRY. I WANT TO PLAY WITH YOU, BUT I HAVEN'T BEEN SLEEPING VERY WELL LATELY...
COLLAPSE
DAAAZE
TOTTER TOTTER
SLOOOOWLY...
SNRRR
WALK WALK WALK
Mi...
Mi...
Mi!
SLWEEP TWALK~! COME ON~! DO IT!
UunNn!~
SHAKE
SHAKE
Nya Nyah~!

Snowball's Feelings

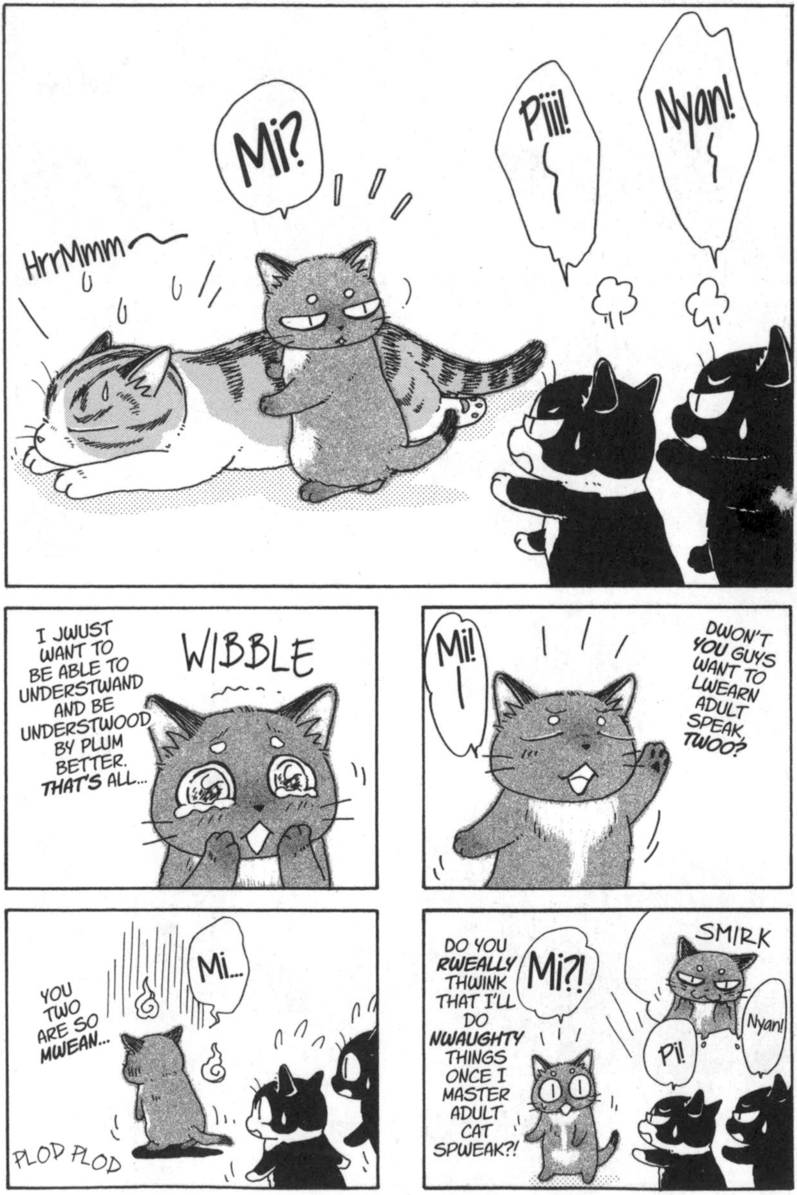

Nyan!
Piii!
Mi?
HrrMmm
Mi!
DWON'T YOU GUYS WANT TO LWEARN ADULT SPEAK, TWOO?
I JWUST WANT TO BE ABLE TO UNDERSTWAND AND BE UNDERSTWOOD BY PLUM BETTER. THAT'S ALL...
WIBBLE
SMIRK
Nyan!
Pi!
Mi?!
DO YOU RWEALLY THWINK THAT I'LL DO NWAUGHTY THINGS ONCE I MASTER ADULT CAT SPWEAK?!
Mi...
YOU TWO ARE SO MWEAN...
PLOD PLOD

Lwet's All Twy Our Bests

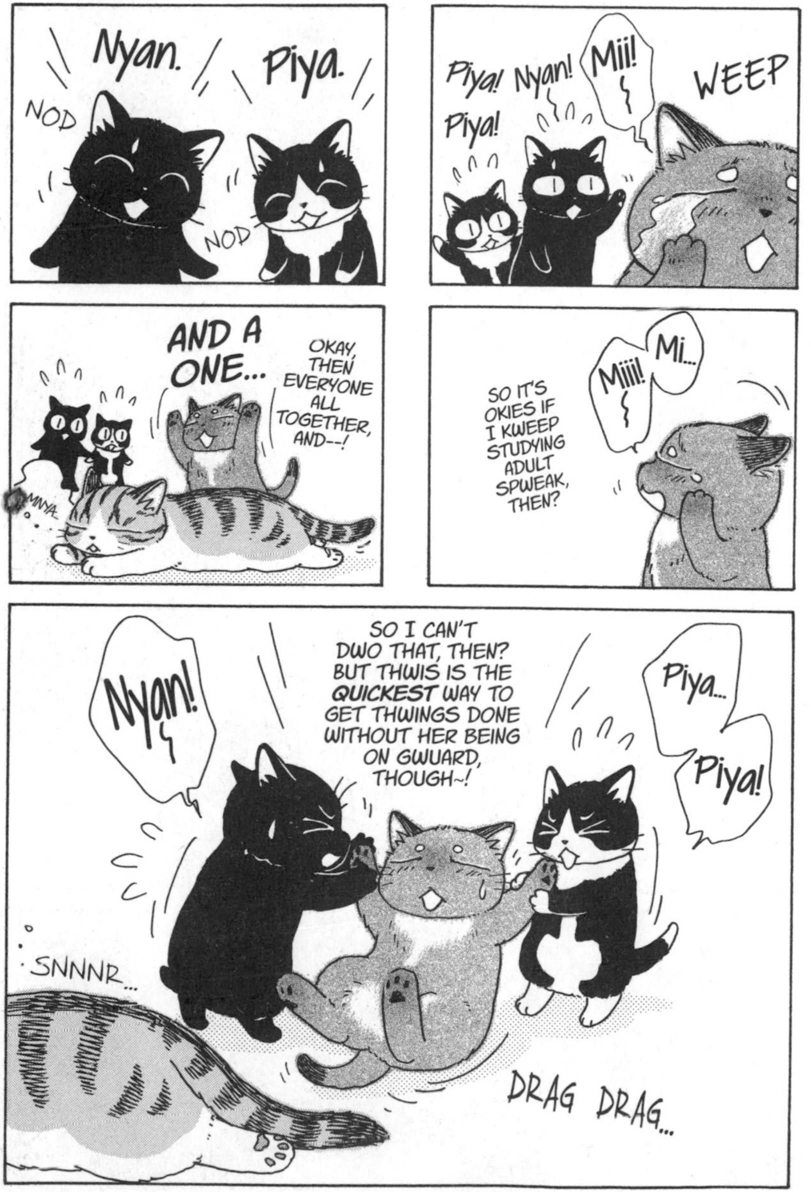
WEEP
Mii!
Nyan!
Piya!
Piya!
Piya.
Nyan.
NOD
NOD
Mi...
Miii!
SO IT'S OKIES IF I KWEEP STUDYING ADULT SPWEAK, THEN?
OKAY, THEN EVERYONE ALL TOGETHER, AND--!
AND A ONE...
Mnya.
Piya...
Piya!
SO I CAN'T DWO THAT, THEN? BUT THWIS IS THE **QUICKEST** WAY TO GET THWINGS DONE WITHOUT HER BEING ON GWUARD, THOUGH~!
Nyan!
SNNNR...
DRAG DRAG...

Snowball's True Feelings

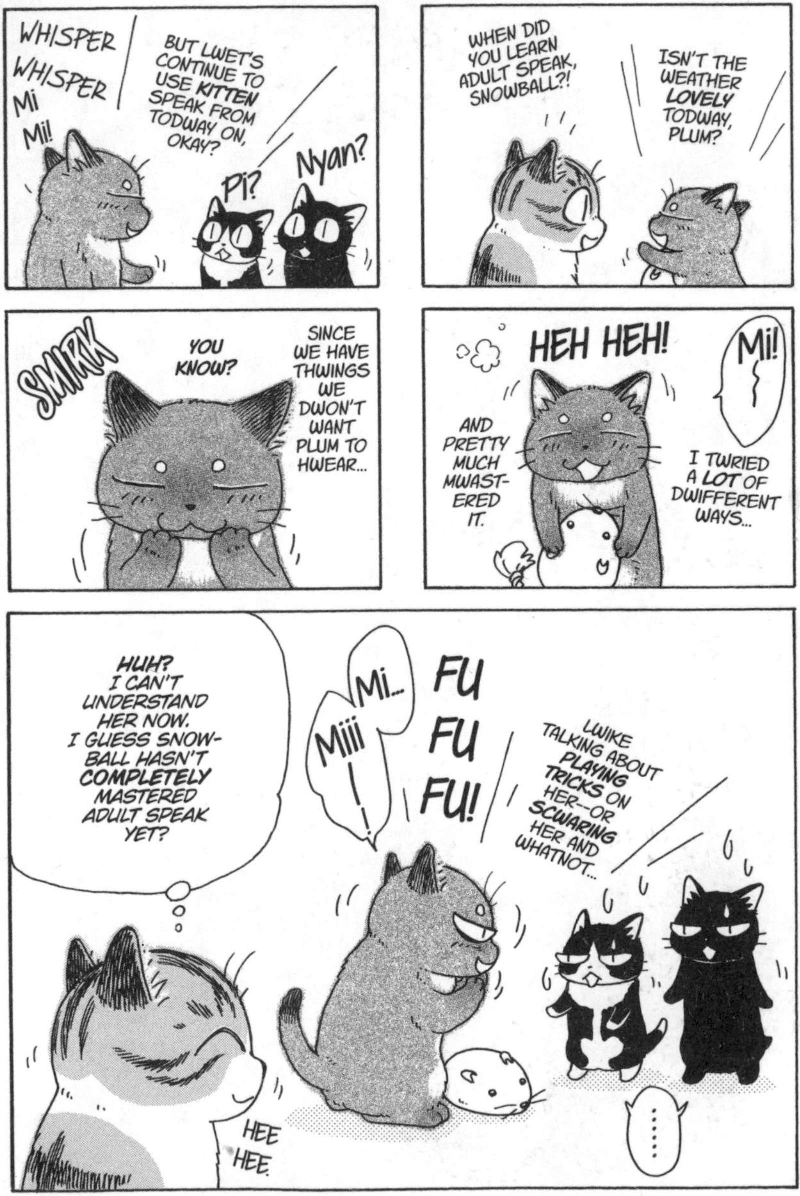
ISN'T THE WEATHER LOVELY TODWAY, PLUM?
WHEN DID YOU LEARN ADULT SPEAK, SNOWBALL?!
BUT LWET'S CONTINUE TO USE KITTEN SPEAK FROM TODWAY ON, OKAY?
WHISPER WHISPER
Mi Mi!
Nyan?
Pi?
Mi!
I TWRIED A LOT OF DWIFFERENT WAYS...
HEH HEH!
AND PRETTY MUCH MWASTERED IT.
SINCE WE HAVE THWINGS WE DWON'T WANT PLUM TO HWEAR...
YOU KNOW?
SMIRK
LWIKE TALKING ABOUT PLAYING TRICKS ON HER--OR SCWARING HER AND WHATNOT...
FU FU FU!
Mi...
Miii!
HUH? I CAN'T UNDERSTAND HER NOW. I GUESS SNOWBALL HASN'T COMPLETELY MASTERED ADULT SPEAK YET?
......
HEE HEE.

THE END

CHAPTER 27
Valentine's Day

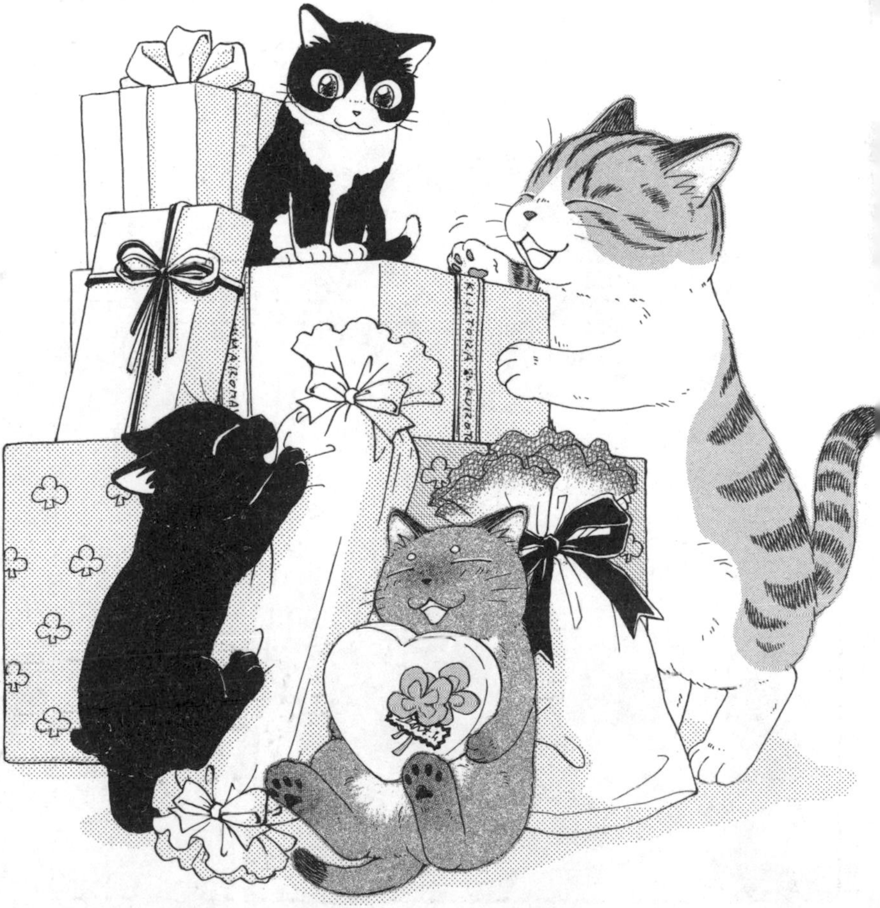

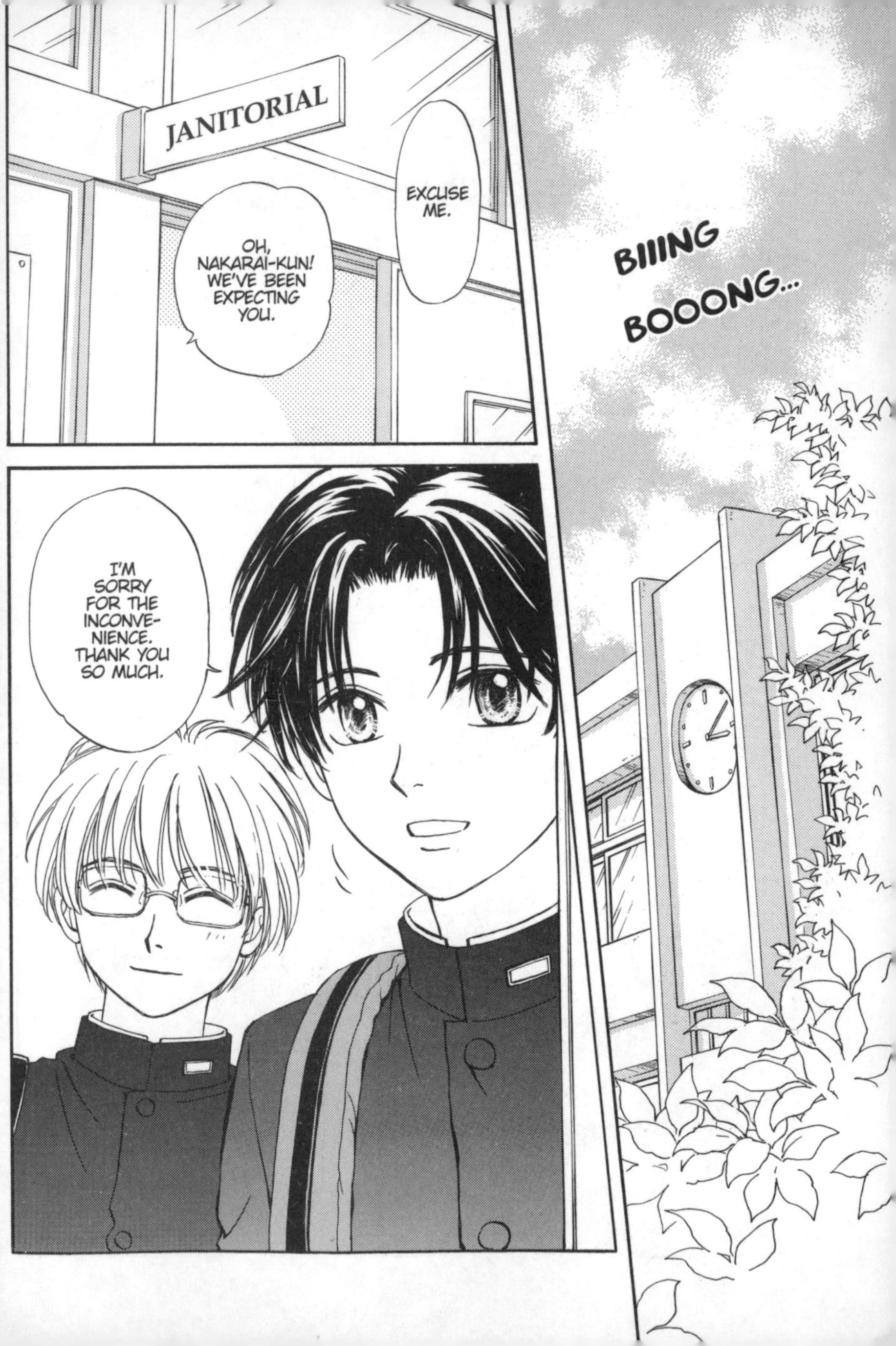
BIIING
BOOONG...
JANITORIAL
EXCUSE ME.
OH, NAKARAI-KUN! WE'VE BEEN EXPECTING YOU.
I'M SORRY FOR THE INCONVE-NIENCE. THANK YOU SO MUCH.

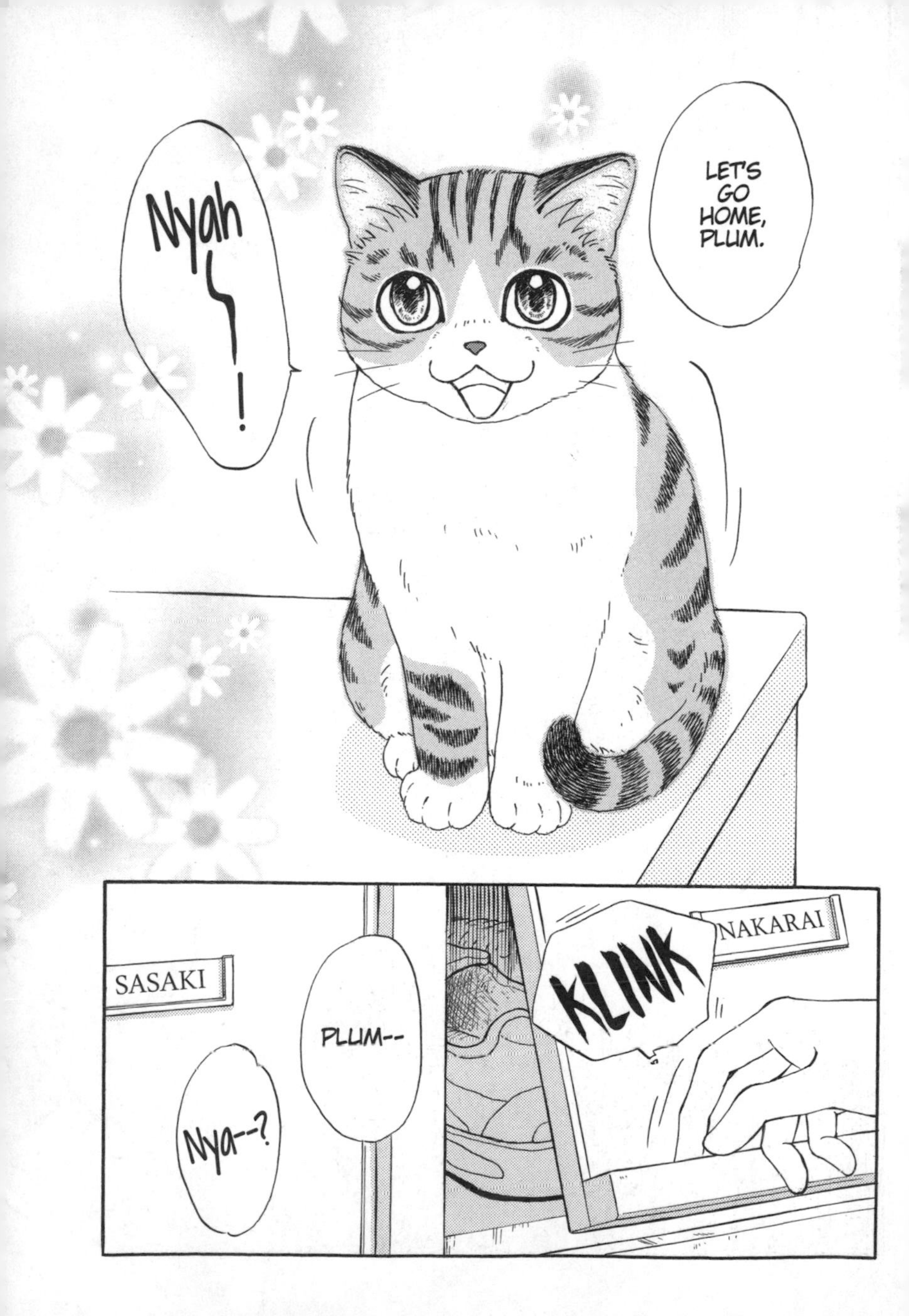
LET'S GO HOME, PLUM.
Nyah~!
KLINK
NAKARAI
PLUM--
SASAKI
Nya--?

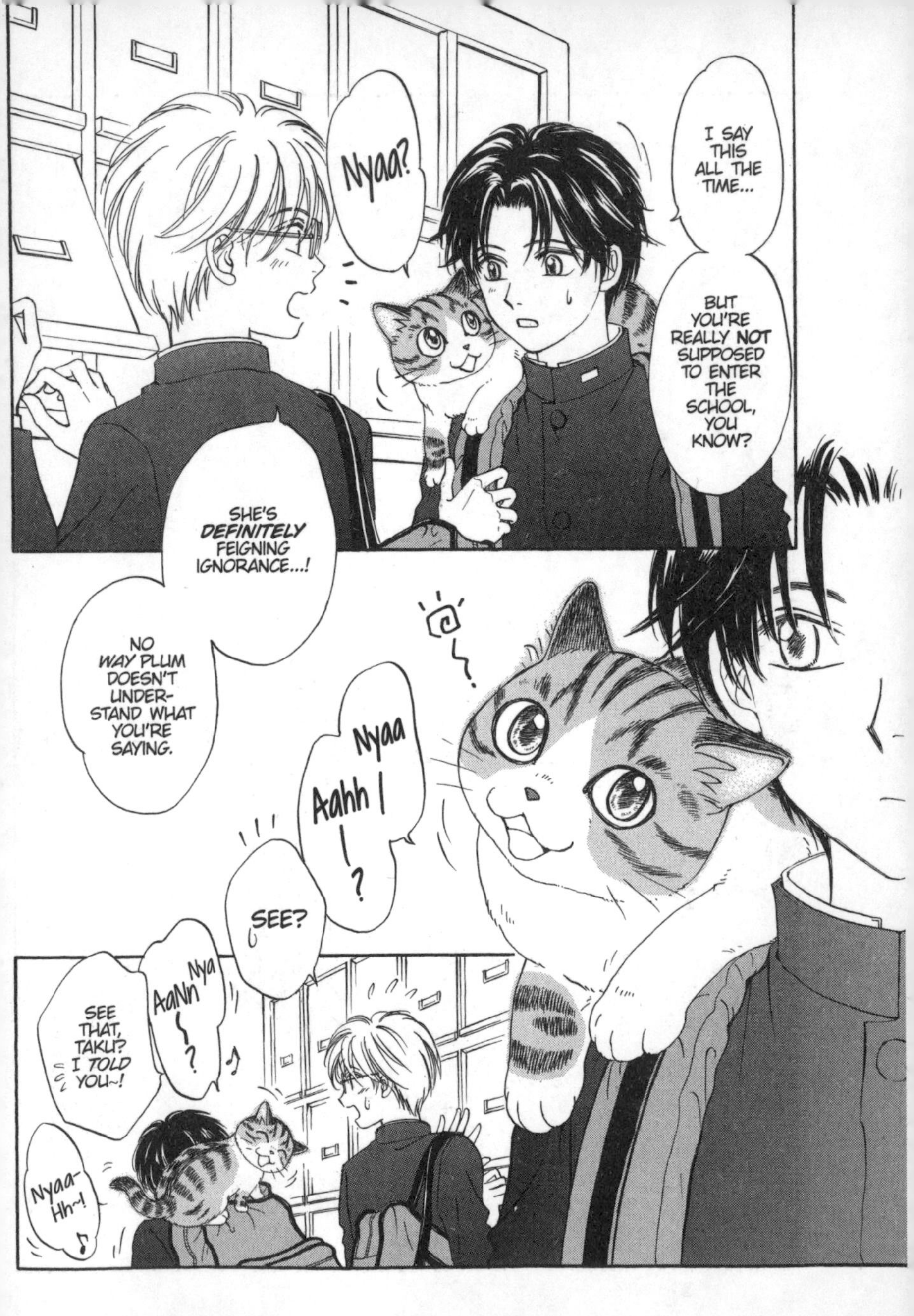
I SAY THIS ALL THE TIME...
BUT YOU'RE REALLY NOT SUPPOSED TO ENTER THE SCHOOL, YOU KNOW?
Nyaa?
SHE'S DEFINITELY FEIGNING IGNORANCE...!
NO WAY PLUM DOESN'T UNDERSTAND WHAT YOU'RE SAYING.
Nyaa Aahh !?
SEE?
Nya AaNn ~?
SEE THAT, TAKU? I TOLD YOU~!
Nyaa-Hh~!

PLUM, DON'T MESS WITH UEHARA LIKE THAT, OKAY?
Nyah!
EH ...?!
SHE WAS MESSING WITH ME?
TMP TMP
PLUUU-UUM.
SO MEAN~!
Nyaha.
BUT SO CUUUTE~!
Nyah...
NYA!

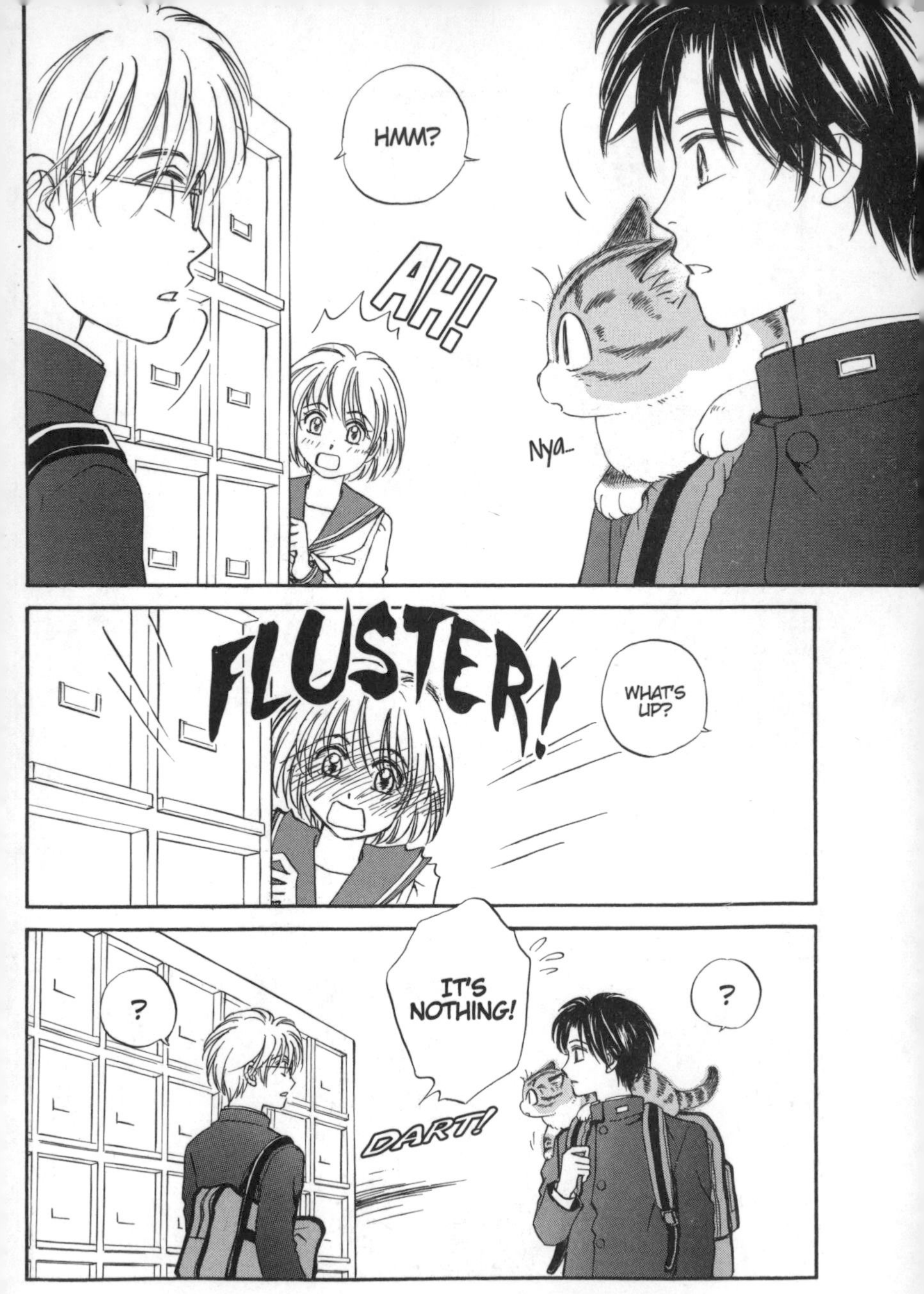
HMM?
AH!
Nya...
WHAT'S UP?
FLUSTER!
?
IT'S NOTHING!
DART!
?

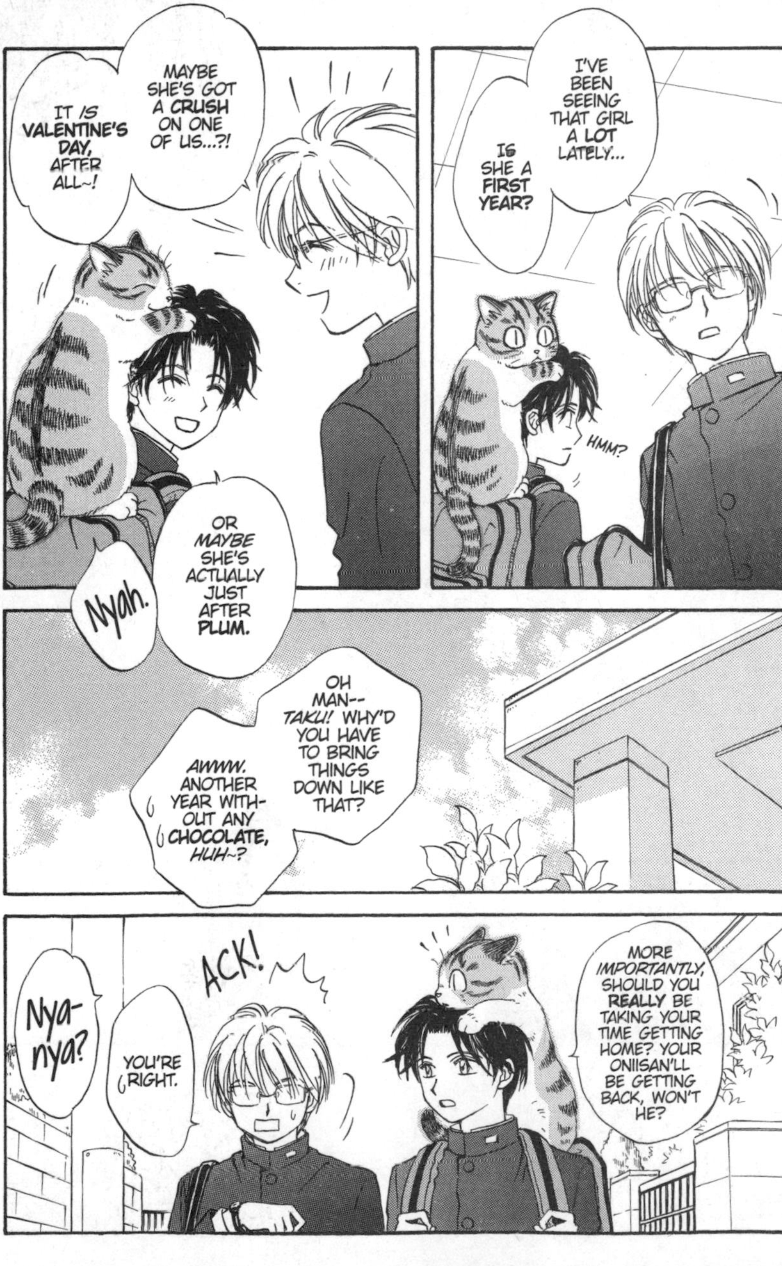
I'VE BEEN SEEING THAT GIRL A LOT LATELY...
IS SHE A FIRST YEAR?
HMM?
MAYBE SHE'S GOT A CRUSH ON ONE OF US...?!
IT IS VALENTINE'S DAY, AFTER ALL~!
OR MAYBE SHE'S ACTUALLY JUST AFTER PLUM.
Nyah.
OH MAN-- TAKU! WHY'D YOU HAVE TO BRING THINGS DOWN LIKE THAT?
AWWW. ANOTHER YEAR WITH-OUT ANY CHOCOLATE, HUH~?
MORE IMPORTANTLY, SHOULD YOU REALLY BE TAKING YOUR TIME GETTING HOME? YOUR ONIISAN'LL BE GETTING BACK, WON'T HE?
ACK!
YOU'RE RIGHT.
Nya-nya?

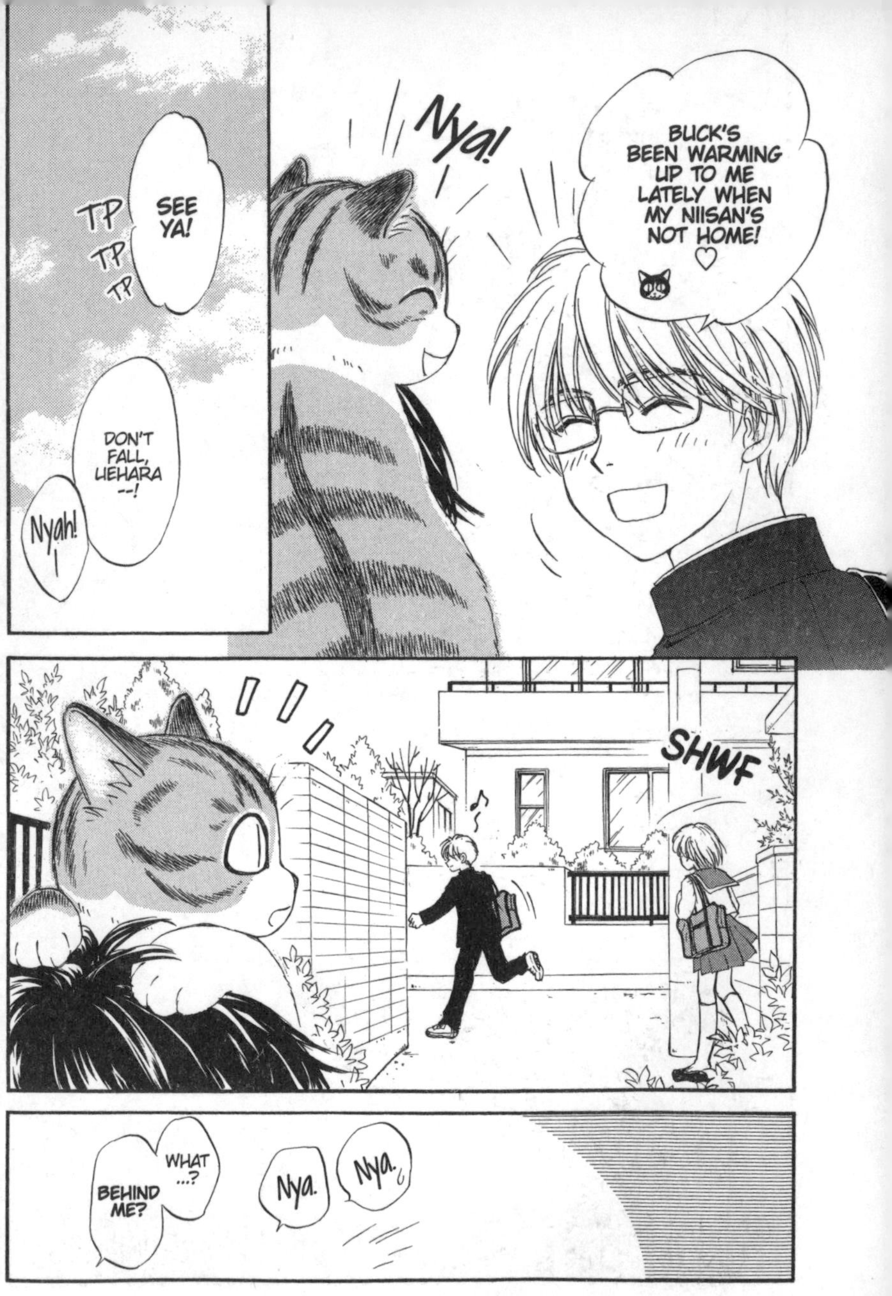
Nya!
BUCK'S BEEN WARMING UP TO ME LATELY WHEN MY NIISAN'S NOT HOME! ♡
SEE YA!
TP TP TP
DON'T FALL, UEHARA --!
Nyah!
SHWF
Nya.
Nya.
WHAT ...?
BEHIND ME?

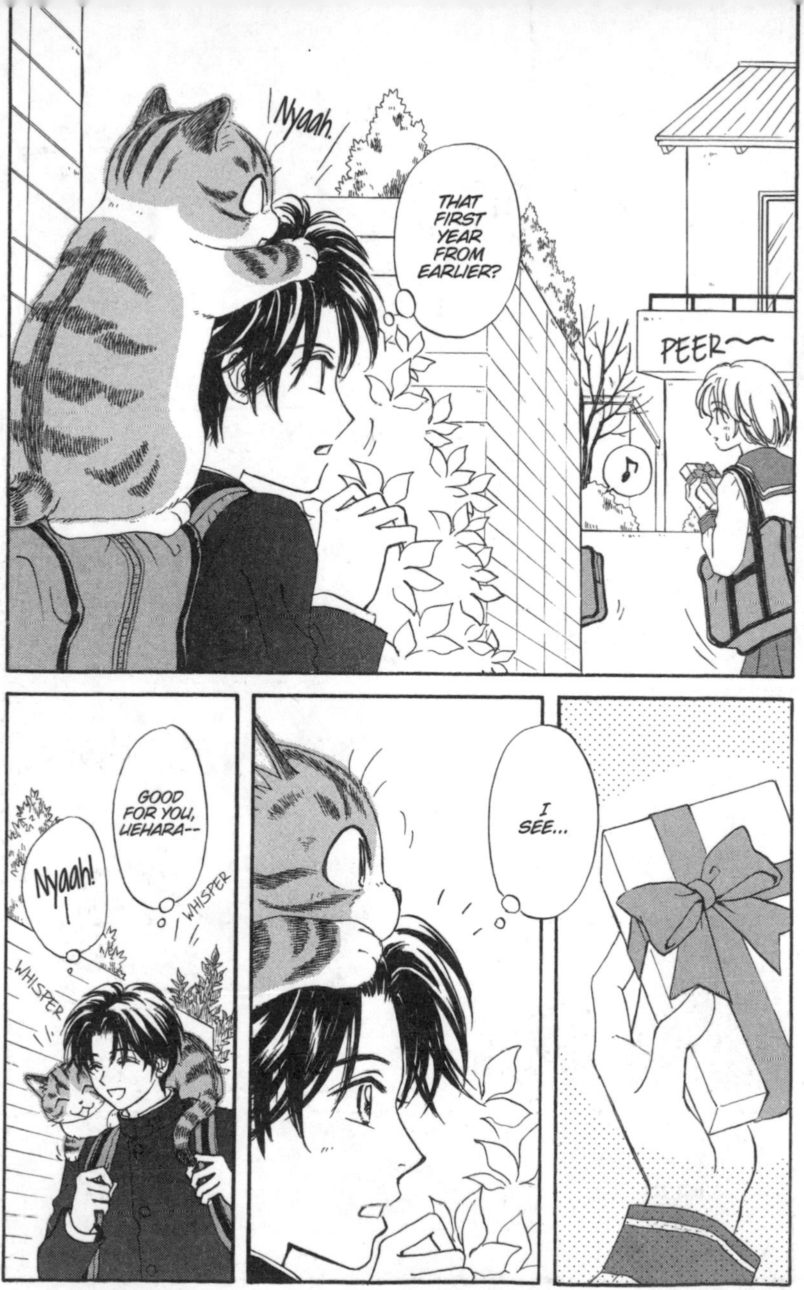
PEER~~
THAT FIRST YEAR FROM EARLIER?
Nyaah.
I SEE...
GOOD FOR YOU, UEHARA--
WHISPER
Nyaah!
WHISPER

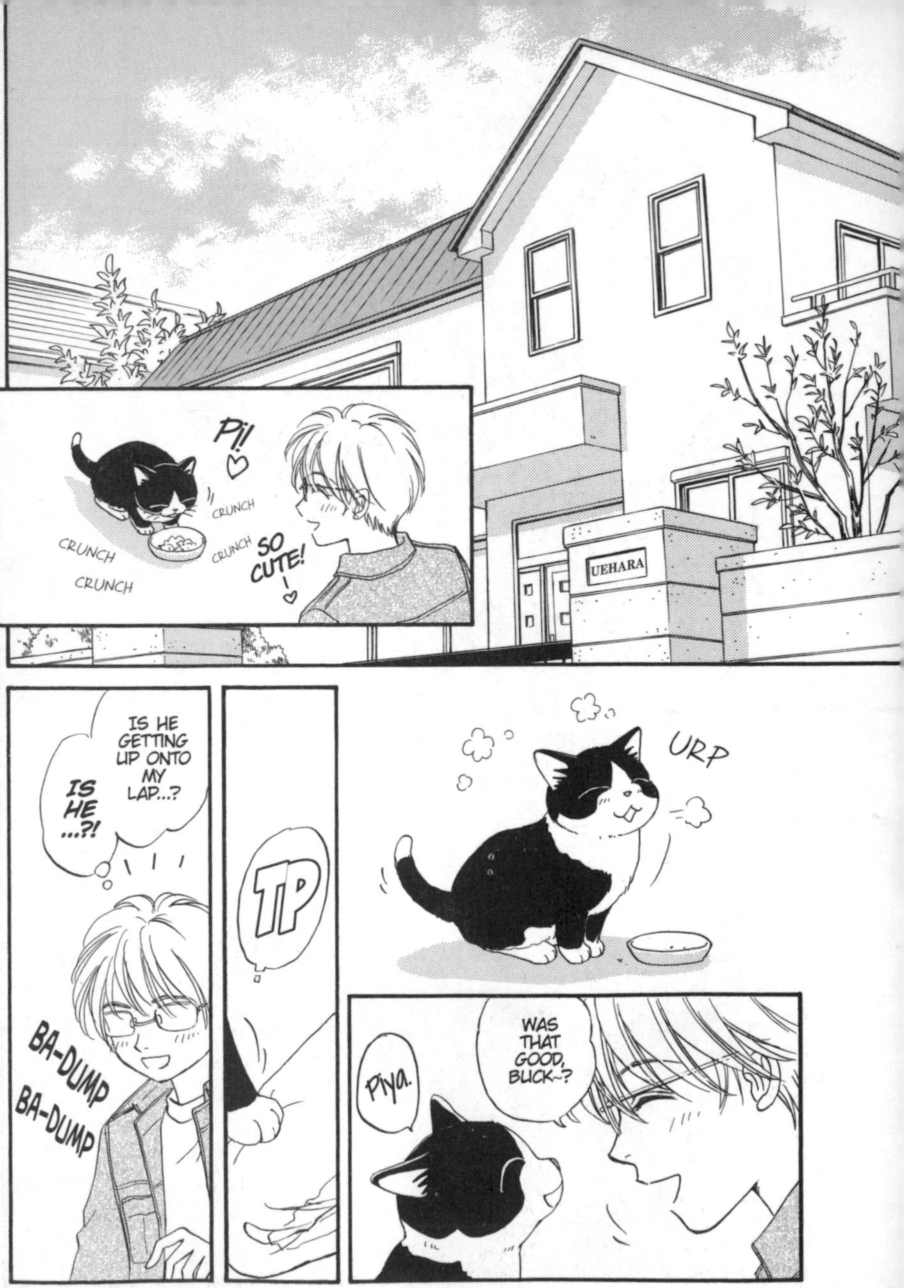
UEHARA
SO CUTE!
Pi!
CRUNCH
CRUNCH
CRUNCH
CRUNCH
URP
WAS THAT GOOD, BUCK~?
Piya.
TP
IS HE GETTING UP ONTO MY LAP...?
IS HE ...?!
BA-DUMP
BA-DUMP

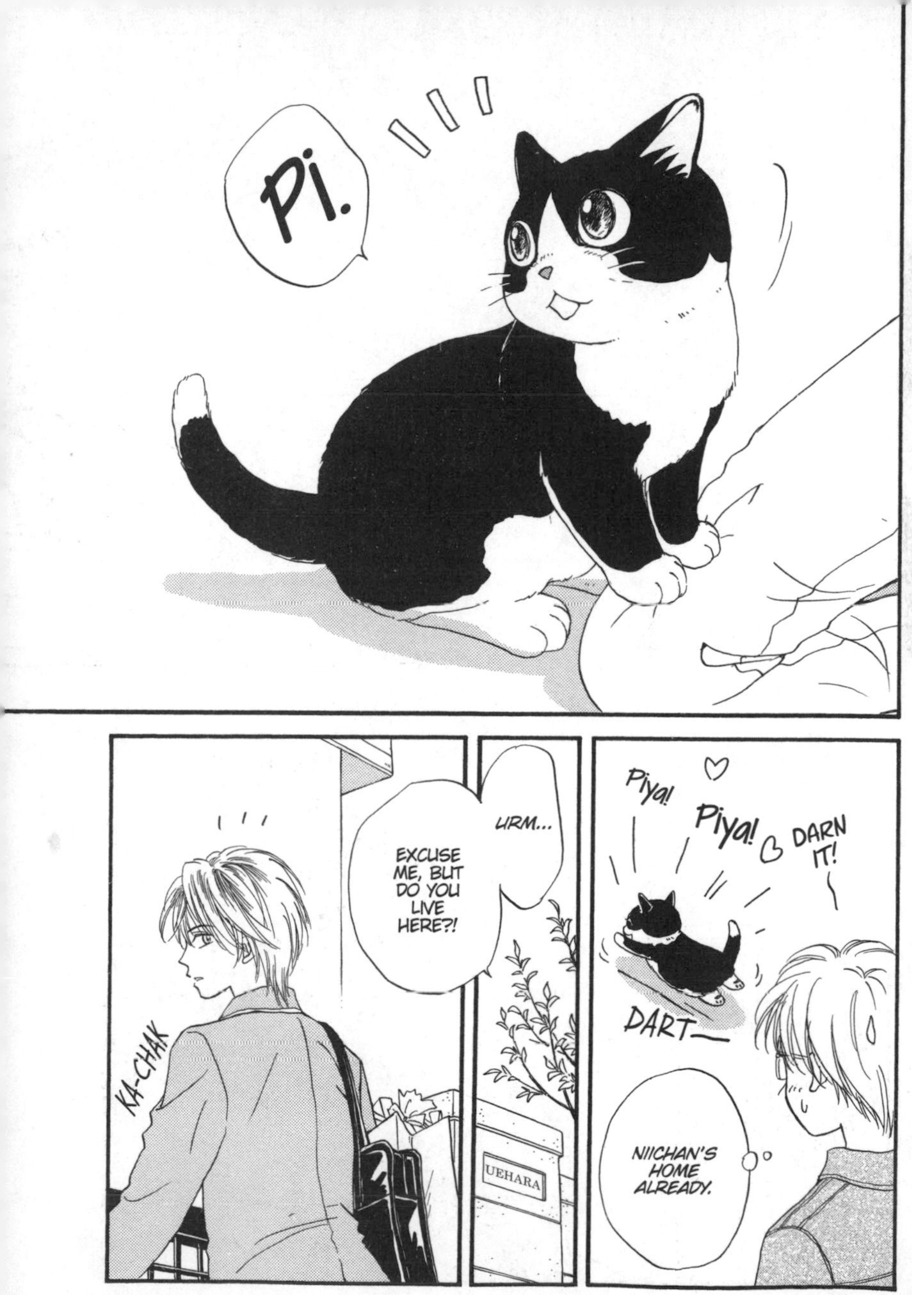
Pi.
Piya!
Piya!
DARN IT!
DART—
NIICHAN'S HOME ALREADY.
URM...
UEHARA
EXCUSE ME, BUT DO YOU LIVE HERE?!
KA-CHAK

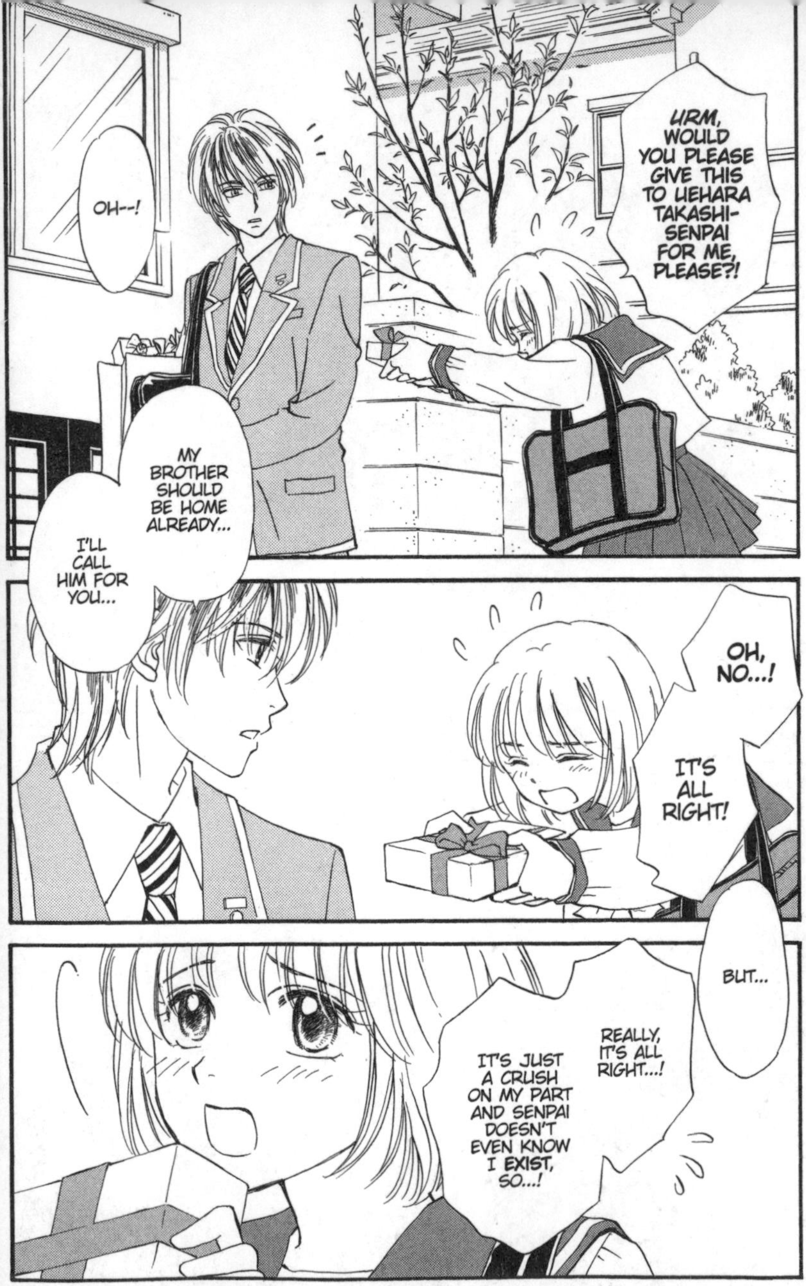
URM, WOULD YOU PLEASE GIVE THIS TO UEHARA TAKASHI-SENPAI FOR ME, PLEASE?!
OH--!
MY BROTHER SHOULD BE HOME ALREADY...
I'LL CALL HIM FOR YOU...
OH, NO...!
IT'S ALL RIGHT!
BUT...
REALLY, IT'S ALL RIGHT...!
IT'S JUST A CRUSH ON MY PART AND SENPAI DOESN'T EVEN KNOW I EXIST, SO...!

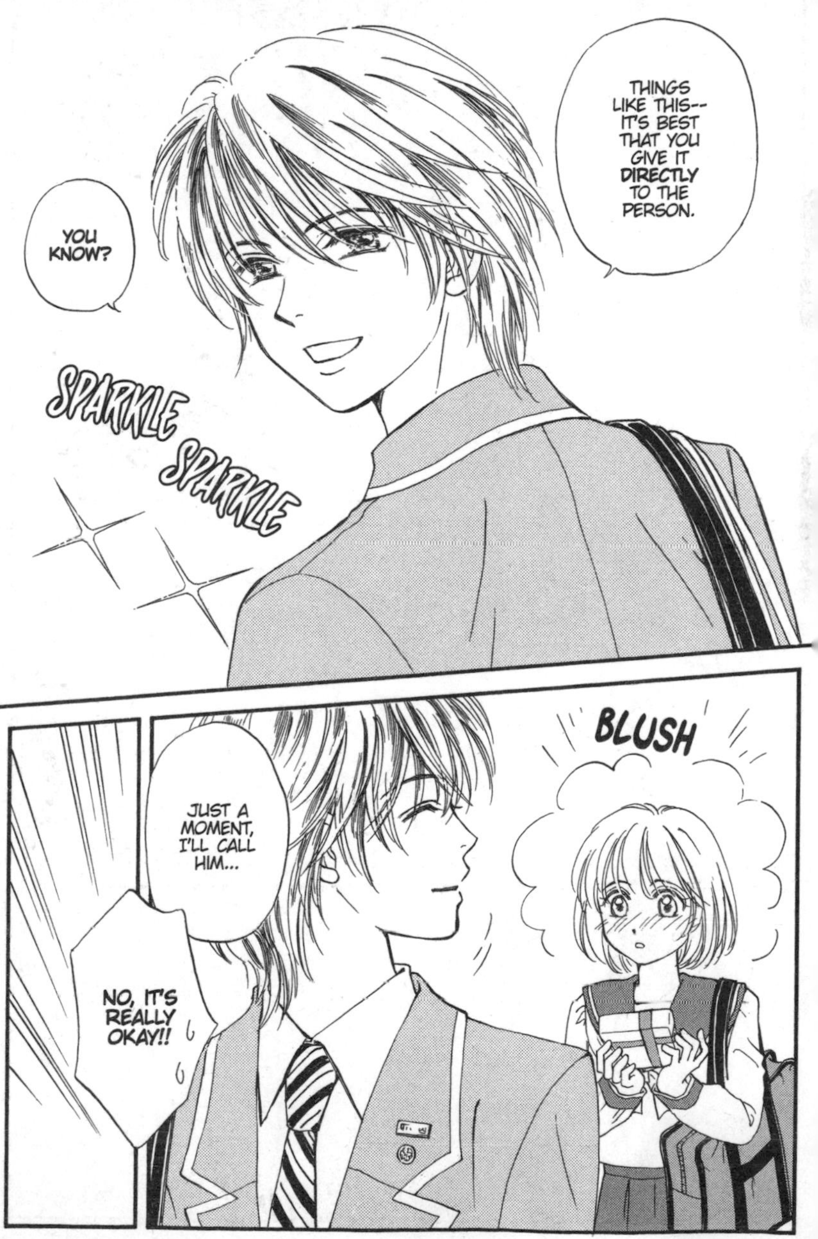
THINGS LIKE THIS-- IT'S BEST THAT YOU GIVE IT **DIRECTLY** TO THE PERSON.
YOU KNOW?
SPARKLE
SPARKLE
BLUSH
JUST A MOMENT, I'LL CALL HIM...
NO, IT'S REALLY OKAY!!

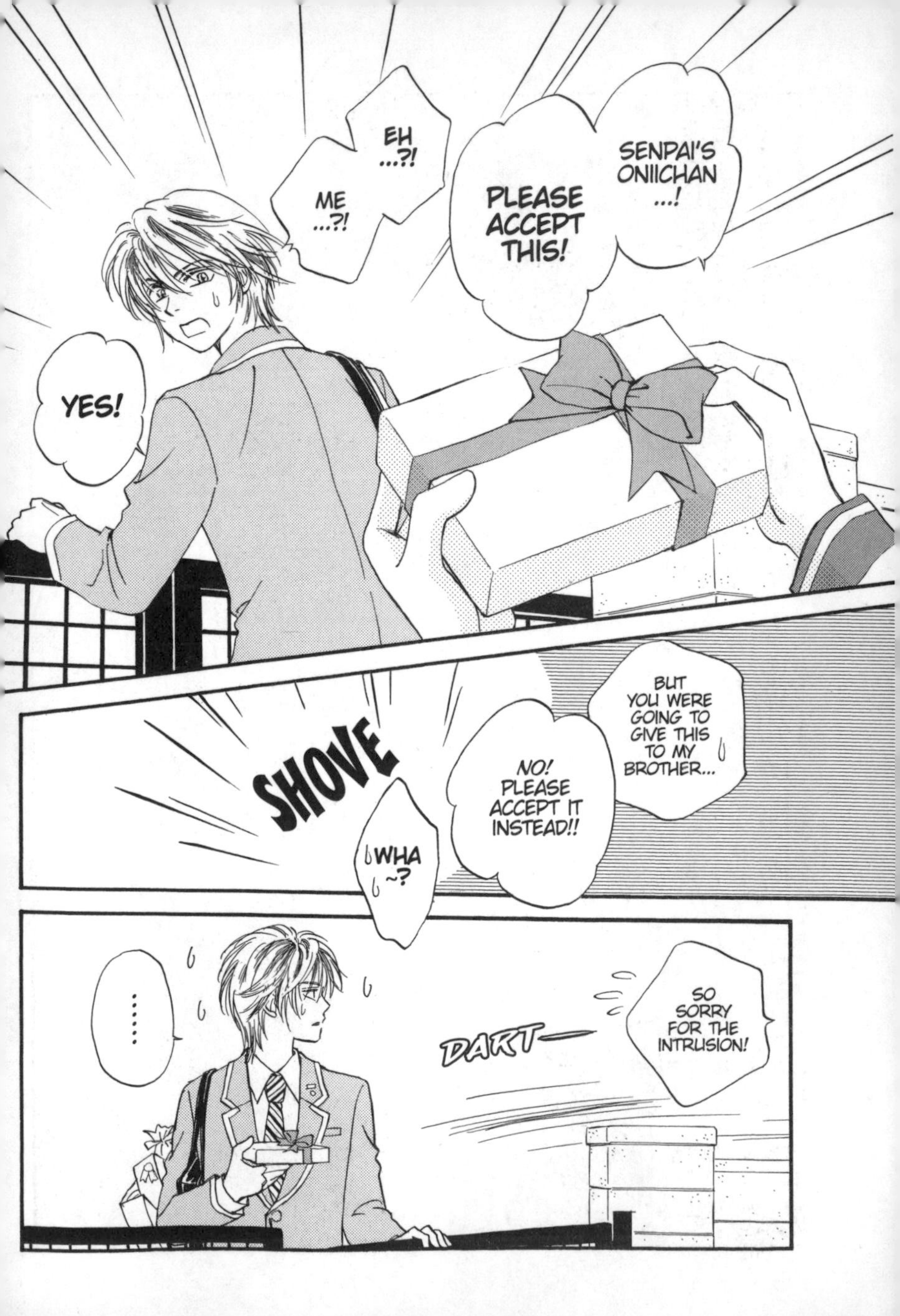
SENPAI's ONIICHAN ...!
PLEASE ACCEPT THIS!
EH ...?!
ME ...?!
YES!
BUT YOU WERE GOING TO GIVE THIS TO MY BROTHER...
NO! PLEASE ACCEPT IT INSTEAD!!
SHOVE
WHA ~?
SO SORRY FOR THE INTRUSION!
DART—
......

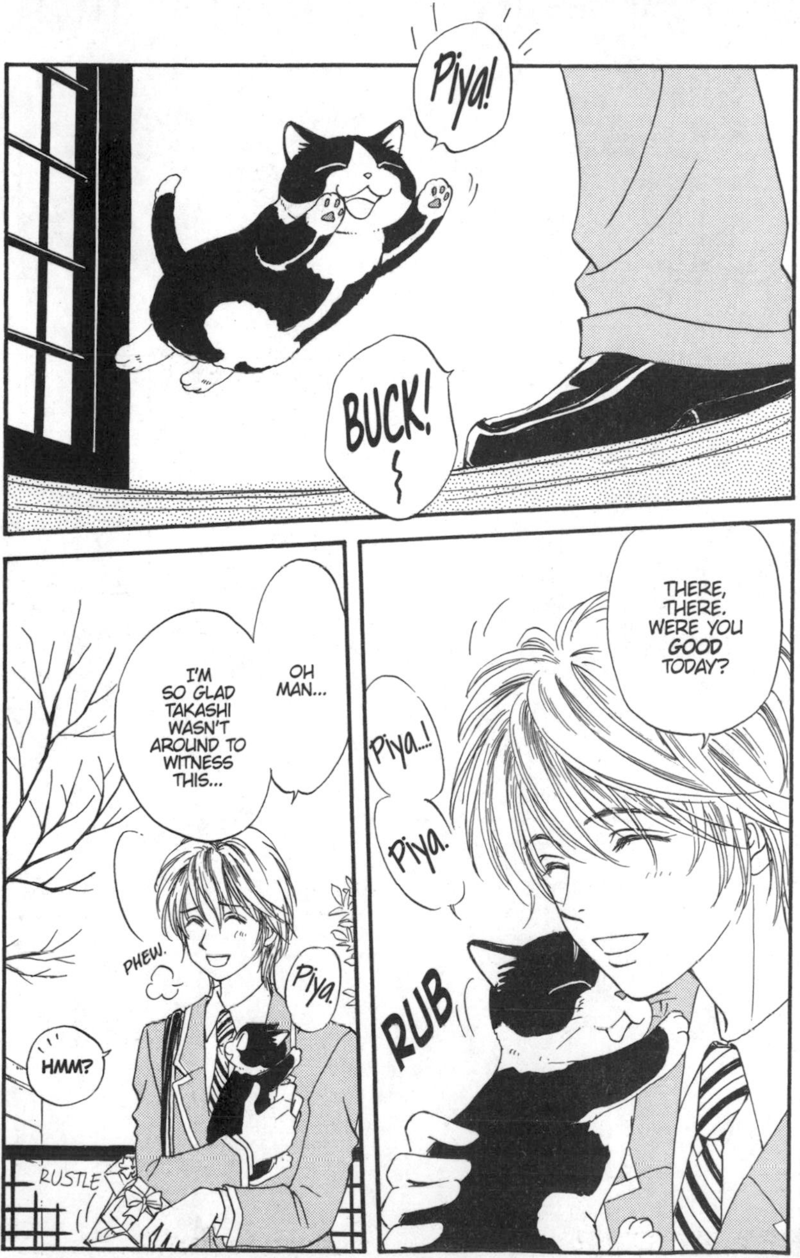
Piya!
BUCK!
THERE, THERE. WERE YOU GOOD TODAY?
Piya..!
Piya.
RUB
OH MAN...
I'M SO GLAD TAKASHI WASN'T AROUND TO WITNESS THIS...
PHEW.
Piya.
HMM?
RUSTLE

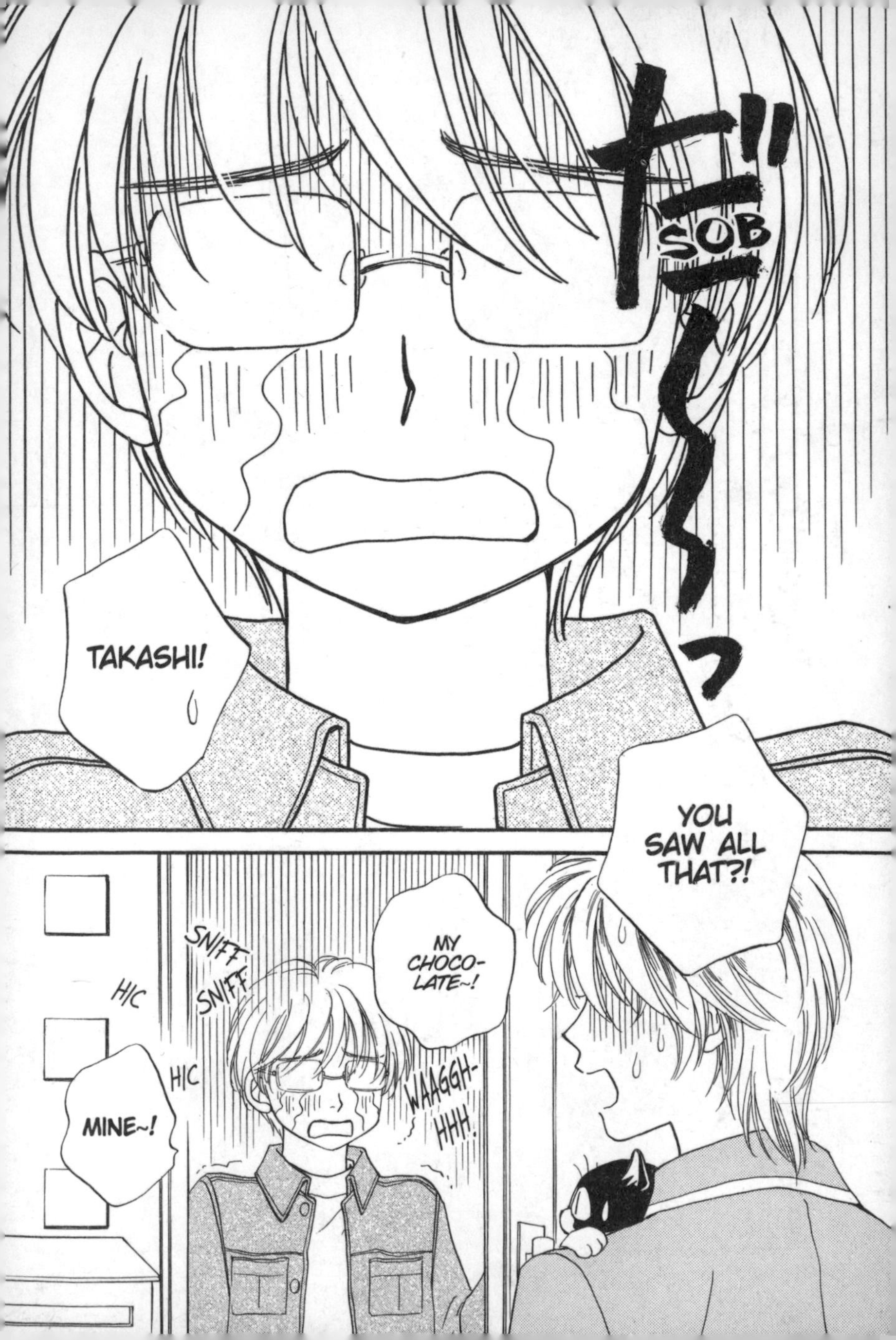
SOB
TAKASHI!
YOU SAW ALL THAT?!
WAAGGH-HHH
MY CHOCO-LATE~!
SNIFF SNIFF
HIC
HIC
MINE~!

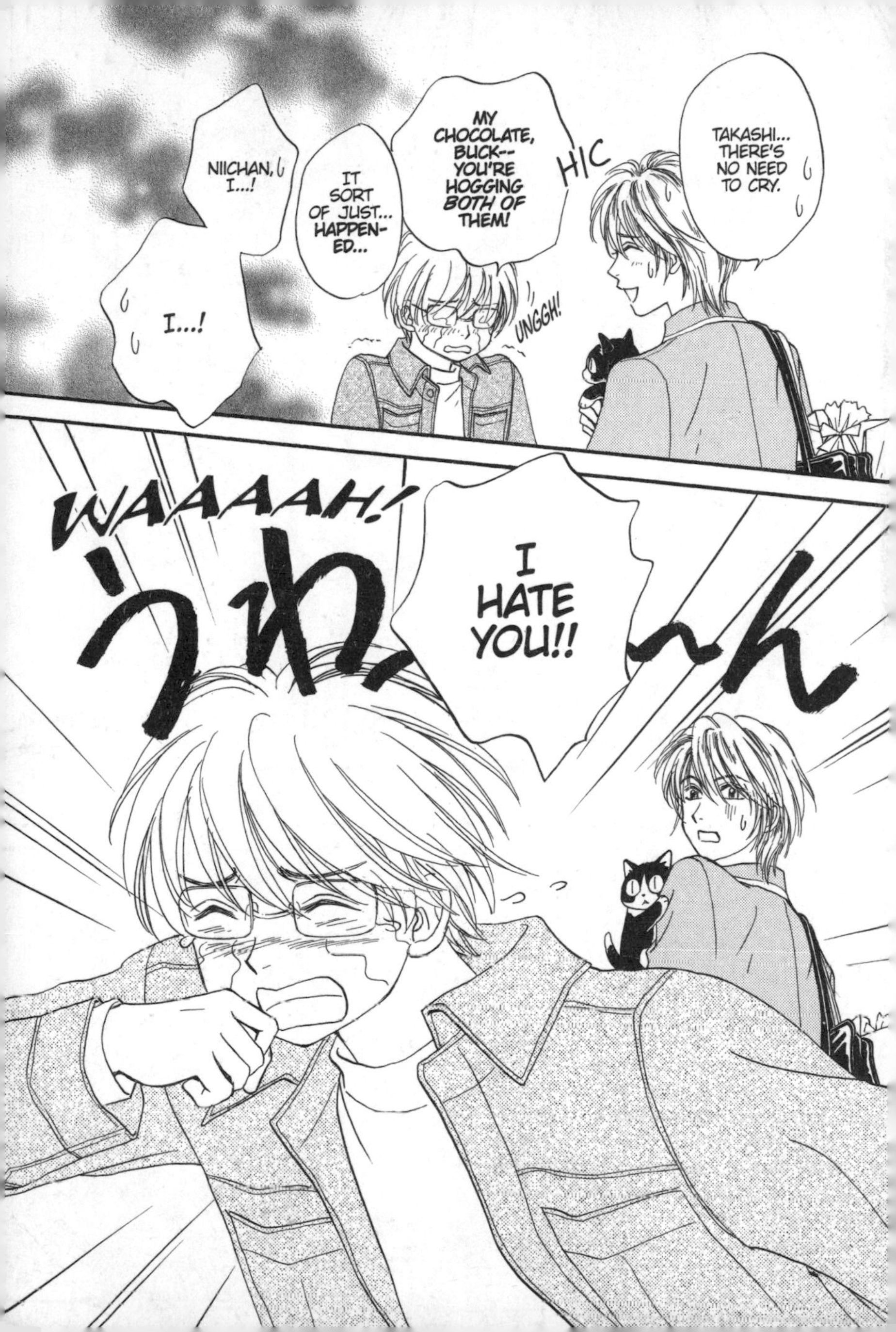
TAKASHI... THERE'S NO NEED TO CRY.
H/C
MY CHOCOLATE, BUCK-- YOU'RE HOGGING BOTH OF THEM!
UNGGH!
IT SORT OF JUST... HAPPEN-ED...
NIICHAN, I...!
I...!
I HATE YOU!!
WAAAAH!
うわ〜ん

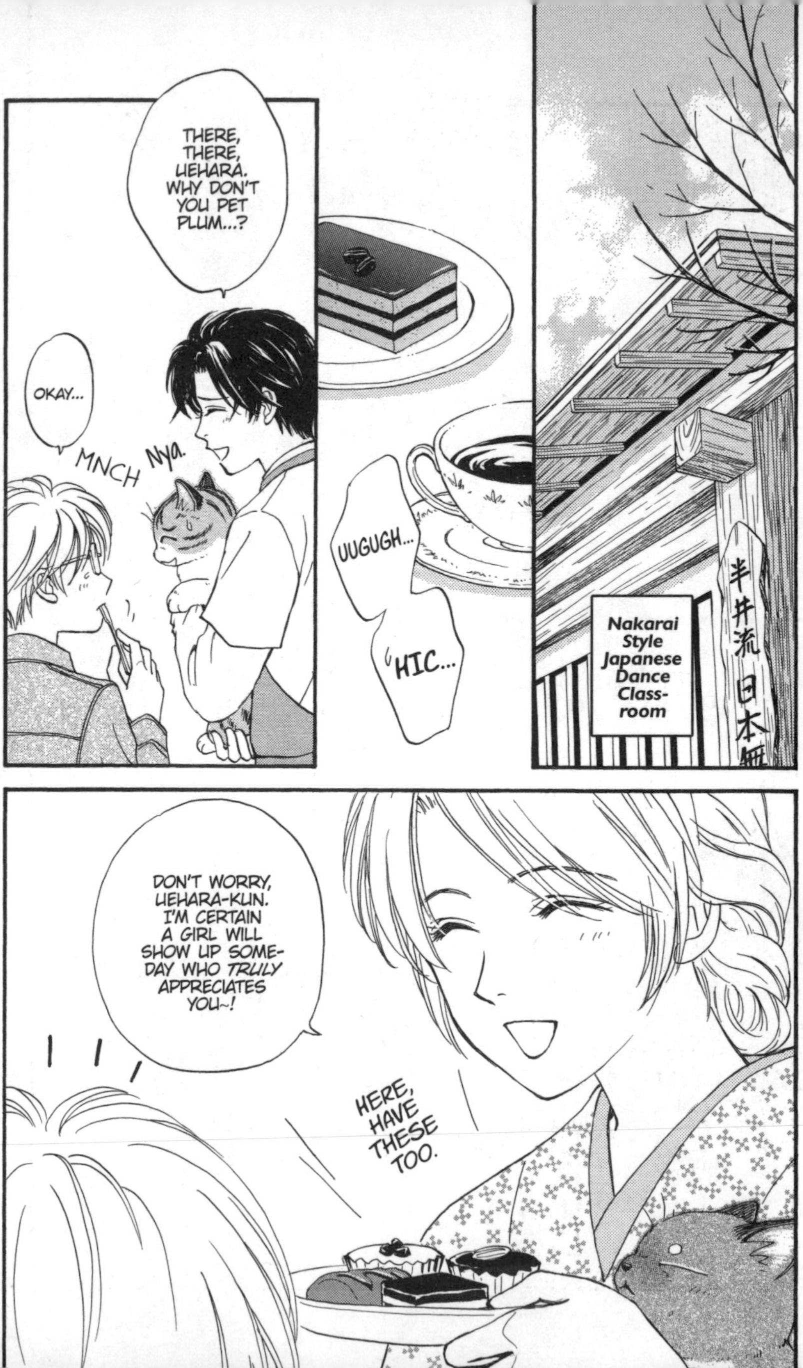
Nakarai Style Japanese Dance Class- room
半井流日本舞
UUGUGH...
HIC...
THERE, THERE, UEHARA. WHY DON'T YOU PET PLUM...?
OKAY...
Nya.
MNCH
DON'T WORRY, UEHARA-KUN. I'M CERTAIN A GIRL WILL SHOW UP SOME-DAY WHO TRULY APPRECIATES YOU~!
HERE, HAVE THESE TOO.

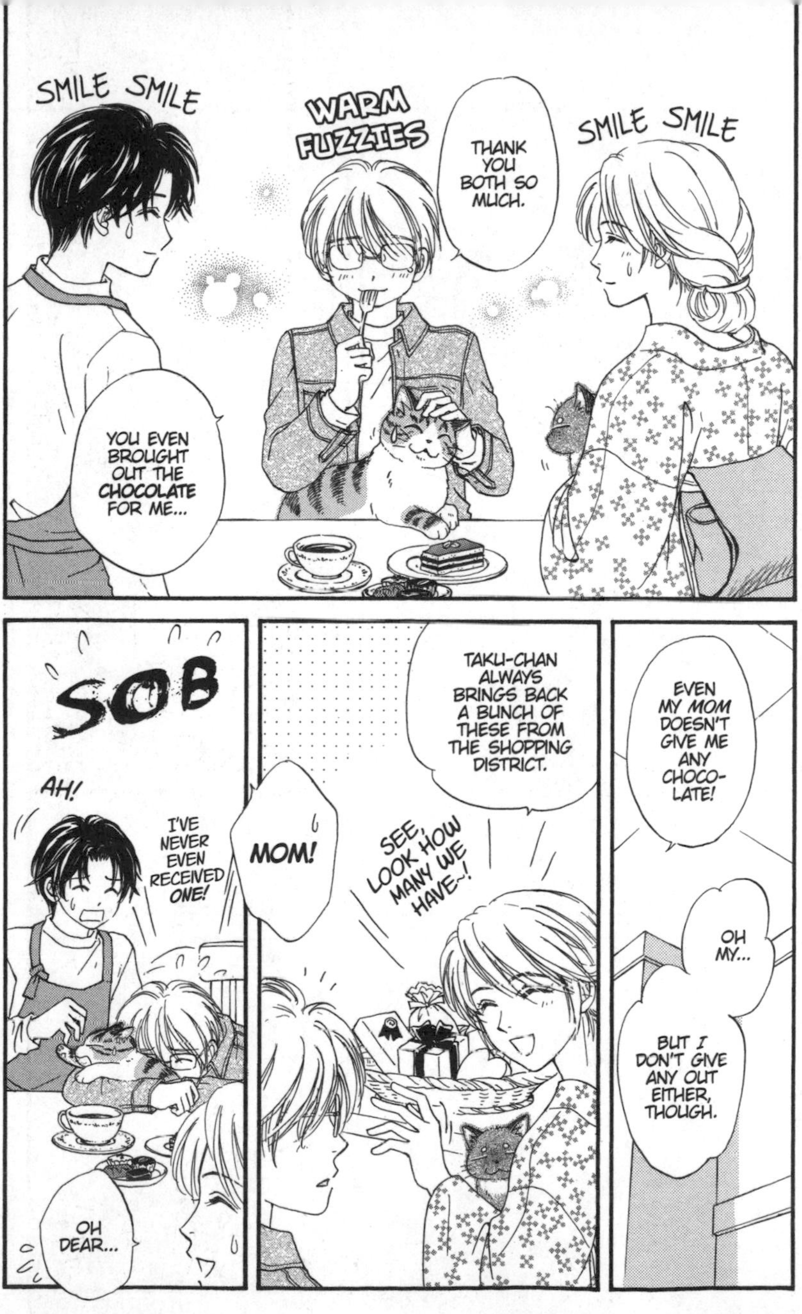
SMILE SMILE
THANK YOU BOTH SO MUCH.
WARM FUZZIES
SMILE SMILE
YOU EVEN BROUGHT OUT THE CHOCOLATE FOR ME...
EVEN MY MOM DOESN'T GIVE ME ANY CHOCO-LATE!
OH MY...
BUT I DON'T GIVE ANY OUT EITHER, THOUGH.
TAKU-CHAN ALWAYS BRINGS BACK A BUNCH OF THESE FROM THE SHOPPING DISTRICT.
SEE, LOOK HOW MANY WE HAVE~!
MOM!
SOB
I'VE NEVER EVEN RECEIVED ONE!
AH!
OH DEAR...

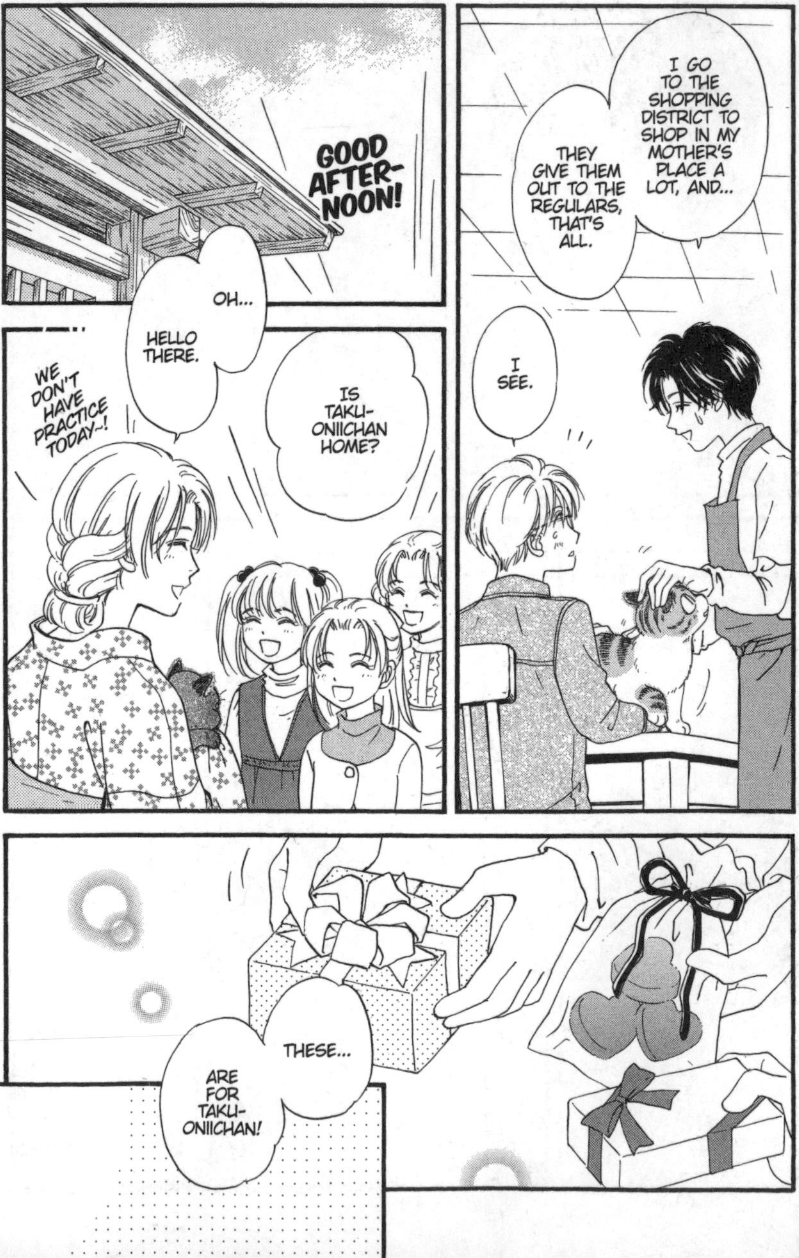
I GO TO THE SHOPPING DISTRICT TO SHOP IN MY MOTHER'S PLACE A LOT, AND...
THEY GIVE THEM OUT TO THE REGULARS, THAT'S ALL.
I SEE.
GOOD AFTER-NOON!
OH...
HELLO THERE.
IS TAKU-ONIICHAN HOME?
WE DON'T HAVE PRACTICE TODAY~!
THESE...
ARE FOR TAKU-ONIICHAN!

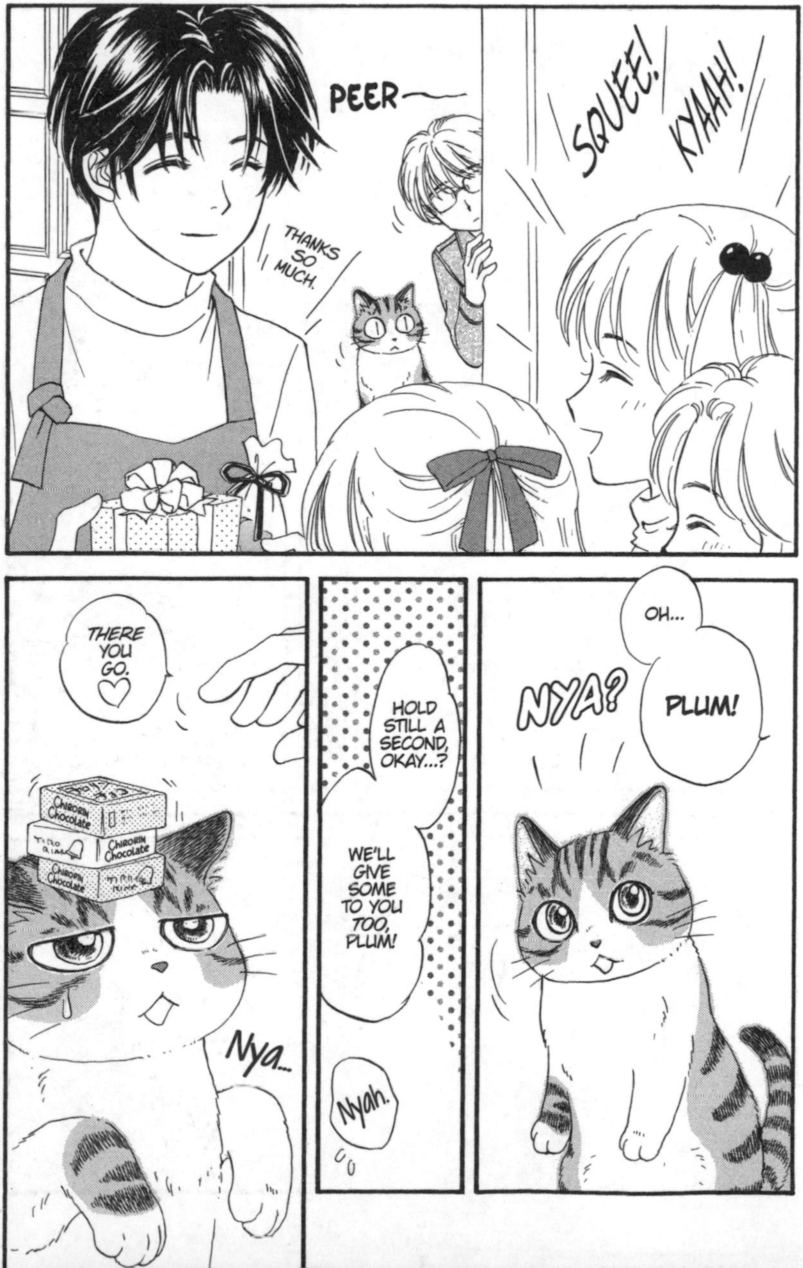
KYAAH!
SQUEE!
PEER—
THANKS SO MUCH.
OH...
PLUM!
NYA?
HOLD STILL A SECOND, OKAY...?
WE'LL GIVE SOME TO YOU TOO, PLUM!
Nyah.
THERE YOU GO. ♡
CHIRORIN Chocolate
CHIRORIN Chocolate
CHIRORIN Chocolate
Nya...

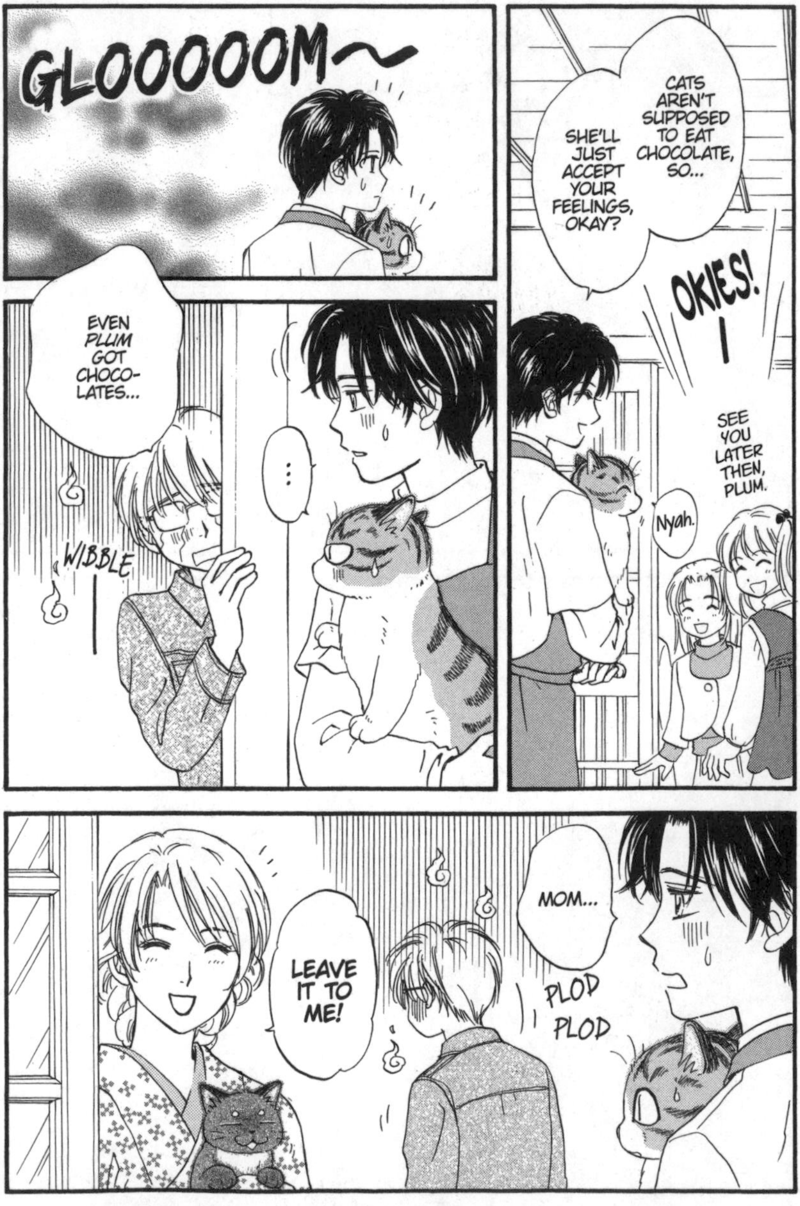
CATS AREN'T SUPPOSED TO EAT CHOCOLATE, SO...
SHE'LL JUST ACCEPT YOUR FEELINGS, OKAY?
OKIES!
SEE YOU LATER THEN, PLUM.
Nyah.
GLOOOOOM~
...
EVEN PLUM GOT CHOCO-LATES...
WIBBLE
MOM...
PLOD PLOD
LEAVE IT TO ME!

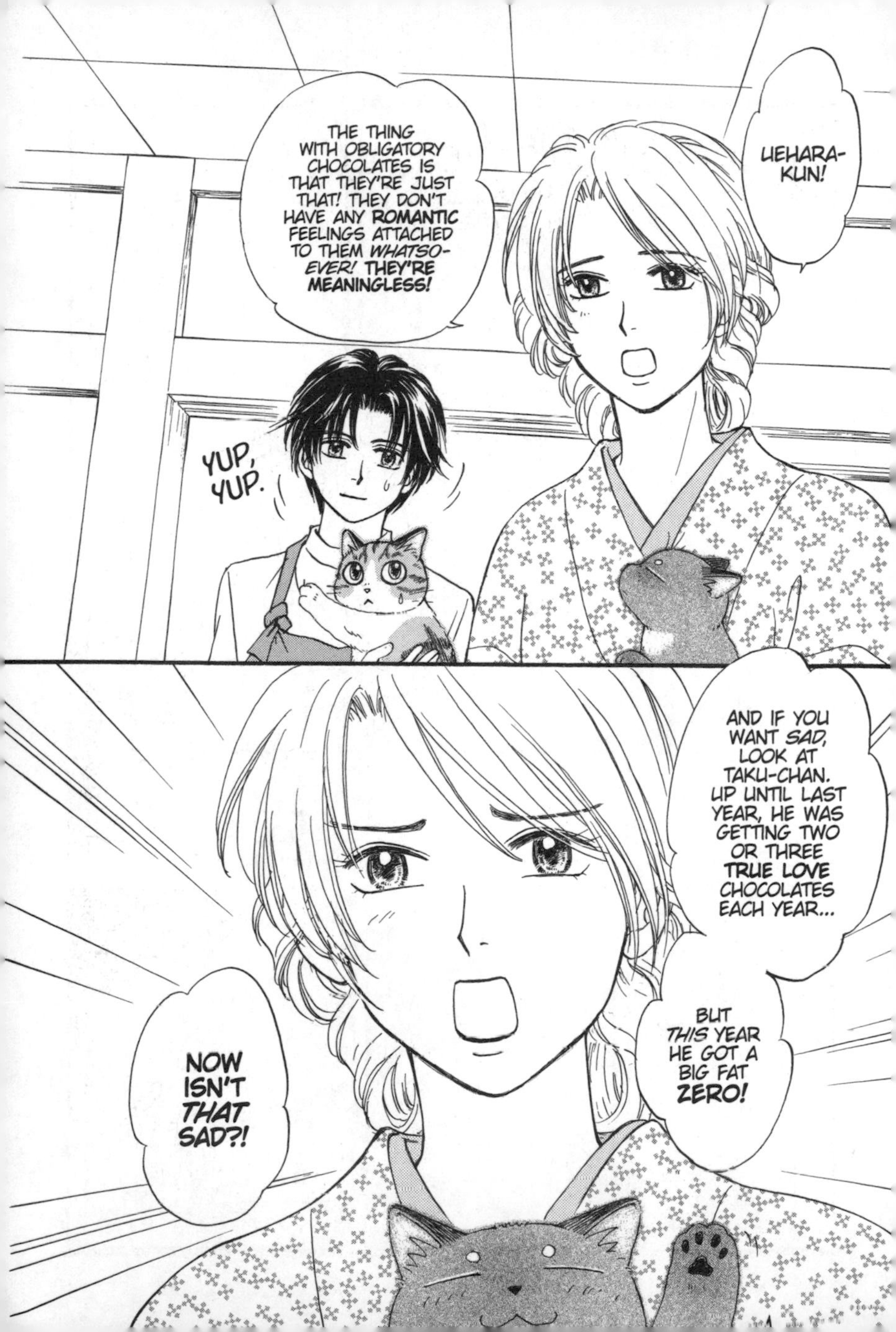
UEHARA-KUN!
THE THING WITH OBLIGATORY CHOCOLATES IS THAT THEY'RE JUST THAT! THEY DON'T HAVE ANY ROMANTIC FEELINGS ATTACHED TO THEM WHATSO-EVER! THEY'RE MEANINGLESS!
YUP, YUP.
AND IF YOU WANT SAD, LOOK AT TAKU-CHAN. UP UNTIL LAST YEAR, HE WAS GETTING TWO OR THREE TRUE LOVE CHOCOLATES EACH YEAR...
BUT THIS YEAR HE GOT A BIG FAT ZERO!
NOW ISN'T THAT SAD?!

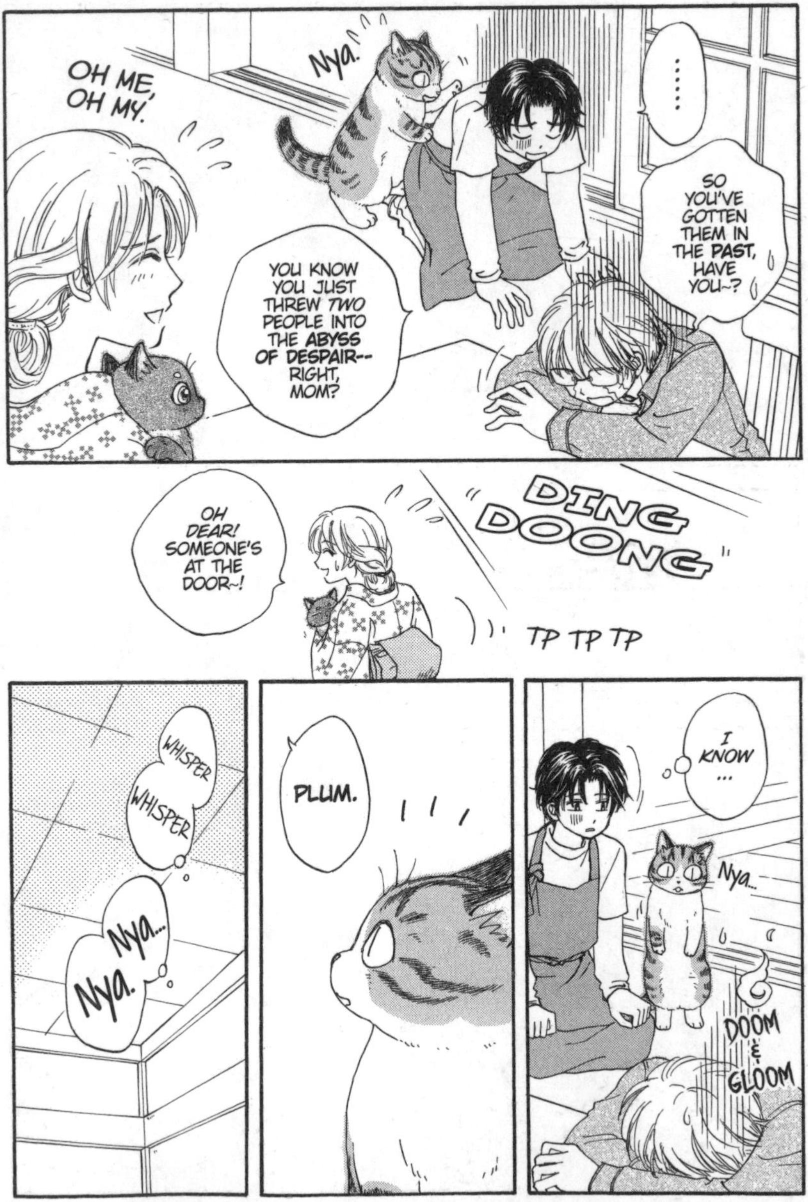
......
SO YOU'VE GOTTEN THEM IN THE PAST, HAVE YOU~?
Nya.
YOU KNOW YOU JUST THREW TWO PEOPLE INTO THE ABYSS OF DESPAIR-- RIGHT, MOM?
OH ME, OH MY.
DING DOONG
OH DEAR! SOMEONE'S AT THE DOOR~!
TP TP TP
I KNOW ...
Nya...
DOOM & GLOOM
PLUM.
WHISPER
WHISPER
Nya...
Nya.

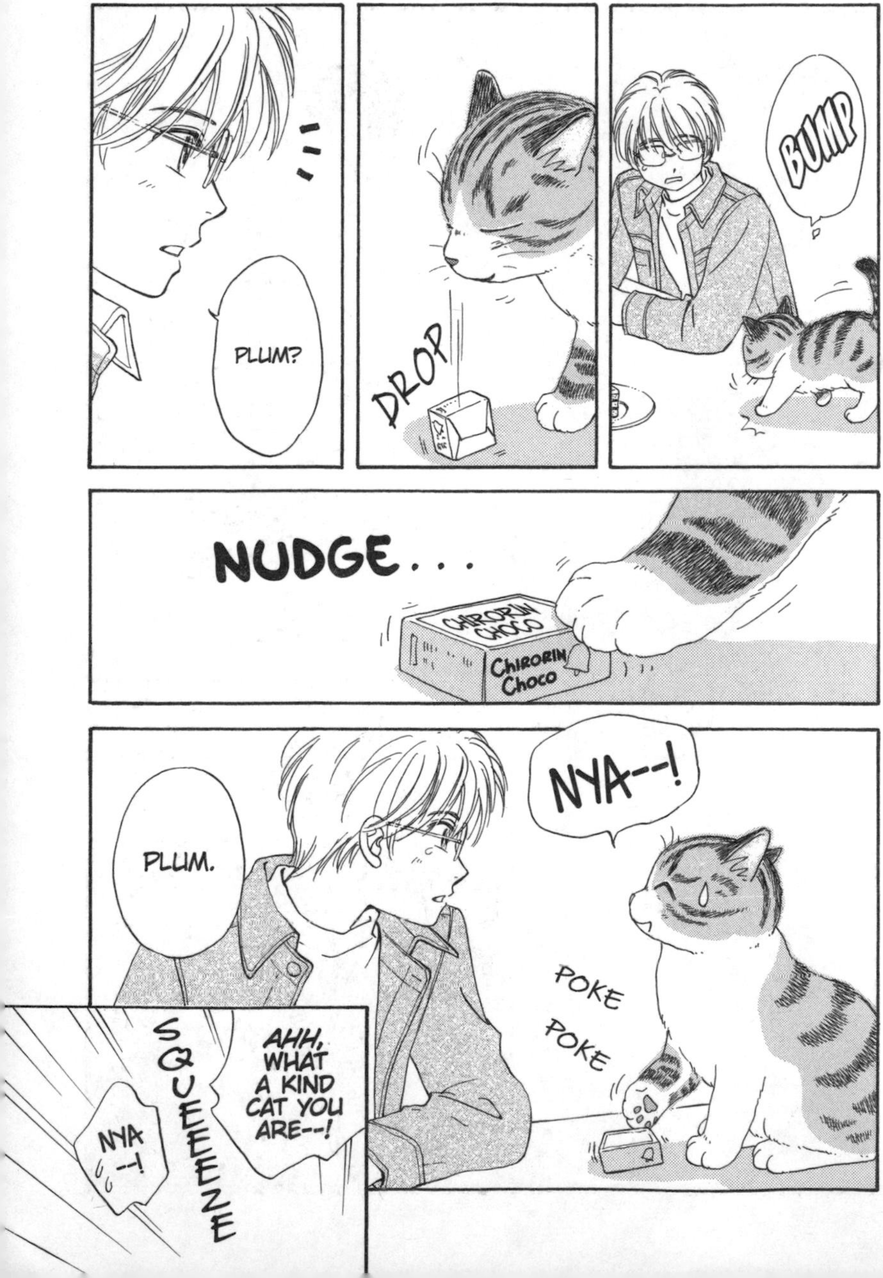
BUMP
DROP
PLUM?
NUDGE...
CHIRORIN CHOCO
CHIRORIN CHOCO
NYA--!
POKE
POKE
PLUM.
AHH, WHAT A KIND CAT YOU ARE--!
SQUEEEEZE
NYA--!

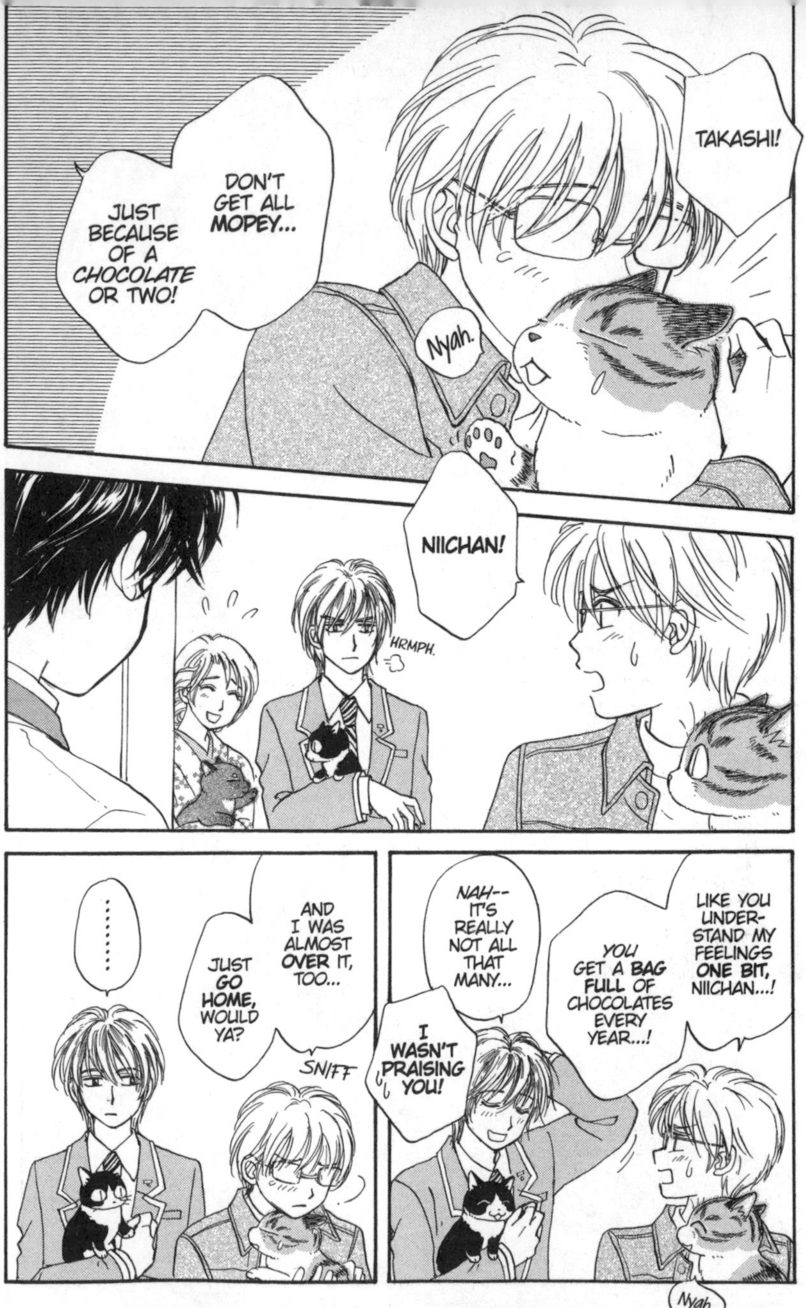
TAKASHI!
DON'T GET ALL MOPEY...
JUST BECAUSE OF A CHOCOLATE OR TWO!
Nyah.
NIICHAN!
HRMPH.
LIKE YOU UNDER-STAND MY FEELINGS ONE BIT, NIICHAN...!
YOU GET A BAG FULL OF CHOCOLATES EVERY YEAR...!
NAH-- IT'S REALLY NOT ALL THAT MANY...
I WASN'T PRAISING YOU!
Nyah.
AND I WAS ALMOST OVER IT, TOO...
JUST GO HOME, WOULD YA?
SNIFF
......

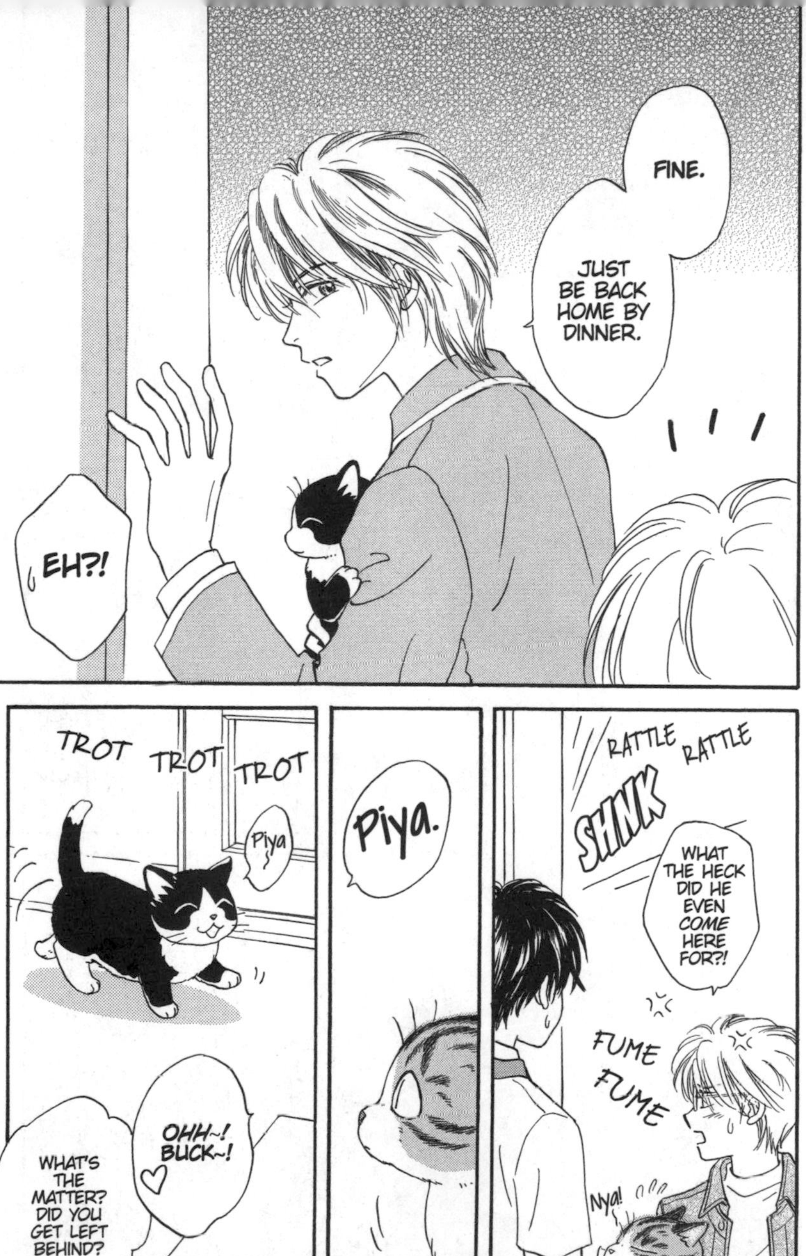
FINE.
JUST BE BACK HOME BY DINNER.
EH?!
RATTLE RATTLE
SHNK
WHAT THE HECK DID HE EVEN COME HERE FOR?!
FUME FUME
Nya!
Piya.
TROT TROT TROT
Piya
OHH~! BUCK~!
WHAT'S THE MATTER? DID YOU GET LEFT BEHIND?

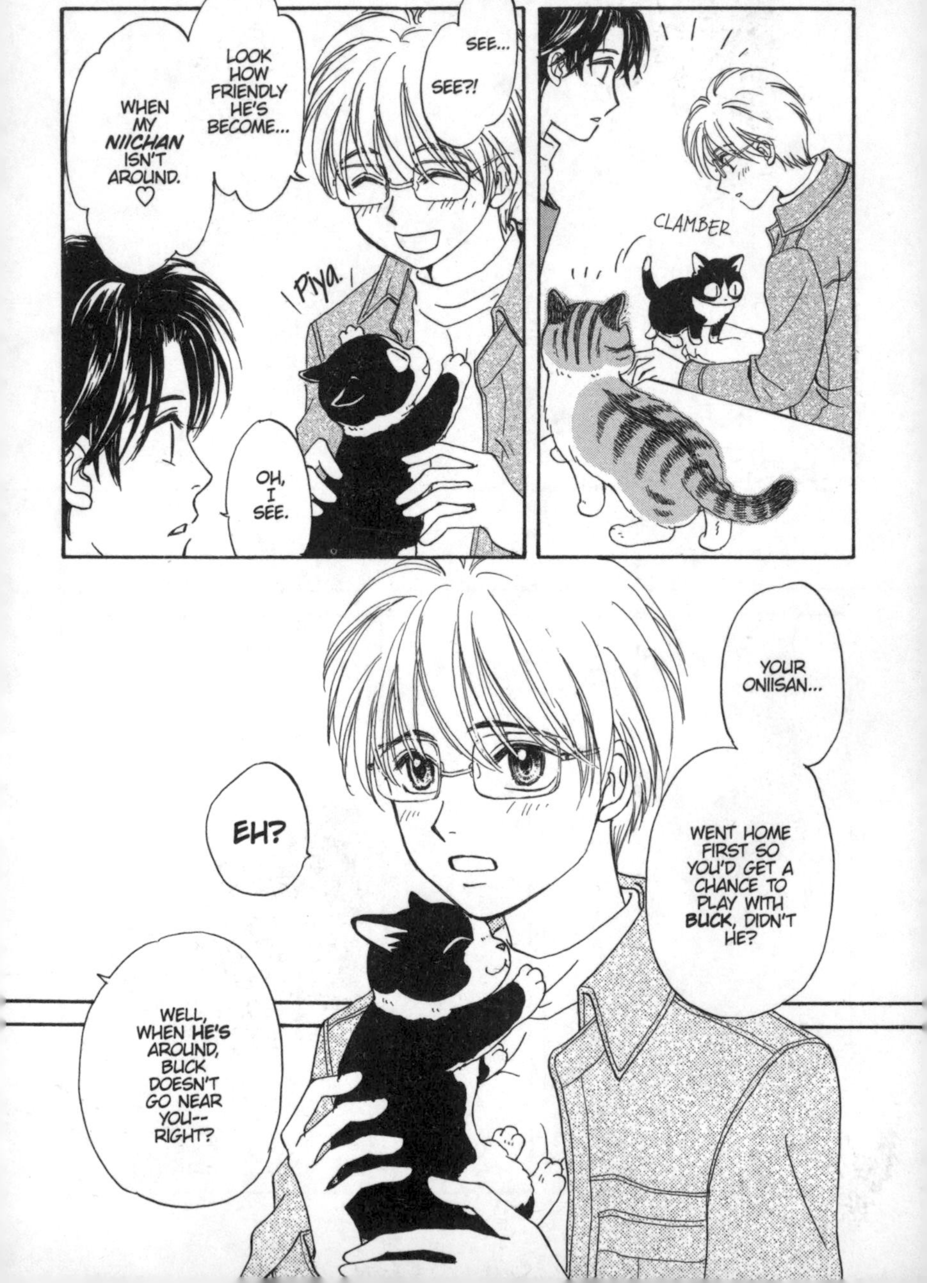
CLAMBER
SEE...
SEE?!
LOOK HOW FRIENDLY HE'S BECOME...
WHEN MY *NIICHAN* ISN'T AROUND. ♡
Piya.
OH, I SEE.
YOUR ONIISAN...
WENT HOME FIRST SO YOU'D GET A CHANCE TO PLAY WITH **BUCK**, DIDN'T HE?
EH?
WELL, WHEN HE'S AROUND, BUCK DOESN'T GO NEAR YOU-- RIGHT?

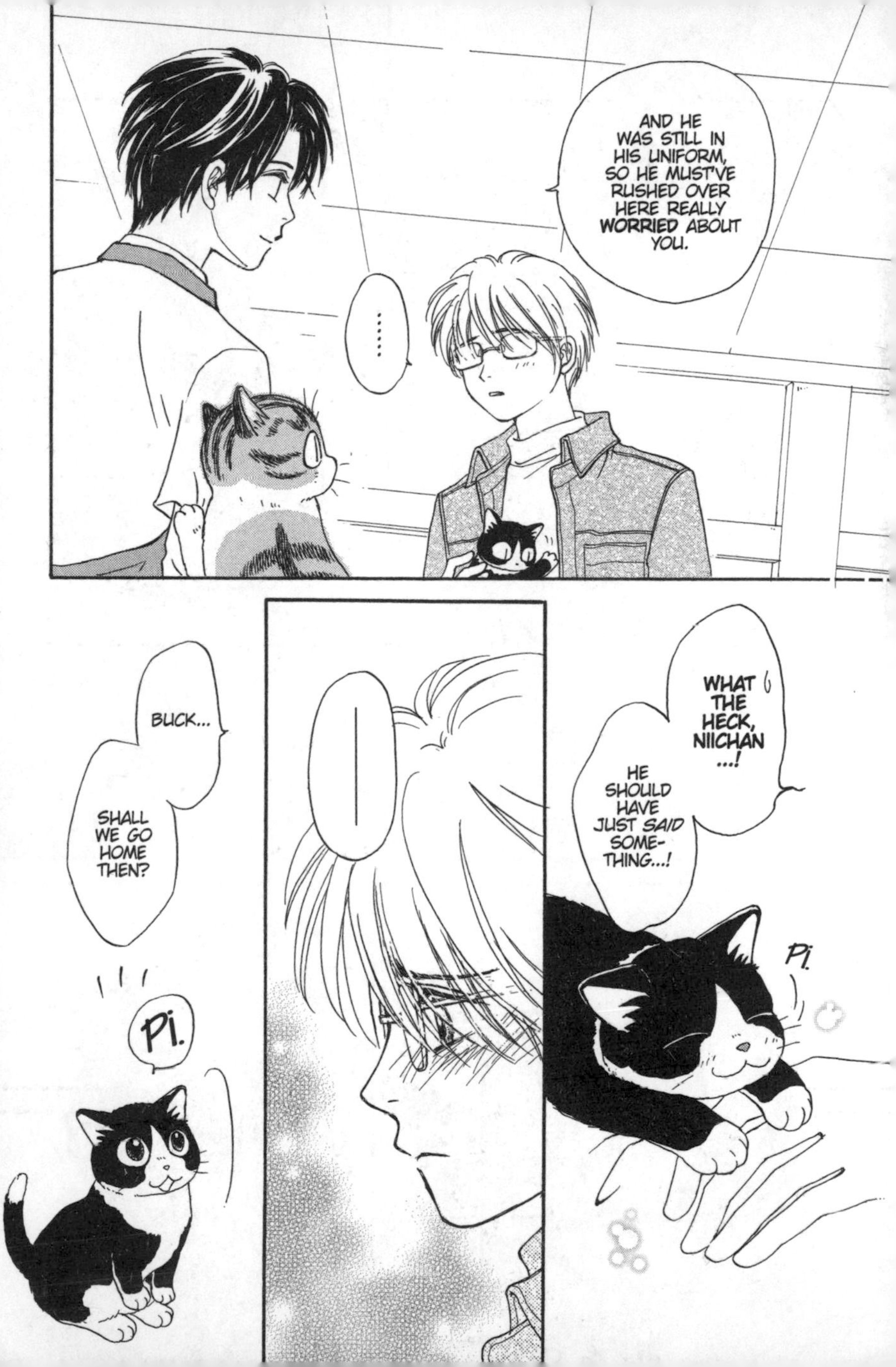
AND HE WAS STILL IN HIS UNIFORM, SO HE MUST'VE RUSHED OVER HERE REALLY **WORRIED** ABOUT YOU.
......
WHAT THE HECK, NIICHAN ...!
HE SHOULD HAVE JUST *SAID* SOME-THING...!
Pi.
BUCK...
SHALL WE GO HOME THEN?
Pi.

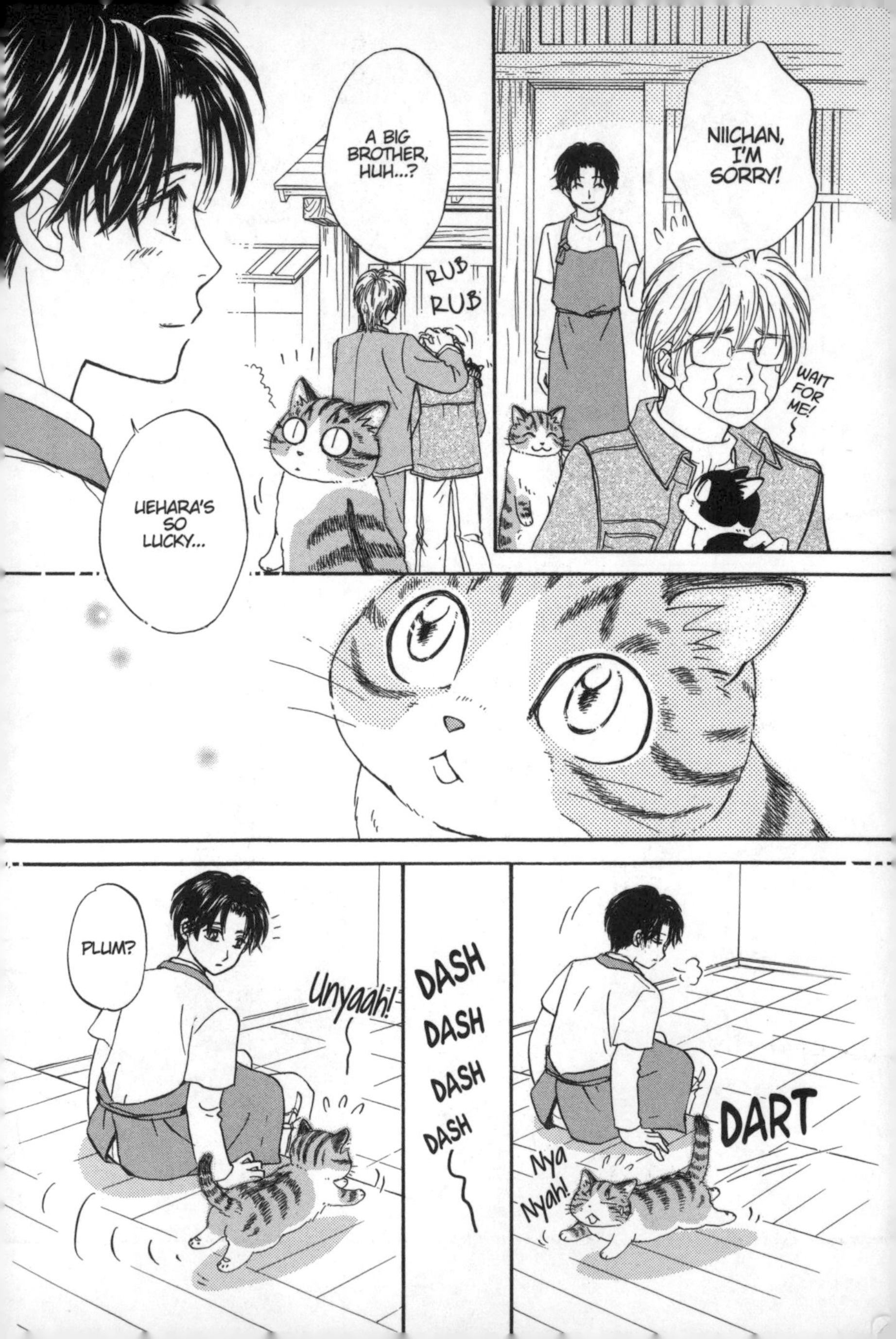
NIICHAN, I'M SORRY!
WAIT FOR ME!
A BIG BROTHER, HUH...?
RUB RUB
UEHARA'S SO LUCKY...
DART
Nya Nyah!
DASH DASH DASH DASH
PLUM?
Unyaah!

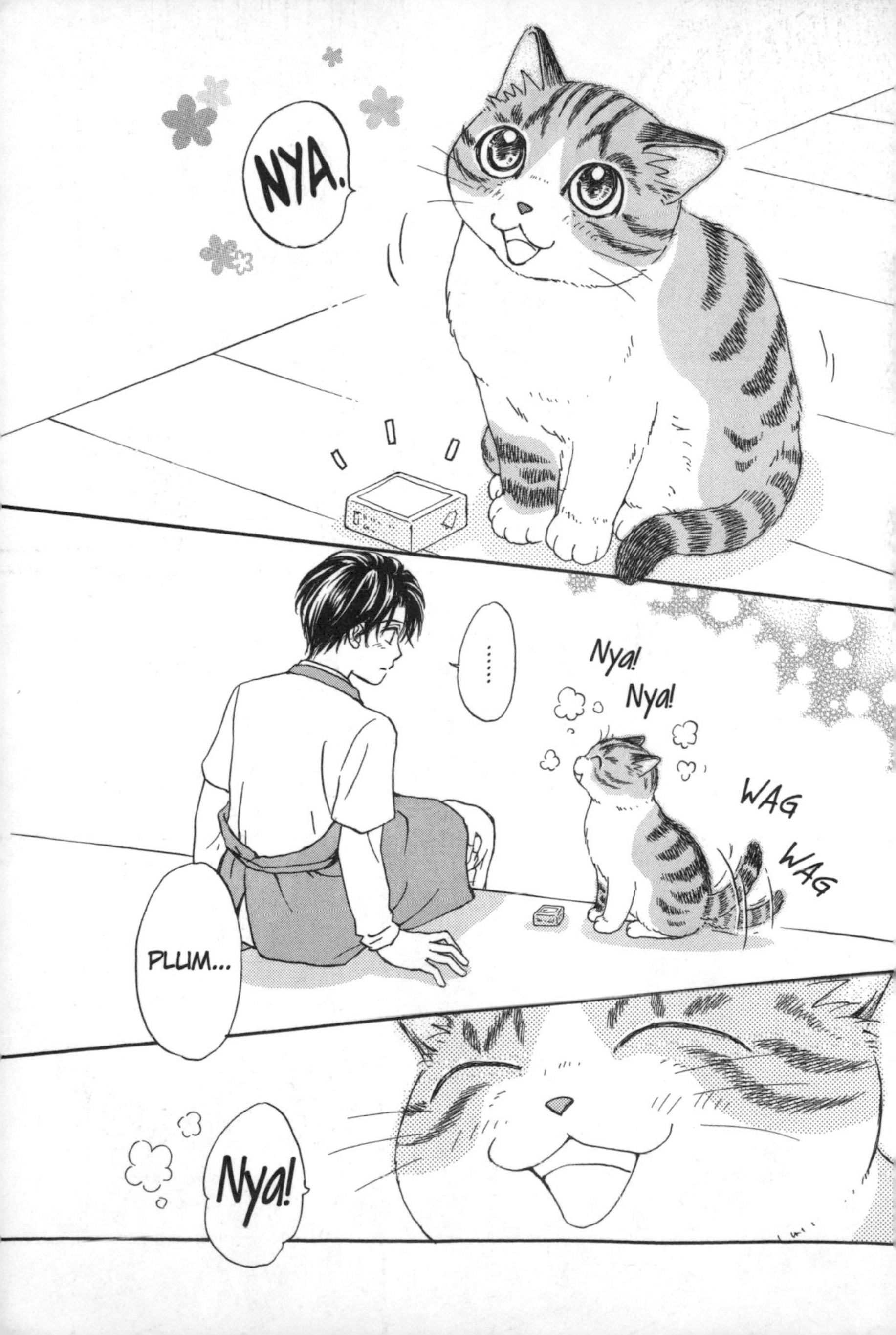
NYA.
Nya!
Nya!
WAG
WAG
......
PLUM...
Nya!

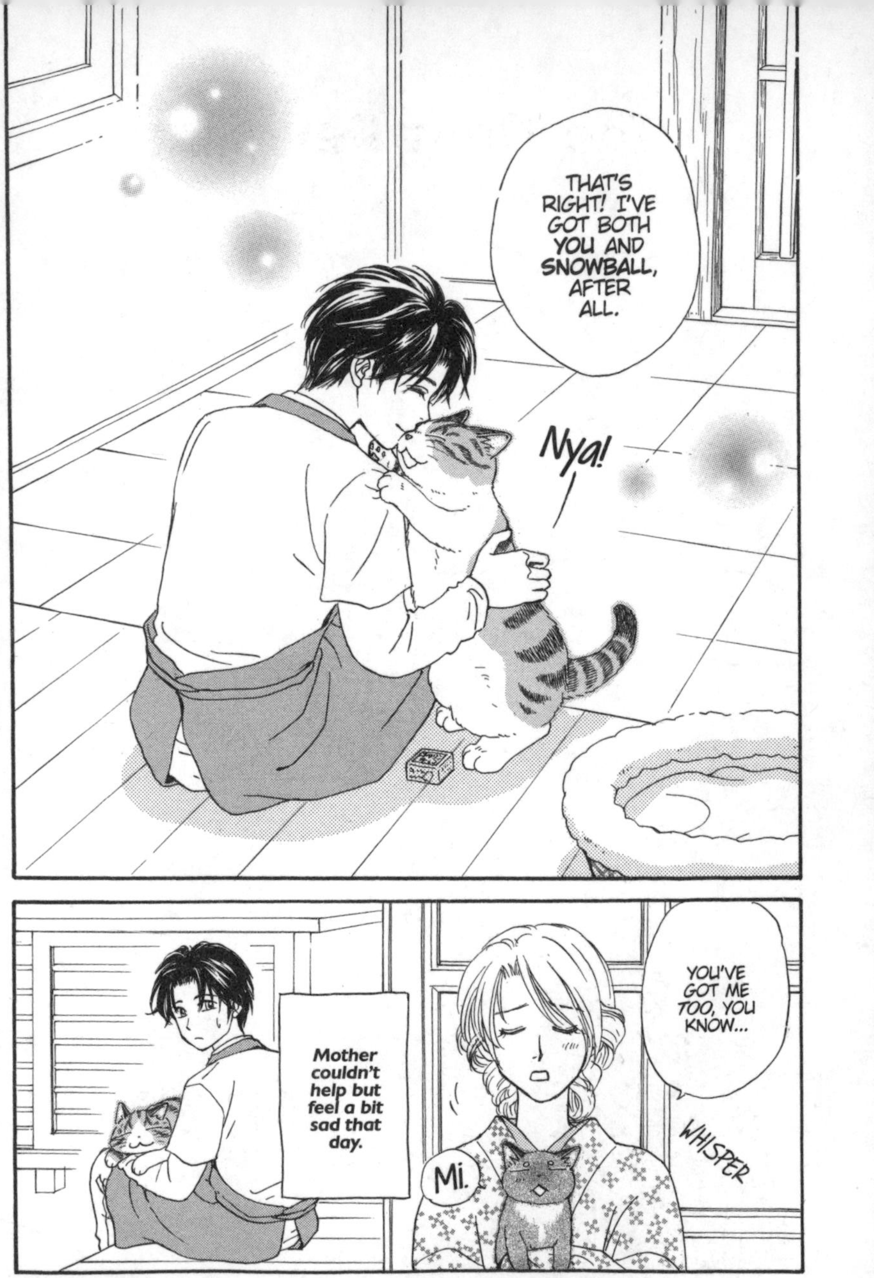
THAT'S RIGHT! I'VE GOT BOTH YOU AND SNOWBALL, AFTER ALL.
Nya!
YOU'VE GOT ME TOO, YOU KNOW...
WHISPER
Mi.
Mother couldn't help but feel a bit sad that day.

THE END

The Three Penguins

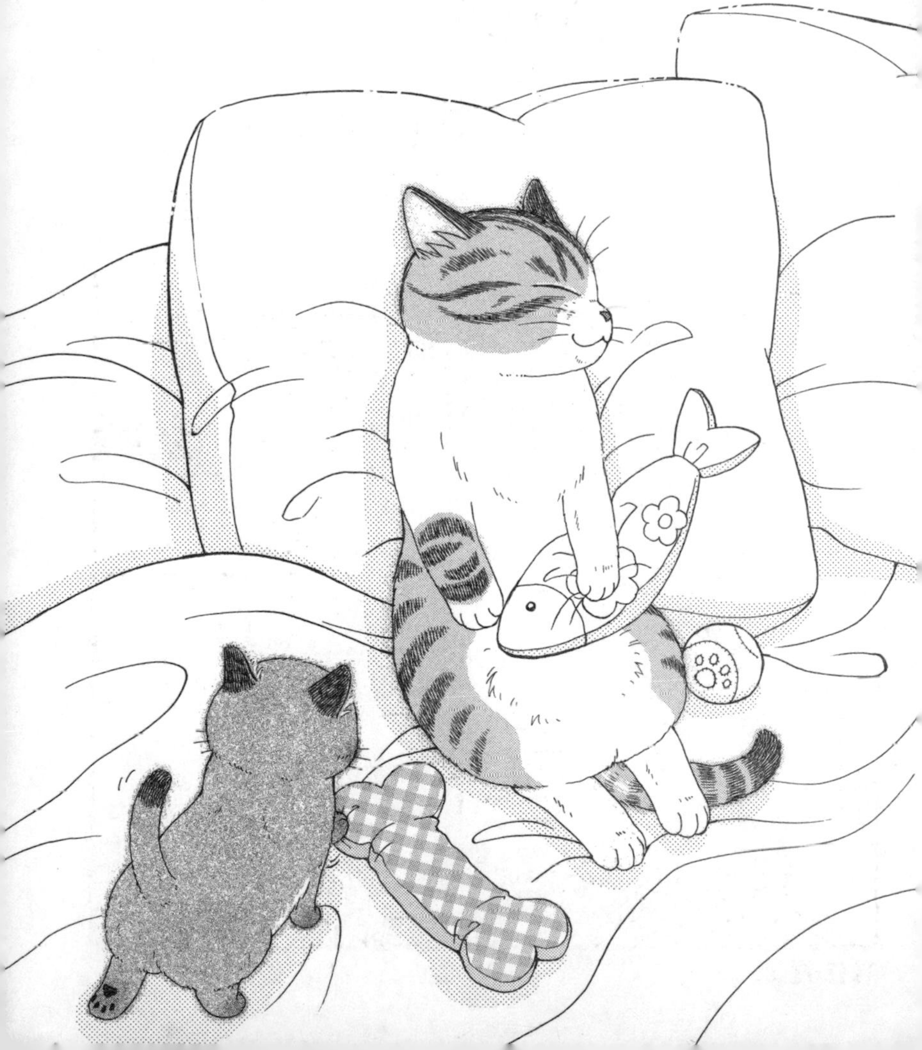

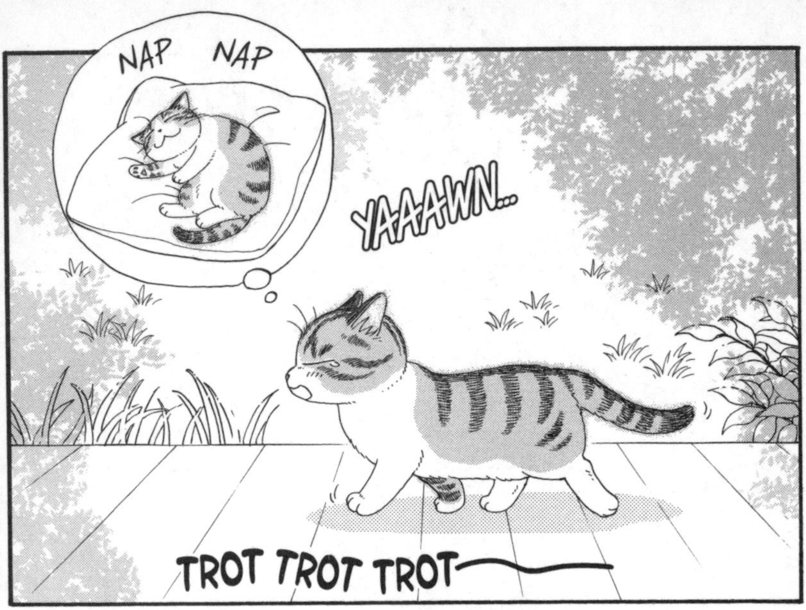
NAP NAP
YAAAWN...
TROT TROT TROT
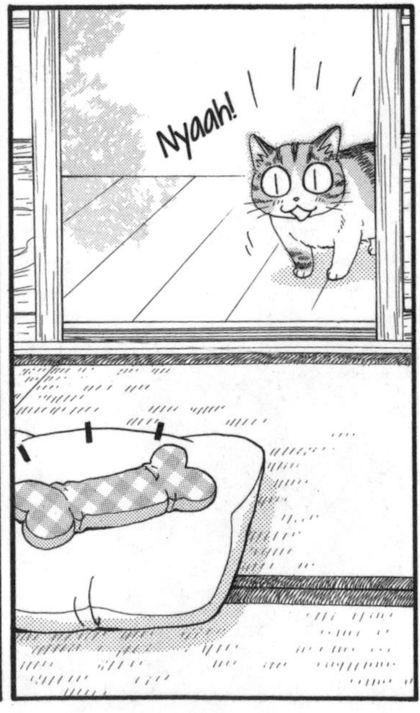
Nyaah!
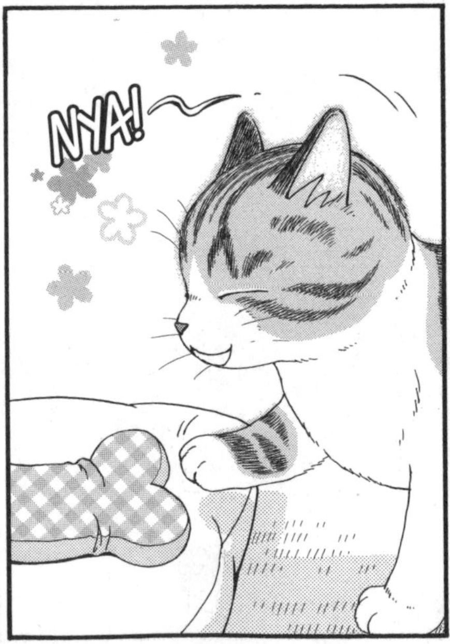
NYA!

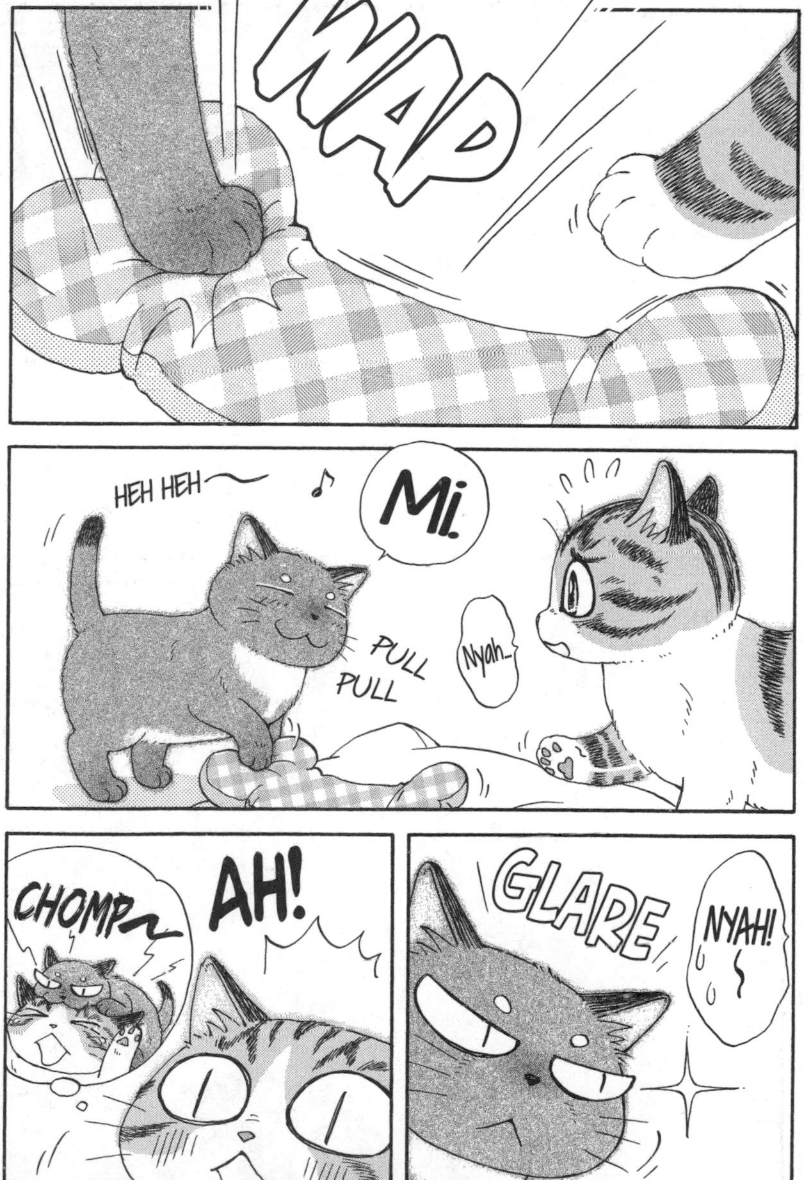
WAP
Mi.
HEH HEH~ ♪
Nyah...
PULL PULL
NYAH!
GLARE
AH!
CHOMP~

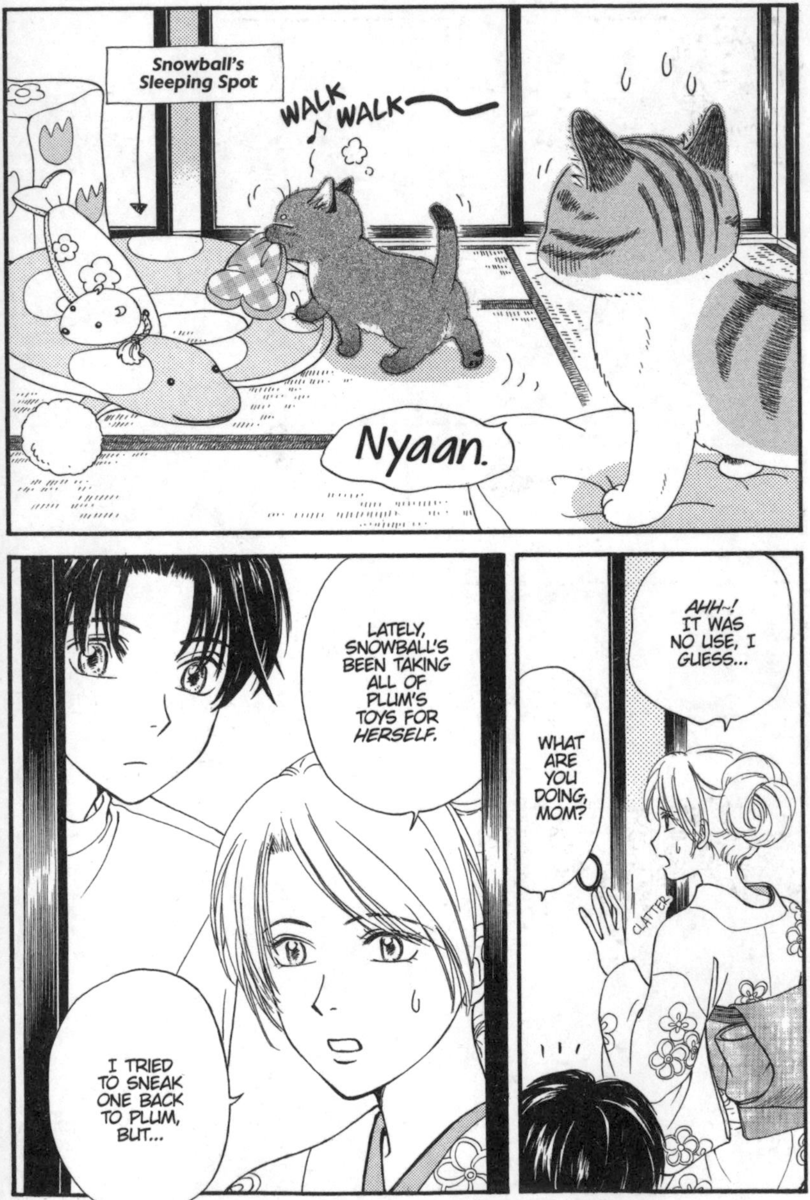
WALK ♪ WALK
Snowball's Sleeping Spot
Nyaan.
AHH~! IT WAS NO USE, I GUESS...
WHAT ARE YOU DOING, MOM?
CLATTER
LATELY, SNOWBALL'S BEEN TAKING ALL OF PLUM'S TOYS FOR *HERSELF*.
I TRIED TO SNEAK ONE BACK TO PLUM, BUT...

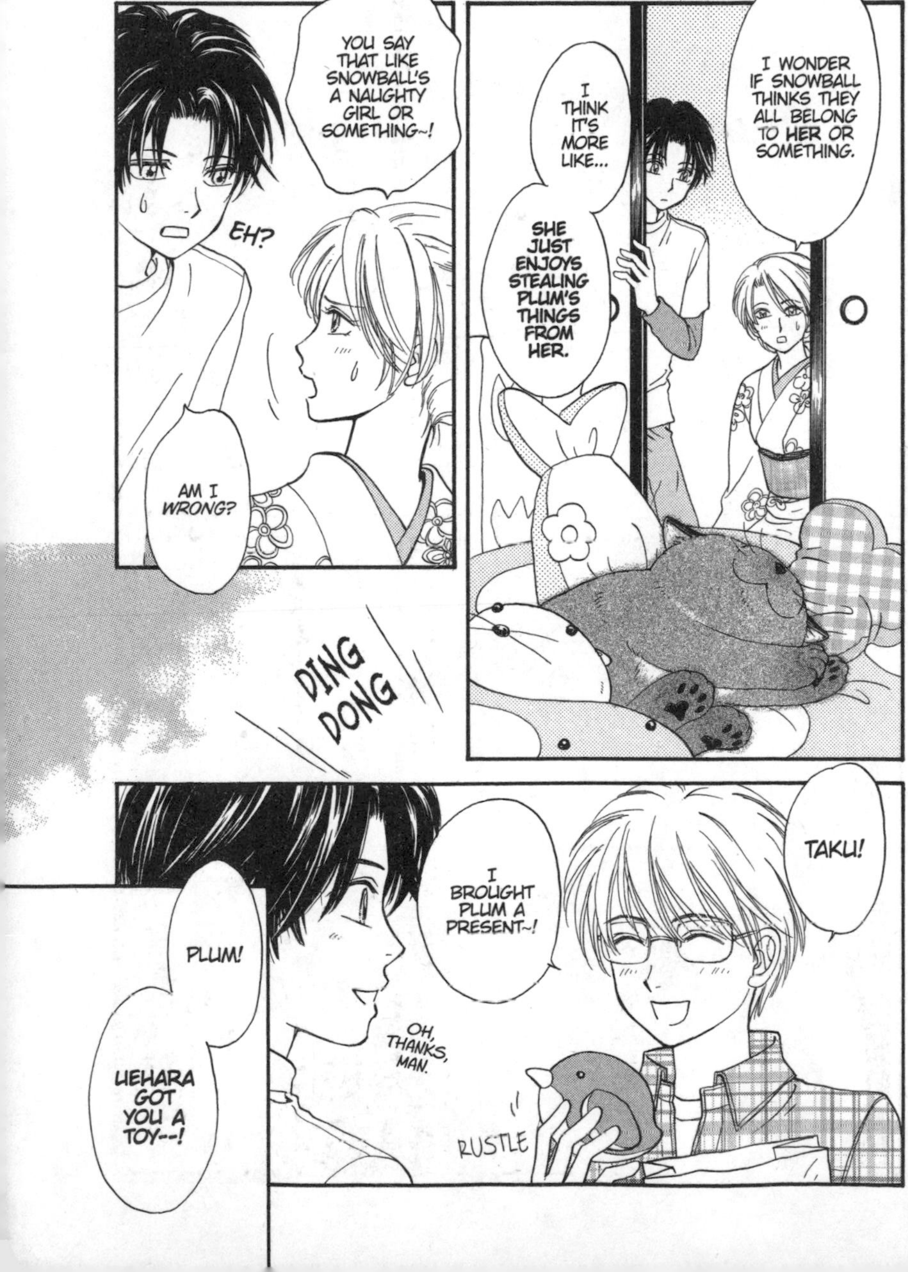
I WONDER IF SNOWBALL THINKS THEY ALL BELONG TO HER OR SOMETHING.
I THINK IT'S MORE LIKE...
SHE JUST ENJOYS STEALING PLUM'S THINGS FROM HER.
YOU SAY THAT LIKE SNOWBALL'S A NAUGHTY GIRL OR SOMETHING~!
EH?
AM I WRONG?
DING DONG
TAKU!
I BROUGHT PLUM A PRESENT~!
OH, THANKS, MAN.
RUSTLE
PLUM!
UEHARA GOT YOU A TOY--!

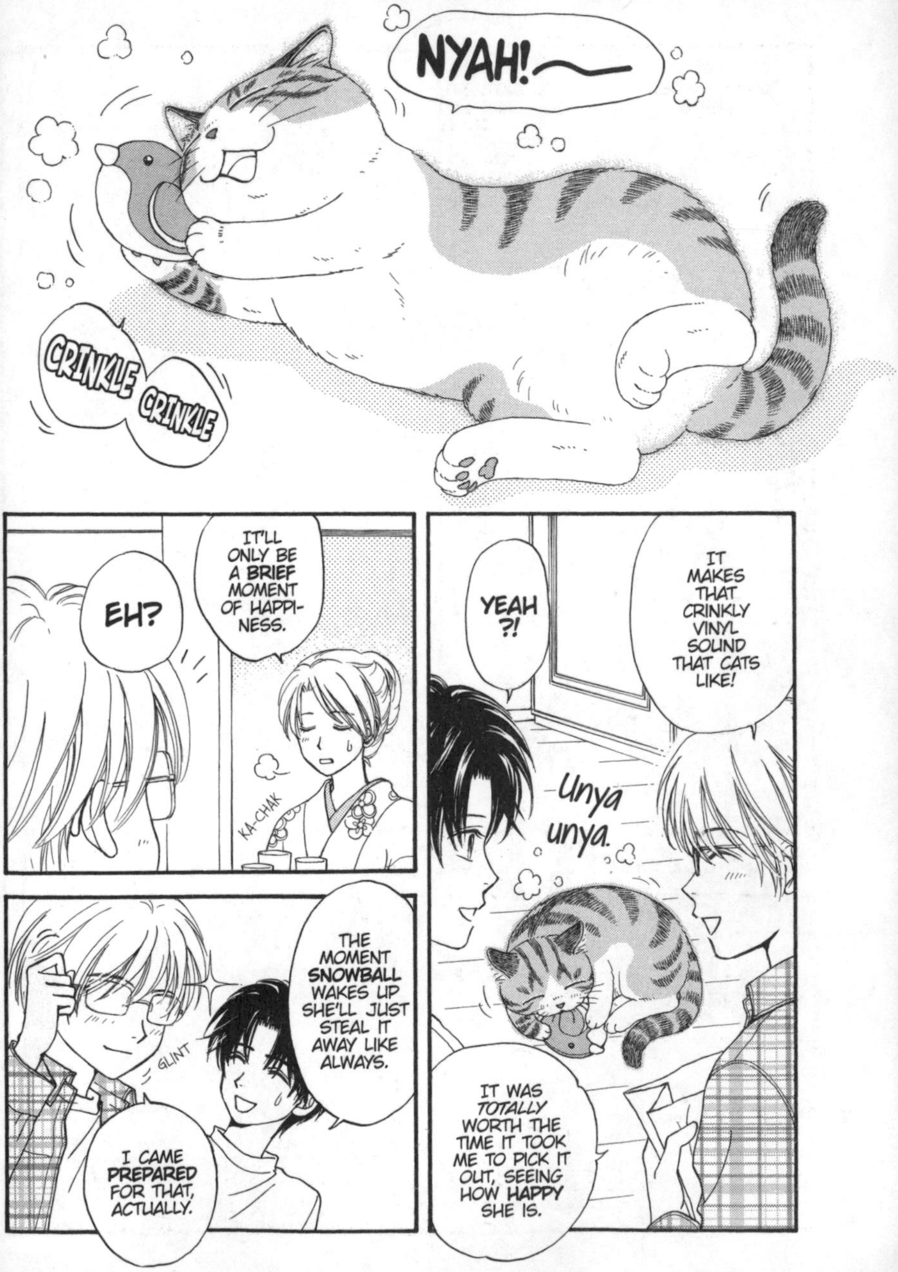
NYAH!~
CRINKLE CRINKLE
IT MAKES THAT CRINKLY VINYL SOUND THAT CATS LIKE!
YEAH?!
Unya unya.
IT WAS TOTALLY WORTH THE TIME IT TOOK ME TO PICK IT OUT, SEEING HOW HAPPY SHE IS.
IT'LL ONLY BE A BRIEF MOMENT OF HAPPINESS.
EH?
KA-CHAK
THE MOMENT SNOWBALL WAKES UP SHE'LL JUST STEAL IT AWAY LIKE ALWAYS.
GLINT
I CAME PREPARED FOR THAT, ACTUALLY.

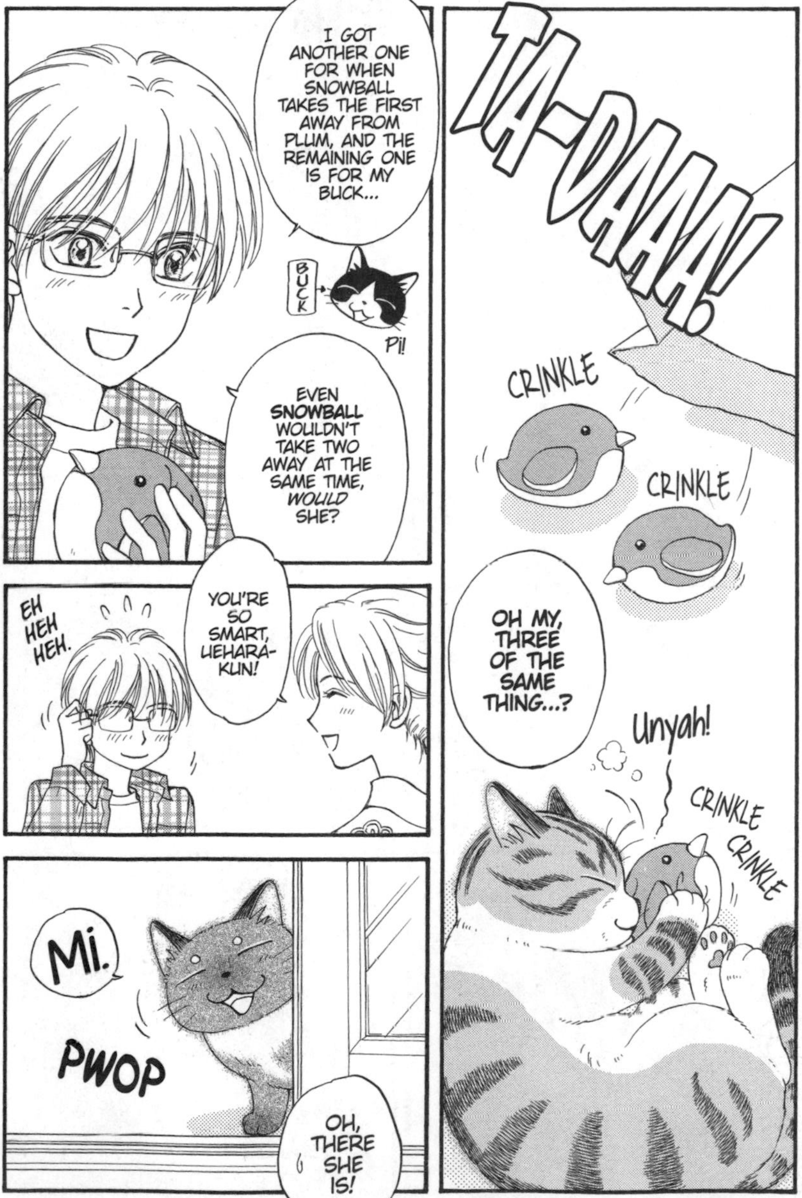
TA-DAAA!
CRINKLE
CRINKLE
OH MY, THREE OF THE SAME THING...?
Unyah!
CRINKLE CRINKLE
I GOT ANOTHER ONE FOR WHEN SNOWBALL TAKES THE FIRST AWAY FROM PLUM, AND THE REMAINING ONE IS FOR MY BUCK...
BUCK
Pi!
EVEN SNOWBALL WOULDN'T TAKE TWO AWAY AT THE SAME TIME, WOULD SHE?
YOU'RE SO SMART, UEHARA-KUN!
EH HEH HEH.
Mi.
PWOP
OH, THERE SHE IS!

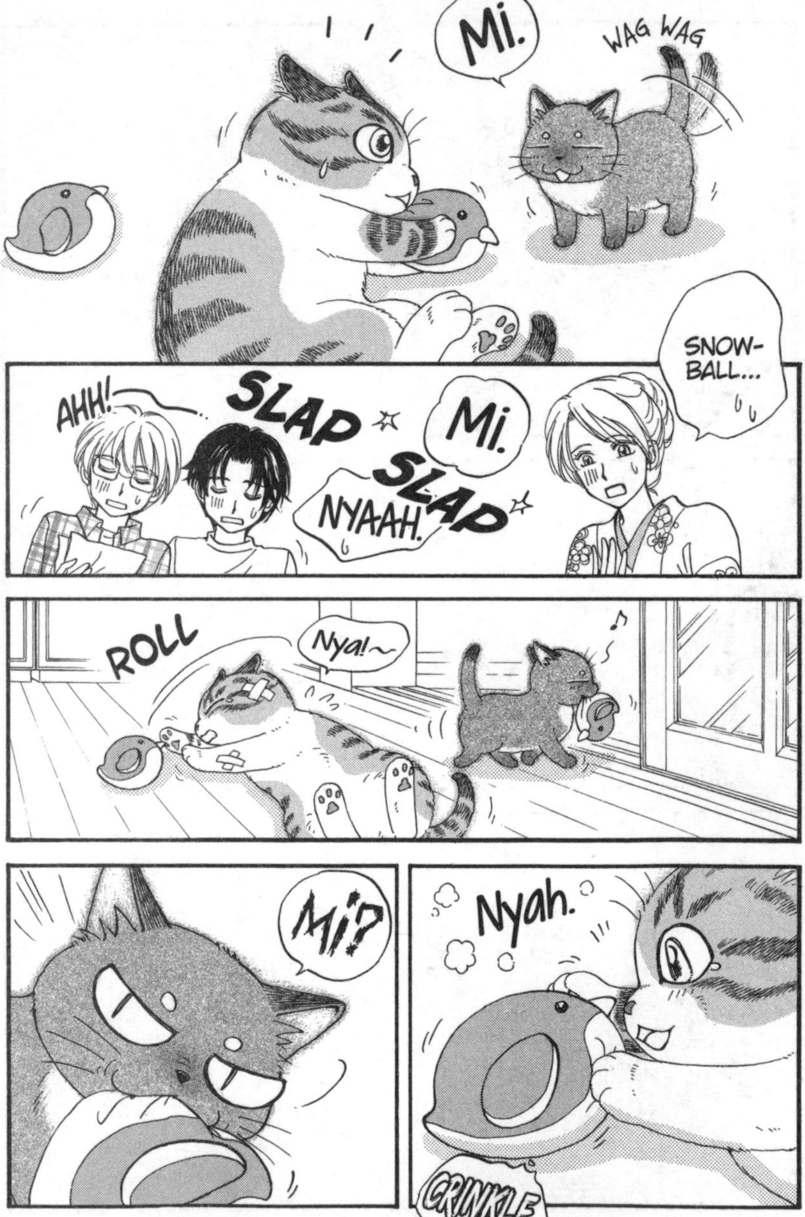
WAG WAG
Mi.
SNOW-BALL...
Mi.
SLAP
SLAP
NYAAH.
AHH!
Nya!~
ROLL
Nyah.
CRINKLE
Mi?

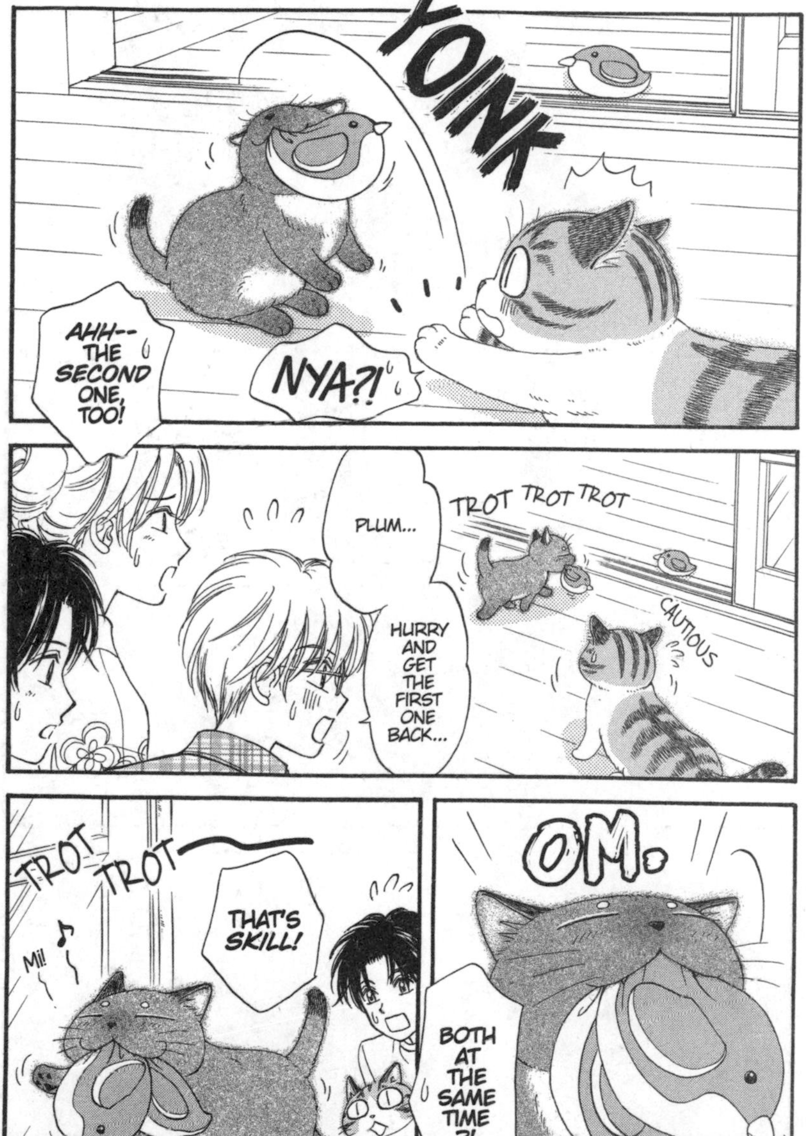
YOINK
NYA?!
AHH-- THE SECOND ONE, TOO!
TROT TROT TROT
CAUTIOUS
PLUM...
HURRY AND GET THE FIRST ONE BACK...
OM.
BOTH AT THE SAME TIME ?!
THAT'S SKILL!
TROT TROT—
MI! ♪

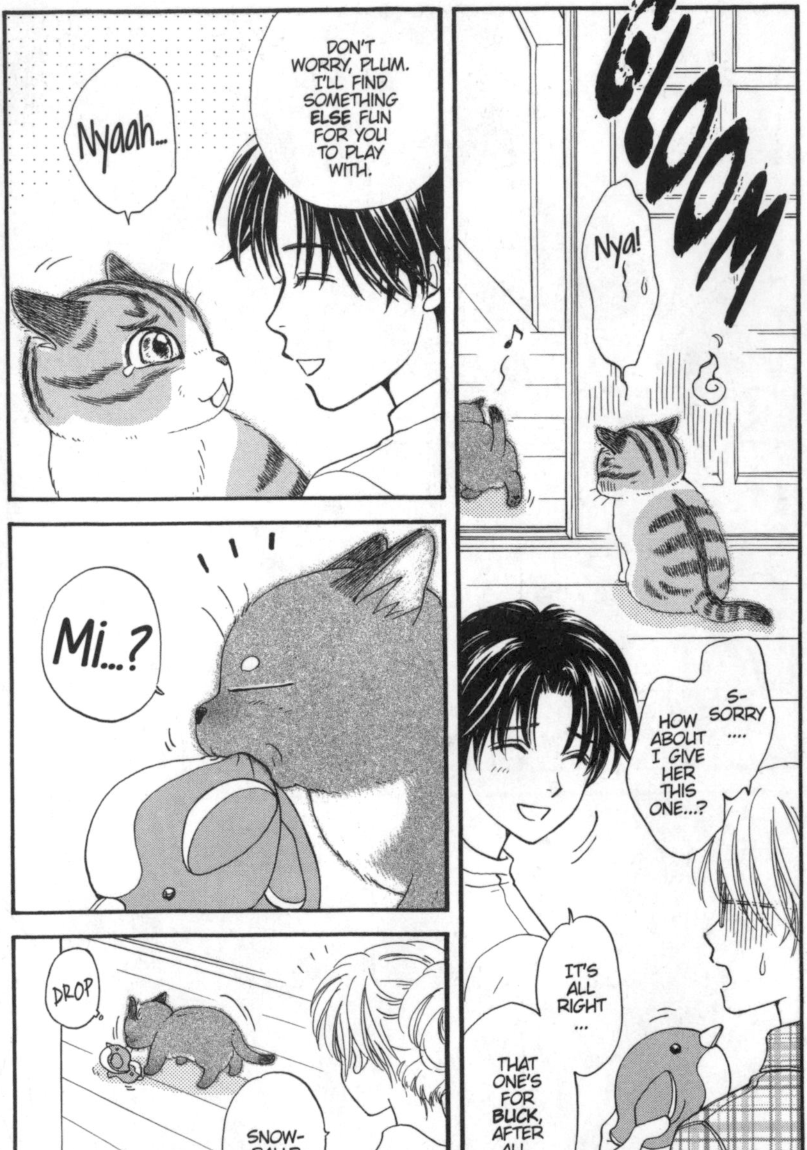
GLOOM
Nya!
S-SORRY ....
HOW ABOUT I GIVE HER THIS ONE...?
IT'S ALL RIGHT ...
THAT ONE'S FOR BUCK, AFTER ALL.
DON'T WORRY, PLUM. I'LL FIND SOMETHING ELSE FUN FOR YOU TO PLAY WITH.
Nyaah...
Mi...?
DROP
SNOW-BALL?

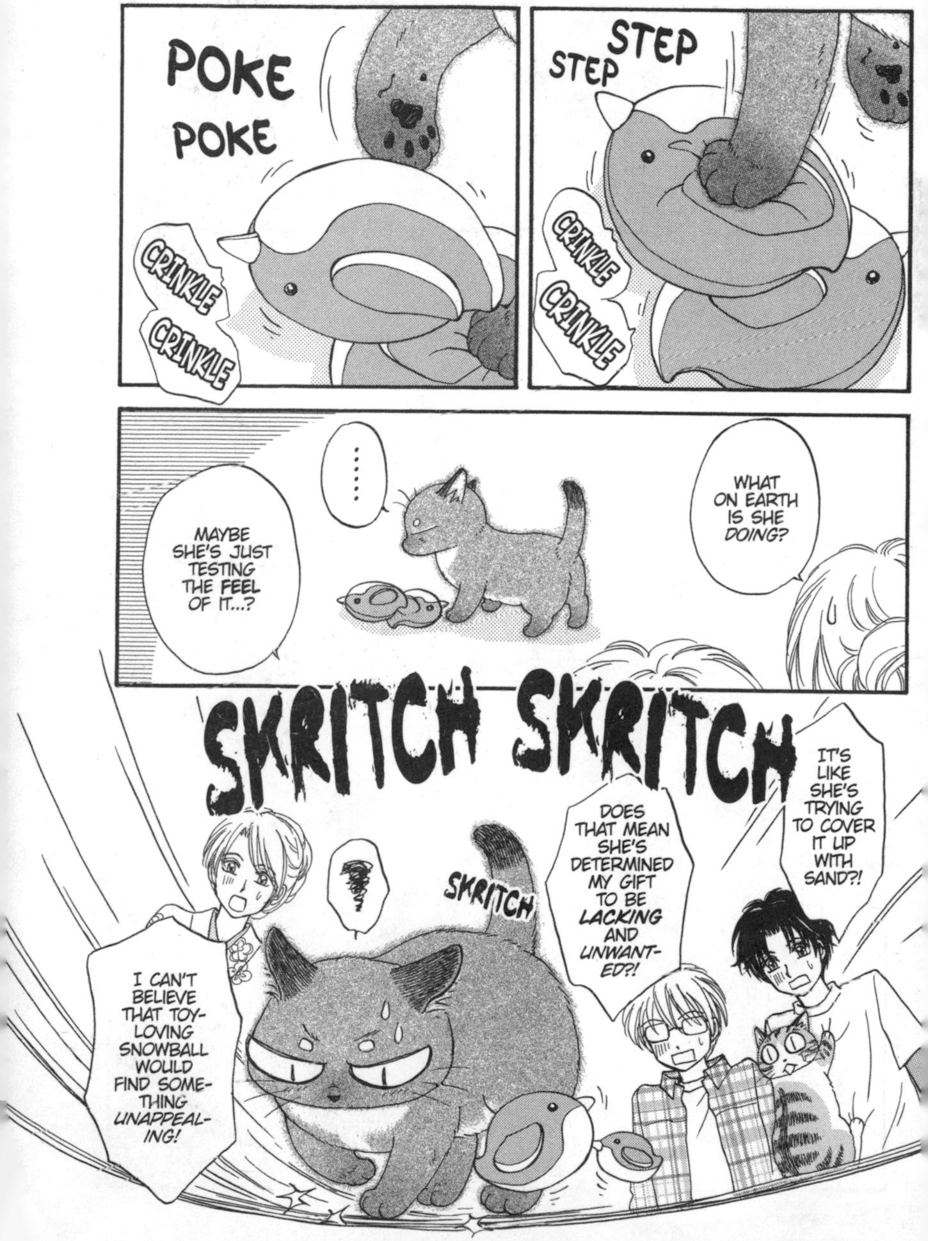
STEP STEP
CRINKLE CRINKLE
POKE POKE
CRINKLE CRINKLE
WHAT ON EARTH IS SHE DOING?
......
MAYBE SHE'S JUST TESTING THE FEEL OF IT...?
SKRITCH SKRITCH
IT'S LIKE SHE'S TRYING TO COVER IT UP WITH SAND?!
DOES THAT MEAN SHE'S DETERMINED MY GIFT TO BE LACKING AND UNWANTED?!
SKRITCH
I CAN'T BELIEVE THAT TOY-LOVING SNOWBALL WOULD FIND SOMETHING UNAPPEALING!

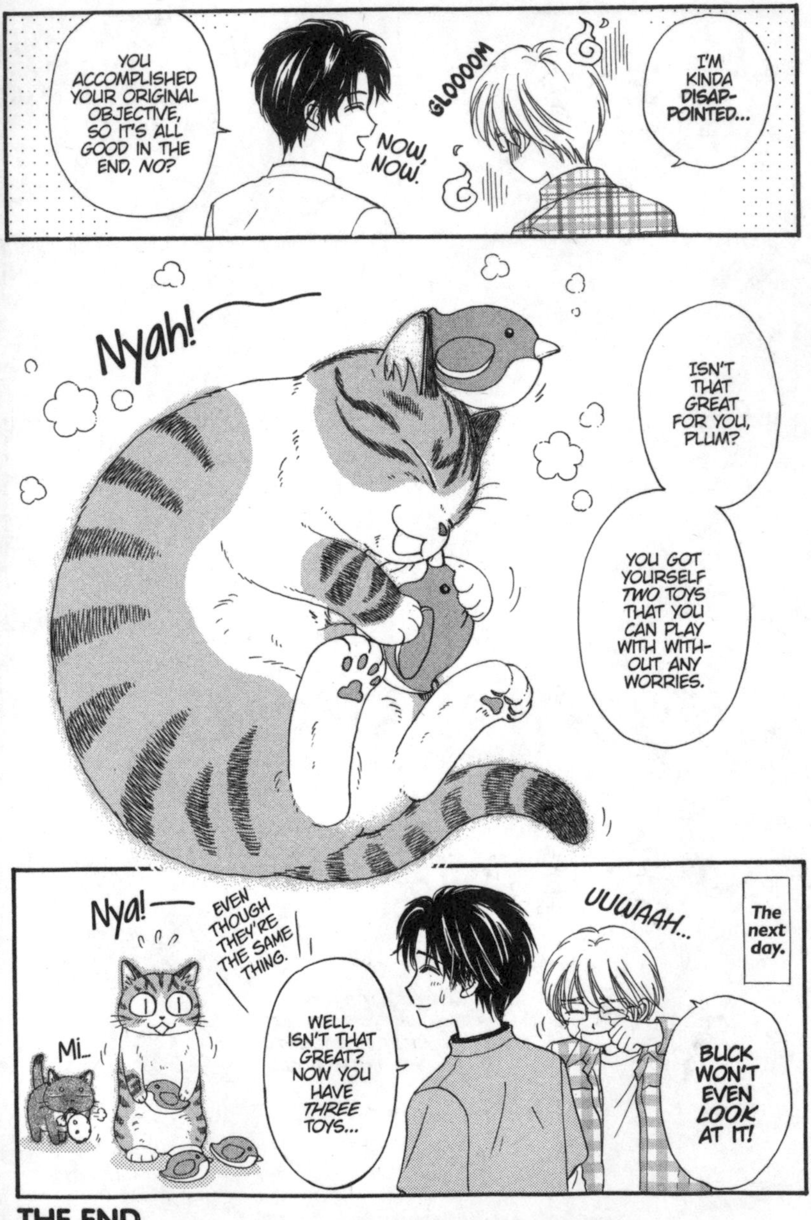
I'M KINDA DISAPPOINTED...
GLOOOOM
NOW, NOW!
YOU ACCOMPLISHED YOUR ORIGINAL OBJECTIVE, SO IT'S ALL GOOD IN THE END, *NO*?
ISN'T THAT GREAT FOR YOU, PLUM?
YOU GOT YOURSELF *TWO* TOYS THAT YOU CAN PLAY WITH WITHOUT ANY WORRIES.
Nyah!
The next day.
UUWAAH...
BUCK WON'T EVEN *LOOK* AT IT!
WELL, ISN'T THAT GREAT? NOW YOU HAVE *THREE* TOYS...
EVEN THOUGH THEY'RE THE SAME THING.
Nya!
Mi...

THE END

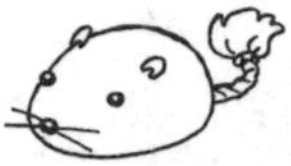

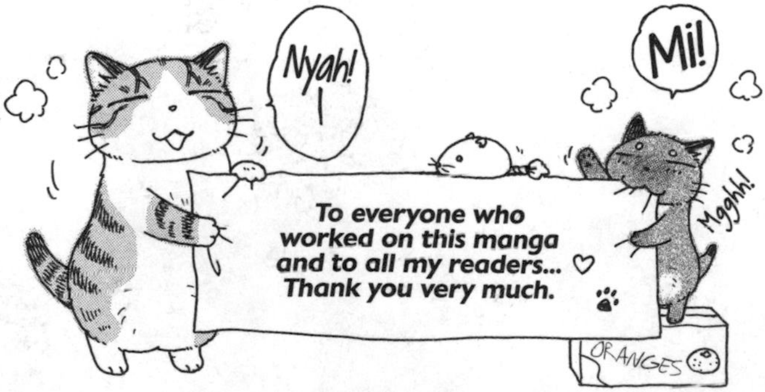
Mi!
Mgghh!
Nyah!
To everyone who worked on this manga and to all my readers... ♡ Thank you very much.
ORANGES

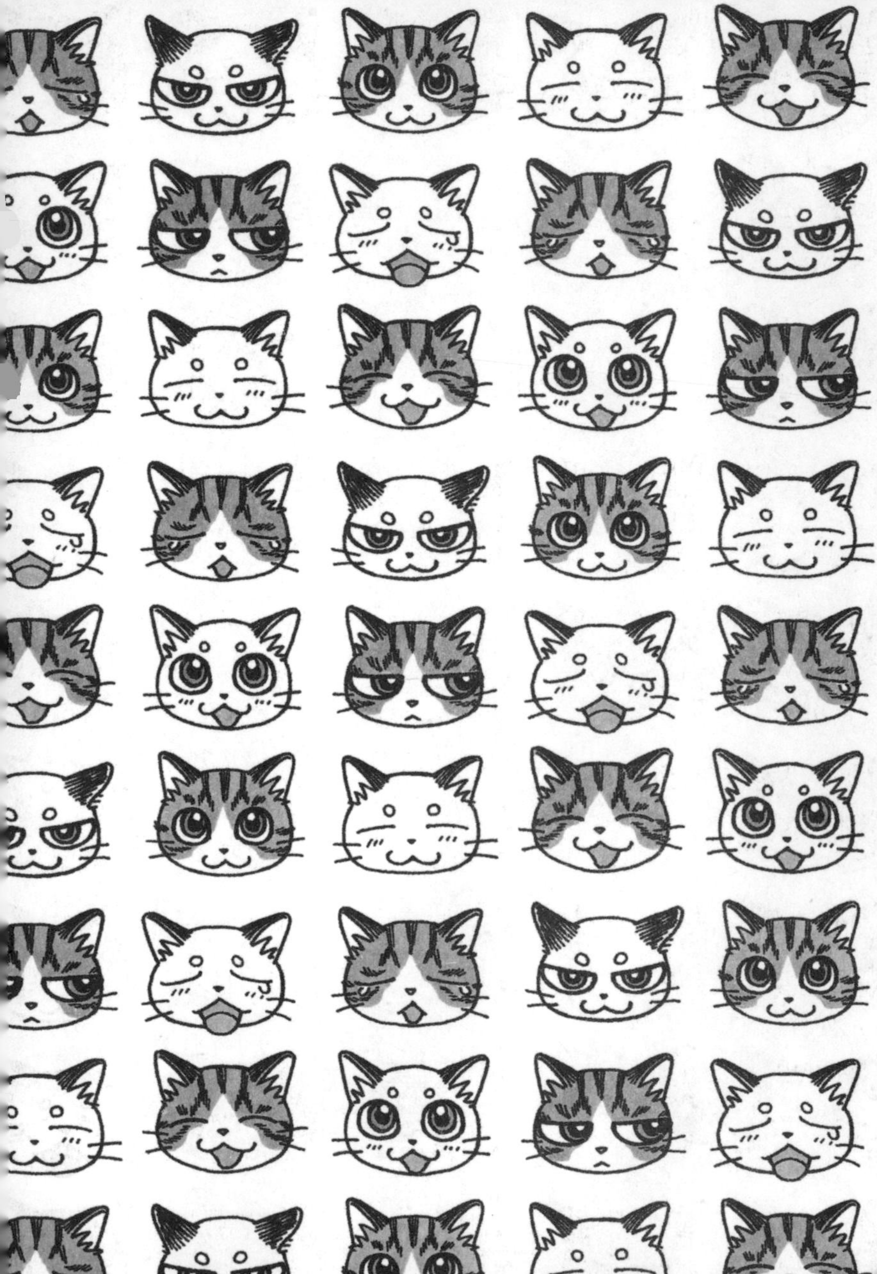